SEXUAL BEHAVIOR:

PHARMACOLOGY AND BIOCHEMISTRY

Sexual Behavior: Pharmacology and Biochemistry

Edited by

Merton Sandler, M.D.
Professor of Clinical Pathology
The Bernhard Baron Memorial
Research Laboratories
Queen Charlotte's Maternity Hospital
London, England

G. L. Gessa, M.D.
Professor of Pharmacology
Cagliari University School
of Medicine
Cagliari, Sardinia, Italy

Raven Press ▪ New York

Made in the United States of America

International Standard Book Number 0–89004–005–2
Library of Congress Catalog Card Number 74–14478

*ISBN outside North and South America
only: 0–7204–7545–7*

Preface

Today it seems that nearly every aspect of human life can be influenced by drugs. They can control sleep, hunger, aggression, and other behavior patterns. They have helped us not only to treat abnormal conditions, but also to unravel the biochemical basis of behavior—and the evidence in support of "chemical coding" of behavior is mounting rapidly.

Although the search for drugs capable of influencing (stimulating) sexual behavior has gone on since ancient times, any scientific approach to this problem has been hindered by puritan arguments and attitudes. Indeed, until lately, research on animal sexual behavior was largely concerned with hormonal and neuroanatomic matters and the clinical literature on sexual pharmacology dealt mainly with the negative influence of drugs on fertility and ejaculation, with occasional anecdotal reports of positive effects on libido.

Recently, however, scientific interest in the pharmacology of sexual behavior has been given impetus by the discovery of drugs that can stimulate or inhibit such behavior. It is particularly important that these compounds appear to interact selectively with one or another brain neurotransmitter. It seems, therefore, that sexual behavior not only depends on classic hormonal influences but is under monoaminergic control as well. In fact, the functional interplay of hormones with monoamines in controlling sexual behavior has been the leitmotiv of the symposium on which this volume is based. Another important aspect of the field that has been under scrutiny is our present knowledge of the morphologic substrates that underlie copulatory behavior; the importance of suitable methodologic approaches has been emphasized.

Although psychiatrists have tended to discourage the tendency of research workers to interpret their animal findings in human terms, they are now beginning to accept that developments in the neurochemistry of sexual behavior may provide a physical basis for our understanding of certain disturbances that had previously been considered psychogenic. Indeed, animal models may well have much to offer. Impotence and premature ejaculation, for example, are not exclusively human conditions but have also been noted in the laboratory rat. This entire area of research is developing rapidly and it seems likely that there will be further important developments in the foreseeable future.

M. Sandler
G. L. Gessa
November, 1974

Contents

Sexual Behavior: Pharmacology and Biochemistry, edited by M. Sandler and G. L.
Gessa. Raven Press, New York © 1975.

Brain Mechanisms of Primal Sexual Functions and Related Behavior

Paul D. MacLean

Laboratory of Brain Evolution and Behavior, National Institute of Mental Health, Bethesda,
Maryland 20014

Contrasted with the neuroendocrinologic aspects of sexual behavior, almost nothing was known until recent years about specific brain structures involved in such elemental sexual functions as penile erection and seminal discharge. Although the brain had been extensively explored by electrical stimulation, there was hardly a reference to this particular topic. In his classic treatise of 1909, von Bechterew referred to Pussep's finding that electrical stimulation of the anterior thalamus in dogs resulted in penile erection.

I undertook work on this problem in connection with experiments that had been suggested by my elaboration upon the Papez theory of brain mechanisms of emotion (Papez, 1937; MacLean, 1949). Because of the highly organized forms of behavior required for the preservation and procreation of the species, it seemed probable that systematic exploration of the forebrain by electrical stimulation might reveal structures involved in elemental and perhaps more complex forms of sexual behavior.

RELEVANCE OF ANIMAL EXPERIMENTATION

Because animal experimentation provides our only systematic knowledge of brain functions, the use of findings on animals may be justifiable for drawing inferences about the workings of the human brain. At the molecular or cellular levels, discoveries in animals are readily acknowledged as applicable to human biology. But somewhat ironically, there is widespread belief that behavioral and neurologic observations on animals have little or no human relevance. Perhaps such an attitude stems from a failure to recognize that in its evolution, the human brain expands in hierarchic fashion along the lines of three basic patterns, which are labeled reptilian, paleomammalian, and neomammalian in Fig. 1. Markedly different in chemistry and structure, and in an evolutionary sense countless generations apart, the three cerebrotypes constitute, so to speak, three brains in one, a "triune" brain (MacLean, 1970, 1973c). Because of the respective similarities in chemistry and anatomic organization of the three basic evolutionary formations, the comparative experimental approach can give important leads with respect to elemental functions of the human brain.

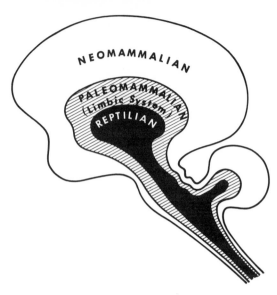

FIG. 1. Diagram of the hierarchy of three basic cerebrotypes that provide the anatomic and chemical "blueprints" for the evolution of the human brain. Radically different in chemistry and structure, and in an evolutionary sense countless generations apart, the three formations constitute three brains in one, a "triune" brain. (From MacLean, 1967*b*.)

I first describe our findings on the cerebral representation of penile erection with respect to each of the three main evolutionary formations. Then I summarize the results of experiments concerning somatosensory aspects of genital function and seminal discharge. Finally, I describe ablation experiments on the mammalian counterpart of the reptilian brain pointing out that in social communication genital manifestations may have other than purely sexual significance.

METHODS

For the stimulation experiments a stereotaxic platform with electrode guides was chronically fixed above the scalp on four screws that were previously cemented in the skull (MacLean, 1967*a*). This device avoids open surgery; it also provides a closed system for millimeter-by-millimeter exploration of the brain with stimulating and recording electrodes while the monkey sits in a special chair and is periodically given its favorite forms of fluid and nourishment. After each experiment the monkey is returned to its home cage. Stimulation was performed at each locus with three sets of stimulus parameters. The magnitude of erection was graded on a scale of ± to 5+, and a positive response was characterized as one that could be obtained repeatedly at a regular latency. When stimulation elicited seminal discharge, the presence of spermatozoa was confirmed by microscopic examination. Experiments were spaced 2 to 4 days apart and no more than

8 to 10 tracks were explored in a single animal. The location of all points of stimulation was confirmed histologically.

PENILE ERECTION

Neomammalian Formation

The neomammalian formation consists of the most highly evolved form of cortex—the neocortex—and of structures of the brainstem with which it is primarily connected. In operations for treatment of epileptic disorders, Penfield stimulated the greater part of the human neocortex, as well as limbic cortex of the insulotemporal region, but he never elicited signs or symptoms of a sexual nature (Penfield and Jasper, 1954). Woolsey, Marshall, and Bard (1942) demonstrated in the macaque that tactile stimulation of the genitalia evoked potentials in the parietal cortex on the medial wall of the hemisphere. In the squirrel monkey, we stimulated, millimeter-by-millimeter, all of the medial frontal and parietal neocortex (MacLean and Ploog, 1962; Dua and MacLean, 1964). Stimulation of the transitional region between medial frontal cortex and limbic cortex of the anterior cingulate gyrus evoked full penile erection (Dua and MacLean, 1964). We did not explore the somatomotor areas of the lateral convexity, but stimulation of the middle segment of the cerebral peduncle, which contains efferent fibers from that region, failed to induce erection.

Limbic System

In all mammals, most of the phylogenetically old cortex is contained in a large convolution that Broca (1878) called the great limbic lobe because it surrounds the brainstem. In 1952 I suggested the term "limbic system" (MacLean, 1952) as a designation for the limbic cortex and structures of the brain with which it has primary connections. This anatomically and functionally integrated system represents an inheritance from paleomammalian forms. In the last 40 years evidence has accumulated that the limbic system derives information in terms of emotional feelings that guide behavior required for self-preservation and the preservation of the species (MacLean, 1962, 1973c).

It will help to visualize oral-genital relationships, which are discussed later, if the findings on the limbic system are described with respect to three of its main subdivisions. Figure 2 illustrates that the limbic lobe has the shape of a ring and that the medial forebrain bundle is a major line of communication between the limbic cortex and structures of the brainstem. In contrast to the neocortex, the limbic cortex has numerous connections with the hypothalamus, which plays a major role in integrating the performance of brain mechanisms involved in self-preservation and the preservation of the species. It should be noted that the two upper branches of the medial forebrain meet with descending fibers from the olfactory bulb and feed into the lower and upper halves of the ring through the

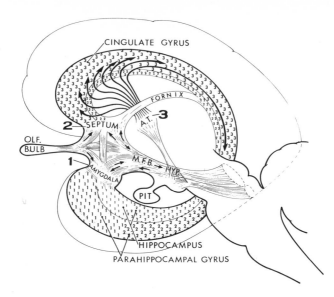

FIG. 2. Diagram of three main corticosubcortical subdivisions of the limbic system. Note how the major pathway of the third subdivision (3) bypasses the olfactory apparatus. See text regarding evolution of oral–genital relationships. HYP, Hypothalamus; M.F.B., medial forebrain bundle; OLF, olfactory; PIT, pituitary. (After MacLean, 1958.)

amygdala (1) and the septum (2), whereas the third large pathway (3) branches lower down from the hypothalamus and bypasses the olfactory apparatus.

Clinical and experimental findings have indicated that the subdivision identified with the amygdala is involved with feelings and behavior that ensure self-preservation (cf. MacLean, 1958). Neural excitation in this circuit results in responses related particularly to the oral aspects of feeding, fighting, and self-protection.

The neighboring subdivision associated with the septum, on the contrary, appears to be involved with expressive and feeling states that are conducive to sociability and the procreation of the species (MacLean, 1957, 1962). With respect to genital function, we found that stimulation of the lower part of the septum and the adjoining medial preoptic area elicited full erection (MacLean and Ploog, 1962). In a number of instances, stimulation within the dorsal psalterium or fimbria of the hippocampus resulted in recruitment of hippocampal potentials and penile erection (MacLean, Denniston, Dua, and Ploog, 1962). The next section discusses other evidence of hippocampal influence on sexual functions.

In the third subdivision of the limbic system (Fig. 2), positive loci for erection were found in the mammillary bodies, along the course of the mammillothalamic tract, in the anterior thalamus, and in the pregenual cingulate and subcallosal cortex, which are known to receive projections from the anterior thalamic nuclei.

Both the second and third subdivisions of the limbic system articulate with the part of the medial dorsal nucleus that projects to the posterior part of the

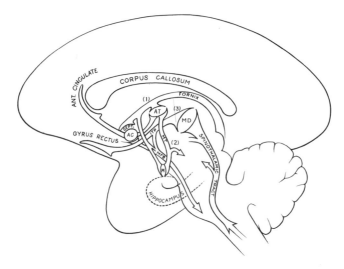

FIG. 3. Anatomic diagram of cerebral circuits involved in elemental sexual functions. AC, Anterior commissure; AT, anterior thalamic nuclei; ITP, inferior thalamic peduncle; M, mammillary bodies; MD, medial dorsal nucleus; MFB, medial forebrain bundle; MT, mammillothalamic tract; SEPT, septum. (From MacLean, 1962.)

gyrus rectus. Stimulation at loci in either of these structures (Fig. 3) was highly effective in eliciting penile erection.

As diagrammed in Fig. 3, the results of stimulation indicated that the main effector pathway from the medial septopreoptic region follows the medial forebrain bundle, whereas that from the midline thalamus runs in the inferior thalamic peduncle before it joins the medial forebrain bundle. After following the medial forebrain bundle to the ventral tegmental area, the main effector pathway turns abruptly toward the lateral part of the substantia nigra, then descends through the ventrolateral part of the pons, and enters the medulla near the exit of the sixth nerve and lateral to the pyramids (MacLean, Denniston, and Dua, 1963).

Hippocampal Influences

The hippocampus contains the so-called archicortex of the limbic lobe. Stimulation at positive points in the pregenual cingulate cortex and subcallosal region resulted in a buildup of high-voltage potentials in the hippocampus that coincided with the appearance of penile erection (Dua and MacLean, 1964). Stimulation at positive sites in the septum and anterior thalamus commonly led to the development of self-sustained hippocampal afterdischarges associated with throbbing of the penis and an increase in size of the erection (MacLean and Ploog, 1962). Afterward spiking activity might appear in the hippocampus and persist for periods up to 10 min, during which time there would be waxing and waning of penile erection. In view of the known hippocampal projections to the septum and anterior thalamus, these findings suggest that the hippocampus exerts a modulatory influence on genital tumescence. We have since demonstrated in the squirrel monkey that hippocampal volleys elicit short latency responses of single units in the septum and in the contiguous parts of the medial preoptic area (Poletti, Kinnard, and MacLean, 1973). In a parallel anatomic study it was shown for the first time in a primate that the fornix projects to the medial preoptic region. As mentioned previously, electrical stimulation in the medial preoptic region elicits full erection.

It is also of interest to mention here some ancillary observations on the effects of depositing α-MSH and β^{1-24}-ACTH in the septopreoptic region and hypothalamus of the squirrel monkey. These experiments were suggested by G. L. Gessa, who, in extending the original findings of Ferrari, Floris, and Paulesu (1955), demonstrated that the intracisternal or intracerebral application of peptides possessing the activities of these hormones results in yawning, stretching, and penile erection in such diverse species as rats, rabbits, cats, dogs, and vervet monkeys (see Gessa, Vargiu, and Ferrari, 1966; Gessa, Pisano, Vargiu, Crabai, and Ferrari, 1967). As briefly noted in earlier work (MacLean, 1973*d*), Kinnard and I found that deposits in solid form of one of these hormones in the septopreoptic region resulted in episodes of stretching, yawning, scratching of the body, and full penile erection. All manifestations of the syndrome were present after 1 to 1½ hr and persisted for nearly 6 hr. The peak activity occurred in about 3 hr, with episodes timed as frequently as twice per minute. Deposits of the hormones 1 mm from the third ventricle in the ventromedial nucleus of the hypothalamus and premammillary region were ineffective.

Recently it has been found that the medial septopreoptic region plays an important role in sexual differentiation of some rodents and that it exerts a regulatory influence on the tonic and cyclic secretion of gonadotropin, respectively, in the male and female (see Gorski, 1971, for review). It therefore seems likely that in addition to its influence on genital function, the hippocampus may also affect the regulation of the release of gonadotropin. In view of limbic system involvement in emotional behavior, these findings suggest neural mechanisms by which either the agreeable or disagreeable aspects of affective experience could influence genital and gonadal function.

The Striatal Complex

The major counterpart of the reptilian forebrain in mammals is represented by the olfactostriatum, corpus striatum (caudate + putamen), globus pallidus, and satellite gray matter. In addition to a high content of cholinesterase, the striatum has large amounts of serotonin and dopamine, the latter deriving from the recently discovered dopaminergic pathway from the substantia nigra.

We have not systematically explored the striatal complex, but stimulation at many points within the caudate, putamen, and globus pallidus elicited no genital responses (MacLean and Ploog, 1962).

GENITAL SENSATION AND SEMINAL DISCHARGE

As already mentioned, electrical stimulation at some sites resulted in throbbing penile erection that persisted for many seconds after the termination of the stimulus. Despite the orgastic appearance, ejaculation was never observed under these conditions. Seminal discharge, sometimes preceding erection, was elicited only in those cases in which the electrodes proved upon reconstruction to lie along the course of the spinothalamic pathway (Fig. 3) and its ancient medial ramifications into the caudal intralaminar region of the thalamus (MacLean, Dua, and Denniston, 1963). Characteristically, as the electrode approached one of these points, the monkey would begin to scratch in the region of the chest or abdomen and then, with the electrode at the critical locus, scratch the genitalia. It was shown, however, that emission containing motile sperm could occur independently of scratching. The thalamic structures involved in these manifestations lie in close relationship to the part of the midline thalamus involved in penile erection. These experiments provide a first indication of pathways and brain structures involved in sensorimotor aspects of elemental sexual functions.

Robinson and Mishkin (1966) reported a single case of a macaque that ejaculated following self-stimulation through an electrode in the medial preoptic area. According to Herberg (1963), stimulation in the posterior hypothalamus of rats may induce ejaculation.

ORAL–GENITAL FACTORS IN FEEDING AND AGGRESSION

With regard to oral–genital relationships, it is significant that slow frequency stimulation of the amygdala may elicit first either facial or alimentary responses such as biting, chewing, and salivation followed 30 or more sec later by penile erection (MacLean, 1962), presumably resulting from recruitment of neural activity in related structures involved in genital function. The close relationship between oral and genital functions seems to be attributable to the olfactory sense, which, dating far back in evolution, is involved in both feeding and mating.

These considerations are also relevant to orosexual factors in aggressive and combative behavior. Suppose for the moment that in Fig. 2 we used the shield of Mars (○) as a symbol for plotting points at which stimulation elicited oral or facial responses and his sword (↗) as a symbol for genital responses. The symbols for shield and sword, respectively, would be seen to cluster in the region of the amygdala and the septopreoptic area. Traced caudally along the converging pathways from the amygdala and septum the symbols would unite and show a reconstitution of the warrior Mars (♂) in a region, which Hess and Brügger (1943) proved to be involved in the expression of angry and defensive behavior.

In the squirrel monkey, stimulation within a narrow compass of this region elicits penile erection, angry behavior, biting, and chewing (MacLean and Ploog, 1962; MacLean, Denniston, and Dua, 1963).[1] As fighting is a preliminary to both feeding and mating, the same mechanisms for combat appear to be involved in each situation.

PENILE ERECTION IN AGGRESSIVE AND OTHER BEHAVIOR

During the bucking and locking of horns while defending its territory called a "lek," the Uganda kob often develops penile erection (Buechner, Morrison, and Leuthold, 1966). The same autonomic manifestation may be seen in the chimpanzee during its raucus display (Van Lawick-Goodall, *personal communication*). The squirrel monkey, which we have studied extensively, provides an excellent example of multiple ways in which the genital may be used in social communication. This monkey variously uses a genital display in a show of aggression, courtship, and greeting (MacLean, 1962; Ploog and MacLean, 1963). There is evidence that it is an innate form of behavior (Ploog, Hopf, and Winter, 1967). It is of comparative interest that the aggressive display may involve grinding of the teeth, recalling that bruxism and penile erection have been observed in man during REM (rapid eye movement) sleep correlated with dreaming (Fisher, Gross, and Zuch, 1965).

I have described one variety of squirrel monkey that will display to its reflection in a mirror (MacLean, 1964). We refer to the mirror-displaying animal as the "gothic" type because the ocular patch comes to a peak over the eye much like a gothic arch; we call the other subspecies "roman" because the patch is round like a roman arch. The mirror display is so predictable that I have used it as a test in an attempt to identify brain structures involved in genetically constituted, species-typical forms of behavior. Other manifestations recorded in the display test are urination, vocalization, "thigh-spreading," and scratching.

I have made observations on more than 90 animals. Large bilateral lesions in limbic or neomammalian parts of the brain may have only a transient or no effect on the display. I have found, however, in a study of 14 squirrel monkeys that following large bilateral lesions of the globus pallidus monkeys no longer are inclined to display (MacLean, 1972, 1973a,b). Such animals, however, have proved capable of defending themselves, and even of overpowering the dominant animal, when introduced into an established colony of squirrel monkeys. Without a test of the innate display behavior one might conclude that the operated animals were unaffected by the loss of brain tissue.

These findings are of considerable interest because after 150 years of experimentation remarkably little has been learned about the functions of the striatal complex. The traditional clinical view that it subserves purely motor

---

[1] The original papers must be consulted in regard to other manifestations such as vocalization, urination, cardiac changes, etc., that may at times be elicited in conjunction with penile erection.

functions is not in harmony with findings that large bilateral lesions of the striatal complex may result in no incapacity of movement. The present experiments indicate that the striatal complex is essential for programming highly organized forms of species-typical, ritualistic behavior.

I have since found that small bilateral lesions of pallidal projections in the ansa lenticularis may interfere with the somatic components of the display, whereas small lesions of the medial forebrain bundle initially affect the genital response (1975).

Elsewhere I have discussed the display behavior itself in regard to the significance of phallic representations in mythology; the use of phallic sculptures as territorial markers; the symbolic equivalence of the genital with the "evil eye"; recent reports of similar displays in primitive tribes; and man's adoption of the loincloth (MacLean, 1962, 1973*b*).

SUMMARY

The primate forebrain evolves and expands along the lines of three basic patterns that may be characterized as reptilian, paleomammalian, and neomammalian. The striatal complex (olfactostriatum, corpus striatum, globus pallidus) reflects the organization of a major part of the reptilian forebrain. The limbic system (limbic cortex and its primary nuclear connections) is largely a paleomammalian derivative. The neomammalian formation, comprising the neocortex and its connections, reaches its culmination in the human brain. Radically different in anatomy and chemistry, the three interconnected evolutionary formations constitute a triune brain.

Until recently, there was little direct evidence of a representation of sexual functions in the forebrain. The first part of this chapter summarizes a series of brain stimulation studies in squirrel monkeys on the cerebral representation of elemental sexual functions. The findings are discussed with regard to oro-sexual, as well as aggressive and combative forms of behavior.

Finally, a summary is given of an extensive study in squirrel monkeys that demonstrates for the first time in a mammal that the striatal complex plays a fundamental role in genetically constituted, species-typical, ritualistic behavior. The behavioral observations illustrate that in social communication genital manifestations may have other than sexual significance.

REFERENCES

Broca, P. (1878): Anatomie comparée des circonvolutions cérébrales. Le grand lobe limbique et la scissure limbique dans la série des mammifères. *Rev. Anthropol.,* 1:385.

Buechner, H. K., Morrison, J. A., and Leuthold, W. (1966): Reproduction in Uganda kob with special reference to behavior. In: *Comparative Biology of Reproduction in Mammals,* edited by J. W. Rowlands. Academic Press, New York.

Dua, S., and MacLean, P. D. (1964): Localization for penile erection in medial frontal lobe. *Am. J. Physiol.,* 207:1425–1434.

Ferrari, W., Floris, E., and Paulesu, F. (1955): Sull'effetto eosinofilopenizzante dell' ACTH iniettato nella cisterna magna. *Boll. Soc. Ital. Biol. Sper.,* 31:862.

Fisher, C., Gross, J., and Zuch, J. (1965): Cycle of penile erection synchronous with dreaming (REM) sleep. *Arch. Gen. Psychiatry,* 12:29–45.

Freedman, A. M., Kaplan, H. I., and B. J. Sadock, editors (1975): *Comprehensive Textbook of Psychiatry.* Williams & Wilkins, Baltimore, Maryland *(in press).*

Gessa, G. L., Pisano, M., Vargiu, L., Crabai, F., and Ferrari, W. (1967): Stretching and yawning movements after intracerebral injection of ACTH. *Rev. Can. Biol.,* 26:229–236.

Gessa, G. L., Vargiu, L., and Ferrari, W. (1966): Stretchings and yawnings induced by adrenocortico-trophic hormone. *Nature,* 211:426.

Gorski, R. A. (1971): Sexual differentiation of the hypothalamus. In: *The Neuroendocrinology of Human Reproduction,* edited by H. C. Mack. Thomas, Springfield, Illinois.

Herberg, L. J. (1963): Seminal ejaculation following positively reinforcing electrical stimulation of the rat hypothalamus. *J. Comp. Physiol. Psychol.,* 56:679–685.

Hess, W. R. and Brügger, M. (1943): Das subkortikale Zentrum der affektiven Abwehrreaktion. *Helv. Physiol. Pharmacol. Acta,* 1:33–52.

MacLean, P. D. (1949): Psychosomatic disease and the "visceral brain." Recent developments bearing on the Papez theory of emotion. *Psychosom. Med.,* 11:338–353.

MacLean, P. D. (1952): Some psychiatric implications of physiological studies on frontotemporal portion of limbic system (visceral brain). *Electroencephalogr. Clin. Neurophysiol.,* 4:407–418.

MacLean, P. D. (1957): Chemical and electrical stimulation of hippocampus in unrestrained animals. II. Behavioral findings. *Arch. Neurol. Psychiatry,* 78:128–142.

MacLean, P. D. (1958): Contrasting functions of limbic and neocortical systems of the brain and their relevance to psychophysiological aspects of medicine. *Am. J. Med.,* 25:611–626.

MacLean, P. D. (1962): New findings relevant to the evolution of psychosexual functions of the brain. *J. Nerv. Ment. Dis.,* 135:289–301.

MacLean, P. D. (1964): Mirror display in the squirrel monkey, Saimiri sciureus. *Science,* 146:950–952.

MacLean, P. D. (1967*a*): A chronically fixed stereotaxic device for intracerebral exploration with macro- and micro-electrodes. *Electroencephalogr. Clin. Neurophysiol.,* 22:180–182.

MacLean, P. D. (1967*b*): The brain in relation to empathy and medical education. *J. Nerv. Ment. Dis.,* 144:374–382.

MacLean, P. D. (1970): The triune brain, emotion, and scientific bias. In: *The Neurosciences Second Study Program,* edited by F. O. Schmitt. Rockefeller Univ. Press, New York.

MacLean, P. D. (1972): Cerebral evolution and emotional processes: New findings on the striatal complex. *Ann. N.Y. Acad. Sci.,* 193:137–149.

MacLean, P. D. (1973*a*): Effects of pallidal lesions on species-typical display behavior of squirrel monkey. *Fed. Proc.,* 32:384.

MacLean, P. D. (1973*b*): New findings on brain function and sociosexual behavior. In: *Contemporary Sexual Behavior: Critical Issues in the 1970s,* edited by J. Zubin and J. Money. Johns Hopkins Univ. Press, Baltimore, Maryland.

MacLean, P. D. (1973*c*): A triune concept of the brain and behaviour, Lecture I. Man's reptilian and limbic inheritance; Lecture II. Man's limbic brain and the psychoses; Lecture III. New trends in man's evolution. In: *The Hincks Memorial Lectures,* edited by T. Boag and D. Campbell. Univ. of Toronto Press, Toronto.

MacLean, P. D. (1973*d*): An evolutionary approach to the investigation of psychoneuroendocrine functions. In: *Hormones and Brain Function,* edited by K. Lissak. Plenum, New York.

MacLean, P. D. (1975): Role of pallidal projections in species-typical display behavior of squirrel monkey. *Trans. Am. Neurol. Assoc.,* vol. 100.

MacLean, P. D., Denniston, R. H., and Dua, S. (1963): Further studies on cerebral representation of penile erection: Caudal thalamus, midbrain, and pons. *J. Neurophysiol.,* 26:273–293.

MacLean, P. D., Denniston, R. H., Dua, S., and Ploog, D. W. (1962): Hippocampal changes with brain stimulation eliciting penile erection. In: *Physiologie de l'hippocampe.* Colloques Internationaux du Centre National de la Recherche Scientifique, 107:491–510.

MacLean, P. D., Dua, S., and Denniston, R. H. (1963): Cerebral localization for scratching and seminal discharge. *Arch. Neurol.,* 9:485–497.

MacLean, P. D., and Ploog, D. W. (1962): Cerebral representation of penile erection. *J. Neurophysiol.,* 25:29–55.

Papez, J. W. (1937): A proposed mechanism of emotion. *Arch. Neurol. Psychiat.,* 38:725.

Penfield, W. and Jasper, H. (1954): *Epilepsy and the Functional Anatomy of the Human Brain.* Little, Brown, Boston, Massachusetts.

Ploog, D. W., and MacLean, P. D. (1963): Display of penile erection in squirrel monkey (Saimiri sciureus). *Anim. Behav.,* 11:32–39.

Ploog, D. W., Hopf, S., and Winter, P. (1967): Ontogenese des Verhaltens von Totenkopf-Affen (Saimiri sciureus). *Psychol. Forsch.,* 31:1–41.

Poletti, C. E., Kinnard, M. A., and MacLean, P. D. (1973): Hippocampal influence on unit activity of hypothalamus, preoptic region, and basal forebrain in awake, sitting squirrel monkeys. *J. Neurophysiol.,* 36:308–324.

Robinson, B. W., and Mishkin, M. (1966): Ejaculation evoked by stimulation of the preoptic area in monkey. *Physiol. Behav.,* 1:269–272.

Von Bechterew, W. (1909–1911): *Die Funktionen der Nervencentra,* Vols. I–III. Gustav Fischer, Jena.

Woolsey, C. N., Marshall, W. H., and Bard, P. (1942): Representation of cutaneous tactile sensibility in the cerebral cortex of the monkey as indicated by evoked potentials. *Bull. Hopkins Hosp.,* 70:399–441.

Sexual Behavior: Pharmacology and Biochemistry, edited by M. Sandler and G. L. Gessa. Raven Press, New York © 1975.

Neural Mediation of Steroid-Induced Sexual Behavior in Rats

Julian M. Davidson and Suzanne Trupin

Department of Physiology, Stanford University School of Medicine, Stanford, California 94305

EFFECTS OF SEXUAL BEHAVIOR ON GONADOTROPIN SECRETION

Normal functioning of the reproductive process depends on a complex set of interactions between the environment and the nervous and endocrine systems. One result of these interactions is that reproductive behavior will be manifested under the appropriate circumstances. But behavior is more than just a "product" of neuroendocrine activity. Information arising from behavioral and social stimuli acts back not only to influence the individual's further behavior directly, but also to alter endocrine secretion in such a way as to change both its reproductive physiology and its further behavioral responses.

These interactions are portrayed diagrammatically in Fig. 1 as a set of connections between a neuroendocrine and a behavioral feedback loop. This brief chapter considers some of the relationships expressed by the arrows connecting these two loops. The arrow depicting effects of behavior on the neuroendocrine loop symbolizes processes that are only beginning to be understood. One example is the observation that the probability of achieving successful pregnancy in rats depends upon receipt by the copulating female of a sufficient degree of genital-tract stimulation from the male (Wilson, Adler, and LeBoeuf, 1965). A critical number of intromissions is required for achievement of normal pregnancy, apparently through promotion of sperm transport as well as adequate preparation of the uterus for successful implantation (Adler, 1969; Chester and Zucker, 1970).

Another neuroendocrine reflex whereby behavioral stimuli can have important effects on reproductive function is that of coitus-induced ovulation. It is now abundantly clear that this reflex can be induced readily in at least one "spontaneously ovulating" species, the laboratory rat, if any of a variety of methods are used to block spontaneous ovulation while maintaining sexual receptivity (refs. in Davidson, Smith, and Bowers, 1973). In the constant light-exposed female rat, plasma LH (and prolactin) rises 10 min after onset of mating and peaks in 1 hr (Brown-Grant, Davidson, and Greig, 1973; Davidson et al., 1973); changes in hypothalamic LFR content precede the LH surge (Smith and Davidson, 1974).

The idea that another spontaneously ovulating species, the human, also can

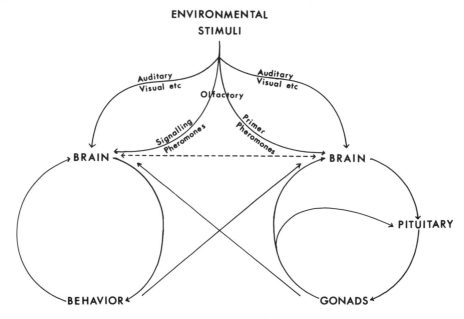

FIG. 1. Environmental stimuli, including "social" stimuli from sexual and nonsexual partners, influence brain mechanisms controlling sexual behavior and the reproductive system, each of which is part of a "feedback loop." The two loops are interconnected by the effects of gonadal hormones on sexual behavior and effects of coitus-derived stimuli on neuroendocrine activity. (From Bermant and Davidson, 1974.)

show this neuroendocrine reflex under certain circumstances has been promoted by various authors (refs. cited in Jochle, 1973). However, as yet, increases in gonadotropin secretion have not been demonstrated to result from coitus in humans. Table 1 shows pre- and postcoital levels of plasma gonadotropins in

TABLE 1. *Plasma FSH, LH, and testosterone in human males and females shortly before coitus and about 20 min after its termination**

Hormone	Female		Male	
	Pre	Post	Pre	Post
LH (ng LER-960/ml)	1.36 ± 0.42 (5)	1.33 ± 0.18 (5)	0.95 ± 0.07 (7)	0.99 ± 0.06 (7)
FSH (ng LER-1366/ml)	2.57 ± 0.73 (5)	2.97 ± 0.65 (5)	1.83 ± 0.24 (5)	1.71 ± 0.12 (5)
Testosterone (ng/ml)	—	—	5.7 ± 1.2 (6)	5.0 ± 0.6 (6)

Mean ± SE.
* All males and all except one female experienced orgasm. One female was in midcycle, and the rest were perimenstrual. Numbers of subjects in parentheses. All determinations were by radioimmunoassay.

young men and women (see table footnote for details of the study). No significant changes in FSH or LH in either sex were observed following coitus. Independent of this work, another group has failed recently to find effects of coitus on serum FSH or LH in women (Stearns, Winter, and Faiman, 1973). These data are not sufficient to negate the possibility that "paracyclic ovulation" may occur in women under different circumstances; more extensive studies at various stages of the menstrual cycle are required.

Several reports in recent years (e.g., Fox and Fox, 1971) have suggested the possibility of coitus-induced increases in testosterone secretion in men. In our small study, plasma testosterone also was measured in men. As shown in Table 1, no significant effects on release of this hormone was observed. Whereas these data indicate that large changes in testosterone are unlikely, small effects might be found with repetitive sampling procedures.

NEURAL MEDIATION OF THE ANDROGENIC ACTIVATION OF SEXUAL BEHAVIOR

Actions of steroid hormones on brain and behavior are diagrammed in Fig. 1. In this context, we have observed that implants of crystalline testosterone propionate (TP) in the anterior hypothalamic–preoptic area (AHPO) restore male copulatory behavior, including the ejaculatory response in castrated rats (Davidson, 1966; Johnston and Davidson, 1972). Similar implants of dihydrotestosterone (DHT) (or systemic injections) are ineffective, so that 5α reduction apparently is not a necessary step in the action of testosterone on brain receptors underlying behavior, as it seems to be for androgen action on the prostate.

Hypothalamic implants do not completely restore sexual behavior either in terms of numbers of animals which respond or the quality of the behavior in those that do respond (Davidson, 1966; Johnston and Davidson, 1972). Although there are various possible explanations for this finding, it was of particular interest to determine whether it was due to lack of androgenic stimulation at the periphery (particularly the penis), as the possible behavioral importance of this type of action of androgen is an important and unsettled question (see Bermant and Davidson, 1974). The apparent ineffectiveness of DHT on the brain has led us to utilize it in studying this question.

It was reasoned that if the failure of hypothalamic testosterone implants to fully restore copulatory behavior was due to lack of androgen at the periphery, then supplementing an implant with systemic administration of DHT should result in full behavioral activation. The data from a similar study are shown in Fig. 2. DHT was administered either in daily subcutaneous injections (100 μg/day) of the propionate or as the free alcohol in silastic capsules (30 mm in length, 1.6 mm i.d.). The two treatments (commenced 7 to 10 days before TP implantation) resulted in similar accessory sexual gland weights, and the combined autopsy data are *seminal vesicles:* vehicle, 101.2 ± 7.1 mg (SE); DHT, 304.7 ± 16.2; *ventral prostate:* vehicle, 69.4 ± 7.5; DHT, 293.1 ± 21.8. It is seen that systemic TP (100 μg/per 100 gm) results in complete restoration of ejaculatory responses by 2

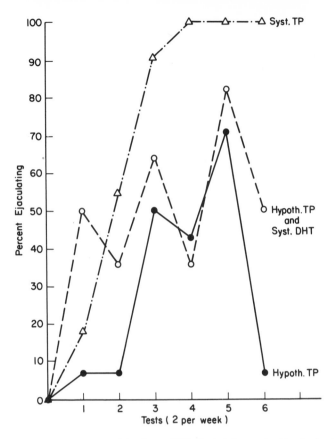

FIG. 2. Effects of daily subcutaneous injections of TP; single intracerebral implants of crystalline TP (200 µg) in the AHPO region plus systemic (s.c.) DHT; or AHPO implants of TP plus s.c. vehicle, on the sexual behavior of castrated male rats. Tests were terminated after 15 min in the absence of intromission or 30 min in the absence of ejaculation.

weeks after the onset of treatment. Neither AHPO implants of TP nor such implants supplemented with adequate systemic doses of DHT had effects that approached 100% restoration of copulatory behavior. Futhermore, although the DHT seemed to augment behavior on the first, second, and last tests, in the intervening period there were no significant differences that could be attributed to DHT action. Because earlier experiments (Bloch and Davidson, 1971) showed that even double (anterior and posterior hypothalamic) implantation of choles-terol did not prevent normal activation of sexual behavior by systemic TP, the failure to even approach 100% activation with TP implants is not caused by production of lesions in the brain. The explanation for the present findings may be that a certain concentration of androgen receptors for male sexual behavior may exist in parts of the brain other than the AHPO. They do not support the necessity for androgenic stimulation of the penis in adulthood, although they do not eliminate its possible role in this respect.

Knowledge of the behavioral ineffectiveness of DHT in rats has stimulated interest in the possibility that conversion to estrogen may be necessary for the behavior-stimulatory action of androgen on the brain, as DHT is not aromatizable. Whereas estrogen administration alone is relatively ineffective in stimulating male sexual behavior in rats, several groups have shown recently that combinations of estrogen with dihydrotestosterone (both administered systemically) are remarkably effective in this respect (Baum and Vreeburg, 1973; Larsson and Sodersten, 1973; Feder, Naftolin, and Ryan, 1974). Some years ago, we found that large implants of estradiol benzoate (EB) in the AHPO did not restore intromissions or ejaculations in castrated male rats (Davidson, 1968, *unpublished observations*). Accordingly, we performed experiments in which AHPO implants of EB were combined with subcutaneous implants of DHT in silastic capsules (similar to those used in the above experiment) and studied the effects of this combination on sexual behavior in rats castrated on day 30.

As shown in Fig. 3, the combined EB–DHT treatment produced levels of male

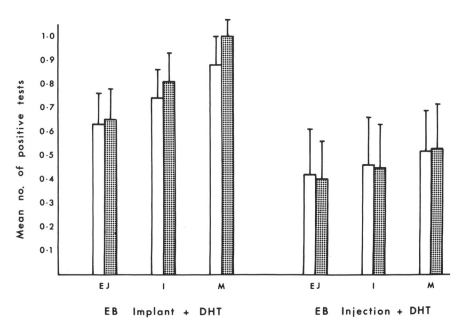

FIG. 3. Effects of combinations of AHPO implants of EB (fused to the tips of 22 gauge tubing) or s.c. EB injections (0.5 μg/day) plus DHT in silastic capsules (see text) on sexual behavior in castrated male rats. 1.0: the response was shown on all tests by all rats. Open bars represent mean responses on tests conducted on days 11, 14, 16, 18, 21, 23, 25, and 28 after implantation. Shaded bars show results from 10 tests conducted during 1 month after removal of DHT (on day 29). DHT was implanted 10 days before EB; a test conducted 7 days after DHT implantation was almost entirely negative. Vertical lines are standard errors. EJ, ejaculations; I, intromissions; M, mounts. Tests as in Fig. 2.

copulatory behavior similar to those obtained with intrahypothalamic implants of TP alone several weeks following the onset of treatment (in addition to which levels were maintained longer). Other groups of animals were treated with low doses of EB injected s.c. (0.5 μg/day) combined with the same DHT treatments as in the case of the brain implants. The latter animals responded with lower levels of behavior than when AHPO implants of EB were used. The surprising outcome of these experiments, however, was that when testing was continued for 4 weeks after removal of the DHT capsules, there was no decrease in the levels of ejaculations, intromissions, or mounts observed either with the implants or injections of EB (see Fig. 3). This puzzling finding suggests that the effectiveness of the combined EB–DHT treatment is not to be explained by any simple hypothesis involving direct activation of behavior by means of aromatized metabolites at the brain level and 5α-reduced metabolites acting peripherally. It does rather suggest that DHT may act in conjunction with estrogen to "trigger" behavioral responsiveness independent of *concurrent* stimulation of the periphery. Evidence that DHT may synergize with estrogen at the level of the brain has most recently been presented by Baum, Sodersten, and Vreeburg (1974).

FUNCTIONAL CHARACTERISTICS OF ANDROGEN "RECEPTORS"

The broken line connecting the two loops of Fig. 1 symbolizes the uncertain relationship between the putative hypothalamic receptors mediating male sexual behavior, and the other negative feedback receptors, which inhibit the secretion of gonadotropins. We have compared the functional characteristics of these two anatomically contiguous systems in other publications (Davidson, Johnston, Bloch, Smith, and Weick, 1971; Davidson, Cheung, Smith, and Johnston, 1973); relevant comparisons are summarized in Table 2.

TABLE 2. *Characteristics of androgen "receptors" for negative feedback (LH) and sexual behavior*

Parameter	Feedback	Behavior
Location	MBH–pituitary	AHPO
Sensitivity		greater
Postcastration		
hyposensitivity	?	+
Dihydrotestosterone	+	−
Antiandrogenicity of:		
Cyproterone	+	−
Flutamide	+	−

One of the interesting ways in which these two androgen actions differ in the rat is in their responses to the potent antiandrogen cyproterone. Despite its strong antagonistic actions on the classic androgen target tissues and the negative feedback regulation of gonadotropins (Bloch and Davidson, 1967; Von Berswordt-Wallrabe and Neumann, 1967) it has no antiandrogenic effects on the behavior of experienced adult male rats (refs. cited in Bloch and Davidson, 1971).

Recently, a new antiandrogen, which differs from cyproterone in being non-steroidal, but is equipotent in antiandrogenicity, has been developed (Neri et al., 1972). In preliminary experiments with this compound, flutamide (4'-nitro-3'-trifluoromethylisobutyranilide) we have found that it shares the differential actions mentioned above for cyproterone. Large daily doses (50 mg/kg) of fluta-mide had no adverse effects on any aspect of male sexual behavior in adult rats over a 4-week period of administration. At the end of that period, however, plasma LH had risen to the level expected after the rats had been castrated for an equal length of time. Furthermore, plasma testosterone concentration had reached the impressively high mean titer of about 25 ng/ml (normal value in intact males is 2 to 3 ng/ml).

These experiments, still in progress, thus extend the concept that feedback and behavior receptors respond very differently to antiandrogens beyond the previous studies, which utilized biologic end points rather than radioimmunoassay. They show that the properties of the antiandrogen cyproterone are not merely an idiosyncracy of one molecular type, as they are shared by an antiandrogen of quite different molecular structure.

ACKNOWLEDGMENTS

This work was supported by grants HD 00778 and MH 1778 from the NIH. The technical assistance of Ann Bergfors and Dorothy Tallentire is gratefully acknowledged. We are also most grateful for the help of Dr. M. M. Grumbach and Dr. S. L. Kaplan (University of California, San Francisco) who performed the assays on blood from human subjects.

REFERENCES

Adler, N. T. (1969): Effects of the male's copulatory behavior on successful pregnancy of the female rat. *J. Comp. Physiol. Psychol.,* 69:613–622.

Baum, M. J., and Vreeburg, J. T. M. (1973): Copulation in castrated male rats following combined treatment with estradiol and dihydrotestosterone. *Science,* 182:283–284.

Baum, M. J., Sodersten, P., and Vreeburg, J. T. M. (1974): Mounting and receptive behavior in the ovariectomized female rat: Influence of estradiol, dihydrotestosterone, and genital anesthetization. *Horm. Behav.,* 5:175–190.

Bermant, G., and Davidson, J. M. (1974): *Biological Bases of Sexual Behavior.* Harper and Row, New York.

Berswordt-Wallrabe, R. von, and Neumann, F. (1967): Influence of testosterone antagonist (cyproter-one) on pituitary and serum FSH-content in juvenile male rats. *Neuroendocrinology,* 2:107–112.

Bloch, G. J., and Davidson, J. M. (1967): Anti-androgen implanted in brain stimulates male reproduc-tive system. *Science,* 155:593–595.

Bloch, G. J., and Davidson, J. M. (1971): Behavioral and somatic responses to the antiandrogen cyproterone. *Horm. Behav.,* 2:11–25.

Brown-Grant, K., Davidson, J. M., and Greig, F (1973): Induced ovulation in albino rats exposed to constant light. *J. Endocrinol.,* 57:7–22.

Chester, R. V., and Zucker, I. (1970): Influence of male copulatory behavior on sperm transport, pregnancy, and pseudopregnancy in female rats. *Physiol. Behav.,* 5:35–43.

Davidson, J. M. (1966): Activation of the male rat's sexual behavior by intracerebral implantation of androgen. *Endocrinology,* 79:783–794.

Davidson, J. M., Cheung, C., Smith, E. R., and Johnston, P. (1973): Feedback regulation of gonado-tropins in the male. *Advan. Biosci.,* 10:63–72.

Davidson, J. M., Johnston, P., Bloch, G. J., Smith E. R., and Weick, R. F. (1970): Comparative responses to androgen of anatomic, behavioral and other parameters. *Exc. Med. Int. Congr. Ser.,* 184:727–730.

Davidson, J. M., Smith, E. R., and Bowers, C. Y. (1973): Effects of mating on gonadotropin release in the female rat. *Endocrinology,* 93:1185–1192.

Feder, H. H., Naftolin, F., and Ryan, K. J. (1974): Male and female sexual responses in male rats given estradiol benzoate and 5α-androstane-17β-ol-3-one propionate. *Endocrinology,* 94:136–141.

Fox, C. A., and Fox, B. (1971): A comparative study of coital physiology, with special reference to the sexual climax. *J. Reprod. Fertil.,* 24:319–336.

Jochle, W. (1973): Coitus-induced ovulation. *Contraception,* 7:523–564.

Johnston, P., and Davidson, J. M. (1972): Intracerebral androgens and sexual behavior in the male rat. *Horm. Behav.,* 3:345–357.

Larsson, K., and Sodersten, P. (1973): Sexual behavior in male rats treated with estrogen in combina-tion with dihydrotestosterone. *Horm. Behav.,* 4:289–299.

Neri, R., Florance, K., Koziol, P., and Van Cleave, S. (1972): A biological profile of a nonsteroidal antiandrogen SCH 13521-(4'-nitro-3'-trifluoromethylisobutyranilide). *Endocrinology,* 91:427–437.

Smith, E. R., and Davidson, J. M. (1974): Luteinizing hormone releasing factor in constant light exposed rats: Effects of mating. *Neuroendocrinology,* 14:129–138.

Stearns, E. L., Winter, J. S. D., and Faiman, C. (1973): Effects of coitus on gonadotropin, prolactin and sex steroid levels in man. *J. Clin. Endocrinol. Metab.,* 37:687–691.

Wilson, J. R., Adler, N., and LeBoeuf, B. (1965): The effects of intromission frequency on successful pregnancy in the female rat. *Proc. Natl. Acad. Sci. U.S.,* 53:1392–1395.

Sexual Behavior: Pharmacology and Biochemistry, edited by M. Sandler and G. L. Gessa. Raven Press, New York © 1975.

Drugs and Sexual Motivation in the Female Rat

Bengt J. Meyerson

Department of Medical Pharmacology, University of Uppsala, Uppsala, Sweden

Modern neuropharmacology provides several interesting tools to be used in the investigation of sexual behavior. For some compounds the action is sufficiently well understood for their effects on sexual behavior to be able to provide information about the neurophysiologic processes involved in the production and maintenance of this behavior. Knowledge about basic neurophysiologic and psychopharmacologic mechanisms related to sexual behavior is of course, necessary for a future specific pharmacotherapy of sexual disorders.

A prime difficulty when taking the step from pure behavior studies to behavior pharmacology is to find relevant parameters to measure the effect of drugs on behavior. The methods must be chosen taking into account the unavoidable necessity of running large series, dose-response curves, time-response relationships, and the use of many different agents.

Most investigations on the pharmacology of sexual behavior have been concerned with copulatory behavior. This behavior pattern is relatively easy to define and record as it represents an easily recognizable hormone-dependent motor pattern. In the female rat an antagonistic action of 5-hydroxytryptamine on copulatory behavior has been proposed based upon the effect of neuropharmacologic agents with different actions on CNS monoaminergic mechanisms. (For reviews see Meyerson, Eliasson, Lindström, Michanek, and Söderlund, 1973; Meyerson, Carrer and Eliasson, 1974.) It could be assumed that copulatory behavior is preceded by a physiologic state that brings the subject actively to seek sexual contact. This urge to seek sexual contact will in the following discussion be called sexual motivation. It is probably wise to distinguish the eagerness to seek sexual contact (sexual motivation) from the intensity of the copulatory behavior (lordotic behavior, mounting, etc.). To analyze the effects of hormones and drugs on sexual motivation, we employed techniques to measure the urge of the female rat to seek contact with a sexually active male. The methods differ with respect to the behavior the subject has to perform to reach contact with the incentive object.

BEHAVIOR TECHNIQUES USED

Details of the techniques used and environmental conditions are described elsewhere (Meyerson and Lindström, 1973a). The animals used were ovariectomized Sprague-Dawley rats (purchased as specific pathogen-free, 250 to 300 g), which were kept under reverse daylight regimen (12 hr light and 12 hr darkness); the tests were conducted during the dark period of the cycle.

Sexual Motivation

The *increasing barrier technique* was used to record how much of an aversive stimulus the female was willing to take to reach contact with the sexually active male (Fig. 1). The animal had to pass from one cage (starting cage) through the grid to a second cage (goal cage), which held the sexually vigorous male. The grid current was increased stepwise every second time the animal crossed. The animal was allowed 15 sec in the goal cage and was then replaced in the starting cage again until it was no longer willing to cross (i.e., after 5 min had been spent in the starting cage). Before the experiment started, the animals were subjected to a standardized training procedure. The time spent before the animal crossed the grid (hesitation time) and the amount of the grid current the subject was willing to take was recorded by an electromechanical device.

In the *open-field method* the animals were observed on a circular observation arena. The sexually active male was placed in a mesh cage in the center of the field. A wall running straight across the field dividing it into two semicircular observation areas where two animals could be tested simultaneously. The circumference of each semicircular field held a mesh cage, which held a spayed estradiol benzoate + progesterone-treated female. The animal under study was free to move around and the location was recorded photographically by a movie camera located in the center of the box, once every minute for 60 min per test session. The only light source was a 60-W lightbulb behind an infrared filter. Location is expressed in terms of percentage of the records in which the animal was located in a certain area. In later studies we replaced the photographic recording with an electromechanical device that consists of microswitches connected to 36 10×10 cm aluminum plates that constitute the floor of the field. The location of the test subject was recorded every second in this apparatus and printed out on a recorder (Sodeco) every 5 min. The locomotor activity in the field was recorded by a count each time the animal closed a microswitch. Location in the male or female vicinity means for both recording systems that the experimental subject was located within 10 cm from the cages that held the incentive animals.

The *runway-choice method* was designed to investigate the choice between sexually active male versus an estrous female in a run-and-choose situation. The experimental animal was placed in a runway, which at the far end led the animal to two separate goal cages, one holding a vigorous male and the other one an estrous female. Each experimental female was subjected to 20 consecutive trials each test session. The number of trials the female entered one of the goal cages and the percentage of these trials the female entered the goal cage with a male were recorded.

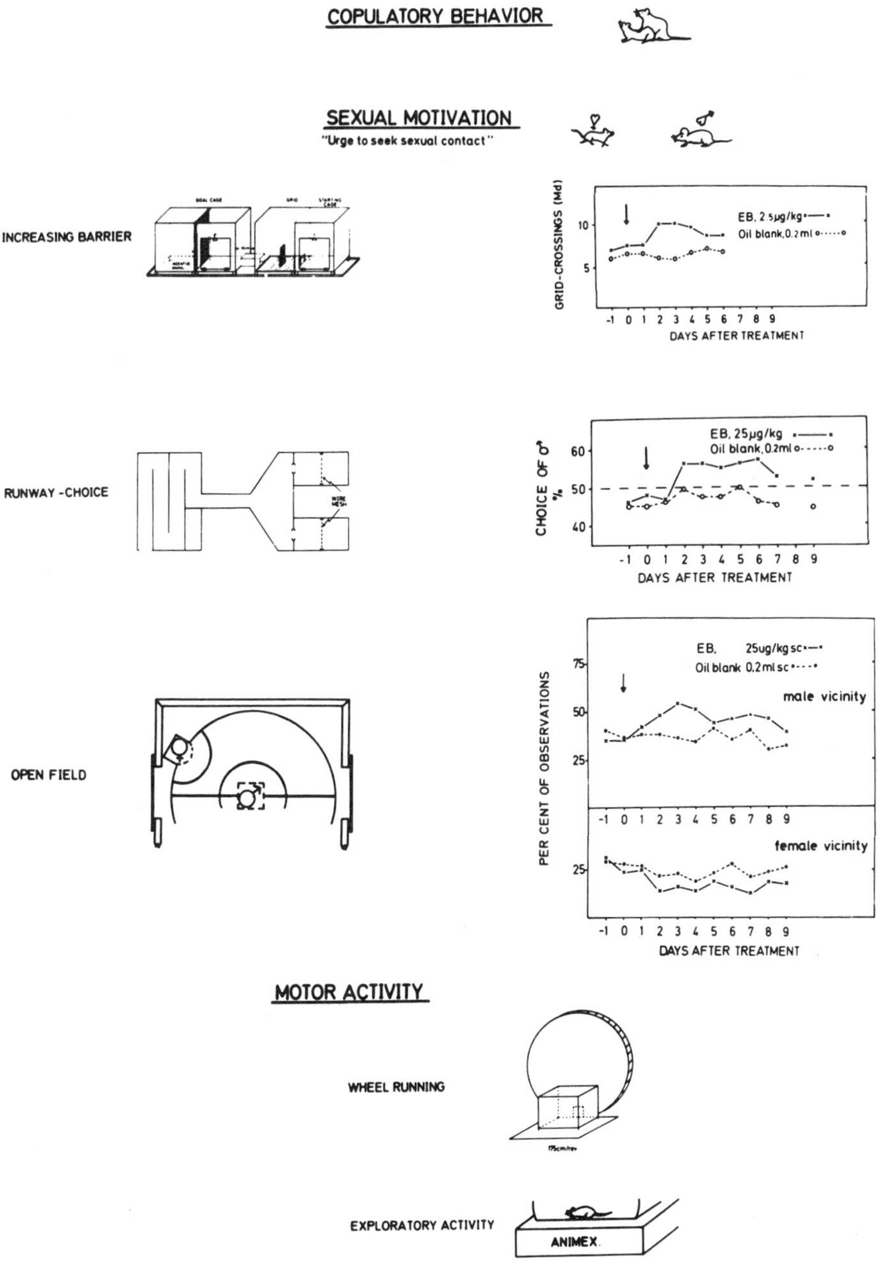

FIG. 1. Behavior techniques used. (A detailed description of the procedures is given in Meyerson and Lindström, 1973a.)

Statistically significant differences were tested by the Wilcoxon matched pairs signed-ranks test, or Mann-Whitney U test (Siegel, 1956).

Copulatory Behavior

Lordotic response on mounting by a male was tested by transferring the female to an observation cage that held a sexually active male. Copulatory behavior was induced by a single injection of estradiol benzoate followed 48 hr later by progesterone (0.4 mg/rat). The hormones were dissolved in olive oil. The first test was conducted 4 hr after the progesterone treatment (preinjection test, see Table 1).

Motor Activity

The techniques used to study sexual motivation also give some information about the motor ability of the tested animals. The hesitation times in the increasing barrier technique, the locomotor activity in the open field, and the number of trials the subject completes running through the runway and entering the goal cage in the run-and-choose technique, will point to whether motor ability is impaired. However, to guide the choice of appropriate dose regimen, the studies on the effect of neuropharmacologic agents start by a test of locomotor activity measured by an Animex activity meter (Farad, Stockholm) and by a wheel-running apparatus (Fig. 1). In the Animex meter, one subject at a time was placed for 10 min in an empty Macrolon® cage (42 X 27 X 15h cm). The activity measured during this time mainly reflects the animal's exploration of the cage. The running wheel was adjoining a 25 X 25 X 25 cm cage in which the animal had free access to food and water. The number of revolutions (every 175 cm) per 12 hr (the dark period) was recorded (Table 2).

EFFECTS OF HORMONES

It is well established that copulatory behavior in the female rat is dependent on gonadal hormones. The state that brings the female animal to seek contact with a sexually active male was shown in the 1920s in studies using extracts of hormones and intact animals; a relationship between gonadal hormones and sexual motivation in the female rat was proved (Nissen, 1929). With the techniques we use, there has been a constant finding that during the proestrous–estrous state of the estrous cycle the female seeks more contact with the male than during the diestrous state of the cycle (Table 3, Meyerson and Lindström, 1973a; Eliasson and Meyerson, 1974). In ovariectomized subjects estradiol benzoate induced an obvious increase in the amount of aversive stimuli the subject was willing to stand to reach contact with a sexually active male (the increasing barrier technique); the female spent more time sitting close to the male as measured by the open-field technique, and in the runway-choice situation there was

TABLE 1. The effect of pargyline+ Ro 4–4602+ 5-HTP on estradiol+ progesterone-activated copulatory behavior in ovariectomized rats

Treatment	Lordosis response[a] %				N	Animex activity[b] (counts/10 min mean ± S.E.M.)	N
	Pre-inj.	Hr after last inj.					
		$\frac{1}{2}$	$1\frac{1}{2}$	3			
Pargyline (25) and Ro 4–4602 (25) and							
5-HTP (2.5)	73	77	68	45[+]	22	981 ± 49	6
(5.0)	63	73	33[++]	17[++]	30	563 ± 171 [+]	6
Saline 0.2 ml	75	89	85	79	48	950 ± 49	6
Pargyline (10) and Ro 4–4602 (25) and							
5-HTP (5.0)	85	100	95	95	19	803 ± 36	9
Saline 0.2 ml	88	88	88	88	12	850 ± 65	6
Saline 0.2 ml	75	79	79	79	24	852 ± 53	12

[a] Estradiol benzoate (10 μg/kg s.c.) was followed 48 hr later by progesterone (0.4 mg/rat). The preinjection test was performed 4 hr and the $\frac{1}{2}$-hr test 6 hr after the progesterone injection. All injections were s.c. except 5-HTP and saline, which were given i.p. The estimate of the percentage of lordosis responses is based on the number of animals showing a positive lordosis response after at least 2 out 5–6 mounts. Significant difference between 5-HTP treatment and saline tested by χ^2: +, $p < 0.05$ ++, $p < 0.01$.

[b] Animals run in the Animex meter were treated in the same way as those tested for lordotic response. Tests were performed for 10 min 3 hr after 5-HTP injection. Significance was tested by Mann Whitney U-test.

TABLE 2. *Locomotor activity in ovariectomized rats after treatment with estradiol benzoate and* p-*chlorophenylalanine methylester HCl (PCPA)*

		Day				
		1	2	3	4	
		PCPA (mg/kg i.p.)				
Activity	Group	100	50	50	50	N
		% increase from preexp. level mean ± S.E.M.				
Wheel-running[a]	Exp. animals	41 ± 12	35 ± 15	98 ± 32	110 ± 31	6
	Controls	85 ± 24	143 ± 37	245 ± 60	415 ± 202	6
	(p)	NS	0.02	0.05	NS	
Animex[b]						
(counts/10 min)	Exp. animals	865 ± 26	810 ± 26	788 ± 32	886 ± 58	12
	Controls	880 ± 48	770 ± 37	830 ± 83	920 ± 60	12
	(p)	NS	NS	NS	NS	

[a] The number of revolutions per 12 hr was recorded. Estradiol benzoate (5 μg/kg s.c.) was given at day 1. The increased activity in controls after the estrogen treatment was significant from day 2 ($p < 0.01$). Recordings were taken during five consecutive days before the estrogen was given (preexperimental period). The experimental period wheel activity is expressed as percentage of the average preexperimental period activity. Controls preexperimental activity: 469 ± 203. Experimentals: 462 ± 150 rev/12 hr. Statistical significance was tested by Student's *t*-test.

[b] Estradiol benzoate (10 μg/kg) was given at day 0. PCPA was injected 5 hr before test.

TABLE 3. *Changes during the estrous cycle*

		Vaginal smear			% increase of response		
Methods	Measurements	D_1	P	E	$(E/D_1 - 1)$ 100	P	N
Open field	% of observation with female in male vicinity	40	55	58	45	<0.01	7
Increasing barrier	Average number of crossings	7.6	8.5	11.4	50	<0.01	10
Runway choice	% choice of male versus female	56.2	71.2	68.1	21	<0.05	11

All subjects had a regular five-day cycle of the D, D, P, E^1, E^2 type. Data taken from Meyerson and Lindström, 1973; Eliasson and Meyerson, 1975.

an increase in the number of trials the male was chosen versus an estrous female (Meyerson and Lindström, 1973a).

Testosterone propionate had an effect similar to estradiol benzoate (Meyerson, Lindström, Nordström, and Ågmo, 1973) but the nonaromatizable androgen, dihydrotestosterone benzoate, was ineffective in producing an effect on sexual behavior (McDonald and Meyerson, 1973). The antiestrogen, MER-25, has been shown effectively to inhibit the estrogen-activated copulatory behavior in the female rat (Meyerson and Lindström, 1968). In addition, the estrogen-induced response in the increasing barrier technique was inhibited by pretreatment with MER-25. The testosterone-induced response was delayed but not completely blocked (McDonald and Meyerson, 1973).

THE EFFECT OF NEONATAL TESTOSTERONE TREATMENT

Psychosexual differentiation in the female rat is influenced by androgenic stimulation during a neonatal period around 5 days postpartum (Barraclough and Gorski, 1962; Harris and Levine, 1965; Gerall and Ward, 1966). Later, female copulatory behavior is abolished in the intact female rat as well as hormone-activated behavior in ovariectomized rats. Females were given 1 mg testosterone propionate subcutaneously at 5 days of age and were ovariectomized and tested for sexual motivation as adults. The estrogen-induced urge to seek contact with the male was not seen in these animals even after high doses of estradiol benzoate (100 μg/kg), nor were there any significant effects obtained when the incentive animal was an estrous female (Meyerson and Lindström, 1970, 1973b).

EFFECT OF DRUGS[1]; INCREASED MONOAMINERGIC ACTIVITY

The monoamine oxidase inhibitor pargyline was given together with a peripheral decarboxylase inhibitor (Ro 4–4602; Bartholini and Pletscher, 1968) and the serotonin precursor 5-hydroxytryptophan (5-HTP). The aim of this combination of drugs was selectively to increase the amount of serotonin in the brain and to impair at the same time the synthesis of serotonin outside the blood-brain barrier. The effect of this treatment on the estrogen + progesterone-activated lordotic behavior and exploratory behavior is shown in Table 1. The pargyline (25 mg/kg) + Ro 4–4602 (25 mg/kg) + 5-HTP (2.5 or 5.0 mg/kg) treatment significantly decreased the number of animals that displayed a lordotic response on mounting by a male (Table 1). The effect was most evident at the test performed 3 hr after the 5-HTP injection. At this time the locomotor activity as measured in the Animex activity meter was slightly reduced after 5 but not after 2.5 mg/kg 5-HTP. When the dose of pargyline was reduced to 10 mg/kg in an otherwise analogously conducted experiment, no inhibition of the lordotic response was obtained. The high response shown would rather indicate a stimulatory effect. However, the response of the controls and the preinjection response level were too high to permit a stimulatory effect to be established.

The number of grid crossings performed by an estrogen-treated ovariectomized female to reach contact with a sexually active male is shown in Fig. 2. Estradiol benzoate was given at day 1 and saline or pargyline + Ro 4–4602 + 5-HTP or

---

[1] Drugs injected: Pargyline HCl (Abbott), *N*-(DL-seryl)-*N*-(2,3,4-trihydroxybenzylhydrazine) (Ro 4–4602, Hoffman-La Roche), 5-hydroxy-L-tryptophan methyl ester HCl (5-HTP, Calbiochem), DL-*p*-chlorophenylalanine methyl ester (PCPA, H 69/17, Hässle) were dissolved in saline.

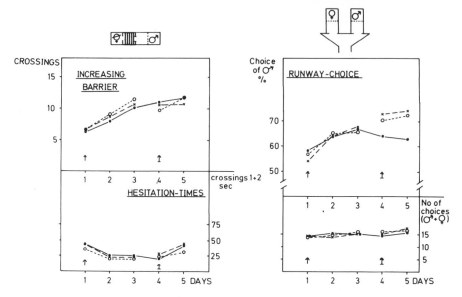

FIG. 2. Effect of pargyline (10 mg/kg) + Ro 4–4602 (25 mg/kg) and 5-HTP (5 mg/kg) (crosses at barred arrow) or saline (0.2 ml) (open circles at barred arrow) on the urge to seek contact with a sexually active male in estrogen-treated ovariectomized rats. Controls had saline (0.2 ml) instead of drug (filled circles at barred arrow). Estradiol benzoate 10 µg/kg was given day 0 (arrow) 4–6 hr before the test session started. Pargyline, Ro 4–4602, 5-HTP, or saline were injected in that order 30 min apart, the last injection 3 hr before the test day 4.

saline were injected 3 hr before the test at day 4. In saline only treated subjects, there is a slight increase of the response from day to day throughout the test period. A decrease is seen in the response between days 3 and 4 after the pargyline + Ro 4–4602 + saline treatment (Fig. 2). The response between days 3 and 4 was significantly different between the pargyline + Ro 4–4602 + saline and saline-only treatment. However, the pargyline + Ro 4–4602 + 5-HTP treatment was not significantly different from the saline-only-treated group, although the increase from days 3 to 4 seen in the saline group was not obtained in the 5-HTP group.

Given a choice between a vigorous male and an estrous female in the runway-choice apparatus, the pargyline + Ro 4–4602 + 5-HTP (5 mg/kg) treatment significantly increased the percentage of trials that the male was chosen. This effect remained the day after the treatment. The 5-HTP treatment increased the response insignificantly from the response achieved by pargyline + Ro 4–4602 + saline. The number of trials that the subject entered the goal cages was not changed by the drug treatment (Fig. 2).

THE EFFECT OF PCPA

The effect of PCPA tested in the increasing barrier apparatus shows an apparent increase of the number of grid crossings performed to reach the sexually active male (Fig. 3). On the first day of treatment there is a slight increase (not statistically significant) in hesitation times, probably due to the fact that the animals were sluggish after 100 mg/kg PCPA. It is interesting that the same dose regimen of PCPA decreased the number of crossings when water was used as reward (Meyerson, Carrer, and Eliasson, 1974) and depressed the estrogen-activated wheel-running motor activity (Table 1) but not the activity measured in the Animex meter. In the open-field technique the estrogen-induced increase in the amount of time spent in the vicinity of the male cage at day 3 was reduced significantly ($p = 0.02$) by the PCPA treatment. Also, the locomotor activity in the open field was reduced at days 1, 2, and 3 ($p < 0.02$). In the runway-choice situation the same treatment regimen was used as increasing barrier and open-field techniques. There was a slight decrement in the number of trials the subject ran into the goal cages at days 2 and 3 in the PCPA experiment. At day 3 there is an evident decrease in the preference for the male ($p < 0.001$).

CONCLUSIONS

When the data from the three different methods of studying sexual motivation are taken together, it is concluded that estrogen treatment induced a clear-cut urge to seek contact with a vigorous male. The effect seen after estradiol benzoate was also achieved by testosterone propionate, but not by the nonaromatizable androgen dihydrotestosterone. Antiestrogen MER-25 was effective in inhibiting the estrogen-activated response and also in delaying the effect of testosterone. These findings are in agreement with the data on estrogen- and testosterone-activated lordotic response in ovariectomized rats (Beach, 1942; Pfaff, 1970; Beyer and Komisaruk, 1971; Meyerson, Nordström, and Ågmo, 1971; Whalen, Battie, and Luttge, 1972). Conversion of testosterone to estradiol has been shown to occur within the CNS (Ryan, Naftolin, Reddy, Flores, and Petro, 1972). It is

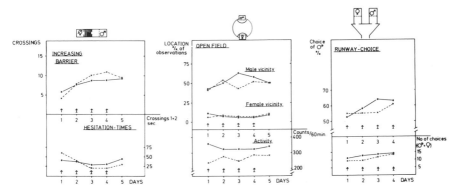

FIG. 3. Effect of PCPA on the urge to seek contact with a sexually active male in estrogen-treated ovariectomized rats. Estradiol benzoate 10 μg/kg was given 4–6 hr before test session day 1 (arrow). PCPA 100 mg/kg was given on day 1 (arrow) and 50 mg/kg on days 2, 3, and 4 (crosses at barred arrow), 5 hr before test session started. Controls had 0.2 ml saline instead of PCPA (filled circles at barred and unbarred arrows).

therefore possible that testosterone is converted to estradiol before producing the effects seen in the tests for sexual motivation. However, further investigations must be conducted before any firm conclusion can be drawn.

In early androgen-treated females that were ovariectomized as adults, estradiol benzoate was ineffective in producing a response in the increasing barrier, open-field, and runway-choice techniques. We have to analyze further different doses used in the early androgen treatment to determine whether the pattern of adult behavior could be changed by administering androgen at different times during the neonatal period.

Experiments on the neuropharmacology of sexual motivation are at a very early phase. Decreased biosynthesis of serotonin by means of PCPA treatment appears to increase the response in the increasing barrier technique. In contrast, the same treatment decreases the location to the vicinity of the male and the preference of a male versus an estrous female measured by the open-field apparatus and the runway-choice techniques, respectively. The reversed effects were obtained by pargyline + Ro 4–4602 treatment. However, the effects achieved by pargyline + Ro 4–4602 + 5-HTP were not significantly different from those seen when the 5-HTP was replaced by saline. Therefore, the role of serotonin in the regulation of sexual motivation in the female rat must be elucidated by further experiments. Perhaps by running different methods in parallel we will find a neuropharmacologic profile to provide evidence of pathways implicated in the condition that brings the animal to seek sexual contact.

ACKNOWLEDGMENTS

This investigation was supported by grants from the Swedish Medical Research Council, B74–04x–64–10C. For generous supplies of hormones we thank Organon, the Netherlands, through Erco, Sweden; Hässle, Sweden, for H 69/17; Abbott for pargyline; and Hoffmann–La Roche for Ro 4–4602.

REFERENCES

Barraclough, C. A., and Gorski, R. A. (1962): Studies on mating behavior in the androgen-sterilized female rat in relation to the hypothalamic regulation of sexual behavior. *J. Endocrinol.* 25:175.

Bartholini, G., and Pletscher, A. (1968): Cerebral accumulation and metabolism of C^{14}-DOPA after selective inhibition of peripheral decarboxylase. *J. Pharmacol. Exp. Ther.,* 161:14–20.

Beach, F. A. (1942): Male and female mating behavior in prepuberally castrated female rats treated with androgen. *Endocrinology,* 31:673–678.

Beyer, C., and B. Komisaruk (1971): Effects of diverse androgens on estrous behavior, lordosis reflex and genital tract morphology in the rat. *Hor. Behav.,* 2:217–225.

Eliasson, M., and Meyerson, B. J. (1975): Sexual preference in female rats during estrous cycle, pregnancy and lactation. *Physiol. Behav. (in press).*

Gerall, A. A., and Ward, I. L. (1966): Effects of prenatal exogenous androgen on the sexual behaviour of the female albino rat. *J. Comp. Physiol. Psychol.,* 62:370–375.

Harris, G. W., and Levine, S. (1965): Sexual differentiation of the brain and its experimental control. *J. Physiol. (Lond.),* 181:379.

McDonald, P., and Meyerson, B. J. (1973): The effect of oestradiol, testosterone and dihydrotestosterone on sexual motivation in the ovariectomized female rat. *Physiol. Behav.,* 11:515–520.

Meyerson, B. J., Carrer, H., and Eliasson, M. (1974): 5-Hydroxytryptamine and sexual behavior in the female rat. In: *Serotonin—New Vistas: Biochemistry and Behavioral and Clinical Studies, Advances in Biochemical Psychopharmacology,* Vol. 11, edited by E. Costa, G. L. Gessa, and M. Sandler, pp. 229–242. Raven Press, New York.

Meyerson, B. J., Eliasson, M., Lindström, L., Michanek, A., and Söderlund, A.-Ch. (1973): Monoamines and female sexual behavior. In: *Psychopharmacology, Sexual Disorders and Drug Abuse,* edited by T. A. Ban, J. R. Boissier, G. J. Gessa, H. Heimann, L. Hollister, H. E. Lehmann, I. Munkvad, H. Steinberg, F. Sulser, A. Sundwall, and O. Vinar. North-Holland Publ., Amsterdam.

Meyerson, B. J., and Lindström, L. (1968): Effects of an oestrogen antagonist ethamoxytriphetol (MER-25) on oestrous behaviour in rats. *Acta Endocrinol.,* 51:41–48.

Meyerson, B. J., and Lindström, L. (1970): Sexual motivation in the estrogen treated ovariectomized rat. In: *Hormonal Steroids* (Proc. IIInd Int. Congr. Hamburg), edited by L. Martini and V. H. T. James. Excerpta Med. Inter. Congr. Ser. No. 219.

Meyerson, B. J., and Lindström, L. (1973a): Sexual motivation in the female rat. *Acta Physiol. Scand.,* Suppl. *389,* 1–80.

Meyerson, B. J., and Lindström, L. (1973b): Sexual motivation in the neonatally androgen-treated female rat. In: *Hormones and Brain Function* (K. Lissák, ed.) Plenum Press, New York.

Meyerson, B. J., Lindström, L., Nordström, E-B, and Ågmo, A. (1973): Sexual motivation in the female rat after testosterone treatment. *Physiol. Behav.,* 11:421–428.

Meyerson, B. J., Nordström, E. B., and Ågmo, A. (1971): Sexual behaviour and testosterone in the female rat. *Acta Pharmacol. Tox.,* 29, Suppl. 4.

Nissen, H. W. (1929): The effects of gonadectomy, vasotomy and injections of placental and orchic extracts on the behavior of the white rat. *Genet. Psychol. Monogr.,* 5:455–547.

Pfaff, D. (1970): Nature of sex hormone effects on the rat sexual behavior: Specificity of effects and individual patterns of response. *J. Comp. Physiol. Psychol.,* 73:349–358.

Ryan, K. J., Naftolin, F., Reddy, V., Flores, F. and Petro, Z. (1972): Estrogen formation in the brain. *Am. J. Obstet. Gynecol.,* 114:454–460i.

Siegel, S. (1956): *Nonparametric Statistics for Behavioral Sciences.* McGraw-Hill, New York.

Whalen, R. E., Battie, L., and Luttge, W. G. (1972): Antioestrogen inhibition of androgen induced sexual receptivity in rats. *Behav. Biol.,* 7:311–320.

Whalen, R. E., and Hardy, D. V. (1970): Induction of receptivity in female rats and cats with estrogen and testosterone. *Physiol. Behav.,* 5:529–533.

Sexual Behavior: Pharmacology and Biochemistry, edited by M. Sandler and G. L. Gessa. Raven Press, New York © 1975.

Methodologic Considerations in the Study of Animal Sexual Behavior

Richard E. Whalen, Boris B. Gorzalka, and Joseph F. DeBold

University of California, Irvine, California 92664

The use of drugs to study sexual function has had a long history. Loewe, for example, reported in 1938 that the ejaculatory reflex in mice is facilitated by parasympathomimetic drugs and is inhibited by parasympatholytic drugs. More recently, in the 1950s the Soulairacs published a number of papers on the effects of various agents on rat copulatory behavior (Soulairac, 1952; Soulairac and Soulairac, 1957, 1961). Throughout the 1960s Meyerson was probably the most active investigator using drugs to dissect the neurologic substrate of sexual behavior (Meyerson, 1964; Meyerson and Lewander, 1970). Today, a large number of investigators (Tagliamonte, Tagliamonte, Gessa, and Brodie, 1969) are actively pursuing the pharmacology of sexual activity.

It would be rewarding if we could draw upon the hundreds of published studies to formulate a clear picture of the chemistry of sexuality. Unfortunately, we cannot do so. The contradictions in the literature are numerous and for the most part unexplained. We would therefore like to consider some of the methodologic problems we face in the analysis of sexual behavior.

Organismic Factors

When studying the pharmacology of sexual behavior the most obvious organismic variable is the species studied. Different species may react somewhat differently to the same drug, but more importantly, different species exhibit different patterns of mating, patterns that are under different degrees of hormonal and environmental control. For example, castration of the male rat results in a relatively rapid decline in mating activity. Prior sexual experience appears to have relatively little effect upon this decline in rats that were sexually vigorous before castration (Rabedeau and Whalen, 1959). In contrast, male cats may contine to copulate for several months following castration, particularly if they are sexually experienced (Rosenblatt and Aronson, 1958). Another example concerns the stimulus control of mating. Male rats distinguish between appropriate and inappropriate sexual stimuli quite well (Beach, 1942) and rarely mount other males, whereas male cats often show male-to-male mounting (Michael, 1961). These studies illustrate the need for considering a variety of organismal factors such as species, initial sexual responsiveness, and sexual experience.

We believe that the organismal factors listed above have contributed to some of the inconsistencies that we find in the literature. Zitrin, Beach, Barchas, and Dement 1970) have also emphasized this point. In our own work (Whalen and Luttge, 1970), we failed to find any effect of parachlorophenylalanine (PCPA) on the probability or frequency of heterosexual interactions in male rats. This contrasts with the findings of Malmnas and Meyerson (1971) who reported that PCPA did indeed increase the probability and frequency of mounting responses displayed by male rats placed with receptive females. The two studies differ in an important way, however. We tested sexually vigorous males; Malmnas and Meyerson tested males that were maintained on submaximal dosages of testosterone such that they were less than sexually vigorous at the time of drug treatment. Therefore, our failure to find a drug facilitation of mating may have been due to the fact that our males were already mating at maximal levels at the time of drug treatment.

This interpretation is also consistent with the findings of Mitler, Morden, Levine, and Dement (1972) who reported that PCPA enhanced sexual activity in male rats that were described as being low to moderately low in sexual vigor prior to drug treatment.

Prior sexual experience may also alter a drug response. Hardy, DeBold, and Eckardt *(unpublished observations)* have found that PCPA increased the mounting of females by inexperienced males, but did not have this effect in sexually experienced males. Therefore, both initial sexual responsiveness and prior sexual experience can influence the response of male rats to PCPA.

DOSE–RESPONSE RELATIONSHIPS

Many of the studies that have been published, including our own, have used a single drug dose to determine the effect of the drug. Such an inadequate pharmacologic analysis can contribute to confusion and misinterpretations. For example, several years ago the senior author examined the effects of graded doses of *d*-amphetamine on mating in male cats. The effects of this drug on the behavior of one male-female pair is illustrated in Fig. 1. As the dose of amphetamine was increased, the frequency of intromissions per test increased dramatically. With still higher doses, however, performance declined and at a dose of 2.0 mg/kg the male failed to mate entirely. Therefore, if a single dose of 0.25 mg/kg had been used the conclusion could have been that activation of the catecholamine system stimulates mating; if a single dose of 1.0 to 2.0 mg/kg had been chosen, the conclusion would have been the opposite.

With respect to more recent studies, Zemlan, Ward, Crowley, and Margules (1973) reported that PCPA facilitated lordosis behavior in estrogen-treated female rats, a finding consistent with the earlier work of Meyerson (1964), but contrary to the findings of Segal and Whalen (1970). Zemlan et al. (1973) suggested that a critical difference between the studies may have been the dose of PCPA (Segal and Whalen used 100 mg/kg, whereas Zemlan et al. administered 316 mg/kg). Their conclusion could have been correct as Koe and Weissman

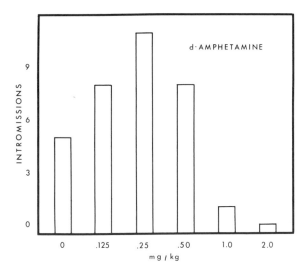

FIG. 1. Effects of various doses of *d*-amphetamine upon the sexual performance of a sexually experienced male cat. The number of intromission responses before the male ceased mating for 30 min is indicated.

(1966) have demonstrated that these two doses of PCPA do indeed differentially deplete brain serotonin at least when given as single injections. To substantiate their conclusion, we have recently replicated the Zemlan et al. (1973) experiment using both doses of PCPA and their treatment schedule (Gorzalka and Whalen, *unpublished),* the results of which are shown in Fig. 2. When the rats were tested for lordotic behavior 66 or 70 hr after PCPA (and 42 or 46 hr after estrogen treatment), neither the low dose of PCPA (100 mg/kg) nor the high dose (316 mg/kg) facilitated lordosis relative to animals treated with estrogen and drug vehicle. Consequently, although drug dose is usually a critical factor, this experiment failed to reveal such an effect with respect to the facilitation of lordosis. However, the study did reveal a dose–response relationship when we tested our animals 74 hr after PCPA and 3 hr after progesterone treatment. (The animals were given 500 µg progesterone 1 hr following the test at hour 70.) The rats treated only with estrogen and progesterone showed a high probability of lordosis. Those treated in addition with a low dose of PCPA showed a moderate inhibition of receptivity whereas those treated with a high dose of PCPA showed a greatly reduced response to progesterone. This latter finding also confirms the earlier observations of Segal and Whalen (1970) and Singer (1972) that chronic administration of PCPA reduces responsiveness to progesterone.

TIME–RESPONSE RELATIONSHIPS

Most of the published research on drugs and sexual activity has been directed toward an analysis of the acute as opposed to the chronic effects of drugs. This has been particularly true in the recent studies of female sexual behavior in which

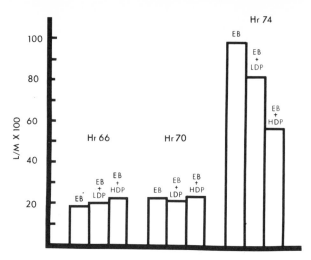

FIG. 2. Effects of parachlorophenylalanine on lordosis behavior in female rats (L/M = lordosis responses/mounts). Animals were administered estradiol benzoate (EB) or EB plus a low dose of PCPA (LDP = 100 mg/kg) or EB plus a high dose of PCPA (HDP = 316 mg/kg). All animals were tested 66 and 70 hr after PCPA treatment. At hour 71 they were given 500 μg progesterone and were tested again at hour 74. All animals were ovariectomized and adrenalectomized.

drugs have been used as substitutes for progesterone in the usual estrogen–progesterone induction of receptivity. A large number of these studies have reported that agents that deplete brain serotonin (reserpine, tetrabenazine, PCPA) can effectively substitute for progesterone, that is, estrogen-treated rats will show lordosis when tested 2 to 8 hr after drug treatment (Meyerson, 1964; Paris, Resko, and Goy, 1971; Eriksson and Södersten, 1973). In contrast, two studies that employed the chronic administration of PCPA failed to demonstrate enhanced lordosis (Segal and Whalen, 1970; Singer, 1972). Moreover, the Zemlan et al. (1973) study and our own replication (Fig. 2) in which the animals were tested 66 to 70 hr after PCPA treatment failed to yield the same results. Hence, several studies in which animals were tested shortly after drug treatment produced drug-facilitated lordosis behavior, whereas two of the three studies in which testing occurred one or more days after drug treatment failed to find facilitation. These observations would suggest that although this reflects only one factor, some of the inconsistencies in the literature may reflect differences in treatment schedules.

Part of the difficulty here seems to be with the incomplete theoretical formulation which investigators have made about the underlying substrate for sexual behavior and how drugs might be interacting with that substrate. For example, there are at least three models used to demonstrate drug action. One could speculate that the drugs work on the hormone-sensitive neurons and do so in the same way as hormones. This model states that the drugs simply mimic or exaggerate normal hormone action. This hypothesis would lead the experimenter to conduct drug experiments that parallel hormone experiments. A common example is the administration of reserpine or PCPA to the estrogen-primed rat with testing following 3 to 5 hr later. Because progesterone is effective within this time range, one would be using the drug to mimic or substitute for the hormone which normally elicits lordosis behavior.

If one were attempting to mimic the effects of testosterone in the male, one would administer the drug chronically or administer the drug in a manner that elicited some chronic change in brain chemistry, as chronic stimulation with testosterone or similar androgens is necessary to maintain mating behavior.

If one were attempting to mimic the effects of estrogen, one might give a single application of the drug followed by testing 18 to 48 hr later, a procedure that is effective in bringing female rats into heat with estrogen.

The point we wish to stress is that the design of the experiment should follow some explicit model of the possible action of the drug. In terms of our first model, that is, that the drug action mimics hormone action, the data do not favor validity of this model. There are two lines of evidence. First, the drugs which have been employed in recent years cannot substitute for testosterone or estrogen in the maintenance of sexual activity. Gessa, Tagliamonte, Tagliamonte, and Brodie (1970) failed to find enhanced male-to-male mounting in castrated rats unless they were also administered testosterone. Similarily, it has been shown that treatments with reserpine or PCPA are behaviorally effective only in estrogen-primed rats. Second, if the model were correct, one would expect that both the hormone and the drug would alter central amine or other chemical levels in the same way. This appears not to be the case (Meyerson, 1964a; Gessa et al. 1970).

A second possible model for the effects of drugs upon sexual behavior might be that amines (or other neurochemicals) modulate the activity of hormone-sensitive cells either directly or indirectly by some afferent collaterals. In this model the hormones might be necessary, but they are not sufficient for the function of the cell. One would not expect any necessary correlation between hormone levels and transmitter levels. With such a model one might design experiments in which the hormone-primed animal was tested at times when the drug was exerting its maximal pharmacologic effect. Zemlan et al. (1973) used this procedure in their study of the effects of PCPA upon lordosis behavior. Zemlan et al. tested their rats 66 to 70 hr after PCPA treatment, a time when, according to Koe and Weissman (1966), serotonin depletion is maximal. Although we failed to replicate their results (Fig. 2), the design of the experiment is clear and is based on the assumption that the maximal behavior effect should be correlated with the maximal pharmacological effect of the drug. The Ahlenius, Engel, Eriksson, Modigh, and Sodersten (1972) and Segal and Whalen (1970) experiments had the same logic.

A third possible model of drug effects might be that the drug enhances the effectiveness of the hormone, that is, that functionally it increases the dose of the hormone. A drug might accomplish this by enhancing hormone-receptor binding, if this is relevant, by slowing hormone metabolism, or by a variety of other means.

With this model one might design experiments in which the drug is combined with subthreshold levels of a hormone, applying the drug at the same time or shortly after the hormone.

These three models of how a drug might alter sexual behavior are by no means exclusive. They were only selected to illustrate how the design of an experiment might be determined by our model of its mechanism of action. We feel that by making our models explicit we can improve our chances of designing appropriate experiments. The importance of this is discussed in the next section.

SPECIFICITY OF DRUG EFFECTS

Probably the greatest difficulty we have in the analysis of drug effects upon behavior concerns the specificity of these effects. There are two concerns here: (1) is there a single unique correlation between a brain effect and a behavioral effect of a drug, and (2) is the behavioral effect of the drug indeed mediated directly by its effect upon brain biochemistry? To frame this question in one concrete way, do PCPA and all other drugs which deplete brain serotonin facilitate lordosis behavior and do they do so because they deplete brain serotonin? Only when such questions can be answered unequivocally can we begin to build a neurochemical model for the substrate of behavior.

A major difficulty is that the drugs we have available are "dirty" in the sense that they do not alter a single neurochemical system. For example, in his early studies Meyerson (1964) reported that reserpine facilitated lordosis. Reserpine, which depletes brain serotonin, also depletes norepinephrine and dopamine. Therefore, a definitive statement about the neurochemical substrate for lordosis could not be drawn.

More recently, PCPA has become the drug of choice in the control of lordosis because of its relatively greater effect upon serotonin than upon norepinephrine or dopamine. Nonetheless, it should be recalled that, according to Koe and Weissman (1966), 4 hr after treatment with PCPA, that is, at a time when animals are commonly tested, brain NE and DA levels were found to be at approximately 85% of control, whereas brain 5-HT levels were at approximately 77% of control. This difference hardly seems striking enough to suggest that the critical amine is serotonin.

Ahlenius, et al. (1972) attempted to disentangle the correlation between behavior change and changes in monoamines by examining both at various times after treatment. They administered PCPA to estrogen-primed rats and either tested them for sexual receptivity 2, 4, 8, 26, and 50 hr after treatment or killed them for amine determinations 2, 8, or 26 hr after treatment. They found that the maximal behavioral effect occurred at hour 2 and then progressively declined, even though brain serotonin levels continued to drop over a 26-hr period. At hour 26 brain serotonin levels were minimal while brain NE or DA levels had returned to normal yet lordosis was infrequent; in fact, it occurred significantly less often than in control rats not administered PCPA. They therefore suggested that the catecholamines, rather than the indoleamine, may mediate lordosis. This correlational approach does have certain advantages, yet the problem remains that the drugs employed do have multiple effects.

Another approach to solving the problem of multiple effects of a drug has been to use several drugs that have a single effect in common, but other effects to different degrees. Meyerson (1964b) employed this approach in his early studies by giving reserpine, tetrabenazine, amine precursors, such as DOPS, DOPA, and 5-HTP, as well as monoamine oxidase inhibitors. These studies yielded relatively consistent results from the pharmacological point of view. However, more recently Meyerson and Lewander (1970) have reported that although both PCPA and α-propyldopacetamide depleted brain serotonin, only the former facilitated lordosis. Such a finding presents a problem for any simple hypothesis about the relationship between brain serotonin and lordosis behavior.

The second part of our question about specificity concerns causality versus correlation. We always face the possibility that the correlations which we observe between behavior and brain levels of presumed neurotransmitters are simply fortuitous and that the chemical changes are not directly related to the changes which we see in behavior. This question has been raised most forcefully with respect to the action of drugs that facilitate lordosis. A number of investigators have argued, for example, that drugs such as reserpine and PCPA facilitate lordosis behavior not through their action on some neural behavior control system but by causing the secretion of progesterone from the adrenal gland. As this point is important for our interpretation of the mechanism of action of these drugs, these studies will be reviewed in detail.

Before discussing the pharmacologic studies, it is valuable to consider whether adrenal activation could play a role in the control of lordosis behavior. In 1969 Feder and Ruf treated ovariectomized rats and guinea pigs with estrogen and with progesterone, ACTH, or oil. Both progesterone and ACTH (but not oil) induced lordosis behavior in both species. ACTH also caused a large increase in plasma progesterone levels. In the same year Resko (1969) confirmed the observation that ACTH stimulates adrenal progesterone secretion. These two studies established the possibility that conditions, such as stress, which cause the release of ACTH, could induce the secretion of behaviorally effective levels of adrenal progesterone.

Based on the above studies, Uphouse, Wilson, and Schlesinger (1970) studied the lordosis-facilitating effects of reserpine in two strains of mice. They found that reserpine induced lordosis in ovariectomized, but not in ovariectomized–adrenalectomized animals.

Paris et al. (1971) expanded upon this work and demonstrated that reserpine would induce lordosis in estrogen-primed ovariectomized rats while increasing plasma progesterone over 300%. These investigators also showed that dexamethasone, which inhibits ACTH secretion by negative feedback, would prevent the effects of reserpine on both behavior and plasma progesterone levels. Finally, they showed that metopirone, a corticotropin stimulator, would mimic the behavioral and endocrine effects of reserpine.

More recently Eriksson and Sodersten have reported that both PCPA and

α-methyltyrosine would facilitate lordosis in adrenally intact rats, but not in adrenalectomized animals (1973).

Finally, our own earlier work (Segal and Whalen, 1970) may be relevant here. We tested our animals approximately 24 hr after each PCPA injection, that is, at a time when adrenal progesterone would presumably no longer be a factor. We found no facilitation of lordosis even though brain serotonin levels were reduced substantially.

The studies reviewed here seem to suggest quite strongly that reserpine and PCPA facilitate lordosis by causing the secretion of adrenal progesterone. Two studies disagree with these findings, Meyerson (1964b) reported that reserpine induced heat in 33 to 42% of his adrenalectomized animals whereas none of the control animals showed lordosis. It should be pointed out, however, that the criterion used for heat was rather an insensitive one—to be considered in heat, the animals were required to show only one lordosis response with eight to 10 mounts by the male. If we had applied this criterion to our own recent study of the effects of PCPA (Fig. 2), we would have found that 50 to 88% of the drug-treated animals were receptive. Moreover, we would have found also that progesterone treatment had no significant effect even in nondrugged animals.

The other report of interest is that of Zemlan et al. (1973) who reported that PCPA facilitated lordosis in adrenalectomized rats. Our failure to replicate their finding, also using adrenalectomized animals, however, leaves the question of the role of the adrenal still open.

At the risk of overemphasizing the role of the adrenal in sexual function (since there is little evidence that it plays a major role under normal conditions), we would like to mention two studies that implicate the adrenal in the effects of pharmacologic manipulations. First, we have recently examined the action of aminophylline (DeBold, Waymire, and Whalen, *unpublished observations*). Aminophylline is an inhibitor of cyclic nucleotide phosphodiesterase, the enzyme which inactivates cyclic $3',5'$-AMP (Butcher and Sutherland, 1962). Cyclic $3',5'$-AMP has been proposed as an intracellular mediator of hormone action and a large body of literature exists to support this (for reviews see Major and Kilpatrick, 1972, or Robison, Butcher, and Sutherland, 1971). We studied the possible role this system might play in the induction of sexual receptivity. Intraperitoneal injections of aminophylline were paired in time with either submaximal doses of estrogen or of progesterone, doses which had been determined earlier to result in a moderate amount of receptivity in female rats. Administration of the phosphodiesterase inhibitor coincident with either estrogen or progesterone increased the probability of lordosis in ovariectomized rats, but this facilitation was absent in ovariectomized–adrenalectomized animals as shown in Table 1. In addition, aminophylline actually inhibited responsiveness to progesterone in these animals.

The effect of aminophylline was also dose-dependent. When the aminophylline dosage was reduced to 75 μM/kg the original increase in receptivity was not seen.

In the second study (Whalen, Neubauer, and Gorzalka, *unpublished observa-*

TABLE 1. *The effects of aminophylline on the probability of lordosis in ovariectomized estrogen- and progesterone-treated female rats*

Hr 0		Hr 45		
Aminophylline (μM/kg)	Estradiol benzoate (μg)	Aminophylline (μM/kg)	Progesterone (μg)	Hr 48 Lordosis/mounts × 100
Adrenally intact rats				
0	2	0	100	34.3
200	2	0	100	73.8
0	8	0	25	26.3
0	8	200	25	51.3
Adrenalectomized rats				
0	10	0	100	94.0
0	10	0	0	30.0
0	10	60	0	12.0
0	10	60	100	14.0

tions) we applied potassium chloride to the cortex of estrogen-primed adrenally intact and adrenalectomized rats. This study follows from the work of Clemens, Wallen, and Gorski (1967) and of Ross and Gorski (1973). Both studies showed that KC1 would facilitate lordosis in the adrenally intact rat. Because cortical application of KC1 presumably depresses cortical function, these studies have contributed to the concept that lordosis behavior is under tonic cortical inhibition. Our data are shown in Fig. 3. As in previous work we found that KC1 applied to the cortex would induce lordosis behavior. This effect, however, was found only in adrenally intact animals. When both sets of animals were administered estrogen and progesterone, both showed high levels of lordosis behavior indicating that adrenalectomy in no way impaired hormone responsiveness. We have tentatively concluded that the KC1 induces lordosis through the ACTH activation of adrenal progesterone.

Based on these several studies we are led to the conclusion that at least in pharmacologic studies, concern with adrenal function constitutes a major methodologic consideration in our analysis of the substrate for female sexual behavior.

THEORETICAL FACTORS

Our final consideration concerns the interpretation of data. Although most of the studies in the recent literature have been theoretically neutral with respect to neurobehavioral mechanisms, these mechanisms are important to consider. A major question concerns the motivation–performance dichotomy. For example, does a drug such as PCPA which increases male-to-male mounting in rats in fact

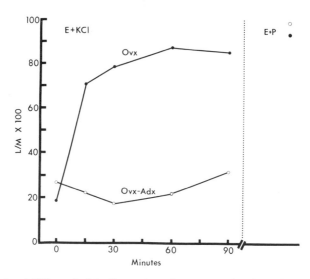

FIG. 3. Effects of KCl applied to the cortex of estrogen-primed ovariectomized (Ovx) or ovariectomized–adrenalectomized (Ovx–Adx) female rats on lordosis behavior (L/M = lordosis responses/mounts). The right panel shows the response of these animals to estrogen and progesterone treatment.

increase "sex drive?" It may, but a simple prepostdrug test is inadequate to establish this conclusion. A number of alternatives are possible. The drug could enhance general arousal and activity. Presumably that is the mechanism by which *d*-amphetamine enhances sexual activity in the male cat (Fig. 1). The drug could have its effects by altering the animal's ability to discriminate appropriate from inappropriate sexual stimuli. The drug could also reduce "fear" or some inhibition of social contact which was learned in other circumstances. These drug effects could enhance sexual activities while being independent of some central motivational system.

With respect to the female, drugs have been reported to increase the probability of lordosis. Does this mean that the drugs increase sexual motivation? This question is pertinent because PCPA at least does not seem to enhance the probability of soliciting behaviors that are often seen in estrogen–progesterone-treated rats (Zemlan et al., 1973). Two alternatives are that the drugs that increase lordosis simply facilitate spinal reflexes or decrease the female's ability to avoid copulation, neither of which need be considered motivational variables. Unfortunately, no one has carried out the extensive motivational analysis, beautifully exemplified by the recent work of Meyerson and Lindström (1973), which is necessary if one is to conclude that drive systems have been altered by a drug.

The inhibition of sexual performance by a drug is particularly difficult to interpret. The drug could make the animal hypoaroused, disoriented, or insensitive to sexual stimuli. For example, olfactory stimuli seem to play a major role in controlling the sexual responses of some species—removal of the olfactory bulbs in male hamsters completely inhibits mating (Murphy and Schneider, 1970). Consequently, a drug that inhibits olfactory ability would be expected to inhibit mating in this species. This general problem exists whenever we administer a drug.

Finally, we face the problem of drug-induced quantitative changes in mating performance. For example, a drug-treated male rat may ejaculate after fewer intromissions than is normal. Does this mean that the animal is hypersexual or hyposexual?

What if a drug increases the frequency of mounts without intromission with no effect upon the frequency of intromission responses? Does this reflect a change in some central state which controls copulatory efficiency or does this mean that the drug has reduced the sensitivity of the penis, a condition that will produce just such an effect?

The answers to these questions are not clear. The questions do, however, remind us that any manipulations that influence sexual behavior could be effecting changes in that behavior by a variety of mechanisms. Often we are overly quick to presume that our manipulation is directly influencing some central mechanism which is specific to sexual behavior without considering the variety of alternatives that are also viable. Ultimately, if we are to understand the biologic substrate of sexual behavior, we must be prepared to consider all levels of the systems involved, sensory input, central states, and effector mechanisms.

REFERENCES

Ahlenius, S., Engel, J., Eriksson, H. Modigh, K., and Sodersten, P. (1972): Importance of central catecholamines in the mediation of lordosis behaviour in ovariectomized rats treated with estrogen and inhibitors of monoamine synthesis. *J. Neural, Transm.*, 33:247–255.

Beach, F. A. (1942): Effects of testosterone propionate upon the copulatory behavior of sexually inexperienced male rats. *J. Comp. Psychol.*, 33:227–247.

Butcher, R. W., and Sutherland, E. W. (1962): Adenosine 3'5' phosphate in biological materials. I. Purification and properties of cyclic 3'5' nucleotide phosphodiesterase and use of this enzyme to characterize adenosine 3'5' phosphate in human urine. *J. Biol. Chem.*, 237:1244–1250.

Clemens, L. G., Wallen, K., and Gorski, R. A. (1967): Mating behavior: Facilitation in the female rat following cortical application of potassium chloride. *Science*, 137:1208–1209.

Eriksson, H., and Sodersten, P. (1973): A failure to facilitate lordosis behavior in adrenalectomized and gonadectomized estrogen-primed rats with monoamine-synthesis inhibitors. *Horm. Behav.*, 4:89–97.

Feder, H. H., and Ruf, K. B. (1969): Stimulation of progesterone release and estrous behavior by ACTH in ovariectomized rodents. *Endocrinology*, 84:171–174.

Gessa, G. L., Tagliamonte, A., Tagliamonte, P., and Brodie, B. B. (1970): Essential role of testosterone in the sexual stimulation induced by *p*-chlorophenylalanine in male animals. *Nature*, 227: 616–617.

Koe, B. K., and Weissman, A. (1966): *p*-Chlorophenylalanine: A specific depletor of brain serotonin. *J. Pharmacol. Exp. Ther.*, 154:499–516.

Loewe, S. (1938): Influence of autonomic drugs on ejaculation. *J. Pharmacol. Exp. Ther.*, 63:70–75.

Major, P. W., and Kilpatrick, R. (1972): Cyclic AMP and hormone action. *J. Endocrinol.*, 52: 593–630.

Malmnas, C. O., and Meyerson, B. J. (1971): *p*-Chlorophenylalanine and copulatory behavior in the male rat. *Nature*, 232:398–400.

Meyerson, B. J. (1964*a*): Central nervous monoamines and hormone induced estrous behaviour in the spayed rat. *Acta Physiol. Scand.*, 63:(Suppl. 241) 1–32.

Meyerson, B. J. (1964*b*): Estrus behaviour in spayed rats after estrogen and progesterone treatment in combination with reserpine and tetrabenazine. *Psychopharmacologia,* 6:210–218.

Meyerson, B. J., and Lewander, T. (1970): Serotonin synthesis inhibition and estrous behavior in female rats. *Life Sci.,* 9:661–671.

Meyerson, B. J., and Lindstrom, L. H. (1973): Sexual motivation in the female rat. *Acta Physiol. Scand.* (Suppl. 389) 1–80.

Michael, R. P. (1961): "Hypersexuality" in male cats without brain damage. *Science,* 134:553–554.

Mitler, M. M., Morden, B., Levine, S., and Dement, W. (1972): The effects of parachlorophenylalanine on the mating behavior of male rats. *Physiol. Behav.,* 8:1147–1150.

Murphy, M. R., and Schneider, G. E. (1970): Olfactory bulb removal eliminates mating behavior in the male golden hamster. *Science,* 167:302–304.

Paris, C. A., Resko, J. A., and Goy, R. W. (1971): A possible mechanism for the induction of lordosis by reserpine in spayed rats. *Biol. Reprod.,* 4:23–30.

Rabedeau, R. G., and Whalen, R. E. (1959): Effects of copulatory experience on mating behavior in the male rat. *J. Comp. Physiol. Psychol.* 52:482–484.

Resko, J. A. (1969): Endocrine control of adrenal progesterone secretion in the ovariectomized rat. *Science,* 164:70–71.

Robison, G. A., Butcher, R. W., and Sutherland, E. W. (1971): *Cylic AMP.* Academic Press. New York.

Rosenblatt, J. S., and Aronson, L. R. (1958): The decline of sexual behavior in male cats after castration with special reference to the role of prior sexual experience. *Behaviour,* 12:285–338.

Ross, J. W., and Gorski, R. A. (1973): Effects of potassium chloride on sexual behavior and the cortical EEG in the ovariectomized rat. *Physiol. Behav.,* 10:643–646.

Segal, D. S., and Whalen, R. E. (1970): Effects of chronic administration of *p*-chlorophenylalanine on sexual receptivity of the female rat. *Psychopharmacologia (Berl),* 16:434–438.

Singer, J. J. (1972): Effects of *p*-chlorophenylalanine on the male and female sexual behavior of female rats. *Psychol. Rep.,* 30:891-893.

Soulairac, A. (1952): La signification physiologique de la période réfractaire dans le comportement sexual du rat mâle. *J. Physiolog. (Paris),* 44:99–113.

Soulairac, A., and Soulairac, M.-L. (1957): Action de l'amphétamine, de l'adrénaline et de l'atropine sur le comportement sexual du rat mâle. *J. Physiolog. (Paris),* 49:381–385.

Soulairac, A., and Soulairac, M.-L. (1961): Action de la réserpine sur le comportement sexuel du rat mâle. *C. R. Soc. Biol. (Paris),* 155:1010–1012.

Tagliomonte, A., Tagliomonte, P., Gessa, G. L., and Brodie, B. B. (1969): Compulsive sexual activity induced by *p*-chlorophenylalanine in normal and pinealectomized male rats. *Science,* 166:1433–1435.

Uphouse, L. L., Wilson, J. R., and Schlesinger, K. (1970): Induction of estrus in mice: The possible role of adrenal progesterone. *Horm. Behav.,* 1:255–264.

Whalen, R. E., and Luttge, W. G. (1970): *p*-Chlorophenylalanine methyl ester: An aphrodisiac? *Science,* 169:1000–1001.

Zemlan, F. P., Ward, I. L., Crowley, W. R., and Margules, D. L. (1973): Activation of lordotic responding in female rats by suppression of serotonergic activity. *Science,* 179:1010–1011.

Zitrin, A., Beach, F. A., Barchas, J. D., and Dement, W. C. (1970): Sexual behavior of male cats after administration of parachlorophenylalanine. *Science,* 170:868–870.

Sexual Behavior: Pharmacology and Biochemistry, edited by M. Sandler and G. L. Gessa. Raven Press, New York © 1975.

Pharmacologically Conditioned Sexual Behavior and Related Phenomena

H. Steinbeck

Department of Endocrine Pharmacology, Schering AG, 1 Berlin 65, Germany

The first conditioning of sexual behavior takes place during sexual differentiation of the fetus. The undeveloped brain of either genetic sex has the capacity of acquiring both directions of psychosexual orientation and eventually any intermediate state between the extremes of total maleness or femaleness (Steinbeck and Neumann, 1973). Normally, androgenic hormones secreted by the fetal testis imprint a masculine pattern of behavioral responses, including sexual performance, to postpubertal hormone levels in connection with an appropriate stimulus, e.g., a female in heat. The organizational influence of androgens on the developing brain was demonstrated experimentally for the first time in female guinea pig fetuses that received injections of testosterone into the amniotic cavity (Dantchakoff, 1938). When adult, these animals responded to testosterone propionate injections with more frequent and intense male-like copulatory activity than normal female controls. These early experiments on guinea pigs have since been confirmed and extended (Phoenix, Goy, Gerall and Young, 1959; Goy, Bridson, and Young, 1964; Goy, 1966). Hence, it has been shown that the differentiation of psychosexual orientation can be influenced by androgen injection in the female guinea pig fetus between the 30th and 50th days of pregnancy.

Experiments on other mammalian fetuses have revealed that each species has its own well-defined period of highest sensitivity of the neural substrate for later behavioral orientation to the organizational influence of testicular hormones (cf. Steinbeck and Neumann, 1973). In the majority of species, the most sensitive period for the hormonal setting of later gender orientation extends prior to birth. This has been demonstrated, in addition to the above-mentioned experiments on guinea pigs, by injection of androgenic hormones into pregnant monkeys (Goy, 1966) and bitches (Beach, Kuehn, Sprague, and Anisko, 1972), and accidentally also into women (Ehrhardt and Money, 1967). In rats and hamsters (Crossley and Swanson, 1968; Eaton, 1970), the time of neural sensitivity for the organizing effect of gonadal hormones extends for some time beyond birth.

Fetuses that are deprived of androgenic hormone influence during the period of neural organization, either naturally in the female or experimentally in the male sex, retain the capacity for feminine psychic responses to appropriate stimulation later in life. The organizational effect of androgens during this time seems to consist not so much of imprinting masculine traits but rather of lifelong destruction of female-type behavioral responses to relevant stimulation. Consequently, the influence of androgens on the developing brain has been termed "defeminization" (cf. Beach et al., 1972).

If the preceding is true, removal of testicular hormonal influence during the sensitive period of brain differentiation must interfere with the development of normal psychoorientation in male fetuses. Indeed this has been found to result from castration of newborn male rats (Grady, Phoenix, and Young, 1965; Whalen and Edwards, 1967). Another approach to androgen influence elimination during the critical period of neural organization has been the treatment of fetal male rats (Neumann and Elger, 1965; Neumann and Elger, 1966; Nadler, 1969), guinea pigs (Goldfoot, Resko, and Goy, 1971) and dogs (Steinbeck and Neumann, 1972, 1973) with an antiandrogen. This method has the advantage over testes removal that "castration" is only temporary; any effect resulting from such treatment is strictly confined to the medication period.

Some years ago, a number of beagle bitches were treated in our laboratories with the antiandrogen cyproterone acetate. The male offspring born to these bitches were morphologically feminized to various degrees, they all had a vagina and no penis (Steinbeck, Neumann, and Elger, 1970). However, these dogs still had their testes, which produced the same amounts of testosterone after puberty as in normal males, as gauged from serum levels by radioimmunoassay. Unlike animals in castration studies, these dogs were under the influence of androgens all the time after antiandrogen treatment was terminated. Earlier observations had revealed that the surviving three dogs showed a certain deviation from normal masculine behavior when they were young adults (Steinbeck and Neumann, 1972, 1973). It seemed worthwhile to do a follow-up study now that the dogs are 6 years of age, in order to find out whether the constant influence of testosterone had any late influence on their behavioral performance.

METHODS

The bitches were injected with a daily dose of 10.0 mg/kg cyproterone acetate from the 23rd day of pregnancy to term; the young were also treated for the first 2 weeks of life. The puppies were delivered by Cesarean section on the 63rd day because cyproterone acetate has such a strong progestational effect that labor could not be initiated. Because milk ejection was also completely blocked, the young were hand-reared, which resulted in only three male survivors. At 2 years of age, these three feminized dogs were accustomed to a 3 × 5-m room and also to the presence of the investigator in the same room, but sitting on a table out of reach. As stimulus females, two spayed bitches were used which had been brought into a highly receptive state by two injections of 0.4 mg/kg estradiol benzoate every other day, and 5.0 mg per animal progesterone 7 days after the first estrogen administration (Beach and Kuehn, 1970). Tests commenced the day after progesterone was given. The bitches could be used without any loss of sexual excitement and without further treatment for more than 8 days. The dogs were allowed 10 minutes of free access to the bitch that was tethered with 2-m leash

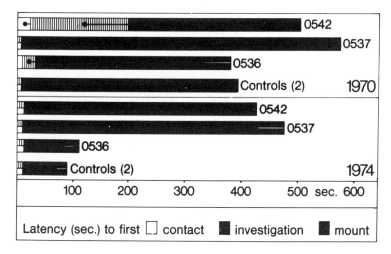

FIG. 1. Masculine sex behavior of feminized dogs. Twelve tests for each feminized dog. Latencies (sec) from the onset of test sessions to first contact with the bitch, first exploration of her genitals, and first rear mount. (Means ± s.d. of means).

to one corner. This time was chosen because in most test sessions, the male controls had achieved intromission long beforehand.

All actions were recorded on a 10-channel Esterline-Angus event recorder, A 620 X.

RESULTS AND DISCUSSION

As in the first study, all three dogs exhibited a great deal of typical masculine behavior in the second series of test sessions. They all mounted the females from the rear with vigorous pelvic thrusting. However, analysis and comparison of the new and old data give certain hints that the behavior is different now from what was reported earlier. In general, the same order of masculinity was found, i.e., dog 0542 had the least scores for male-type behavior, 0537 had more masculine traits but was still distinguishable from controls, whereas 0536 behaved like a normal male. However, an overall increase in masculine components of behavior was noticed in all three dogs. The latency to the first investigation of the bitch's genitals was now the same in all feminized dogs and in the controls (Fig. 1).

Although the latency to the first mount hardly differed from the previous series in dogs 0542 and 0537, they both had an increased readiness to mount, as might be inferred from the higher incidence of mounting, which rose from two out of 12 tests, to seven in 0542 and five in 0537. Dog 0536 again had the same latencies as the controls; he mounted the females in all test sessions. This dog also spent almost as much time with the bitch as controls did (Fig. 2). In this parameter, 0542 again had the lowest scores but the difference compared with controls had become smaller, which is also true for 0537.

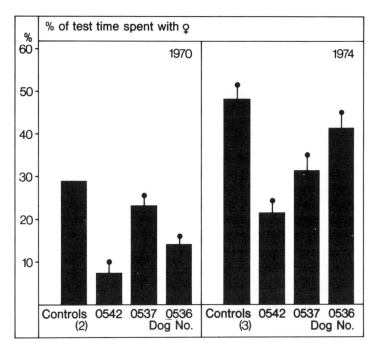

FIG. 2. Mean percentage of test time each dog spent in sex-orientated interactions with the bitch. (Means ± s.d. of means).

An impressive change has taken place in the urinating posture of 0542. Normal dogs attain a sex-specific position of the body when urinating. Males stand upright with one leg lifted but females squat down on the floor. These habits are very reliable signs of psychosexual orientation. In the previous publications (Steinbeck and Neumann, 1972, 1973), 0542 was reported to urinate almost exclusively squatting like a bitch, whereas 0536 and 0537 were mostly standing upright. This behavior did not change in the latter two dogs but 0542 now has masculine attitudes in considerable part (Fig. 3). He is now squatting bitchlike only on about one-third of all occasions.

In conclusion, it is probably reasonable to state that in the feminized dogs, a certain shift toward enhanced masculinity has taken place in the course of the years. To put it another way: the pharmacological conditioning of behavior by cyproterone acetate during the period of psychosexual organization has lost its intensity after years of continuous androgen influence from endogenous sources. Although the above-mentioned data are perhaps too scanty to allow definite conclusions to be drawn, it should be remembered that other authors (Beach and Kuehn, 1970; Beach et al., 1972) found that pre- and postnatal androgen treatment of female dogs was more effective in imposing masculine traits on these dogs than prenatal treatment alone. According to the same group, males castrated at

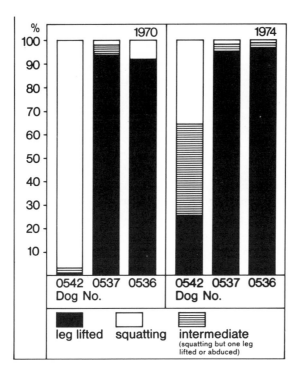

FIG. 3. Frequencies of male or female urination postures of feminized dogs. Number of observations: 259 for 0542; 152 for 0537; 170 for 0536 in 1974, about similar numbers in 1970.

birth reacted to testosterone less well than males castrated in adulthood. Consequently, it seems that even in dogs, the period of neural sensitivity to the organizational influence of androgens is not restricted to intrauterine life. At the moment, it is not clear at which time the process of psychologic defeminization under continous androgen influence is terminated in this species.

REFERENCES

Beach, F. A., and Kuehn, R. E. (1970): Coital behavior in dogs. X. Effects of androgenic stimulation during development on feminine mating responses in females and males. *Horm. Behav.,* 1:347.

Beach, F. A., Kuehn, R. E., Sprague, R. H., and Anisko, J. J. (1972): Coital behavior in dogs. XI. Effects of androgenic stimulation during development on masculine mating responses in females. *Horm. Behav.,* 3:143.

Crossley, D. A., and Swanson, H. H. (1968): Modification of sexual behaviour of hamsters by neonatal administration of testosterone propionate. *J. Endocrinol.,* 41:xiii.

Dantchakoff, V. (1938): Rôle des hormones dans la manifestation des instincts sexuel. *C.R. Acad. Sci. (Paris),* 206:945.

Eaton, G. (1970): Effects of a single prepubertal injection of testosterone propionate on adult bisexual behavior of male hamsters castrated at birth. *Endocrinology,* 87:934.

Ehrhardt, A. E., and Money, J. (1967): Progestin-induced hermaphroditism: IQ and psychosexual identity in a study of ten girls. *J. Sex. Res.,* 3:83.

Goldfoot, D. A., Resko, J. A., and Goy, R. W. (1971): Induction of target organ insensitivity to testosterone in the male guinea-pig with cyproterone. *J. Endocrinol.,* 50:423.

Goy, R. W. (1966): Role of androgens in the establishment and regulation of behavioral differences in mammals. *J. Anim. Sci. [Suppl.]* 25:21.

Goy, R. W., Bridson, W. E., and Young, W. C. (1964): Period of maximal susceptibility of the prenatal female guinea pig to masculinizing effects of testosterone propionate. *J. Comp. Physiol. Psychol.,* 57:166.

Grady, K. L., Phoenix, C. H., and Young, W. C. (1965): Role of the developing rat testis in differentiation of the neural tissues mediating mating behavior. *J. Comp. Physiol. Psychol.,* 59:176.

Nadler, R. D. (1969): Differentiation of the capacity for male sexual behavior in the rat. *Horm. Behav.,* 1:53.

Neumann, F. and Elger, W. (1965): Physiological and psychical intersexuality of male rats by early treatment with an antiandrogenic agent (1.2α-methylene-6-chloro-Δ^6-hydroxy-progesterone-acetate). *Acta Endocrinol. (Copenhagen) [Suppl.],* 100:174.

Neumann, F., and Elger, W. (1966): Permanent changes in gonadal function and sexual behavior as a result of early feminization of male rats by treatment with an antiandrogenic steroid. *Endokrinologie,* 50:209.

Phoenix, C. H., Goy, R. W., Gerall, A. A., and Young, W. C. (1959): Organizing action of prenatally administered testosterone propionate on the tissues mediating mating behavior in the female guinea pig. *Endocrinology,* 65:369.

Steinbeck, H., and Neumann, F. (1972): Aspects of steroidal influence on fetal development. In: *The Effect of Prolonged Drug Usage on Fetal Development,* edited by M. A. Klingberg, A. Abramovici, and J. Chemke. *Advan. Exp. Med. Biol.,* 27:227.

Steinbeck, H., and Neumann, F. (1973): Regulation of sexual behavior. In: *Psychopharmacology, Sexual Disorders and Drug Abuse,* edited by T. A. Ban, J. R. Boissier, G. J. Gessa, H. Heimann, L. Hollister, H. E. Lehmann, I. Munkvad, H. Steinberg, F. Sulser, A. Sundwall, and O. Vinar, p. 503. North-Holland Publ. Co., Amsterdam, London.

Steinbeck, H., Neumann, F., and Elger, W. (1970): Effect of an anti-androgen on the differentiation of the internal genital organs in dogs. *J. Reprod. Fertil.,* 23:223.

Whalen, R. E., and Edwards, D. A. (1967): Hormonal determinants of the development of masculine and feminine behavior in male and female rats. *Anat. Rec.,* 157:173.

Sexual Behavior: Pharmacology and Biochemistry, edited by M. Sandler and G. L. Gessa. Raven Press, New York © 1975.

Copulatory Behavior in the Female Rat After Amphetamine and Amphetamine Derivatives

Annika Michanek and Bengt J. Meyerson

Department of Medical Pharmacology, University of Uppsala, Uppsala, Sweden

Copulatory behavior in female rats (lordosis response on mounting by a male) disappears after ovariectomy but can be restored by estrogen followed after a certain time interval by progesterone (Boling and Blandau, 1939; Beach, 1942). As a result of neuropharmacologic studies, an antagonistic relationship between the estrogen plus progesterone-activated copulatory behavior and central nervous monoamines is suggested. This has been shown primarily in the rat, but similar mechanisms also indicated in other species, such as the mouse, hamster, and rabbit (Meyerson, Eliasson, Lindström, Michanek, and Söderlund, 1973). The effect of agents with a selective effect on serotonergic and catecholaminergic mechanisms suggests that in the rat the inhibitory system of female copulatory behavior is particularly sensitive to an increase of serotonergic tone. This fact does not exclude the significance of other inhibitory mechanisms. A possible relationship between central nervous muscarinic and serotonergic mechanisms with regard to inhibition of copulatory behavior was demonstrated by Lindström (1971). In addition, dopamine may be involved as the dopamine agonist apomorphine was shown to decrease the copulatory response in a recent study (Meyerson, Carrer, and Eliasson, 1974). When the effects of monoaminergic drugs on different behavioral parameters are compared, the predominant inhibitory effect seems to be caused by increased serotonergic activity. In an investigation of the effects of imipramine and related tricyclic antidepressants on lordotic behavior, it was found that the compounds inhibited the lordosis response, but no correlation existed between the effectiveness of these compounds on the lordosis response and on catecholamine-dependent behavior patterns (Meyerson, 1966). The present study was designed to investigate the effect of amphetamine and amphetamine derivatives on copulatory behavior in the female rat. The central stimulant effect of amphetamine is mainly correlated with an interaction with catecholaminergic mechanisms. However, there is also evidence that amphetamine can release extragranular stores of 5-hydroxytryptamine (5-HT) into the extraneuronal space (Fuxe and Ungerstedt, 1970). Fenfluramine and parachloroamphetamine interfere with 5-HT mechanisms. Both compounds cause long-lasting depletion of 5-HT stores and increase the serotonin turnover rate (Costa, Gropetti, and Revuelta, 1971; Tagliamonte, Tagliamonte, Perez-Cruet, Stern, and Gessa, 1971; Sanders-Bush, Bushing, and Sulser, 1972). The effect of these compounds on copulatory behavior, motor activity, and the production of stereotype activity was compared in the present study.

BEHAVIOR TESTS

Ovariectomized Sprague-Dawley rats (300 to 350 g) were kept under reversed day–night rhythm (light from 9 P.M. to 9 A.M.) in air-conditioned quarters maintained at 22°C. Rat pellets and water were provided *ad libitum.*

Copulatory Behavior

The tests were conducted during the period of darkness.[1] Copulatory behavior was induced by a single injection of estradiol benzoate, 10 µg/kg s.c., followed 48 hr later by progesterone (0.4 mg/rat s.c.). The first test were conducted 4 hr after the progesterone injection. Female copulatory behavior was tested by transferring the female to an observation cage that held a sexually vigorous male. A clear-cut lordotic response on at least two out of six mounts was scored as positive. Statistical significance was calculated by the chi-square test.

Stereotype Activity

The subject was transferred 45 min before the test to an empty Macrolon® cage (41 X 25 X h 14 cm). Observations for stereotype activity were conducted for 10 sec of each of 10 consecutive min. Stereotype activity in this context is defined as any type of behavior pattern that lasted for 10 sec without variation. Each time the subject fulfilled the criterion for stereotype activity one point was given. Thus, the maximal score possible for an observation period was 10 points.

Exploratory Behavior

Locomotor activity was measured for 10 min in an Animex activity meter (Farad, Stockholm). Movement of an animal across a tuned oscillator coil system results in a change of tuning, which is recorded as a count. One subject at a time was placed in the apparatus. The activity measurements at this time mainly reflect the exploratory behavior of the animal but are also influenced by the stereotype behavior induced by such drugs as amphetamine.

---

[1] Drugs injected: estradiol benzoate and progesterone (N.V. Organon through Erco Ltd, Stockholm, Sweden) were dissolved in olive oil and injected subcutaneously. *d*-Amphetamine sulfate, *l*-amphetamine sulfate (Biochem. Research Foundation, California), fenfluramine HCl (Alfred Benzon, Copenhagen), *dl-p*-chloroamphetamine HCl (Regis Chemical Co.) were dissolved in saline and injected subcutaneously. *dl-α*-Methyl-*p*-tyrosine-methyl ester HCl (Hässle, Sweden) was dissolved in saline and injected intraperitoneally.

EFFECT OF AMPHETAMINE AND AMPHETAMINE DERIVATIVES

The two isomers *d-* and *l-*amphetamine and the derivatives fenfluramine and parachloroamphetamine were tested. The compounds were given 30 to 60 min after a pretest. The pretest was conducted when the optimal response level was not completely established (see controls, Fig. 1). At the time of the first test after

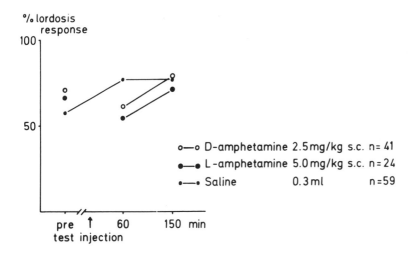

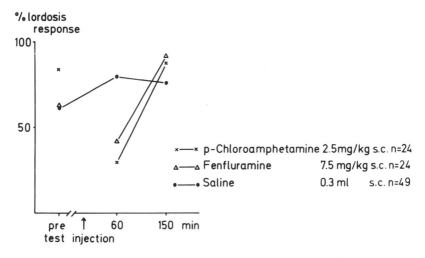

FIG. 1. Effect of *l*-amphetamine, *d*-amphetamine, fenfluramine, and parachloroamphetamine on lordosis response activated by estrogen and progesterone in ovariectomized rats. Estradiol (10 μg/kg) was given at 0 hr; progesterone, 0.4 mg per rat at 48 hr. Tests for lordosis response were conducted between 52 and 56 hr.

drug treatment the lordosis response was fully developed, and it was possible to elicit it at the same level for at least another 1½ hr. All compounds clearly reduced the copulatory response at the test performed 60 min after injection. After 150 min, the response was again unimpaired (Fig. 1). The dose–response relationship can be seen from Table 1. Data are given for tests conducted 60 min after the drug injection. The most effective compound was parachloroamphetamine ($ED_{50} = 2$ mg/kg) followed by *d*-amphetamine ($ED_{50} = 4$ mg/kg), fenfluramine ($ED_{50} = 7.5$ mg/kg) and the least effective was *l*-amphetamine ($ED_{50} = 10$ mg/kg). Locomotor activity, as measured by the Animex device, was significantly increased by all drugs except *l*-amphetamine after doses that also decreased the lordosis response. Parachloroamphetamine (2.5 mg/kg) as well as *d*-amphetamine (2.5 mg/kg) increased motor activity but in different ways. *d*-Amphetamine induces a specific stereotype activity which is not seen after parachloroamphetamine. It is not possible to dissociate this difference in behavior in the Animex meter and therefore stereotype activity was measured by direct observation (Table 1). Stereotype activity was most evident after injection of *d*-amphetamine. In contrast, parachloroamphetamine and fenfluramine did not

TABLE 1. *Effect of amphetamine, parachloroamphetamine and fenfluramine, and d-amphetamine after pretreatment with α-methyl-p-tyrosine, on estradiol + progesterone-activated copulatory behavior, stereotype activity, and locomotor activity in ovariectomized rats*[a]

Treatment	Dose (mg/kg)	Lordosis response	Stereotype activity (points)	Motor activity[b] (counts/10 min)
		% Inhibition		
d-Amphetamine	2.5	24	4.8	814‡ ± 20
	5.0	69‡	8.3‡	—
l-Amphetamine	5.0	24	0.6*	710 ± 36
	10.0	48†	1.6	—
Parachloroamphetamine	2.5	62‡	1.1	820‡ ± 35
	5.0	100‡	1.6	—
Fenfluramine	7.5	50‡	2.1	758‡ ± 50
	10.0	95‡	1.6	—
α-Methyl-*p*-tyrosine +	100	—	—	—
d-amphetamine	5.0	50‡	2.1	—
		% Response		
Saline	0.3 ml	79	1.9	621 ± 26
α-Methyl-*p*-tyrosine	100	100	—	—

[a] Estradiol benzoate (10 μg/kg s.c.) was followed 48 hr later by progesterone (0.4 mg per rat). The effect on lordosis behavior was obtained 60 min after drug injection. Animals received this treatment also when tested for stereotype and motor activity. These tests were conducted 45–55 min after last injection. α-Methyl-*p*-tyrosine was given i.p. 5 hr before the amphetamine treatment. Other treatments were given subcutaneously. Number of subjects tested: Lordosis response: $n = 24$–30, except for α-methyltyrosine: $N = 12$; stereotype activity: $n = 8$; motor activity: $N = 7$–8. Significant difference: (*) $p < 0.05$; (†) $p < 0.01$; (‡) $p < 0.001$.
[b] Mean ± S.E.M.

significantly induce a degree of stereotype activity above what was seen after saline treatment. *l*-Amphetamine (5 mg/kg) significantly decreased stereotype activity. This was due to a restlessness that was qualitatively different from both normal and drug-induced stereotype activity.

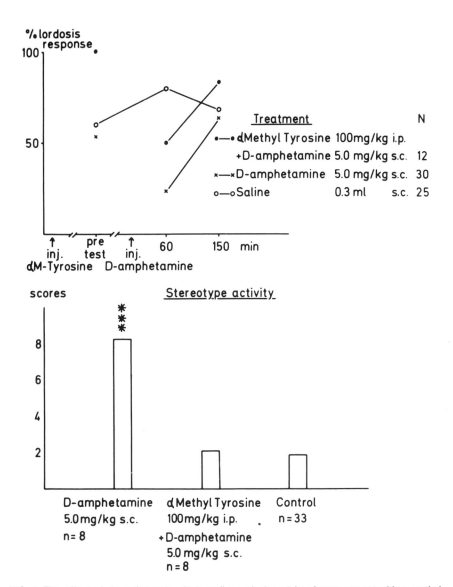

FIG. 2. The effect of *d*-amphetamine (5.0 mg/kg s.c.) given 5 hr after treatment with α-methyl-*p*-tyrosine (100 mg/kg i.p.) on stereotype activity and lordosis response, activated by estrogen and progesterone in ovariectomized rats. Stereotype activity was observed 45–55 min after the *d*-amphetamine injection.

EFFECT OF d-AMPHETAMINE AFTER PRETREATMENT WITH α-METHYL-p-TYROSINE

α-Methyl-p-tyrosine (100 mg/kg) was given i.p. 5 hr before the injection of d-amphetamine (5 mg/kg s.c.). Tests were conducted at 60 and 150 min after the d-amphetamine injection. The inhibitory action of amphetamine on the lordosis response was not significantly different from the effect of d-amphetamine alone. However, comparisons are complicated by the difference in pretreatment response levels. Four hr after treatment with α-methyltyrosine, an evident increase in lordotic response was seen. In contrast, the amphetamine-induced increase in stereotype activity was completely abolished after α-methyl-p-tyrosine pretreatment (Fig. 2).

CONCLUSIONS

Serotonergic as well as catecholaminergic pathways have been suggested to mediate inhibition of lordosis response and induction of stereotype activity (Fog, Randrup, and Pakkenberg, 1967; Meyerson et al. 1973; Weiner, Goetz, Westheimer, and Klawans, 1973). A comparison of the effects of d- and l-amphetamine, fenfluramine, and parachloroamphetamine on lordotic behavior and stereotype activity in the present study revealed that there is no correlation between the effect of amphetamine and amphetamine-like compounds on the lordotic behavior and stereotype activity. The fact that α-methyl-p-tyrosine decreased the d-amphetamine effect on stereotype activity, but not the effect on lordosis response, also suggests that amphetamine may inhibit lordosis response and induce stereotype activity by different mechanisms.

ACKNOWLEDGMENTS

This investigation was supported by grants from the Swedish Medical Research Council B74-04X-64-10C. For generous supplies of hormones we thank Organon, the Netherlands, through Erco, Sweden; Hässle, Sweden for α-methyltyrosine; Alfred Benzon, Denmark for fenfluramine and Regis Chemical Co. for parachloroamphetamine.

REFERENCES

Beach, F. A. (1942): Importance of progesterone to induction of sexual receptivity in spayed female rats. *Proc. Soc. Exp. Biol. Med.,* 51:369–371.
Boling. J. L., and Blandau, R. J. (1939): The estrogen–progesterone induction of mating responses in the spayed female rat. *Endocrinology,* 25:359–364.
Costa, E., Gropetti, A., and Revuelta, A. (1971): Action of fenfluramine on monoamine stores of rat tissue. *Br. J. Pharmacol.,* 41:57–64.
Fog, R., Randrup, A., and Pakkenberg, H. (1967): Aminergic mechanisms in corpus striatum and amphetamine induced stereotyped behavior. *Psychopharmacologia,* 11:179–183.
Fuxe, K., and Ungerstedt, U. (1970): Histochemical, biochemical and functional studies on central

monoamine neurons after acute and chronic amphetamine administration. In: *Central Monoamine Neurons in Amphetamines and Related Compounds,* edited by E. Costa and S. Garattini, p. 257. Raven Press, New York.

Lindström, L. H. (1971): The effect of pilocarpine and oxotremorine in oestrous behaviour in female rats after treatment with monoamine depletors or monoamine synthesis inhibitors. *Eur. J. Pharmacol.,* 15:60–65.

Meyerson, B. J. (1966): The effect of imipramine and related antidepressive drugs on estrous behavior in ovariectomised rats activated by progesterone, reserpine or tetrabenazine in combination with estrogen. *Acta Physiol. Scand.* 67:411–422.

Meyerson, B. J., Carrer, H., and Eliasson, M. (1974): 5-Hydroxytryptamine and sexual behavior in the female rat. In: *Advances in Biochemical Psychopharmacology, Vol. 11: Serotonin—New Vistas,* edited by E. Costa, G. L. Gessa, and M. Sandler, pp. 229–242. Raven Press, New York.

Meyerson, B. J., Eliasson, M., Lindström, L., Michanek, A., and Söderlund, A.-Ch. (1973): Monoamines and female sexual behavior. In: *Psychopharmacology, Sexual Disorders and Drug Abuse,* edited by T. A. Ban, J. R. Boissier, G. J. Gessa, H. Heimann, L. Hollister, H. E. Lehmann, I. Munkvad, H. Steinberg, F. Sulser, A. Sundwall, and O. Vinar, pp. 463–472. North-Holland Publ. Co., Amsterdam, Holland.

Sanders-Bush, E., Bushing, J. A., and Sulser, F. (1972): Long-term effects of *p*-chloroamphetamine on tryptophan hydroxylase activity and on the levels of 5-hydroxytryptamine and 5-hydroxyindole acetic acid in brain. *Eur. J. Pharmacol.,* 20:385–388.

Tagliamonte, A., Tagliamonte, P., Perez-Cruet, J., Stern, S., and Gessa, G. L. (1971): Effect of psychotropic drugs on tryptophan concentration in the rat brain. *J. Pharmacol. Exp. Ther.,* 177: 475–480.

Weiner, W. J., Goetz, C., Westheimer, R., and Klawans, H. L. Jr. (1973): Serotoninergic and antiserotoninergic influences on amphetamine-induced stereotyped behavior. *J. Neurol. Sci.,* 20: 373–379.

Sexual Behavior: Pharmacology and Biochemistry, edited by M. Sandler and G. L. Gessa. Raven Press, New York © 1975.

Influence of Quipazine on Sexual Behavior in Male Rats

Maria Grabowska

Institute of Pharmacology, Polish Academy of Sciences, 31–344 Cracow, Poland

Quipazine, [2- (1-piperazinyl)quinoline maleate], has been described as a drug stimulating both peripheral and central serotoninergic receptors. Data pointing to a stimulatory effect of quipazine on those receptors were obtained from behavioral, biochemical, and EEG studies (Hong and Pardo, 1966; Hong, Sancillo, and Vargas, 1969; Drucker-Colin, Rojas-Ramirez, and Rodriguez, 1972; Rodriguez, Rojas-Ramirez, and Drucker-Colin, 1973; Grabowska, Antikiewicz, and Michaluk, 1974*a, b*). As elevation of brain serotonin level inhibits certain components of animal sexual behavior (Tagliamonte, Tagliamonte, Gessa, and Brodie, 1969; Gessa, Tagliamonte, Tagliamonte, and Brodie, 1970), the stimulation of central serotoninergic receptors by quipazine should give similar results.

The influence of quipazine on two models of pharmacologically induced hypersexuality (Tagliamonte et al., 1969; Gessa et al., 1970) was investigated in rats. Male Wistar rats, weighing 200 to 230 g, were housed in individual cages and treated as described below.

1. *Parachlorophenylalanine, methyl ester hydrochloride (PCPA)* was injected intraperitoneally, at a dose of 100 mg/kg, daily at 8 a.m. for 4 days. 6 hr after the last injection, rats were treated with pargyline hydrochloride (100 mg/kg) and placed in groups of four in observation cages. The number of mountings was registered for 9 hr. Quipazine at a dose of 2.5 or 10.0 mg/kg was injected i.p. 315 min after the beginning of the test.

2. *PCPA,* in a dosage and time schedule described above, was injected for 3 days and testosterone propionate (1.25 mg/kg, s.c.) was administered for 4 days, at noon. Six hr after the last injection of testosterone, rats were placed in groups of four and the number of mountings was registered for 1.5 hr. Quipazine (2.5 mg/kg) and methysergide hydrogen maleate (5.0 mg/kg) were injected 15 and 30 min before the test, respectively.

The rats treated with PCPA and pargyline showed sexual excitement, measured by the number of mountings, up to 30 min after they were placed together. The behavior of animals was exactly as described by Tagliamonte et al. (1969). After the first period of sexual excitation, the rats became quiet, and mountings were almost completely inhibited for about 4 hr. Signs of sexual stimulation then reappeared and were visible until the end of the observation period. Quipazine,

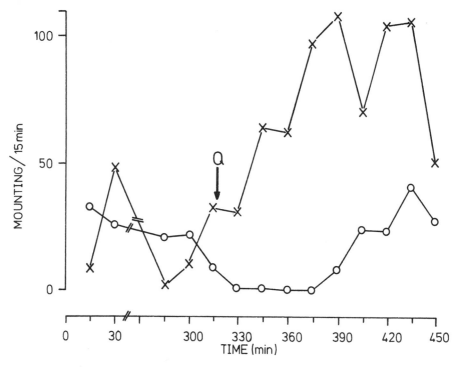

FIG. 1. The influence of quipazine on mounting behavior in rats pretreated with PCPA and pargyline (crosses). Circles show results obtained in rats treated also with quipazine (Q). Each group consisted of eight animals placed four to a cage.

at a dose of 2.5 mg/kg almost completely inhibited mounting behavior (Fig. 1). Higher dosage of the drug (10.0 mg/kg) acted similarly but for a longer period of time. This dose of quipazine, however, is capable of producing stereotyped behavior in rats (Grabowska, Antkiewicz, and Michaluk, 1974a) so that the lower dose of the drug only was used in subsequent experiments.

Rats pretreated with PCPA plus testosterone showed very frequent mountings (Table 1) as described by Benkert and Eversmann (1972) and Gessa et al. (1970). Quipazine (2.5 mg/kg) injected 15 min before the test inhibited mounting behavior almost completely for the first 30 min of observation. Methysergide, given alone, did not affect mounting behavior in PCPA and testosterone-pretreated rats but counteracted quipazine-induced inhibition of mounting frequency (Table 1).

The results revealed that mounting behavior induced by PCPA and pargyline or PCPA and testosterone in isolated male rats was inhibited by quipazine. Similar inhibition of the behavior was observed after administration of 5-hydroxytryptophan (5–HT), the precursor of serotonin (Tagliamonte et al., 1969; Gessa et al., 1970).

The inhibitory effect of quipazine was counteracted by methysergide, a drug believed to block central serotoninergic receptors (Corne, Pickering, and Warner,

TABLE 1. *Influence of quipazine on mounting behavior in male rats*

Drug treatment	Total number of mountings (per 15 min)					
	15 min	30 min	45 min	60 min	75 min	90 min
Testosterone + PCPA	101 (24)	98 (24)	80 (24)	64 (24)	52 (24)	61 (24)
Testosterone + PCPA + quipazine	1 (16)	2 (16)	24 (16)	43 (16)	118 (16)	77 (16)
Testosterone + PCPA + methysergide + quipazine	80 (16)	48 (16)	17 (16)	35 (16)	71 (16)	8 (16)
Testosterone + PCPA + methysergide	103 (8)	65 (8)	38 (8)	74 (8)	—	—

Number of rats is given in parentheses. There were four rats in each cage. For further explanation, see text.

1963; Anderson, 1972). It should be mentioned that behavioral, biochemical, and EEG changes observed after quipazine administration are blocked by serotoninolytics (Hong et al., 1969; Drucker-Colin et al., 1972; Rodriguez et al., 1973; Grabowska et al., 1974 *a,b*).

If we assume that quipazine stimulates central serotoninergic receptors, then the results presented here confirm the inhibitory role of serotonin in sexual behavior, as measured by the number of mountings in isolated male rats.

ACKNOWLEDGMENTS

I would like to thank to Dr. D. A. Stauffer (Miles Laboratories) and Dr. M. Taeschler (Sandoz Company) for generous gifts of quipazine and methysergide, respectively. The technical assistance of Mrs. Martha Golda is gratefully acknowledged.

REFERENCES

Anderson, E. G. (1972): Bulbospinal serotonin-containing neurons and motor control. *Fed. Proc.,* 31:107–112.

Benkert, O., and Eversmann, T. (1972): Importance of the anti-serotonin effect mounting behaviour in rats. *Experientia,* 28:532–533.

Corne, S. J., Pickering, R. W., and Warner, B. T. (1963): A method for assessing the effects of drugs on the central actions of 5-hydroxytryptamine. *Br. J. Pharmacol.,* 20:106–120.

Drucker-Colin, R. R., Rojas-Ramirez, J. A., and Rodriguez, R. (1972): Serotonin-like electroencephalographic and behavioral effects of quipazine. *Fed. Proc.,* 31:270.

Gessa, G. L., Tagliamonte, A., Tagliamonte, P., and Brodie, B. B. (1970): Essential role of testosterone in the sexual stimulation induced by *p*-chlorophenylalanine in male animals. *Nature,* 227: 616–617.

Grabowska, M., Antkiewicz, L., and Michaluk, J. (1974*a*): A possible interaction of quipazine with central dopamine structures. *J. Pharm. Pharmacol.,* 26:74–75.

Grabowska, M., Antkiewicz, L., and Michaluk, J. (1974*b*): The influence of quipazine on the turnover rate of serotonin. *Biochem. Pharmacol. (In press).*

Hong, E., and Pardo, E., G. (1966): On the pharmacology of 2-(1-piperazinyl)quinoline. *J. Pharmacol. Exp. Ther.,* 153:259–265.

Hong, E., Sancillo, L. F., and Vargas, R. (1969): Similarities between the pharmacological actions of quipazine and serotonin. *Eur. J. Pharmacol.,* 6:274-280.

Rodriguez, R., Rojas-Ramirez, J. A., and Drucker-Colin, R. R. (1973): Serotonin-like actions of quipazine. *Eur. J. Pharmacol.,* 24:164–171.

Tagliamonte, A., Tagliamonte, P., Gessa, G. L., and Brodie, B. B. (1969): Compulsive sexual activity induced by *p*-chlorophenylalanine in normal and pinealectomized male rats. *Science,* 166:1433–1435.

Sexual Behavior: Pharmacology and Biochemistry, edited by M. Sandler and G. L. Gessa. Raven Press, New York © 1975.

DRUG–SEX PRACTICE IN THE HAIGHT-ASHBURY or "THE SENSUOUS HIPPIE"

George R. Gay, John A. Newmeyer, Richard A. Elion, and Steven Wieder

Haight-Ashbury Free Medical Clinics, 529 Clayton Street, San Francisco, California 94117

. . . and you will journey down Haight Street, the very nerve center of a city within a city . . . Marijuana, of course, is a household staple here, enjoyed by the natives to stimulate their senses . . .

aph′ro-dis′i-ac [GK. *aphrodisiakos* sexual, fr. *aphrodité* pert, to sensual love]: exciting sexual desire, provocative of or inclined to venery (as by a drug).

Heroes, poets, philanderers, profligates, prophets, and kings have sought love potions or aphrodisiacs for unrecorded centuries, which were supplied promptly thereafter by designated witches, sorcerers, doctors, and chemists. Unfortunately, as natural human passion inevitably waned contrapuntal to decreased sexual gratification, so did the mystique of each proffered specific. Now, street myth and folklore have regenerated interest in use of the vast panoply of drugs currently available to renew and to heighten sexual response by the sophisticated and unsophisticated alike.

The current study was undertaken to review common streetlore of the drug-using counterculture of the 1970s, and hopefully, through applying sound pharmacologic and sociologic principle, to clarify and to distinguish misapprehension and contradiction from reality.

At the outset, it is often difficult to comprehend the multiple variability of action/reaction between an individual and his or her chosen ingested drug(s) —one must attempt, then, to view the pharmacosexual effects of any drug by means of an interacting matrix of human variables: existing sociologic, cultural, and physical settings, as well as psychic and sexual and other physical aspects of the individual set (Simmons, 1966; Mathis, 1970; *Interim Report of the Commission of Inquiry into the Nonmedical Use of Drugs, 1970;* Gay and Sheppard, 1973; Gay and Smith, 1973). First we must consider that the effect of any drug is integrally dose-related, viz. one joint of "grass" may lower inhibitions and make an individual more open to experimentation with an exotic sexual technique, whereas five may make him or her only bleary-eyed and dysfunctional.

Historically, there have been precious few properly controlled and duplicated studies that have examined the sexual aspects of the interaction between an individual and the pharmacologic effect(s) of any specific drug. Most of what we have been told has been gleaned from scattered and ill-documented reports in the media. Marijuana has been long and often ludicrously portrayed as an aphrodisiac of enormous power: ". . . it eliminates the line between right and wrong, and substitutes one's own warped [sexual] desires" (Smith, 1970). Amphetamines as well, in a "proper dosage" have been reported to increase libido and aggressiveness during intercourse (Gay and Sheppard, 1973). Cocaine is also well renowned for aphrodisiac qualities; it is often referred to as the "champagne" of sexual drugs (Gay and Smith, 1973). As one respondent remarked, "Orgasms go better with coke" (Gay and Sheppard, 1973, Freud, 1884). Methaqualone too was originally touted on the street as a "love drug" (Inaba, Gay, Newmeyer, and Whitehead, 1973). "Junk short circuits sex," according to William Burroughs. Of course, it is difficult to generalize on any of these reported effects, for as Greaves has reminded us, both drug use and sexual pathology may result from common, yet unidentified personality variables (Greaves, 1972).

METHODS

This study involved a questionnaire prepared to examine individual subjective experience with regard to the effects of a variety of drugs on sexual habits, e. g., aggressiveness, increase or decrease in libido, pleasure derived, and general sexual experience, practice, beliefs, and attitudes. Questions were worded carefully so as to be clear to all street people and to provoke minimal apprehension. Various questions were scattered throughout the questionnaire to test reliability of response, i.e., to see whether the same information would be given to differently phrased questions. Only three questionnaires had to be discarded with this check. In order to stimulate motivation, participants received two dollars upon completion of their questionnaire.

The questionnaires were distributed randomly to two distinct but slightly overlapping population groups, including 95 subjects in all. One group was from the Heroin Detoxification Clinic at the Haight-Ashbury Free Medical Clinics, which consisted mostly of individuals (over 90%) who had come to the clinic for detoxification from heroin. The other group consisted of clients of the Haight-Ashbury Free Medical Clinics Medical Section, shown in previous studies (Gay and Sheppard, 1973) to serve as an excellent control group, i.e., in age, race, sex, and geographic and sociologic setting (Newmeyer, 1974). The main difference between the two populations appeared to be the use (47 subjects) or nonuse (48 subjects) of heroin. We have adopted Robins' assumption that the "critical point" for involvement with heroin lies around the usage level of 10 or more times in their lives (Robins and Murphy, 1966). Other drug-use factors and sexual attitudes appeared comparable.

In all, 59 men and 36 women were interviewed. Ethnic breakdown revealed 76 Caucasians, nine Blacks, seven Latinos, and three Asians. Over half the sample was never married, around 30% was separated or divorced, and approximately 20% was currently married. Sixty-one subjects were between 21 and 29 years of age, 11 were 20 or younger, 12 were over 30, and 11 failed to report their age. Forty-nine of the sample attended high school or less, with 24 having received a high school degree. Of this latter group, 46 subjects had attended college. Forty-two were currently unemployed, 26 held "middle class' jobs, and 24 held "working class" jobs. (Class distinction for occupations was made according to the W. Lloyd Warner Scale.)

FINDINGS AND DISCUSSION

Tables 1 and 2 show the self-described levels of use of various drugs by our respondent group. Table 1 refers to lifetime history of usage, and Table 2 reveals

TABLE 1. *Level of use of specific drugs: Lifetime use*

Drug	Not at all	Once or twice	3–10 times	11–50 times	Daily
Grass	2	2	6	22	57
Acid	10	12	13	42	12
"Mescaline"*	15	13	26	30	3
MDA	48	20	10	5	0
PCP	33	18	12	10	3
Barbs	18	11	14	35	6
Speed	14	9	12	40	11
Cocaine	16	10	22	34	5
Amyl nitrite	37	21	15	12	1
Heroin	24	11	5	17	30
Methaqualone	32	17	15	22	1
Alcohol	6	7	11	27	36
Tobacco	14	6	2	10	57

* Mescaline is enquoted because analysis has shown samples of drugs sold as "mescaline" actually to be mescaline less than one time in 20. However, "mescaline" usually contains at least LSD; therefore, it is classed among the psychedelic drugs.

TABLE 2. *Level of use of specific drugs: Recent use (past 2 months)*

Drug	Not at all	Once or twice	A few times	A few times a week	Daily
Grass	10	7	19	26	28
Acid	56	15	15	2	1
"Mescaline"*	76	5	5	2	0
MDA	85	1	1	0	0
PCP	80	2	3	0	1
Barbs	50	18	7	10	2
Speed	59	11	10	6	2
Cocaine	42	18	22	5	1
Amyl nitrite	69	11	6	1	1
Heroin	41	7	11	9	21
Methaqualone	56	14	14	3	1
Alcohol	15	12	19	22	21
Tobacco	24	2	3	4	56

* See footnote to Table 1.

usage during the 2 months prior to interview. There appear to be a number of noteworthy facets in these data. Marijuana usage (as expected) is seen to be quite ubiquitous, with 98% of the sample claiming to have used the drug, and 81% claiming to have used it "at least three times in the past two months." Also, the vast majority of subjects admitted to having used one psychedelic or another on at least one occasion, with an astounding 60% describing 11 or more "trips" taken in their lifetimes. Fully two-fifths of the group declared they had used a psychedelic within the past 2 months, seeming to refute recent claims of a virtual disappearance of psychedelic use in the Bay area (Gay, Elsenbaumer, and Newmeyer, 1972). One must consider a temporal situation here as well. It was springtime, with the opportunity for outdoor "tripping" optimal; and with the seasonal appearance of outdoor "rock" and other music festivals, where almost any unknown substance taken to alter consciousness (be it LSD, PCP, "THC" . . . read LSD . . . or otherwise) is regarded a "psychedelic trip" (Newmeyer, 1974a).

The subject group's apparent familiarity with barbiturates and amphetamines is also very extensive, with only about one in five claiming no experience with one or the other drug. However, only a handful of persons reported "daily use" of either drug, and only about one in eight or one in 10 spoke of having used "barbs" or "speed" more than "a few times" in the past 2 months. Such was not the case for cocaine; more than half the group claimed to have used this drug at least once in the past 2 months. Amyl nitrite, methaqualone, and alcohol, in turn, show a usage pattern much as expected, with methaqualone the big "gainer" when compared to results of drug-use surveys conducted in the Haight-Ashbury neighborhood during 1972 (Newmeyer and Gay, 1972). Finally, heroin and tobacco show themselves to be the only true "addictive" drugs, if judged by the frequency-of-use distribution curve. Their distribution is "U-shaped," in that most persons either use daily or not at all, with very few managing the occasional-use pattern that is shown for all the other drugs.

Table 3A shows the extent of use of various drugs "to make sex better." Because of the way this particular questionnaire item was worded, the subjects probably responded in the narrow terms of drugs they specifically employed to improve sex rather than in terms of drugs they have experienced being "high" on during sexual intercourse. The questionnaire did contain a few items that measured this latter phenomenon; unfortunately, these questions were not worded in the same manner for all drugs. The data from these items are given in Table 3B.

The first column of Table 3A shows that, insofar as frequent, deliberate use of drugs to enhance sex is concerned, marijuna is nonpareil. About two respondents in five claimed to use "grass" a few times a week or more often in conjunction with sexual play. For sheer quantitative, everyday importance in the sexual lives of the young, "hip" San Franciscans sampled in this study, grass is quite possibly as significant as all other drugs combined. Seen to play a lesser role in their sexual-enhancement routine are alcohol, tobacco, cocaine, heroin, amphetamines, barbiturates, and methaqualone. That cocaine should appear to be so frequently

TABLE 3A. *Use of specific drugs in sexual situations: Which drugs do you use to make sex better?*

Drug	A few times a week or more	Once or twice or a few times a month	Not at all
Grass	32	22	31
Acid	1	35	50
"Mescaline"*	0	24	58
"Psilocybin"	1	14	74
MDA	1	7	72
PCP	1	7	73
Barbs	5	12	65
Speed	5	18	59
Cocaine	12	30	42
Amyl nitrite	3	9	69
Heroin	13	10	61
Methaqualone	5	11	—
Alcohol	12	23	46
Tobacco	16	2	60

* See footnote to Table 2.

used is testimony to its high reputation as an enhancer of sexual experience; there is little question but that it would supplant grass as the premium pharmacologic adjunct to the erotic practices of our youthful population were cocaine as cheap and readily available as marijuana.

Experimental or occasional use of the psychedelic to enhance sex is seen to have been quite common (column 2 of Table 3A). There are suggestions in the data, as well as commonly voiced subjective statements, that many respondents found the psychedelics to be powerful aids to sexual pleasure, but that the total experience was simply too "heavy" to be engaged in with great regularity.

In table 3B ("drugs causing a "high" during sexual intercourse), the following points emerge.

1. The vast majority of psychedelic "trips" taken by our subjects did not include sexual intercourse. As a rough estimate, one "trip" in eight involved some sort of sexual contact.

2. Roughly four-fifths of the use of barbiturates in conjunction with sex involves swallowing rather than injecting the drug.

3. The preferred mode of amphetamine administration in sexual situations is injection, with the oral route a near second. A small amount of nasal ("snorting") use of speed was reported.

4. "Snorting" of cocaine is the preferred mode of use of that drug in conjunction with sex. A substantial but smaller number of subjects report injecting cocaine, whereas a small number report the oral route for cocaine use.

5. By far the greater portion of heroin use in sexual situations involves the injection route.

TABLE 3B. *Use of specific drugs in sexual situations: Drugs causing a "high" during sexual intercourse*

Questions	More than 25% of the time	Less than 25% of the time	No answer (generally connotes "never" or "don't use")
How often do you get stoned (on grass or hash) for sex?	48	34	18
How often do you have sex while high from this drug?			
Acid	18	52	24
Mescaline	13	50	31
Psilocybin	10	51	33
MDA	7	49	38
PCP	8	50	35
When you take barbs for an evening of sex:			
How often do you shoot?	10	32	53
How often do you take them by mouth?	37	11	47
When you take speed for an evening of sex:			
How often do you shoot?	16	30	49
How often do you take them by mouth?	12	35	48
How often do you snort this drug?	5	41	49
When you take cocaine for an evening of sex:			
How often do you shoot?	22	32	41
How often do you take them by mouth?	6	45	44
How often do you snort this drug?	30	25	40
When you take heroin for an evening of sex:			
How often do you shoot?	38	17	40
How often do you snort this drug?	10	44	41

Mention should also be made of needle-sharing between partners and the psychopharmacologic orgasm (Chessich, 1960). In a study by Chessich, needle-sharing was reported by 50% of the population interviewed, resulting in orgasm 15% of the time. (Orgasm resulted regardless of the material injected. Saline solution or ice water were common substitutes for heroin.) A study by Howard and Borges (1971) indicates that 64% of heroin addicts studied reported sexual overtones concerning needle-sharing, and often allowed themselves to be "fixed" by a member of the opposite sex. Subjects also reported a "boosting effect" while fixing, which consisted of drawing blood in and out of the syringe, "playing with the needle, jacking off the spike . . . a righteous rush."

Table 4 gives the ratings of the effects of specific drugs on sexual functioning. The questions asked were in the form: "Does [specific drug] affect you in any of the following ways?" Five ratings were possible:

  ++ "Increase very much"   rated as a scale of 5
   + "Increase somewhat"   rated as a scale of 4
   0 "No effect"   rated as a scale of 3
   − "Decrease somewhat"   rated as a scale of 2
 −− "Decrease very much"   rated as a scale of 1

The upper figure for each category in Table 4 represents the mean ratings given by all those subjects who responded to a particular item. Mean values greater than 3.0 generally indicate that the effect of the drug was viewed as more "positive" or "potentiating" than not. The lower figure in each category shows the ranking of the 11 drugs in question. For example, in considering "chance of achieving orgasm," cocaine was regarded as the most positive or potentiating, whereas heroin was relegated to the lowest, or eleventh place. The bottom row in Table 4 gives the mean ranking for the 10 questions that were asked with regard to all the drugs.

It is clear, from an inspection of the mean ratings and the mean over-all rankings, that cocaine is the most highly considered drug with regard to sexual functioning.[1]

"Mescaline," acid, and grass or hash are rated next highest in over-all ranking. There is a wide gap between these drugs and the next-most-highly-rated, speed; a similar gap occurs before alcohol and amyl nitrite are reached. PCP is next, ranking far below its fellow psychedelics acid and "mescaline." The peculiar dissociative phenomena as experienced by the PCP "overdose" may be exhibited as a plastic-rigid "marble statue" catatonic-like state far removed, indeed, from the ideal of a "spacey high," which is reported in lower situations. This problem

---

[1] This clearly coincides with Sigmund Freud's view of *Coca As an Aphrodisiac* (Freud, 1884). "The natives of South America, who represented their goddess of love with coca leaves in her hand, did not doubt the stimulative effect of coca on the genitalia. Mantegazza confirmed that the coqueros sustain a high degree of potency and the disappearance of functional weaknesses following the use of coca . . . Among the persons to whom I have given coca, three reported violent sexual excitement which they unhesitatingly attributed to the coca."

TABLE 4. Evaluation of specific drugs on various aspects of sexuality

Questions	Grass, hash	Acid	"Mescaline"	PCP	Barbs	Speed	Cocaine	Amyl nitrite	Heroin	Meth-aqua-lone	Alcohol
1. Makes sex sensual	4.3 (4)	4.3 (3)	4.4 (2)	3.1 (6)	—	3.7 (5)	4.5 (1)	—	2.9 (7)	—	—
2. Makes you sexually more aggressive	—	—	—	—	3.2 (3)	—	—	3.6 (2)	—	3.2 (4)	3.9 (1)
3. Chance of achieving orgasm	3.7 4	3.8 3	3.8 2	3.1 5	2.7 9	3.1 7	4.0 1	3.0 8	2.3 11	2.5 10	3.1 6
4. Sexual desire (makes you horny)	4.0 2	3.9 3	3.9 4	3.2 10	3.2 9	3.6 6	4.3 1	3.4 7	2.9 11	3.4 8	3.9 5
5. Affect your pleasure when touching your partner	4.2 3	4.3 2	4.4 1	3.2 3	2.8 11	3.4 5	4.1 4	3.3 7	3.1 9	2.8 10	3.3 6
6. Affect your pleasure when being touched	4.2 3	4.3 2	4.3 1	3.3 7	2.9 11	3.5 5	4.2 4	3.4 6	3.1 9	3.0 10	3.3 8
7. Ability to maintain an erection (males)	3.5 2	3.1 5	3.2 3	2.8 7	2.6 7	3.2 4	3.7 1	3.0 6	2.5 11	2.6 10	2.8 8
8. Ability to control when you come	3.2 2	3.1 5	3.1 4	3.0 7	2.8 11	3.2 3	3.4 1	2.9 8	2.8 10	3.0 6	2.9 9
9. Desire to have group experience	3.4 2	3.3 3	3.3 4	2.7 10	2.9 9	3.1 7	3.4 1	3.3 5	2.5 11	3.1 8	3.2 6
10. Ability to have sexual fantasies	3.6 4	3.9 2	3.9 1	3.1 8	2.9 11	3.4 5	3.8 3	3.3 6	2.9 10	3.1 9	3.3 7
11. Desire to act out your sexual fantasies	3.6 4	3.8 3	3.9 1	3.2 8	2.8 10	3.4 6	3.8 2	3.3 7	2.8 11	3.1 9	3.4 5
12. Ability to act out your sexual fantasies	3.6	3.6	3.5	2.9	2.9	3.4	3.7	3.2	2.8	2.8	3.2
Mean rating excluding first two questions:	3.69	3.71	3.73	3.06	2.88	3.32	3.83	3.21	2.77	2.92	3.24
Mean ranking excluding first two listed above:	2.8	3.1	2.5	7.8	9.9	5.3	1.9	6.7	10.3	9.1	6.6

of pharmacologic overshooting is often seen with PCP, as well as with the use of "ketamine," a closely related compound, which has recently made its street debut.

At the very bottom of rankings reside three "downer" drugs: methaqualone, barbiturates, and heroin. The low ratings given methaqualone are particularly interesting in that "ludes" had been regarded as something of a "love drug" during the initial stages of its popularity (Inaba et al., 1973). The opinions of those who have actually experienced the conjunction of methaqualone and sex, however, place the drug clearly among the company of the other "downers." One client reported: "Methaqualone is a 'cheap thrill.' It ain't nothin' more than an overpublicized, over-rated and over-glamorized 'red' " Haight Street Mike.

> "There are a lot of reasons why people have taken to methaqualone. There's the attraction of its sensual pleasantness and its mystique as an orgy drug. It does release inhibitions, but for sex it's about the same as alcohol—as Shakespeare said, "It increaseth the desire but taketh away the performance. [For the male that is; it tends to decrease potency.]
>
> George R. Gay
> Senate Subcommittee to Investigate
> Juvenile Delinquency

One recalls that the downers, without exception, have enjoyed the reputation of sexual enhancer among the inexperienced.

A drug-by-drug inspection of Table 4 shows that cocaine is well thought of in practically all respects. Only in "affecting your pleasure when touching your partner" or in "being touched" does cocaine fall behind the psychedelics and cannabanoids, and then only by a small margin: "Intravenous C is electricity through the brain, activating cocaine pleasure connections" (William Burroughs). This confirms the high opinion that the drug–sex connoisseur in the Bay area has for cocaine's effect upon sex, although our subjects did not regard it as entirely unparalleled in this area. The psychedelics (LSD and mescaline) did very well in most respects, falling significantly behind cocaine only with regard to "ability to maintain an erection," "ability to control when you come," and "sexual desire." These problem areas are again often reported as dose-related, with the more generous quantities of the psychedelics appearing, in punching the user's cosmic ticket, to bring about a loss of bodily control and also to redirect one's attention from the usual culturally encouraged channels (sexual desire) into less usual channels (mysticism, internal absorption, universal communion). "As part of this experience with psychedelics, sex is no longer genitally localized" (Ram Dass).

Because most Bay area mescaline is proved on analysis to be LSD in varying doses (Newmeyer, 1974), it is not surprising that the two drugs were rated virtually the same in their effects upon sexual functioning; the slight advantage that mescaline had in some respects may be considered a placebo effect of its advantageous mislabeling.

Marijuana and hashish are regarded almost equally, as are LSD and mescaline; only with regard to sexual fantasy do the psychedelics slightly exceed the cannabinoids, whereas only with regard to "ability to maintain an erection" do the cannabinoids exceed the psychedelics by a similar margin.

The amphetamine group is the only drug category, in addition to those already mentioned, that has "positive" (above 3.0) mean ratings in all areas queried. In no regard, however, is the mean judgment for speed more than two-thirds of a point above the neutral point. Speed is relatively poorly thought of in comparison to grass or hash, as concerns touching or being touched sexually and with regard to "making sex sensual." As expected, speed does relatively well in the ego-related "control" areas (questions 7, 8, and 12). "Speed makes strange bedfellows" (Haight Street proverb).

Amyl nitrite and alcohol were rated very much the same by respondents—relatively weak in the "control" areas, and relatively strong with respect to promoting sexual desire and sexual aggressiveness, with alcohol exceeding amyl nitrite in both areas. Amyl nitrite or "poppers" have been popular with the Bay area gay male community for at least 5 years (Gay and Sheppard, 1973) and are generally employed during intercourse to bring about an especially powerful and overwhelming orgasm. It is therefore surprising that amyl nitrite should have been graded, by our respondents, as low as it was on items 2, 3, 4, 7, 8, and 12. However, it is evident from the data that our subject population, which is approximately 70% heterosexual, has had only limited experience with this particular drug, and it appears that much of this experience involves the use of poppers at an inappropriate time. One female experimenter reported: "I was wondering when to pop the popper, before I came or when I was over the hill, so I popped and then forgot to come." Only 29 persons had had experience with amyl nitrite, and of these only seven claimed they used the drug "just prior to orgasm" (the optimum time, according to *cognoscenti*), as opposed to earlier or later during intercourse.

None of the mean ratings for PCP falls more than one-third of a point away from the neutral point. PCP is rated relatively strongest with respect to touching and being touched, and is relatively weak with regard to "desire to have group sexual experience." Experience with PCP in sexual situations appears to be rather limited (see Table 3A). A low titration dose by "horning" (or smoking) may create a pleasurable sexual situation but, again, overdose is common among the unsophisticated and the drug glutton and may create bizarre and ineffectual sexual experiences.

The three categories of downer drugs are ranked in the last three places for nearly all of the sexual behavior items. On two items PCP manages to get into this basement fellowship, and on the "ability to control when you come" item, methaqualone is actually ranked sixth from the top (however, this particular item had the narrowest over-all range, with no drug regarded as significantly effective one way or the other). There were a few interesting differences within the downer group: heroin was regarded significantly more negatively than barbiturates in the effect on one's "chance of achieving orgasm"; heroin was placed well below methaqualone as concerns effect upon sexual desire; heroin had a slightly better reputation as far as touching and being touched are concerned; methaqualone and barbiturates were both thought to be more effective than heroin in increasing the "desire to have group sexual experience"; methaqualone did slightly better than the other two downers as regards "desire to act out your sexual fantasies." There is no question that the downers have a poor reputation with our respondents in all areas of sexual functioning. Over-all, 22 out of 33 mean ratings for downers were below the 3.0 neutral point. Even the "passive" sexual-response items, such as question 5, show no particular strength for this class of drugs. However, it should be pointed out that our subject group was fairly well experienced sexually and very liberal in their attitudes, as compared to the total population of young Americans. This means that the capacity of downer drugs to disinhibit one's sexual behavior, i.e., to weaken the inhibitive effect of moral restraint, social fears, or physical distaste, is fairly inoperative as far as our respondents are concerned. With a more uptight, sexually inhibited group of Americans, the importance of downers—and alcohol—in encouraging sexual acting-out would be much greater.

As far as alcohol is concerned, a common viewpoint of our respondents is: "Alcohol makes for sloppy sex." As for barbiturates users:

> Goof ball bums . . . they got no class to them . . . they stagger, fall off bar stools . . . drop food out of their mouths . . . the next step down is coal gas and milk, or sniffing ammonia in a bucket— "The scrubwoman's kick."
>
> William Burroughs

Table 5 records the responses of the group to a number of questions concerning the relationship of various drugs to specific sexual situations. It is significant that for all these questions except the first, the respondent was encouraged to name more than one drug, up to a minimum of three. Hence, the more articulate respondents may tend to be overrepresented. Moreover, because pharmacologically we are dealing with more than one type of cannabinoid, of psychedelic, and of sedative hypnotic, reports on these drug categories represent some crossover and overrepresentations, for example, such responses as MDA, peyote, THC, and LSD would be credited four times in the psychedelic category. This situation occurred fairly rarely, however. It is also important to realize that the subject group has had more extensive experience with some drugs (cannabinoids, alcohol, heroin) than with others (methaqualone, amyl nitrite), so that the latter may appear to get the less than their "fair" number of mentions.

The question "If you could do any drug of your choice or have sex with anyone of your choice, which would you do?" was answered in favor of the sexual contact by three out of four respondents. Nearly all who would prefer to use a drug chose either heroin or cocaine. These are intriguing findings—that anyone would choose a drug in this situation would surprise many young Americans brought up to regard sex as the essence of one's fantasy life. In this regard, it is interesting to note that exactly half the subject group claimed they enjoyed sex more while straight than while high. However, half the group reported that the quality of their sex life had changed since they began using drugs—with nearly three-fourths of these subjects reporting that the change was for the better.

More than two out of five respondents said that the sexual contacts they had

TABLE 5. *Total number of mentions of drug types in relation to certain sexual situations*

Remarks	Grass, hash	Psyche-delics	Barbs	Speed	Cocaine	Amyl nitrite	Heroin	Meth-aqualone	Alcohol	Sedative hypnotics
Would choose this drug over having sex with anyone of my choice	1	1	0	2	6	0	11	0	0	1
More likely to have sex with a partner whom I would not be attracted to while straight, when using this drug	6	10	4	6	11	0	13	5	14	2
This drug increases the aggressiveness of intercourse	17	13	3	12	17	1	13	2	10	0
I sometimes use this drug in the middle of intercourse	0	0	0	6	4	1	3	0	0	2
This drug makes it more difficult to achieve an orgasm	2	3	4	13	6	1	33	4	13	3
I would use this drug(s) tonight	47	13	3	3	24	2	31	4	11	7
This drug has caused loss of erection	2	3	6	14	5	1	20	2	9	1
This drug affects my ability to maintain an erection	4	2	4	10	7	1	18	1	10	0
This drug has been helpful in trying something new, in the evaluation of my sexual behavior	13	6	1	6	9	1	7	1	7	1
If I wanted to be sure to satisfy my partner, I would offer him or her	44	23	3	8	32	2	10	3	9	0
If I wanted to be sure to satisfy my sexual partner I would take myself	39	20	4	8	27	2	15	3	11	3
This drug, in my experience, makes me lose interest in sex	4	17	14	20	0	0	39	1	12	0
This drug increases my chances of experiencing multiple orgasms	25	21	1	12	19	2	7	0	6	2
This drug, in combination, is most effective to increase the pleasure of sexual experience	44	22	5	9	33	1	15	1	12	1
This drug, in combination is most effective to decrease sexual appetite	3	9	14	15	4	0	30	2	9	3

were related to drug-using situations on the majority of occasions. A similar proportion, however, reported that their sexual contacts were related to drug use "quite seldom" or never. In this regard, it is worth noting that many drugs were judged more or less equally for their aphrodisiac quality, or "seducing" capacity, that is, for making one "more likely to have sex with a partner whom I would not be attracted to while straight." Alcohol, cocaine, heroin, and the psychedelics all received frequent mention.

With regard to the "control" aspects of sexual functioning—maintaining an erection for males, and achieving orgasm for both sexes—heroin is by far the most commonly named as a detractor. It is interesting that speed and alcohol are the next-most-often named culprits, both well ahead of barbiturates, methaqualone, and other sedative hypnotics in times mentioned. This is puzzling as Table 4 shows "barbs" and methaqualone to be rated lower than speed and alcohol as regards control over erection and orgasm. A few subjects named cocaine as providing problems in this area. These answers, when qualified, indicated that such depressant effects were most often experienced in currently physically exhausted individuals. Few had anything negative to say about the cannabinoids or the psychedelics, in spite of the widespread use of these drugs (especially the cannabinoids) in sexual situations. Again, the dose-related factor must be recognized; as the individual takes "one toke over the line" he or she is more likely to act out the role of inebriated house guest than that of lover.

The cannabinoids, the psychedelics, speed, cocaine, heroin, and alcohol all were mentioned by at least 10 respondents as drugs that "increase the aggressiveness of intercourse." In contrast, for barbiturates, methaqualone, and other sedative hypnotics each was named by no more than three respondents in this regard. There seems to be a distinction between the "up" and the "down" drugs here, but it is noteworthy that grass, heroin, and alcohol should fall on the "up" side in that they are more than occasionally mentioned as enhancers of sexual aggressiveness. It is surprising that amyl nitrite should be named by only a single respondent as a sexual-aggressiveness enhancer.

In response to the question, "If you were going to use a drug tonight or a combination of drugs, which would you use?," the order cannabinoids $\gg$ heroin $\geq$ cocaine $>$ psychedelics $\geq$ alcohol was reported. This confirms the findings of other portions of the opinions-about-drugs data; heroin, of course, has its unusually high ranking because of the large number of chronic heroin-users in the sample. A very similar ranking, but with heroin dropping from second to fourth place, was observed in replies to the questions, "If you wanted to be sure to satisfy your partner, which drug would you offer him or her?," and "If you wanted to be sure to satisfy your partner which drug would you take yourself?"

Surprisingly, both grass–hash and the psychedelics exceed cocaine in the number of mentions in response to, "Which drugs increase your chances of experiencing multiple orgasms?" It is possible that cocaine would occupy first place if it had been experienced as widely by the subject group as had marijuana, but it may also well be that the sensitivity-enhancing qualities of the cannabinoids and psychedelics are more important in repeated orgasms than is the energizing quality of cocaine.

With regard to "losing interest in sex" or "decreasing sexual appetite," heroin is by far the most commonly cited drug, followed by speed, barbs, the psychedelics, and alcohol. That speed and psychedelics should be named as often as alcohol and barbs here is fascinating; it would be interesting to know if the same psychologic–physiologic "fading-out" were at work with all four drugs, or if perhaps the respondents had experienced a "distracting" or an "anxious" aspect with the use of speed or psychedelics that diverted them from sexual activity. (Exhaustion–paranoia as well as increased dose-response curves also must be considered.)

Table 6 records the data from a few miscellaneous questions posed with regard to drug–sex situations. The responses to the "active–passive partner for the evening" item was pretty much as expected; use of speed engenders a predominant preference for the active role; use of heroin or barbs brings on a preference

TABLE 6. *Miscellaneous questions concerning drug use in sexual situations*

1. When having sex with this drug do you prefer to be:
   a. The more active partner for that evening
   b. The more passive partner for that evening

Agent	Active	Passive
Barbiturates	15	21
Speed	33	12
Amyl nitrite	13	11
Heroin	19	30
Alcohol	33	33

2. How often do you lose interest in sex after taking this drug?

Drug	25% or more of the time	Less than 25% of the time
Barbiturates	27	16
Speed	16	32
Heroin	35	18

3. Are you more selective with whom you trip, or with whom you have sex?

Trip	Sex
23	42

4. Does cocaine increase your chances of multiple orgasms?
   Yes: 33
   No: 23

5. Does cocaine increase your aggressiveness during the sex act?
   Yes: 33
   No: 22

6. Have you ever lost an erection while doing cocaine (males)?
   Yes: 14
   No: 25

for the passive role; use of amyl nitrite or alcohol leaves the users (aroused, but) evenly split as to which role they would prefer. The "loss of interest in sex after taking this drug" question, also, gave data pretty much as expected: unlike Table 5, here at least, the indication was that barbs are a more "antierotic" drug than is speed. We were surprised to find that twice as many people were "more selective about whom they have sex with" than whom they trip with. The items concerning cocaine elucidate the somewhat high regard our respondents have for its enhancement of certain realms of sexual functioning.

SUMMARY

Certain generalizations are appropriate concerning psychosocial and pharmacosexual effects as elicited in this drug–sex survey. Cocaine, marijuana, certain psychedelics, amphetamines (in small doses), heroin, and alcohol were found to possess particular aphrodisiac qualities. These phenomena as described included an increase in libido, enhanced enjoyment of sex, and the lowering of inhibitions. Peripheral effects such as increasing the chances of multiple orgasm were reported in the instances of the cannabinoids, the psychedelics, and cocaine.

Also, certain drugs were noted to decrease sexual activity. Two mechanisms are apparent here: that of diminishing basic desire, and that (particularly in the male) of decreasing potency. The groups of drugs most prominently mentioned in this regard include barbiturates, methaqualone, heroin, and large doses of amphetamine or alcohol.

It is interesting to note that heroin and alcohol are found to be described both as sexual stimulants and depressants. The case for alcohol can almost assuredly be explained as being dose-related, but the case for heroin is more difficult to explain. There has been voluminous speculation that heroin may be used as an anesthetic for the strong feelings associated with sexual arousal (De Leon and Wexler, 1973). Heroin would indeed allay the fears of an individual concerning sex and would make him or her her more likely to engage in and (sic) to enjoy intercourse. "If all pleasure is relief from tension, junk affords relief from this whole life process . . . junk suspends the whole cycle of tension." (William Burroughs). Mathis attributes the heroin addict's use of heroin to an avoidance of sex, as a consequence of a distorted sexual identity (Mathis, 1970). Heroin thus eliminates sexual desire or rather is substituted for it. Freud's classic reports tend to substantiate this opinion (Freud, 1898).

> Searching examination generally shows that . . . narcotics are intended as substitutes (directly or indirectly) for. . . missing sexual gratification, and whenever normal sexual life cannot be re-established a patient who has been weaned from habit may be expected quite certainly to slide back into it.

It is also interesting to note the generally high opinion held of psychedelics in conjunction with sexual activity—a previous study (Gay and Sheppard, 1973) had indicated that subjects were seldom coordinated enough during their trip to experience effective intercourse. The subjects in this study appear to be more sophisticated in their experience with the psychedelics (LSD in particular) and repeatedly reported its aphrodisiac qualities. The transpersonal nature of this experience has been discussed widely. Grof has described feelings of "high levels of sexual excitement and a wild, dynamic ecstasy" during this transpersonal stage (Grof, 1970). Alpert (Baba Ram Dass) also discussed the sexual implication of LSD, ". . . psychedelics offer the possibility of enriching the sexual life of the average individual and show some promise in alleviating sexual pathology" (Alpert, 1969). Leary has stated

> the LSD experience is . . . about . . . Merging, yielding, flowing, union, communion. It's all lovemaking. You make love with candlelight, with sound waves from a record player, with the trees. You're in pulsating harmony with all the energy around you . . . compared with sex under LSD, the way you've been making love—no matter how ecstatic the pleasure you think you get from it— is like making love to a department store storewindow dummy.
>
> (T. Leary, 1968)

CONCLUSION

Whatever our end point, we certainly are now dealing with an experienced and sophisticated drug–sex-wise young population. With all types of drugs now readily available, we must bring ourselves to the realization of a new era of liberated drug–sex experimenters.

> I wanted to smoke dope, take dope, lick dope, suck dope, fuck dope, anything I could lay my hands on, I wanted to do it.
>
> (Janis Joplin)

The extraordinarily high level of "street" experimentation that has taken place during the 1960s and 1970s is counterposed to the paucity of scientific data available. It is our hope that the findings of our Haight-Ashbury population will contribute to some clarification of the ambiguities that so cloud this area of research.

> Some men need some killer weed,
>   and some men need cocaine
> Some men need some cactus juice
>   to purify their brain
>
> Some men need 2 women
>   and some need alcohol
> Everybody needs a little something
>   but Lord I need it *all* . . .
>   Shel Silverstein

ACKNOWLEDGMENTS

The authors are particularly grateful for the help of Jean McKenzie and Lois Mack.

BIBLIOGRAPHY REFERENCES

Alpert, R. (1969); *Lectures (unpublished)*.

Chessich, R. C. (1960): The "pharmacogenic orgasm" in the drug addict. *Arch. Gen. Psychiatry,* 3:545–556.

De Leon, G., and Wexler, H. K.: Heroin addition: Its relation to sexual behavior and sexual experience. *J. Abnorm. Psychol.* 81:36–38.

Freud, S. (1984): *Ueber Coca*. Reprinted by Dunequin Press, 1963.

Freud, S. (1898): *Collected Papers: Sexuality in the Etiology of the Neuroses.*

Gay, G. R., Elsenbaumer, R., and Newmeyer, J. A. (1972): A dash of M*A*S*H: The Zep and the Dead: Head to head. *J. Psychedelic Drugs,* 5:193–203.

Gay, G. R., and Sheppard, C. W. (1973): Sex-crazed dope fiends—Myth or reality? *Drug Forum,* 2:125–140.

Gay, G. R., and Smith, D. E. (1973): A free clinic approach to drug abuse. *Prev. Med.* 2:543–553.

Greaves, G. (1972): "Sexual disturbances among chronic amphetamine users. *J. Nerv. Ment. Dis.* 155: 363–365.

Grof, S. (1970): The use of LSD in psychotherapy. *J. Psychedelic Drugs,* 3:52–62.

Howard, J., and Borges, P (1971): Needle sharing in the Haight: Some social and psychological functions. *J. Abnorm. Psychol.* 4:71–80.

Inaba, D., Gay, G. R., Newmeyer, J. A., and Whitehead, C. (1973): Methaqualone Abuse: Luding out. *JAMA,* 224:1505–1509.

Interim Report of the Commision of Inquiry into the Nonmedical Use of Drugs (1970): Crown Copyrights, Ottowa.

Leary, T. (1968): *Politics of Ecstacy.* Putnam, New York.

Mathis, J. L. (1970) Sexual aspects of heroin addiction. *Med. Aspects Human Sexuality,* iv:98–109.

Newmeyer, J. A. (1974a): "The Boys meet the Dead: Notes on the continued flourishing of the psychedelic era. Haight-Ashbury Free Medical Clinics, San Francisco, California.

Newmeyer, J. A. (1974b): "Five years after: Drug use and exposure to heroin among the Haight-Ashbury Free Medical Clinic clientele. *J. Psychedelic Drugs,* 6:61–66.

Newmeyer, J. A., and Gay, G. R. (1972): The traditional junkie, the Aquarian-age junkie, and the Nixon-era junkie. *Drug Forum,* 2:17–30.

Robins, L., and Murphy, G. (1966): Drug use in a normal population of young Negro men. *Am. J. Public Health,* 57:1580–1596.

Simmons, J. L., and Winograd, B. (1966): *It's Happening.* Marc-Laird, Santa Barbara, California.

Smith, R. C. (1970): In: *The New Social Drug,* edited by D. E. Smith. Prentice-Hall, Englewood Cliffs, New Jersey.

Sexual Behavior: Pharmacology and Biochemistry, edited by M. Sandler and G. L.
Gessa. Raven Press, New York © 1975.

Role of Biogenic Amines in the Modulation of Aggressive and Sexual Behavior in Animals and Man

Guy M. Everett

Department of Pharmacology, University of California, San Francisco, California 94143

The interrelation of aggressive and sexual behavior has been noted in literature and science from time immemorial. In a recent book called *Animals at War* (Barber, 1972), the behavioral changes with increased fighting and aggressive display in mating season are outlined for many species of animals and birds. Although specific hormonal changes have been studied in some species to try to account for these behavioral responses, the important role of brain biogenic amines is only now receiving attention in this area.

We propose that Nature in her wisdom has found ways of using the same neurohormones to control both sexual and aggressive behavior. Thus, Hate and Love are indeed closely related even at the biochemical level.

The possible relationship of brain amines to aggression was first realized from studies of the taming effects of reserpine on monkeys and other animals in conjunction with the biochemical correlate of marked depletion of biogenic amines. Because of the depletion of three putative transmitters—dopamine, norepinephrine, and serotonin—the problem of which one was most important in motor and aggressive behavior was resolved by single replacement studies of these transmitters; their specific precursors were administered to replace the depleted transmitter in the brain (Everett and Toman, 1959).

In the mouse L-3,4-dihydroxyphenylalanine (L-DOPA) increases levels of dopamine and returns the reserpine-depleted animal to normal activity. With large doses of L-DOPA in normal ICR mice, brain dopamine levels markedly increase, and at this time irritability and aggressive fighting behavior appear in this usually benign strain of mouse (Everett and Borcherding, 1970). This was the first evidence for a role of dopamine in aggressive behavior.

In the reserpine-treated monkey, a return of motor and normal aggressive behavior is also obtained after giving L-DOPA. Although minute amounts of norepinephrine are also formed after L-DOPA, it seems unlikely that this transmitter is more than secondarily involved in these dramatic behavioral changes. This is also supported by the finding that dopamine β-hydroxylase inhibitors do not prevent the effects of L-DOPA in restoring motor behavior. In such experiments, dopamine is formed but norepinephrine is not. Furthermore, administration of dihydroxyphenylserine, a direct precursor of norepinephrine, produces slight sedation in normal animals and no reversal of reserpine depression.

If brain serotonin is replaced by administration of its precursor, 5-hydroxytryptophan (5-HTP), to reserpine-depleted mice or monkeys, one does not get a return of normal motor or aggressive behavior. Large doses of 5-HTP cause abnormal limb abduction and tremor in both mice and monkeys. In normal animals, 5-HTP causes decreased motor activity, and also inhibits aggressive and sexual behavior.

Studies of the transmitters in normally aggressive animals have received little or no attention. Everett (1973) reported much higher brain dopamine levels in Balb mice when compared with benign C57B16 and ICR strains. Balb males are usually aggressive to other males and to anyone handling them.

Old (30-week) ICR males kept in groups show remarkable behavioral changes with marked increases in aggressive behavior and a 42% increase in brain dopamine compared with young adults. The old females also show increases in dopamine but do not become aggressive, supporting the importance of hormonal factors in aggressive responses.

Other evidence for the involvement of dopamine in aggressive behavior comes from studies of apomorphine, a drug considered to mimic dopamine. In rats apomorphine enhances aggressive behavior and also increases sexual behavior. The highly effective blocking action of haloperidol against aggressive activity (a specific dopamine-blocking drug) lends further evidence to the dopamine theory of aggressive behavior.

Specific studies of the interrelation of aggressive and sexual behavior to brain amines have not been carried out although ancillary observations have supported the close relation of the two behaviors.

Studies with PCPA in rats have shown that depletion of serotonin results in increased sexual behavior. In confirmatory studies we also observed aggressive rearing and confrontation by male rats but no direct fighting. The PCPA-treated rat is also irritable and difficult to handle and struggles considerably.

This evidence suggests that serotonin, "the civilizing neurohormone" (Everett), is a major inhibitor of both aggressive and sexual activity whereas dopamine is the primal motor mobilizing neurohormone for both aggressive and sexual behavior.

The fact that all aspects of the sexual act in addition to mounting (e.g., number of intromissions and number of ejaculations and shortening of the fatigue period are enhanced suggests that we are indeed dealing with global and fundamental neuromodulator systems in the control of sexual behavior (Gessa and Tagliamonte, 1974).

Although the human pharmacologic data are fragmentary, we can extend this hypothesis to man. Gay and Sheppard (1972) have summarized some relevant data in this area.

In Table 1 I have compiled a list of drugs and precursors which have been shown to affect sexual or aggressive behavior or both in animals and man. Thus, L-DOPA can produce increased aggressive and sexual behavior in animals and also has been reported to increase aggression and sexual interest in man, including priapism in some cases.

TABLE 1. *Effect of drugs on aggressive and sexual behavior in animals and man*

Drug	Modulator	Behavioral effect	
		Aggressive	Sexual
L-DOPA	Dopamine	+	+
Amphetamine	Dopamine	+	+
PCPA	Serotonin (depleted)	+	+
Amantadine	Dopamine	?	+
Morphine	Dopamine	?	+
Cocaine	Dopamine	?	+
Amyl nitrite	?	?	+
Barbiturates	?	+	−
Haloperidol	Dopamine	−	−
Phenothiazines	Dopamine	−	−
5-HTP	Serotonin	−	−
Reserpine	Dopamine, norepinephrine, serotonin (depleted)	−	−

Single doses of amphetamine increase aggression in men and women, and given intravenously can cause erection and spontaneous orgasm. PCPA in rats causes marked increases in sexual mounting and affects other aspects of the sexual act as well. These animals also show aggressive behavior. In man the action of PCPA on sexual behavior is equivocal and will require further study (Benkert, 1973).

Morphine may cause aggressive behavior in cats and in humans. Addicts describe its effects as a "cerebral orgasm" without peripheral involvement. Although the picture is complex, dopamine is probably involved in these morphine actions. In morphine withdrawal priapism is often observed.

Cocaine produces central stimulation and aggressiveness in man. It is also considered an aphrodisiac and is used for this purpose. Amyl nitrite has not been studied in animals for behavioral effects, but it is used by many men as an enhancer of ejaculation and sensory awareness (Everett, 1972).

Barbiturates may produce marked aggressive activity in man. The mechanism of action is obscure as is the case of aggression under alcohol in some individuals. Both classes of drugs have effects on biogenic amine systems and further studies along these lines are definitely indicated.

I have listed four drugs that block aggressive and sexual behavior. Haloperidol dramatically blocks aggressive and violent activity in animals and man and also greatly reduces sexual activity. The phenothiozines are equally effective. Both of these groups are powerful blockers of dopamine receptors. These drugs have been used to reduce or block undesirable compulsive sexual activity in man.

In animals, 5-HTP increases brain serotonin and decreases motor activity and behavior of all kinds including sexual activity. Reserpine also decreases aggressive and sexual behavior by depleting the brain of these transmitters, especially dopamine.

The picture is far from complete, but the evidence is compelling that the serotonin and dopamine systems of the brain are important in the modulation and control of aggressive and sexual behavior. It should be emphasized that the final behavioral output involves the balance between these two systems.

I have not discussed the important role of acetylcholine in these behavioral states. Certainly cholinergic interneurons are present in many of these systems and other neurotransmitters may also be involved.

The complex interrelation of these biogenic amine modulators with the endocrine system is of course essential in determining the final behavioral pattern. The further integration of these two major areas of research will be essential to the elucidation of all forms of behavior.

REFERENCES

Barber, C. (1971): *Animals at War.* Harper and Row, New York.

Benkert, O. (1973): Pharmacology experiments to stimulate human sexual behavior. In: *Psychopharmacology, Sexual Disorders and Drug Abuse,* pp. 489–496. North-Holland Publ. Co., Amsterdam-London.

Everett, G. M. (1972): Effects of amyl nitrite ("Poppers") on sexual experience. *Medical Aspects of Human Sexuality,* 6:146–150.

Everett, G. M. (1973): Genetic factors in the control of biogenic amines and brain excitability. In: *Frontiers in Catecholamine Research,* pp. 657–659, edited by E. Usdin and S. H. Snyder. Pergamon Press, New York.

Everett, G. M., and Borcherding, J. W. (1970): L-DOPA: Effect on concentration of dopamine, norepinephrine and serotonin in brains of mice. *Science,* 168:849–850.

Everett, G. M., and Toman, J. E. P. (1959): Mode of action of rauwolfia alkaloids and motor activity. In: *Biological Psychiatry,* p. 75, edited by J. H. Masserman. Grune & Stratton, New York.

Gay, G. R., and Sheppard, C. W. (1972): Sex in the drug culture. *Medical Aspects of Human Sexuality,* 6:28–47.

Gessa, G. L., and Tagliamonte, A. (1974): Possible role of brain serotonin and dopamine in controlling male sexual behavior. In: *Serotonin—New Vistas,* pp. 217–228, edited by E. Costa, G. L. Gessa, and M. Sandler. Raven Press, New York.

Sexual Behavior: Pharmacology and Biochemistry, edited by M. Sandler and G. L.
Gessa. Raven Press, New York © 1975.

The Mystique of Social Drugs and Sex

Leo E. Hollister

Medical Investigator, Veterans Administration Hospital, Palo Alto, California 94304 and
Associate Professor of Medicine and Psychiatry, Stanford University School of Medicine,
Stanford, California 94305

Sexual behavior, ordinarily thought of simply as "doing what comes naturally," turns out to be much more complex. It is dependent upon a complex
interplay of biogenic amines and hormones within the body, as well as such
extraneous influences as psychologic conditioning, physical health, and prevailing
mood and circumstances. Although few persons are so unlucky as to be completely lacking in sexual drive, the variations in its intensity are enormous among
different individuals. Variations in the expression of sexual drive are becoming
increasingly recognized and quite possibly promoted by extensive publicity.

To set drugs within such a complicated framework of behavior is not an easy
task. With so many variables operating simultaneously, most of which cannot
be controlled, it is not simple to assess the influence of drugs on "normal" sexual
behavior in any scientific fashion. Drugs used socially have been alleged to have
three major beneficial effects on sexual behavior: (1) to promote increased libido;
(2) to increase sexual performance; (3) to increase sexual pleasure. Each of these
manifestations is somewhat interdependent, so that the specific mechanisms by
which these various claims are realized may overlap.

Search for the Perfect Aphrodisiac

During most of his recorded history, man has searched for drugs that would
achieve one or all of the sexual benefits described above. The history of
aphrodisiacs includes a multiplicity of natural materials to which have been
ascribed special sexual properties. The search for the "fountain of youth" must
certainly have been prompted, to a great extent, by the attendant prolongation
of sexual vigor. No one seems ever to have shown much interest in prolonging
old age.

Sex hormones are the most popularly prescribed treatments for enhancing
sexual vigor. Estrogens are given to women and androgens to men with the hope
that declining sexual activity in the middle and latter years of life can be prevented
or remedied. Except in clear cases of deficiency of either type of hormone,
evidence for the desired effect is scanty. A popular remedy for impotence consists
of a combination of two old drugs reputed to be sexual stimulants, strychnine
and yohimbine. The former is thought to act as an excitant of the whole neuraxis,

especially the spinal cord. Yohimbine acts by producing a state of parasympathetic predominance and vasodilatation. Recent reports of the use of pituitrin for impotence are difficult to evaluate and the rationale is unclear.

Although it is to be expected that those who find that the years have taken some toll of their sexual vigor might seek out drugs to stimulate its renewal, such a search by young persons seems hardly necessary. If, indeed, one were to find a drug that would have this effect for either or both sexes, most appropriately its use would be limited to those over 40 years of age. As most nonapproved social drugs are used by young people, the recurrent claims made for these drugs as sexual stimulants can only be viewed either as a highly desired effect or as a way of proselytizing drug use to the older generation.

APPROVED SOCIAL DRUGS AND SEXUAL BEHAVIOR

Alcohol, caffeine, and nicotine are the major approved social drugs of the western world. Few of their users would contend that these drugs do very much for their sex lives, although that was not always the case.

Alcohol has long been recognized as a disinhibiting agent that might "provoke lechery" but detract from its performance. The Ogden Nash couplet about seduction put it more briefly: "Candy is dandy, but liquor is quicker." Long-term use of alcohol may lead to premature loss of virility, possibly on a neurogenic basis. One such alcoholic was quoted: "I started out Early Times, but quickly wound up as Old Grandad" (Lemere and Smith, 1973). Loss of sexual desire and frigidity may also occur in women who are chronic alcoholics.

Caffeine has been condemned as leading to immorality, when the word almost exclusively denoted sexual immorality whereas it also has been described as hot, black water whose property is "to sterilize nature and extinguish carnal desires" (Lewin, 1931a). Probably both assessments are inaccurate. The stimulant effect of caffeine might be beneficial for enhancing sexual performance in someone who may otherwise be uninterested because of physical or mental fatigue. No specific effect of caffeine on sexual function has been demonstrated.

Nicotine use has been said to be associated with an occasional reduction or loss of "sexual generative power" but without any specific proof for this assertion (Lewin, 1931b). Most of the effects of tobacco use may be psychologic. The advertising slogan for a cigarette directed at the market for women, "You've come a long way, baby," contrasts the attitudes toward women who smoke today with those attitudes that prevailed 60 years ago. The original liberation of women, which occurred in the 1920s, was characterized by the flapper with a cigarette holder in hand. More than we appreciate, smoking by women has been linked symbolically with increasing sexual freedom and civil rights.

NONAPPROVED SOCIAL DRUGS AND SEXUAL BEHAVIOR

The general history of these drugs is that at some time one or another representative of each class obtains a reputation as a "sex drug." These reputations derive entirely from those who advocate the use of the drug for other purposes as well. For someone who wishes to proselytize the use of a new drug, surely one of the most effective arguments for its use would be an augmentation of sexual power. Evidence in support of most of these claims is scanty, with the scientific evidence often tending to indicate an opposite effect.

Opiates

The general impression, based on almost all possible evidence, is that opiates seriously impair sexual functions. Although it has been said sometimes that opiates may enhance sexual enjoyment initially, such a process holds only with small doses which act as disinhibiting agents. As tolerance or physical dependence develops, sexual life suffers. Chronic opiate dependence is associated with such a marked reduction in sexual performance that one of the beneficial effects of methadone maintenance programs has been its restoration. Often this fact is commented upon by the patient's mate. Methadone itself, which has effects similar to those of opiates, may impair sexual performance, so that improvement is by no means complete. Often this side effect is not really appreciated until methadone doses are sharply reduced or the drug is withdrawn.

A few years ago, opiate-dependent patients treated with a narcotic antagonist, cyclazocine, reported that it was an aphrodisiac that markedly improved their sexual functioning. Such beneficial effects can be ascribed either to complete withdrawal from any use of opiates, or possibly to a precipitation of a mild withdrawal reaction with concomitant parasympathetic overactivity in patients with residual physical dependence to opiates. The phenomenon of increased sexual desire from narcotic antagonists has not been seen in nonopiate dependent individuals.

Clinical reports of endocrinologic or metabolic complications of opiate abuse have been exceedingly rare despite the diverse actions of morphine on release of adrenocorticotrophic hormone, pituitary gonadotropins, thyrotropin, and vasopressin. Addicts show a partial decrease in gonadotropin release manifested by decreased urinary excretion of 17-ketosteroids; response to exogenous chorionic gonadotropins is increased (Eisenman, Fraser, Sloan, and Isbell, 1958). It is tempting to relate diminished gonadal activity to the loss of sexual desire universally experienced by addicts, but part of the decrease may be due to the orgastic sensation evoked by each successive intravenous bolus of heroin and its subsequent sedation. Diminished or absent menstrual periods, infertility, and spontaneous abortion are frequent in addicted women and may be regarded as evidence of diminished release of pituitary gonadotropins (Stoffer, 1968).

Barbiturates and Other Sedatives

Just as with alcohol, sedatives may enhance sexual behavior by virtue of their disinhibiting function. Abuse of sedatives often mimics that of alcohol abuse, the desired goal being a similar state of intoxication.

Scarcely any contentions were made that sedatives provided sexual benefits until the recent episode of abuse of methaqualone in the United States (Inaba, Gay, Newmayer, and Whitehead, 1973). Although this sedative drug had been widely abused on two continents before making its way to the United States, it took the ingenuity of our drug-using culture to spread the word that this drug had mystical sexual properties. Concomitant with rapid increase in use of the drug were a spate of rumors about how this drug added a new dimension to sex. It was given the epithet "love drug"; enjoying sex while "luded out" (the name deriving from one of the commercial names for the drug) represented a new frontier of sexual ecstasy. Certainly one can imagine no possible way in which spread of use of a drug could be more quickly promoted than by such rumors. At present, use of the drug seems to be decreasing and claims for its special sexual properties are seldom heard. No one who took the drug as a prescription sedative-hypnotic ever noticed such effects. Methaqualone resembles many prior drugs of this class, being a totally unneeded addition to a plethora of such agents.

Barbiturates are said to decrease release of pituitary gonadotropins, in a manner similar to morphine. One is forced to conclude that for most people, except those who require loss of inhibition, sexual performance under the influence of sedative drugs is more likely to be diminished rather than enhanced.

Amphetamines and Other Stimulants

During the 1940s and 1950s, when abuse of amphetamines was exclusively by the oral route and doses were measured in tens of milligrams, they were alleged to incite young people to sexual orgies. Whereas amphetamine use may have been associated with such group behavior, the latter was motivated for other reasons. If you are going to have an orgy, what better drug to take than one that produces euphoria and increased mental alertness and delays fatigue and the need for sleep or food? This pattern of stimulant use was worldwide, being observed in youngsters in Japan taking methamphetamine or, later on, those in Sweden using the amphetamine surrogate phenmetrazine.

During the past decade, use of stimulants has changed. Taking drugs is episodic, the route of administration is intravenous and repetitive, and doses are measured in hundreds or thousands of milligrams per day. Many other drugs may also be tried, including heroin. The effects obtained from intravenous injection of massive doses of amphetamines are qualitatively different from those obtained from smaller oral doses (Kramer, Fishman, and Littlefield, 1967). Just as with heroin, an initial "rush," described as a visceral numbness and tingling akin to a diffuse orgasm, is experienced followed by the customary signs of excessive stimulation, sympathetic nervous system overactivity, and peculiar stereotyped grimacing movements. Injections are taken periodically to repeat the pleasurable aspects of the "rush." Under such circumstances, it should not be surprising that amphetamine used in this way substitutes for, rather than enhances, sexual behavior.

A recent fad in the use of stimulants has been the rediscovery of cocaine. This powerful stimulant, similar in many respects to the amphetamines, may be taken in small doses by intranasal "snuffing" to enhance sexual activity already planned or anticipated. The sympathomimetic effects of the drug may result in delayed ejaculation. Chronic sustained dosage of cocaine produces psychic effects that may overpower any others, and a loss of sexual desire is to be expected. The vasoconstrictive effects of the drug might conceivably impair potency in someone with extensive atherosclerosis of the lower aorta or the blood vessels arising from it.

Hallucinogens

The present wave of drug abuse was led by the popularization of hallucinogens, particularly mescaline and lysergic acid diethylamide by the two prophets of psychedelia, Huxley and Leary. The major benefit to be derived from their use was initially reputed to be a "cleansing of the doors of perception" or an exploration of the inner mind. Predictably, it was not long before devotees of the use of these drugs ascribed special sexual effects to them as well. Certainly, sexual congress under the influence of these drugs must have been different from usual, considering the vast array of somatic, perceptual, and psychic symptoms that relatively modest doses produced in the majority of people (Hollister, 1968).

Just as with other claimed effects of these drugs, assertions about their sexual effects, being entirely subjective, are impossible either to prove or to disprove. In matters such as this, what is in the eye of the beholder, is. Some of the amphetamine-like effects of these drugs might contribute to an increased sexual interest. Paresthesias and floating sensations might be expected to enhance some of the phenomena of orgasm. One of the major problems associated with hallucinogenic drugs is that the abundance of sensory inputs may diminish appreciation of any single one, so that rather than being "turned on" sexually, it is equally possible that one might be "turned off." Many of my experimental subjects have told me that when they had thoughts of sex while under the drug, the idea of being able to accomplish the act seemed preposterous.

Marihuana

Long before the present resurgence in use of cannabis, much of its use was based on the notion that it enhanced sexual behavior. The effects of the drug are complex, having some elements of stimulants, sedatives, and hallucinogens, so that all the possible ways that the above drugs might enhance sex might occur with marihuana. Common doses of cannabis are quite small, so that disinhibition and expectation may play the greatest role in the drug's averred sexual benefits. With larger doses, the reverse situation might occur, so that absorption with what is happening inside oneself may lead to neglect of the interpersonal relationship that sexual intercourse requires. The Indian Hemp Drugs Commission of 1894 reported that hemp drugs have "no aphrodisiac power whatever; and, as a matter of fact, they are used by ascetics in this country with the ostensible object of destroying sexual appetite."

That so many drugs with divergent pharmacologic effects should all enjoy a reputation as sexual superchargers suggests that their effects may be illusory. One cannot help but wonder whether there is not some pervasive myth of the perfect orgasm that keeps driving people to "gild the lily" with drugs. Marihuana is known to have a strong placebo effect, especially in chronic users, many of whom are able to attain satisfactory "highs" with marihuana which contains virtually no active materials. Truly, these are instances of mind over matter.

That one's general pattern of sexual behavior could be changed by marihuana use is entirely possible. The thorny question is how often is the taking of the drug related to the conscious adoption of a life-style in which many behaviors are altered, including that of drug-taking? Reports of promiscuous or polymorphous sexual behavior in chronic marihuana users are frequent, but it is difficult to separate cause from effect (Kolansky and Moore, 1971).

A new finding should raise a new note of caution in those who would espouse marihuana use as a way to sexual salvation. Chronic marihuana use (4 days a week for a minimum of 6 months, without the use of other drugs) was associated with decreased plasma testosterone levels in young men as compared to similar controls, a finding that was dose-related, and reversible when marihuana was discontinued. Six of the 17 men showed oligospermia and two were impotent (Kolodny, Masters, Kolodner, and Toro, 1974). Thus, the most recent experimental evidence on the effects of marihuana on sexual function, at least in men, confirms the opinion of the Indian Hemp Commission.

Inhalants

The use of inhalant gases to "get high" is scarcely new. Nitrous oxide, ether, and chloroform were widely used for this purpose soon after their introduction. Descriptions of the effects obtained by some of the users suggest that the gates of paradise had been opened (Smith, 1972). Perhaps it is a reflection of those more sedate times that no mention ever was made of further enhancing the paradisical visions by concomitant sexual intercourse.

More recently, a large group of volatile hydrocarbon solvents has been abused. These include toluene, xylene, benzene, carbon tetrachloride, naphtha, and gasoline. Another group of such compounds is largely used as refrigerants or aerosol propellants. The pattern of use has been unusual in that most users fall into a group under the age of 14 years or younger. Perhaps because of the callow subjects involved, there has been little reputation of these agents as sexual stimulants (Cohen, 1973).

Contrary to the above-mentioned drugs, amyl nitrite has become an extraordinarily popular sex drug. Formerly, its use was limited solely to providing relief of attacks of angina pectoris. For such use, it was packaged in fragile glass vials covered by finely spun cloth. These vials could be easily crushed in one's hand, which allowed the drug to be inhaled immediately. As relief of anginal attacks was not much more quickly obtained from this cumbersome method of drug administration than from sublingual doses of nitroglycerin, the preparation enjoyed only a small but level rate of use for many years. Several years ago, the sales curve of amyl nitrite took a sharp rise entirely due to the new use of the drug.

The usual pattern of use is for one or both partners to inhale the drug as orgasm approaches. The vasodilating effect may lessen the intensity of erection of the male or active partner, in which case judicious use might provide a means for delaying orgasm and ejaculation. The most common side effect is severe headache from dilation of blood vessels in the extracranial circulation, the typical nitrite headache. This discomfort is short-lived and probably not dangerous. Hypotension, tachycardia, and diminished cardiac output may present dangers to persons with known or latent cardiac disease.

So far as one can tell, it is impossible to answer questions about the epidemiology of this use of amyl nitrite. It is probably much more prevalent among male homosexuals than among other groups (Everett, 1972).

As is the case with many drugs alleged to enhance sexual pleasure, the rationale is sometimes difficult to explain. The sole pharmacologic action of the drug is smooth muscle relaxation, which accounts for its strong vasodilating effect. Vasodilation is manifested by a drop in blood pressure with an increase in pulse rate and by cutaneous flushing. Abruptly lowered blood pressure produces a feeling of giddiness, which may actually proceed to syncope should the dose be too large. Quite possibly, this feeling of dizziness and faintness accounts for the purported increase in the intensity of orgasm. Cutaneous vasodilation may also increase sensitivity of the skin, which could play a lesser role in enhancing pleasure.

CONCLUSION

Just as man continually seeks drugs to change his perceptions, he pursues drugs to improve his sexual behavior. Quite often, the same drug may be used for both purposes. Many of the currently used social drugs are averred to enhance sexual drive, performance, or enjoyment. Such claims are impossible to disprove, but as fashions in the use of drugs for sexual purposes change rapidly, one surmises that the presumed benefits are more illusory than real.

REFERENCES

Cohen, S. (1973): The volatile solvents. *Public Health Rev.* 2:185–214.
Everett, G. M. (1972): Effects of amyl nitrite ("poppers") on sexual experience. *Medical Aspects of Human Sexuality,* 6:146–150.
Eisenman, A. J., Fraser, H. F., Sloan, J., and Isbell, H. (1958): Urinary 17-ketosteroid excretion during a cycle of morphine addiction. *J. Pharmacol. Exp. Ther.,* 124:305–311.

Hollister, L. E. (1968): *Chemical Psychoses. LSD and Related Drugs.* Charles C. Thomas, Springfield, Illinois.

Inaba, D. S., Gay, G. R., Newmayer, J. A., and Whitehead, C. (1973): Methaqualone abuse. "Luding out." *JAMA,* 224:1505–1509.

Kolansky, H., and Moore, W. T. (1971): Effects of marihuana on adolescents and young adults. *JAMA,* 216:486–492.

Kolodny, R. C., Masters, W. H., Kolodner, R. M., and Toro, G. (1974): Depression of plasma testosterone levels after chronic intensive marihuana use. *New Engl. J. Med.,* 290:872–874.

Kramer, J. C., Fishman, V. S., and Littlefield, D. C. (1967): Amphetamine abuse. *JAMA,* 201: 305–309.

Lemere, F., and Smith, J. W. (1973): Alcohol-induced sexual impotence. *Am. J. Psychiat.,* 130:212.

Lewin, L. (1931a): *Phantastica. Narcotic and Stimulating Drugs. Their Use and Abuse,* p. 257. Reprinted by Dutton, New York, 1964.

Lewin, L. (1931b): *Phantastica. Narcotic and stimulating drugs. Their Use and Abuse,* p. 316. Reprinted by Dutton, New York, 1964.

Smith, P. B. (1972): *Chemical Glimpses of Paradise.* Charles C. Thomas, Springfield, Illinois.

Stoffer, S. S. (1968): A gynecological study of drug addicts. *Am. J. Obstet. Gynecol.,* 101:779–783.

Sexual Behavior: Pharmacology and Biochemistry, edited by M. Sandler and G. L. Gessa. Raven Press, New York © 1975.

Categories of Interest in the Scientific Search for Relationships (i.e., Interactions, Associations, Comparisons) in Human Sexual Behavior and Drug Use

Vincent Nowlis

Fellows Program, Drug Abuse Council, Washington, D. C., and Department of Psychology, University of Rochester, Rochester, New York

The area at the intersection of the sets of events in human sexual behavior and drug use may be divided into four regions. The region of most frequent interest is that of the effect of drug use on sexual behavior, both objective and subjective. By subjective, I mean the private, conscious events (awarenesses of pleasure, pain, fantasy, memory, perception) that occur in sexual experience.

A second and widely ignored region is that of the effect of sexual behavior and experience on drug use and on the objective and subjective effects of single or repeated usage. In one sense, this region is the reverse of the first region.

The third and broadest region includes the many associations and correlations between drug use and sexual behavior. I refer to the many ways in which these two sets of phenomena tend to be associated or occur together in daily life; in marital and other associations; in life-styles and subcultures; in the developmental life histories of children, adolescents, and adults; in clinical and criminal records; and in a variety of prejudicial stereotypes in popular myths, and in folklore, ancient and modern, in all parts of the world.

A fourth region includes instances in which some component or attribute of one set of phenomena (i.e., either drug use or sexual behavior) is identified as similar or equivalent to an attribute of the other set. For example, intravenous injection of heroin or methamphetamine may be accompanied by a "pharmacologic orgasm"; or the altered state of consciousness accompanying normal, undrugged sexual orgasm may have a drug-related meaning or connotation for some.

I find that when all four regions are specified, a search of the international professional literature on drug use and sexual behavior yields many hundreds of references and abstracts. Let us then concentrate on the first region, that of the effect of drug use on human sexual behavior and experience. Once again, however, we must immediately recognize that space permits only outline rather than empirical detail. This outline is developed in a way that illuminates those categories of sexual behavior that must be considered by the researcher on drug use and its effects on human sexuality.

A recurrent theme in mankind's thinking about drug use in relationship to sexual behavior is that of adequacy (and heightening or lowering) of so-called sexual interest, sexual desire, sexual appetite, sexual drive, sexual stimulation, sexual arousal, sexual pleasure, sexual enjoyment, sexual powers, sexual perform-ance, sexual endurance, and libido. These diverse terms, even in some of the very current literature on drugs and sex, are usually so poorly defined that we repeat-edly encounter the statement, "At best, the available evidence is inconclusive." Later we shall note some of the many factors that contribute to the inconsistencies that necessitate such inconclusive statements, but the semantic muddle of unde-fined terms is a major one.

A familiar and powerful model for rendering some order to the analysis of sexual adequacy has been provided by Masters and Johnson (1966, 1970). Their analysis is of a complex set of events, which they call the human sexual response or the sexual response cycle. At one level we see this cycle in five phases: excite-ment, plateau, orgasm, resolution, and refractory. At a more molecular level we see two underlying physiologic mechanisms involved in the responses of various organs to sexual stimulation: vasocongestion and myotonia; that is (1) engorge-ment of blood vessels and increased blood supply to tissues; and (2) increased muscle tension, which when appropriately accumulated is a precursor of orgasm and reduction of tension and congestion. All of this involves patterns of activity in the central and autonomic nervous systems.

This model does not justify making our first priority of research in this area the investigation of the effects of various psychoactive drugs on the physiological mechanisms associated with the sexual response; however, further sophisticated information on these effects is needed. Phylogenesis has given man a tremendous potential for the sexual response to be influenced by and functionally related to (via the cerebral cortex) many originally (ontogenetically) non-sex-related fac-tors, organismic, psychologic, motivational, environmental, interpersonal, social. Through its modification of these acquired or learned relationships a psychoactive drug may at least in principle influence human sexual behavior (often in paradoxi-cal, inconsistent, conflictural, or idiosyncratic ways) independently of or at vari-ance with its more or less direct effects, if any, on the physiologic processes underlying the human sexual response. Similarly, in the treatment of sexual dysfunctions, Masters and Johnson found that control of certain of these factors modified their relationships with human sexual response, thus permitting greater adequacy of response.

In the intact human organism, the sexual response and other sexual behavior and experience occur in a person who:

1. Has the capacity to be aware of the inherent pleasure produced by sexual stimulation, arousal, and orgasm, and to prolong that pleasure, to be reinforced by its occurrence, and to have conscious memories of that pleasure

2. Learns to be sexually stimulated and aroused not only through the eroge-nous zones but also by many nontactile external events and stimuli, and by private conscious events such as fantasies, memories, and perceptions

3. Learns, like other primates, to self-stimulate to orgasm his or her own erogenous zones, often accompanied by attention to erotic objects and, in the human, to erotic fantasy

4. Learns to sexually stimulate a partner through touch, vocalizations, expressions, and other behaviors

5. Learns to be stimulated by others and to be receptive to sociosexual stimulation

6. Learns patterns of social interaction in which there is mutual sexual and other stimulation and sharing between partners; and learns to lead up to, initiate, and participate in such interaction

7. Learns to be aware of and to be discriminative with respect to the physiologic responses underlying the various phases of the sexual response and associated responses

8. Learns, through socialization involving aversive sanctions applied to sexual behavior, inhibiting patterns of conflict, anxiety, guilt, and shame which then occur when a sequence of sexual behavior and its accompaniments are thought of, begin to occur, or do occur; in reducing the emotional tension generated by such inhibition of conflict, he or she may learn various sex-related avoidances, compulsions, and obsessions

9. Learns sociosexual interactions involving the stimulation of some level of sexual response in self or others, which are reinforcing because they reduce or otherwise modify other motivation systems and emotional dispositions, such as dependency, nurturance, love, social dominance and power, rebellion, social debasement, the need for money and other resources, and such temporary dispositions as hostility, depression, boredom, loneliness, anxiety; or which increase such desired states as relaxation, surgency, playfulness, social affection, concentration, a sense of having the right relationship with a significant other or with significant aspects of the world.

Therefore, in the study of psychoactive drug use and human sexual behavior, whether in the laboratory or clinic or by means of retrospective verbal report through interview, questionnaire, life history, or diary, we need to extend the basic model of the sexual response to include at least nine other sets of processes:

1. Consciousness of pleasure

2. Range and pattern of nontactile stimuli (as well as tactile stimuli) both external and in fantasy which have acquired the capacity to stimulate arousal in this person

3. Learned pattern of self-stimulation

4. Learned pattern of stimulating others

5. Learned patterns of receptivity to stimulation by others

6. Learned patterns of sociosexual interaction

7. Capacity to be aware of somatic processes and events

8. Learned patterns of motivational conflict with sexual arousal together with learned avoidances, compulsions, obsessions

9. Learned patterns in which sexual behavior becomes part of other motivational systems

It is important to note that, despite the relatively poor quality of most of the available research and information in this area (effects of drug use in sexual behavior), this expanded model does have some heuristic value. There are reports of sexually relevant drug effects in all nine of these auxiliary components of human sexual behavior and experience.

Let us use marijuana as an example, with no intention to analyze fully all the available information, and depending only and directly on the two excellent studies of Goode (1970) and Tart (1971). Some persons report that sometimes under some circumstances with use of certain amounts of marihuana:

1. There is enhancement both of awareness of sexual pleasure and of the pleasure itself. Orgasm has new pleasurable qualities.

2. Tactile and nontactile sensations take on new, sensual, arousing qualities. Sexual fantasy is enhanced.

3. Tart says: "New and pleasurable qualities to orgasm can occur with masturbation. . .[but this] enhancement does not begin to compare to the enhancement of real [interpersonal] sexuality" (pp. 145–146).

4. The lover reports self and other to be better lovers, with more giving.

5. Both partners are more receptive and responsive.

6. Partners experience closer and enhanced contact in addition to greater sharing of identity and energy in the sociosexual interaction.

7. There is greater awareness of internal organs and their processes.

8. Less inhibition is reported.

9. Expressions of a variety of motivations and emotions occur, putting the sexual episode into larger personal contexts.

Some such effects, for one or more of the nine categories (including the human sexual response) in the expanded model, are reported for many psychoactive drugs, but they are often reported as contradictory, inconclusive, or otherwise ambiguous, with different components of the model showing contrasting effects, partly depending on dosage, within a designated period, an example of which is facilitation of one component and inhibition or depression of another.

REFERENCES

Goode, E. (1970): *Marijuana Smokers.* Basic Books, New York.

Masters, W. H., and Johnson, V. E. (1966): *Human Sexual Response.* Little, Brown, Boston, Massachusetts.

Masters, W. H., and Johnson, V. E. (1970): *Human Sexual Inadequacy.* Little, Brown, Boston, Massachusetts.

Tart, C. T. (1971): *On Being Stoned: A Psychological Study of Marijuana Intoxication.* Science and Behavior Books, Palo Alto, California.

Sexual Behavior: Pharmacology and Biochemistry, edited by M. Sandler and G. L. Gessa. Raven Press, New York © 1975.

Amyl Nitrite ("Poppers") as an Aphrodisiac

Guy M. Everett

Department of Pharmacology, University of California, San Francisco, California 94143

No book on the pharmacology of sexual behavior would be complete without some remarks on the wide use of amyl nitrite as a sexual stimulant. This drug has long been prescribed as a fast-acting vasodilator for the treatment of anginal pain. Its use as a sexual stimulant has received little attention in the medical or pharmacologic literature. There is apparently only one article on amyl nitrite as an aphrodisiac (Everett, 1972) although Hollister (1975) and Gay and Sheppard (1972) also refer to its use as a sexual stimulant.

As previously reported, the greatest use is by young people, particularly the "leather crowd" of homosexual males, but it is also used by heterosexual males of all classes and ages as well. Women apparently do not find it very satisfactory, although here, too, there are exceptions.

Usually, the ampule of amyl nitrite is "popped" (broken or crushed) shortly before orgasm and the volatile fumes inhaled. The drug is also used in inhalers in which a few drops of the drug have been placed on a cotton swab. Special double-nostril types of inhalers are also available.

The reported subjective effects are surprisingly consistent. There is a general report of a greater, more sensual orgasm, which may also be prolonged. Local vasodilation, tachycardia, and increased sensory input might account for these effects, but the additional behavioral changes involving truly wild sexual abandon in a considerable number of users suggest some central effects as well. Amyl nitrite is a "social drug" and is often used in group sex activities with the inhaler being passed among the group. The drug, as might be expected, is often used in conjunction with marihuana.

In some people, amyl nitrite causes severe headache or hypotension. It can also produce loss of erection if hypotension is marked and faintness may be experienced. Painful ocular effects have also been reported. Fortunately, due to the brief duration of action, most of these side effects subside rapidly.

Although this is considered an illicit use of the drug, the number of serious side effects appears to be small. Certainly persons with cardiovascular problems or those getting headaches should not use this drug. Most persons use the drug only occasionally. A few consider it essential to a satisfactory sex life.

Although it is impossible to estimate the number of users of amyl nitrite as a sexual stimulant, it is easily in the thousands. Although far from ideal, and perhaps dangerous to some, there seems little doubt that amyl nitrite is a true aphrodisiac for some people.

A study of the neuropharmacology of amyl nitrite and its effects on the sexual behavior of animals would be of considerable interest.

REFERENCES

Everett, G. M. (1972): Effects of amyl nitrite ("Poppers") on sexual experience. *Medical Aspects of Human Sexuality,* 6:146–150.

Gay, G. R., and Sheppard, C. W. (1972) Sex in the "drug culture." *Medical Aspects of Human Sexuality,* 6:28–47.

Hollister, L. E. (1975) The Mystique of Social Drugs and Sex, this volume.

Sexual Behavior: Pharmacology and Biochemistry, edited by M. Sandler and G. L.
Gessa. Raven Press, New York © 1975.

Monoaminergic and Cholinergic Control of Sexual Behavior in the Male Rat

M.-L. Soulairac and A. Soulairac

Laboratoire de Psychophysiologie, Universite de Paris, Paris, France

Our earlier work showed that hypothalamic structures take part at two different levels in the control of sexual behavior in the male rat (Soulairac and Soulairac, 1956; Soulairac, Soulairac, and Giabicani-Teyssere, 1958). Bilateral lesions
of the preoptic area brought about the complete elimination of copulatory behavior after a latency of about 10 days without any simultaneous change taking place
in the genital tract. Bilateral destruction of the lateral mamillary nuclei and of
the perifornical areas also caused a total disappearance of sexual drive within 2
or 3 days of the intervention, but in this case it was accompanied by major
disturbances in gonadal function. These two types of lesion, however, did not
produce any histologic change in the anterior hypophysis. The administration
to these mutilated animals of chorionic gonadotropin (25 I.U. for 15 days) and
2.5 mg of testosterone per day did not provoke the reappearance of sexual
behavior (Soulairac and Soulairac, 1956b).

The impossibility of establishing hormonal recovery after the destruction of
certain nervous tissues would indicate that the latter must play some functional
part in the initiation of behavior before hormone control occurs. The nervous
functioning of the hypothalamus is ensured by the action of chemical
neuromediators, the chief ones known at present being norepinephrine, dopamine, 5-hydroxytryptamine (5-HT), and acetycholine. Since the initial work of
Hess, numerous neurophysiologic studies have demonstrated the definite adrenergic predominance of the posterior hypothalamus structures and the cholinergic
predominance of the anterior formations. Recent pharmacologic work (Barraclough, 1966) has confirmed this view of the neurohormonal control of ovulation
in the female rat. The present study was undertaken with the object of determining the extent to which adrenergic and tryptaminergic mediation are synergisti-
cally involved with cholinergic mediation in the control of male sexual behavior.

GENERAL METHOD OF STUDY

These investigations were carried out with intact adult male albino rats, 3 to
4 months old, weighing approximately 250 g. The females were rendered
pharmacologically responsive at all times by the administration intramuscularly
of 10 μg estradiol benzoate during the 2 days prior to the tests. It is important

here to specify the experimental technique that we have always employed for evaluating the aggregate of elements that make up male sexual behavior.

Sexual behavior in the rat takes place in an invariable sequence of closely subordinated motor activities. Although the apparent integrity of this drive led a number of authors to study it as a single phenomenon, more exacting analytic examination revealed that each of the motor components had its own individuality and independence, although it remained linked with the others by time. Sexual activity in the rat is normally very important, and over the course of 60 to 90 min a certain number of cycles may be observed, each of which terminates in an ejaculation. Each sexual cycle may be subdivided into the following components:

1. *Intromission:* Characterized by the mounting of the female, the development of pelvic movements, and the introduction of the penis into the vagina. A distinction must be made between the more vigorous and better adapted true intromissions that are followed by the licking of the penis by the male, and the false intromissions during which there is no insertion of the penis and no licking.

2. *Ejaculatory latency:* The period during which the intromissions take place.

3. *Ejaculation:* Easily distinguished by a certain motor daze on the part of the male and verifiable by the presence of a vaginal plug of semen.

4. *Refractory period:* The resting phase between the completion of ejaculation and the recommencement of the intromissions.

The number of intromissions required for an ejaculation is an important parameter. The ejaculation, in fact, represents the motor culmination of a genital reflex of which the penile intromissions (sensory stimulations) are the afferent component. Therefore, the fewer the intromissions required to provoke an ejaculation, the greater the sensitiveness of the reflex centers. The number of true intromissions required for an ejaculation thus provides an indirect means of estimating the changes in the thresholds of response of the genital reflexes and of their level of excitability. The false intromissions may be regarded as badly focused copulatory activities, and they seem to indicate a motor discoordination.

Ejaculatory latency may be looked upon as an index of the excitability of the neuromotor mechanisms of coitus. The number of ejaculations over a given period of time are an indication of the sexual response capacity of the animal.

Finally, the refractory periods that follow successive ejaculations do not vary in a random manner, but according to a geometric progression. They indicate the presence of a temporary inhibition phenomenon, a sort of deafferentiation, more or less similar to a focalized sleep, which, moreover, causes the appearance of large, slow waves on the electrocorticogram (Soulairac, 1952).

The parameters that have been considered above are illustrated in graphs in which the abscissa represents time in minutes and the ordinate the number of intromissions. For purposes of simplicity, each behavior cycle of the test has been portrayed subsequently as a triangle of which one side represents time in minutes,

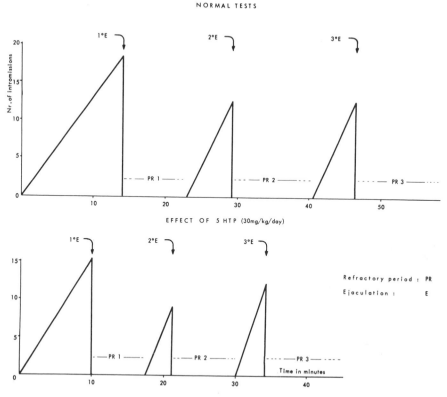

FIG. 1. Effect of 5 HTP on sexual behavior of male rat. *(Upper)* Sequence of the different components of normal sexual behavior during an experimental test (mean of eight rats): in ordinate, cumulative number of intromissions; in abscissa, time in minutes. *(Lower)* Effect of 5 HTP: decrease of the ejaculatory latencies without marked change of the number of intromissions.

the other the cumulative value of the intromissions, whereas the length of the hypotenuse gives a direct indication of the intensity of the neuromotor activity (Fig. 1).

In all the experiments described, each animal always acted as its own control and the statistical evaluation of the results was made according to the method of matched samples.

THE ROLE OF THE BIOGENIC AMINES

Many researchers have confirmed our own earlier findings that the pharmacologic agents that alter the metabolism of cerebral monoamines will change certain of the elements of male sexual behavior (Soulairac and Soulairac, 1957). This monoaminergic control was demonstrated either by the use of pharmacologic substances that stimulated or inhibited the liberation of the monoamines or acted upon monoamine-sensitive nervous structures, or by the administration of biochemical precursors of the physiologic monoamines. Two groups of cerebral monoamines were studied in this connection: the catecholamines and 5-HT (serotonin).

Action of Exogenous Adrenergic Substances

Three substances were used parenterally:

Norepinephrine (50 and 100 μg/kg i.p.) brought about the disappearance in 10 to 15 min of all sexual behavior for several hours, after which normal sexual drive reappeared. This temporary inhibitory effect could be obtained even on a male that had already begun normal copulatory activity. Control tests showed that similar manipulation of the animal with an injection of saline interrupted sexual behavior for only a few minutes.

Epinephrine produced much more complex effects, depending upon the dose given. At high doses (100 μg/kg), the animal quickly stopped all sexual activity, exhibited a generalized stuporous inhibition, and usually fell asleep in the experimental cage; at lower doses (50 μg/kg), the sexual changes were interesting to analyze: there was a significant increase in the number of ejaculations, which rose from an average of 3.1 to 5.0 without any change in the number of intromissions, and only a very small reduction in the ejaculatory latencies; there was no change in the refractory periods. This action, which only affected the number of ejaculations, might represent a nonspecific effect of epinephrine on general activity and, in particular, on the temporary reduction of capacity to become fatigued.

d-Amphetamine. As is well known, *d*-amphetamine is a powerful activator of arousal, which provokes a state of diffuse hyperactivity in the animal. Its action upon sexual behavior varied with the time at which it was administered. A dose of 2 mg/kg i.p., given 15 min before the test, produced an initial phase of generalized hyperactivity, followed by a very definite increase in sexual behavior as shown by a significant increase in the number of ejaculations; a very large decrease in refractory periods; a small simultaneous reduction in the number of intromissions and ejaculatory latencies. When the same dose of amphetamine was continued daily, new sexual changes were observed between the 4th and 5th days—intense general excitation continued, but sexual behavior diminished very markedly, sometimes disappearing entirely. The animal, which had been very active, seemed no longer to be able to focus its attention upon the receptive female. A curious side effect was also observed—erection was seen to persist after ejaculation (Table 1).

Action of Adrenergic Blocking Substances

Three antiadrenergic substances were tested: dihydroergotamine (DHE) and dibenamine, which block α-adrenoreceptors, and propranolol, a β-adrenoreceptor blocking agent.

TABLE 1. Effects of adrenoceptor-stimulating and receptor-blocking drugs on sexual behavior of male rat

	No. ejac.	1st ejaculation				2nd ejaculation				3rd ejaculation			
		E.L.	t	w	R.P.	E.L.	t	w	R.P.	E.L.	t	w	R.P.
						Adrenoceptor-stimulating drugs							
Normal	3.09	14.31	19.0	5.52	6.74	9.43	11.56		7.57	6.2	9.70		10.57
Epinephrine (50 µg/kg)	5.0	11.67	14.42	11.57	6.33	6.50	12.67		7.33	6.1	9.40		10.67
P	0.05	N.S.	N.S.	N.S.	0.02	0.10	N.S.	N.S.	N.S.	N.S.	N.S.	N.S.	N.S.
Normal	2.99	15.31	21.74		7.62	7.05	12.37		11.06	6.77	13.38		15.67
d-Amphetamine (2 mg/kg)	3.84	9.16	14.55		5.65	5.88	12.10		6.64	4.80	10.30		9.90
P	0.05	N.S.	N.S.	N.S.	0.02	N.S.	N.S.	N.S.	0.02	N.S.	N.S.	N.S.	0.02
Normal	2.03	19.20	21.76		7.70	10.12	12.03		8.38	—	—		—
Iproniazid (25 mg/kg, 3 days)	3.60	14.80	15.60		6.60	6.75	7.0		6.75	—	—		—
P	0.02	0.05	N.S.	N.S.	N.S.	0.10	0.02	0.02	N.S.	—	—	—	—
						Adrenoceptor-blocking drugs							
Normal	3.81	38.74	19.57		9.31	7.95	11.05	2.60	11.50	6.86	10.8	3.92	14.27
DHE (0.6 mg/kg)	4.85	29.57	10.72		7.57	9.14	8.86	10.57	8.72	4.0	6.66	3.67	9.6
P	0.05	N.S.	0.01	N.S.	N.S.	N.S.	N.S.	N.S.	N.S.	0.01	0.02	N.S.	0.10
Normal	3.12	44.5	19.8		10.14	9.0	10.59	2.78	12.56	10.57	14.24	4.78	21.33
Dibenamine (0.3 mg/kg)	4.57	21.6	10.9		7.07	6.07	8.14	2.92	10.71	5.57	7.78	4.21	17.50
P	0.10	0.05	0.02	N.S.	N.S.	0.10	N.S.	N.S.	N.S.	0.05	0.05	N.S.	N.S.
Normal	3.64	38.6	20.8	7.1	9.4	9.1	11.5	3.9	11.8	10.7	15.1	6.5	17.5
Propranolol (3 mg/kg)	4.45	15.5	12.3	5.1	7.9	7.1	9.4	4.4	9.1	7.0	7.7	4.9	13.0
P	N.S.	0.01	0.05	N.S.	N.S.	N.S.	N.S.	N.S.	N.S.	N.S.	0.05	N.S.	N.S.

DHE (0.6 mg/kg i.p.): Administered 15 min before the test, significantly increased the number of ejaculations, modifying the ejaculatory latencies only from the 3rd ejaculation. The number of true intromissions was reduced, while the increase in false intromissions was not significant. It was only after the third ejaculation that a significant reduction in refractory period was observed.

Dibenamine (0.3 mg/kg i.p.): Given 15 min before the test, also provoked an increase in number of ejaculations. All the ejaculatory latencies and the number of true intromissions were significantly reduced. The false intromissions and refractory periods remained unchanged.

Propranolol (3 mg/kg i.p.): Administered twice: 30 min and immediately before the test, provoked only minor changes. The number of ejaculations and the duration of refractory periods did not change; the latency of the first ejaculation and the number of true intromissions were very significantly reduced; during subsequent ejaculations there was a general reduction of latencies and intromissions, but the differences did not prove to be statistically significant (Table 1).

Action of a Monoamine Oxidase Inhibitor

In this experiment, iproniazid was used at a dose of 25 mg/kg, administered subcutaneously. The effects upon sexual behavior varied with the period of continued administration. After 3 days, there was a very significant increase in the number of ejaculations; the number of intromissions and the various latencies of ejaculation very definitely diminished; no change was observed in the refractory periods. After a more prolonged administration (as from the 6th day), very different variations occurred—the animals showed great activity and very high excitation, but in 60% of the cases, the behavior test was completely negative with no intromissions having taken place; in 40% of the animals the number of ejaculations was considerably reduced to a single ejaculation in the first hour, but this occurred after a markedly reduced number of intromissions (10.5 rather than 21.7), which seemed to indicate that a facilitation of genital reflexes still persisted. After receiving the same dose of iproniazid daily for 14 days, there was a practically normal resumption of all the elements of sexual behavior.

Action of Tryptaminergic Mediators

Tryptaminergic changes were brought about by using substances that participate directly in the 5-HT metabolic cycle. We employed successively 5-hydroxytryptophan (5-HTP) the precursor of 5-HT to increase its level in the organism; methysergide, an inhibitor of tryptaminergic receptors; and parachlorophenylalanine (PCPA), which inhibits the endogenous synthesis of 5-HT by blocking tryptophan 5-hydroxylation (Table 2).

Action of 5-HTP: This was administered at a dose of 30 mg/kg i.p. for 20 consecutive days, thus enabling the chronologic development of sexual behavior

TABLE 2. *Effects of tryptaminergic drugs on sexual behavior of male rat*

	No. ejac.	1st ejaculation				2nd ejaculation				3rd ejaculation			
		E.L.	t	w	R.P.	E.L.	t	w	R.P.	E.L.	t	w	R.P.
Normal	3.06	14.13	18.58		8.92	6.31	12.72		11.4	5.81	12.82		11.92
5-HTP (30 mg/kg)	3.37	21.0	17.79		9.89	4.0	7.44		13.06	3.68	10.28		10.51
P	N.S.	N.S.	N.S.		N.S.	0.05	0.02		N.S.	0.10	0.05		0.10
5-HTP (30 mg/kg, 15 days)	4.08	10.17	15.36		7.42	3.65	9.4		8.86	4.27	12.34		10.80
P	0.02	0.10	N.S.		0.10	0.02	0.02		0.02	0.02	N.S.		N.S.
Normal	3.02	26.5	18.2		7.02	7.0	7.75		9.25	6.4	8.51		—
Methysergide (8 mg/kg)	5.20	16.4	16.4		6.51	6.0	8.10		7.90	6.7	11.5		10.8
P	0.01	N.S.	N.S.		N.S.	N.S.	N.S.		N.S.	N.S.	N.S.		
Methysergide (18 mg/kg)	3.60	32.8	9.6		8.6	10.0	7.2		10.2	5.4	6.6		—
P	N.S.	N.S.	N.S.		N.S.	N.S.	N.S.		N.S.	N.S.	N.S.		
Normal	2.64	32.2	16.0	6.7	8.41	8.50	10.4	2.07	11.35	6.70	10.3	1.9	12.9
PCPA (100 mg/kg, 24 hr)	6.05	9.4	8.6	4.2	5.08	3.4	5.8	2.12	5.94	2.34	3.4	0.8	6.82
P	0.001	0.001	0.01	N.S.	0.01	0.01	0.05	N.S.	0.05	0.05	0.10	N.S.	0.001
PCPA (100 mg/kg, 3 days)	5.80	9.5	9.5	7.5	4.91	4.65	5.8	7.78	7.02	2.67	2.67	4.8	7.82
P	0.01	0.01	0.001	N.S.	0.001	N.S.	0.05	N.S.	0.01	N.S.	0.10	N.S.	0.05
PCPA (100 mg/kg, 7 days)	4.80	8.5	5.0	5.8	5.41	4.49	5.8	3.45	5.85	3.24	3.50	3.1	7.32
P	0.01	0.01	0.001	N.S.	0.05	0.10	N.S.	N.S.	0.05	0.10	0.05	0.05	0.05
PCPA (100 mg/kg, 9 days)	2.14	11.4	10.9	6.5	9.91	4.60	4.52	3.39	10.85	8.40	6.10	3.2	21.02
P	N.S.	0.05	0.01	N.S.	N.S.	N.S.	0.10	N.S.	N.S.	N.S.	0.10	N.S.	N.S.

to be observed. Immediate action, i.e., 1½ hr after the injection: no change in the number of ejaculations; a significant reduction of intromissions as from the 2nd ejaculation; a highly significant shortening of ejaculatory latencies; refractory periods virtually unchanged (Soulairac and Soulairac, 1971) (Fig. 1).

Long-term action between 10 and 20 days after the onset of treatment: highly significant increase in ejaculations; reduction in ejaculatory latencies without change in number of intromissions; shortening of refractory periods. The animals responded very actively to the specific sexual stimuli and even gave evidence of a real hyperactivity because they achieved an equal number of intromissions within a shorter period of time (Fig. 1 and Table 2).

Action of Methysergide: This was administered in solution subcutaneously in varying doses: 4, 8, 13, and 18 mg/kg, 3 hr before the sexual behavior test. A rest period of 4 to 8 days was allowed between each test.

It will be observed that the only significant change in sexual behavior really consisted of an increase in number of ejaculations, and then only at the 4- and 8-mg/kg dosage level. At higher dosage, these changes disappeared and sexual behavior parameters showed no differences from those of normal animals. A check carried out during the experiment showed that the increase in the number of ejaculations was indeed connected with the administration of methysergide, because the control tests performed between the treatment tests gave normal results.

However, it should be noted that, despite only a slight change in the specifically sexual parameters the behavior pattern as a whole revealed some fairly definite modifications: the rats showed an intense general activity, often poorly focused and sometimes presenting an incomplete sexual behavior pattern whereas at the 18 mg/kg dosage level, an entirely abnormal hypersensitivity occurred. The animals that were accustomed to the experimental procedures were violently startled by the least noise (Table 2).

Action of Parachlorophenylalanine (PCPA): Administered at a daily dose of 100 mg/kg i.p. 24 hr before the first test, the injections being repeated every day at the same dose. Behavior tests were made after 72 hr (100 mg × 3), 168 hr (100 mg × 7) and 216 hr (100 mg × 9). The animals were then sacrificed for determination of hormone levels and histologic examination of various organs.

Twenty-four hours after administration of 100 mg PCPA, all sexual behavior parameters had improved: the number of ejaculations was more than doubled; ejaculatory latencies were very much reduced; the number of true intromissions to obtain an ejaculation was much lower; false intromissions did not vary and were greatly reduced; refractory periods were greatly shortened. This improvement was largely sustained after 72 hr of treatment, except for shortening of ejaculatory latencies, which was no longer significant. It should be recorded that during refractory periods, the animals were not inactive as they usually were, but continued to show a more or less well-orientated activity. In addition, during this stage of treatment with PCPA, the rats were particularly sensitive to handling, to which they reacted aggressively.

Even with nonresponsive females, the male rats exhibited a very definite domination.

After 7 days of treatment, the improvement in behavior was still definite but had dropped in absolute value, particularly in the number of ejaculations. After 9 days of treatment, i.e., at a cumulative dosage of 900 mg: the number of ejaculations returned to normal; the ejaculatory latency and the number of intromissions for the first ejaculation remained reduced; refractory periods had become normal, the animal presenting a marked muscular hypotonia. Out of the six animals receiving this treatment, two that were previously very active gave entirely negative results (Fig. 2 and Table 2).

Action of Psychotropic Substances Operating upon Cerebral Biogenic Amines

Three substances were examined: reserpine, the depleting effects of which on norepinephrine and serotonin stores are well known; lysergic acid diethylamide (LSD 25); and chlorpromazine, a major sedative (Table 3).

Action of Reserpine: At a low dose (0.25 mg/kg/day) for 15 days there was a very significant increase in number of ejaculations whereas the number of intromissions was reduced and ejaculatory latencies shortened. Refractory periods were little affected. At a higher dosage (0.6 mg/kg/day) 48 hr after the first administration, sexual behavior was increased as with the low dosage, especially insofar as the number of ejaculations was concerned. This facilitation was transient and all the tests carried out on the 4th day were negative. The animals showed no tendency to sexual activity and often seemed to be in a stuporous condition throughout the test. These effects appeared to be linked to the action of the reserpine, because 5 days after stopping the treatment, sexual behavior returned to normal. It should be noted that with animals receiving 0.5 mg/kg/day for 8 consecutive days, histologic examination revealed significant spermatogenic changes and alterations in the interstitial tissue of the testis, as had been reported by Tuchmann-Duplessis (1956) and Khazan, Sulman, and Wimik, (1960). In addition, certain localized cellular anomalies were observed in the lateral mammillary nuclei in the region of the posterior hypothalamus (Soulairac and Soulairac, 1961, 1962).

Action of LSD 25: This was an interesting substance to study because behavioral and electrophysiologic effects similar to those produced by amphetamine previously had been reported at fairly low dosage. At a dose of 50 μg/kg i.p. given 15 min before the test, there was a definite increase in the various elements of sexual behavior: an increase in number of ejaculations; a reduction in number of intromissions; a shortening of ejaculatory latencies; a reduction in refractory periods. The action on sexual behavior was very similar to that produced by low doses of amphetamine.

Action of Chlorpromazine: This substance was examined because it is known

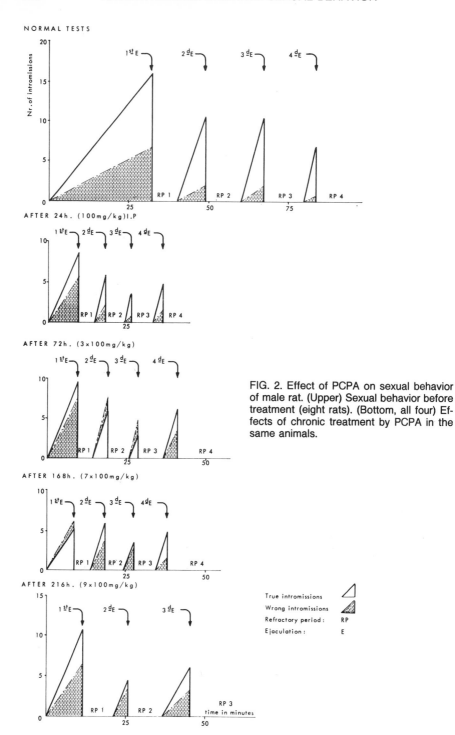

FIG. 2. Effect of PCPA on sexual behavior of male rat. (Upper) Sexual behavior before treatment (eight rats). (Bottom, all four) Effects of chronic treatment by PCPA in the same animals.

TABLE 3. *Effects of various drugs on sexual behavior of male rat*

	No. ejac.	1st ejaculation				2nd ejaculation				3rd ejaculation			
		E.L.	t	w	R.P.	E.L.	t	w	R.P.	E.L.	t	w	R.P.
Nicotine (cholinergic)													
Normal	3.74	35.2	17.5	6.8	9.0	8.5	10.7	4.0	10.9	8.7	11.8	5.7	18.0
Nicotine (0.62 mg/kg)	5.21	19.1	13.2	3.7	6.7	5.4	9.1	1.8	7.8	5.1	8.9	1.9	11.5
P	0.01	0.05	0.01	N.S.	0.02	0.05	N.S.	N.S.	0.01	0.10	N.S.	0.10	0.5
Reserpine													
Normal	2.50	17.1	18.1		7.99	9.9	10.95		9.48	8.17	12.72		8.71
Reserpine (250 µg/kg)	3.83	12.0	13.0		6.17	5.6	6.57		8.08	4.8	6.33		9.59
P	0.02	0.05	0.05		0.02	0.02	0.02		0.05	0.05	0.05		N.S.
LSD 25													
Normal	2.13	22.3	25.2		7.66	11.3	17.4		8.57	—	—		—
LSD 25 (50 µg/kg)	3.30	14.8	18.9		5.90	5.0	8.5		6.87	—	—		—
P	0.02	N.S.	N.S.		0.02	0.05	0.10		N.S.	—	—		—
Chlorpromazine													
Normal	2.94	16.0	14.9		8.0	7.4	11.6		9.5	—	—		—
Chlorpromazine (3 mg/day, 2 days)	2.13	13.3	20.1		8.62	10.4	16.7		14.6	—	—		—
P	0.05	N.S.	0.05		N.S.	N.S.	0.10		0.05	—	—		—

to possess adrenolytic properties and to reduce the reactivity of the reticular structures of the brainstem. It is also known that, it operates upon synaptic transmission by blocking catecholaminergic receptors.

The drug was administered subcutaneously at 3 mg/day for periods of 5 consecutive days, separated by 2 days of rest. This treatment was continued for 5 weeks. General analysis of the results showed that its action was rapidly reversible because the 2-day periods without treatment were usually sufficient to reestablish a normal condition. It was also observed that sensitization to the action of chlorpromazine appeared to arise, as the effects during the 4th and 5th periods were more pronounced than those during the first two periods.

Following each chlorpromazine treatment, there was a progressive reduction in number of ejaculations; the number of intromissions increased greatly without there being any increase in periods of ejaculatory latency; and refractory periods were significantly increased.

THE ROLE OF CHOLINERGIC MEDIATION

Anticholinergic Substance

From among the numerous anticholinergic drugs available, we chose atropine because even in quite high dosage, it did not provoke toxic phenomena in the rat, which might upset a behavioral study. The atropinized animal was hyperactive, in a state of diffuse vigilance and gave an electroencephalographic sleep-wave pattern.

We used atropine sulfate at 10 mg i.p. per rat. Under these conditions it was seen that the male, when presented with a receptive female, displayed no sexual behavior after a period of from 10 to 15 min. Despite this lack of interest, however, he remained quite agitated, ceaselessly running about the experimental apparatus and sniffing repeatedly everywhere. Such behavior clearly did not correspond to a neuromotor inhibition.

In other experiments, we gave identical doses of atropine to animals during sexual intercourse, with the result that all elements of sexual behavior disappeared very quickly. If the rat treated with atropine was kept in the experimental apparatus with a female, it was observed that after about 2 hr, sexual behavior began again and quickly assumed normal proportions. According to our experimental data, this lapse of time corresponded to the end of the atropine action. The administration of amphetamine (0.6 mg/kg i.p.) after the extinction of sexual behavior by atropine, produced a very accentuated general activity, but never provoked a reappearance of sexual behavior.

Action of Cholinergic Stimulation

Our previous work (Soulairac, 1963) had demonstrated the difficulty of producing cholinergic stimulation capable of changing sexual behavior without disturbing at the same time the fundamental psychomotor activities of the animal. The administration of acetycholine produced reactions that were too violent and transient, while the use of anticholinesterases such as eserine and prostigmine provoked peripheral vegetative reactions that were often so intense that the animal was unable to exhibit any completed form of behavior whatever.

We chose nicotine (tartrate) as an acetylcholine stimulating substance that exerted its peripheral effects on the postganglionic neurons in a classic manner. Behavioral research on the central nervous system had shown that nicotine cholinergic receptors existed (Schechter and Rosecrans, 1971). More recent but unpublished work (Soulairac and Soulairac, 1974, *unpublished results*) had demonstrated the action of nicotine at similar dosage on alimentary behavior. It was also observed that there was a correlation between the stimulating effects of nicotine on activity and accumulation of 5-HT, which indicated that nicotine could interfere with this chemical system.

In our studies, the animals received 1.2 or 0.6 mg/kg of nicotine tartrate subcutaneously 30 min prior to the test (Table 3).

Action of Nicotine at 1.2 mg/kg: Very soon after the injection, the animals suffered motor disturbances, tremor and muscular twitches, and for 2 or 3 hr showed no signs of sexual behavior despite the presence of highly receptive females.

Action of Nicotine at 0.6 mg/kg: At this dose we obtained entirely different results, for there appeared a highly significant facilitation of all the components of sexual behavior, especially for the first three ejaculations: an increase in the number of ejaculations; a drop in ejaculatory latencies; a reduction in number of intromissions; and a reduction in refractory periods (Fig. 3).

DISCUSSION

These experiments demonstrate that central monoaminergic and cholinergic influences have major effects upon sexual behavior of the male rat. The fact that the actions observed commonly depend on drug dosage suggests that it probably plays a modulating role.

Our experimental results have been confirmed by a number of different workers (Bignami, 1966; Dewsbury and Davis, 1970; Malmnäs, 1973). If the biogenic amines and acetylcholine have an important influence upon male sexual behavior, the various mediators appear to act upon elements that are often very different. Analysis indicates that some of these mediators show a certain specificity.

To arrive at a general appreciation of sexual behavior, it is important to stress the significance of the parameters involved. In cases of overall facilitation an increase in number of ejaculations was noted in addition to a reduction in number of both true and false intromissions, a shortening of periods of ejaculatory latency, and a reduction of refractory periods. Actually, fewer intromissions during a shorter period of time indicate an improvement in the genital reflexes leading to ejaculation. Shortening of the refractory period denotes a diminishing of

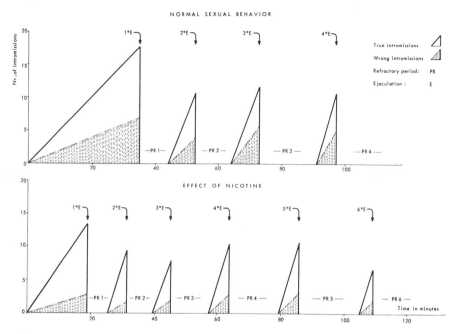

FIG. 3. Effect of nicotine on the sexual behavior of male rat. (Upper) Normal behavior (eight rats). (Lower) Sexual behavior of the same animals after a single administration of 0.6 mg/kg of nicotine tartrate (30 min prior to the test).

psychomotor postejaculatory inhibition whereas an increase in the number of ejaculations is in accordance with a heightened excitability of the genital reflex centers. Therefore, we have the apparent paradox that an increase in the number of intromissions or of ejaculatory latencies signifies a lowering of excitability of the consummating sexual structures, despite the fact that the overall copulatory exercise seems to show an improved performance. This would indicate that a dissociation of behavioral components could exist, each one of them being able to perform experimentally as a distinct motor scheme. This may suggest the concept of an ejaculatory threshold, the height of which is directly proportional to the number of intromissions required to produce an ejaculation. The isolated lengthening of ejaculatory latencies represents a reduction in neuromotor activity.

If the above criteria are used, it will be evident that any pharmacologic action that produces a moderate elevation of monoaminergic tonus will give rise to a precocious and generally overall improvement in sexual behavior. The opposite effects are often obtained by the use of high doses over a prolonged period.

The short-term actions of amphetamine and iproniazid are very similar to each other. Using amphetamine, Bignami (1966) obtained similar results at low dosage (0.5 mg/kg), but these effects disappeared and were replaced by inhibition when the dose was raised to 2 mg/kg. Given over a long period, however, amphetamine fairly quickly brought about complete inhibition whereas iproniazid at the dosage employed and after 5 to 9 days of treatment decreased sexual behavior, which, however, reverted to normal on the 14th day. This temporary inhibition might be compared with the experimental results of Malmnäs (1973), which showed a marked reduction in sexual behavior after strong doses of pargyline and niala- mide. Similar inhibitory effects were reported by Tagliamonte, Tagliamonte, and Gessa (1971) and by Dewsbury, Davis, and Jansen (1972). Epinephrine at low dosage acted only upon the number of ejaculations, while, like norepinephrine, at high dosage it entirely inhibited sexual behavior.

A definite involvement of the cerebral monoamines were again revealed by the administration of reserpine. At low dosage there was permanent facilitation whereas high dosage brought about total inhibition after a transient facilitating period of 24 hr.

These results were confirmed by Dewsbury and Davis (1970) and Dewsbury (1971) who suggested that reserpine has a specific facilitatory effect upon fre- quency of intromission. This view would fit in with the hypothesis that a high level of cerebral monoamines inhibits ejaculation. Using large doses (0.5 mg/kg), Malmnäs (1973) obtained complete suppression of sexual behavior in the cas- trated testosterone-treated rat. Because of the double action of reserpine, which depletes both catecholamine and 5-HT stores, it is difficult to decide which of the two actions is directly involved in the different components of sexual behavior.

The action of the catecholamines is complicated by the presence of two types of adrenergic receptor. Research had shown that alpha and beta hypothalamic adrenoceptors play an antagonistic role in the control of feeding behavior (Leibo- witz, 1970). It is also possible that a balance exists between α- and β-adrenergic activity in sexual behavior. The results obtained with α- and β-blocking sub- stances appear to indicate that the inhibition of α-adrenoceptors by DHE and dibenamine brings about an increase in sexual behavior, by an increase in particu- lar in ejaculations and a reduction in intromissions. In contrast, the blocking of β-adrenoceptors with propranolol only partially changes the behavior, a finding confirmed by Malmnäs (1973). It might therefore be suggested that sexual behav- ioral facilitation depends upon β-adrenergic stimulation, powerful stimulation of the α-receptors inhibiting all behavioral responses. These observations might offer an explanation for the totally suppressive action of norepinephrine, an exclusively α-agonist, and the mixed responses of epinephrine and amphetamine, both of which are α- and β-agonists. Such ambivalence could also explain the variations in experimental results with doses administered and duration of treat- ment periods.

The serotoninergic effect is very much more difficult to understand. Like Tagliamonte et al. (1969, 1971), we found that PCPA has a facilitation action during the first 7 days of administration. If this treatment is continued, behavior becomes comparable with normal on the 9th day. Our results with 5-HTP and methysergide are not as easy to explain. The immediate action of 5-HTP is to reduce the number of intromissions and the period of ejaculatory latency, without changing the number of ejaculations or the duration of refractory periods. This effect, therefore, represents an isolated improvement of copulatory behavior. Under conditions of continued administration, all the component elements are changed after 15 days in favor of a total behavior facilitation. It is obvious that these results are not easy to reconcile with the effects of PCPA and that they leave the question of the influence of 5-HT on sexual behavior unresolved. In addition, inhibition of tryptaminergic receptors by methysergide brings about relatively unimportant changes only in sexual behavior: the effect depends essentially upon the dose given, and only the number of ejaculations is significantly increased at 4 and 8 mg/kg.

The participation of a certain degree of adrenergic stimulating action is again apparent under the action of LSD 25 and chlorpromazine: that of LSD 25 closely resembles the action of amphetamine on the behavior sequence at the beginning of its administration, although the electrophysiologic responses are somewhat different. Gaddum (1957) demonstrated that it was not a case of antagonism with 5-HT and that the adrenomimetic effects of LSD 25 did not change the thresholds of direct stimulation of the mesencephalic reticular formation, but significantly lowered the threshold of awakening provoked by an afferent sensory stimulation. If an attempt is made to associate these results with our own data obtained with α-adrenoreceptor blocking substances, the presence of a β-adrenoreceptor stimulating action of LSD 25 is suggested. At all events, it seems difficult at the present time to retain the view that $\alpha + \beta$-catecholaminergic stimulation represents a facilitating factor in sexual behavior. Specific facilitation might arise from the β-adrenergic system, inhibition depending upon the α-adrenergic system. Mixed stimulation might bring about an increase in the level of generalized arousal, permitting a subsequent functioning of the specific structures.

Chlorpromazine appears to act by blocking adrenergic receptors and lowering the level of generalized arousal.

Although there are far fewer experimental results on cholinergic mediation, those that do exist are particularly convincing and demonstrate the close dependence of male sexual behavior upon cholinergic activation (Bignami, 1966; Singer, 1968). The action of an anticholinergic substance such as atropine not only inhibits sexual behavior, but exerts a similar effect upon a number of fundamental behavioral reactions (hunger, thirst, pain) as well as upon acquired behavior (conditioning and learning). Cholinergic stimulation by nicotine gives particularly clear-cut results that confirm its leading role in the realization of behavior (Bignami, 1966; Soulairac and Soulairac, 1972).

Three types of neurochemical mediation control male sexual behavior and these can be schematically divided into two principal systems: a monoaminergic system represented by the adrenergic and serotoninergic involvement in control of the genital reflexes and the release of the specific neuromotor activities; a cholinergic system, which is indispensable to the functioning of the monoaminergic system. In other words, the monoaminergic system is necessary but insufficient on its own for the complete realization of sexual behavior. A comparison of the results of hypothalamic lesions and of pharmacologic actions indicates that the monoaminergic system acts upon posterior hypothalamic structures (mammillary and perifornical areas). The cholinergic system probably activates anterior hypothalamic structures, principally the preoptic areas. In this behavioral scheme, these anterior structures represent a discriminatory and integrating device that receives all the sensory stimuli which initiate the behavior. The posterior structures might be regarded as a sort of common final-path upon which the very elaborate stimuli of the anterior region play the role of releasers for neuromotor realization of the behavior pattern.

ACKNOWLEDGMENTS

The authors would like to thank Mrs. F. Bonhomme and J. Ernest for their invaluable technical assistance.

REFERENCES

Barraclough, C. A. (1966): Modifications in the CNS regulation of reproduction after exposure of prepubertal rats to steroid hormones. *Rec. Progr. Horm. Res.,* 22:503–539.

Bignami, G. (1966): Pharmacologic influences on mating behavior in the male rat. Effects of d-amphetamine, LSD-25, strychnine, nicotine and various anticholinergic agents. *Psychopharmacologia,* 10:44–58.

Dewsbury, D. A. (1971): Copulatory behavior of male rats following reserpine administration. *Psychon. Sci.,* 22:177–179.

Dewsbury, D. A., and Davis, H. N., Jr. (1970): Effects of reserpine on the copulatory behavior of male rats. *Physiol. Behav.,* 5:1331–1333.

Dewsbury, D. A., Davis, H. N., Jr., and Jansen, P. E. (1972): Effects of monoamine oxidase inhibitors on the copulatory behavior of male rats. *Psychopharmacologia,* 24:209–217.

Gaddum, S. H. (1957): Serótonin-LSD Interactions. *Ann. N.Y. Acad. Sci.,* 66:643–647.

Khazan, N., Sulman, F. G., and Wimik, H. Z. (1960): Effect of reserpine on pituitary gonadal axis. *Proc. Soc. Exp. Biol. Med.,* 105:201–204.

Leibowitz, S. F. (1970): Hypothalamic β-adrenergic "satiety" system antagonizes an α-adrenergic "hunger" system in the rat. *Nature,* 226:963–964.

Malmnäs, C. O. (1973): Monoaminergic influence on testosterone activated copulatory behavior in the castrated male rat. *Acta Physiol. Scand.,* Suppl: 395:1–128.

Schechter, M. D., and Rosecrans, J. A. (1971): Behavioral evidence for two types of cholinergic receptors in the CNS. *Europ. J. Pharmacol.,* 15:375–378.

Singer, J. J. (1968): The effects of atropine upon the female and male sexual behavior of female rats. *Physiol. Behav.,* 3:377–378.

Soulairac, A. (1952): La signification de la période réfractaire dans le comportement sexuel du rat mâle. *J. Physiol. (Paris),* 44:99–113.

Soulairac, A., and Soulairac, M.-L. (1956a): Modifications du comportement sexuel et du tractus génital du rat mâle après lésions hypothalamiques. *C. R. Soc. Biol. (Paris),* 150:1097.

Soulairac, A., and Soulairac, M.-L. (1956b): Effets des lésions hypothalamiques sur le comportement sexuel et le tractus génital du rat mâle. *Ann. Endocrinol.,* 17:731–745.

Soulairac, A., and Soulairac, M.-L. (1957): Action de l'amphétamine, de l'adrénaline et de l'atropine sur le comportement sexuel du rat mâle. *J. Physiol. (Paris),* 49:381–385.

Soulairac, A., and Soulairac, M.-L. (1961): Action de la réserpine sur le comportement sexuel du rat mâle. *C.R. Soc. Biol. (Paris),* 155:1010–1013.

Soulairac, A., and Soulairac, M.-L. (1962): Effets de l'administration chronique de réserpine sur la fonction génitale du rat mâle. *Ann. Endocrinol.,* 23:281–292.

Soulairac, A., and Soulairac, M.-L. (1971): Action de la sérotonine sur le comportement sexuel du rat mâle. *C. R. Soc. Biol. (Paris),* 165:253–256.

Soulairac, A., Soulairac, M.-L., and Giabicani-Teysseyre, J. (1958): Modifications du comportement sexuel du rat mâle après lésions hypothalamiques. Pathologia Diencephalica, pp. 623–630. Springer-Verlag, Wien.

Soulairac, M.-L. (1963): Etude expérimentale des régulations hormono-nerveuses du comportement sexuel du rat mâle. *Ann. Endocrinol. (Paris),* Suppl. 3, 24:1–98.

Soulairac, M.-L., and Soulairac, A. (1972): Action de la nicotine sur le comportement sexuel du rat mâle. *C. R. Soc. Biol. (Paris),* 166:798–802.

Tagliamonte, A., Tagliamonte, P., and Gessa, G.-L. (1971): Reversal of pargyline induced inhibition of sexual behavior, in male rats by *p*-chlorophenylalanine. *Nature,* 230:244–245.

Tagliamonte. A., Tagliamonte, P., Gessa, G.-L., and Brodie, B. B. (1969): Compulsive sexual activity induced by *p*-chlorophenylalanine in normal and pinealectomized male rats. *Science,* 166:1433–1435.

Tuchmann-Duplessis, H. (1956): Action de la réserpine sur le testicule et le tractus génital du rat. *C. R. Acad. Sci., (Paris),* 242:1651–1653.

Sexual Behavior: Pharmacology and Biochemistry, edited by M. Sandler and G. L.
Gessa. Raven Press, New York © 1975.

Role of Brain Serotonin and Dopamine in Male Sexual Behavior

G. L. Gessa and A. Tagliamonte

Institute of Pharmacology, University of Cagliari, Cagliari, Italy

A great deal of experimental evidence indicates that sexual behavior in male rats is stimulated by treatments that either decrease brain serotonin concentration or elevate that of brain dopamine. In contrast, male sexual behavior is suppressed by treatments that either elevate brain serotonin levels or block brain dopamine receptors. Consequently, we have proposed a theory according to which male sexual behavior is reciprocally controlled by a central serotoninergic inhibitory and dopaminergic stimulatory mechanism (Gessa and Tagliamonte, 1974a,b). This chapter presents further evidence in support of this hypothesis and critically evaluates the literature on the subject.

INHIBITORY ROLE OF BRAIN SEROTONIN IN MALE SEXUAL BEHAVIOR

Effect of Parachlorophenylalanine on the Sexual Behavior of the Male Rat

Parachlorophenylalanine (PCPA) stimulates copulatory behavior in male animals (Sheard, 1969; Tagliamonte, Tagliamonte, Gessa, and Brodie, 1969; Ferguson, Henriksen, Cohen, Mitchell, Barchas, and Dement, 1970; Hoyland, Shillito, and Vogt, 1970; Shillito, 1970; Perez-Cruet, Tagliamonte, Tagliamonte, and Gessa, 1971; Salis and Dewsbury, 1971). This finding contains a basic implication; as PCPA is the most potent and specific inhibitor of tryptophan hydroxylase (Koe and Weissman, 1966), its aphrodisiac effect may be causally related to the resulting decrease in brain serotonin synthesis. The effect of PCPA on male sexual behavior has therefore been extensively studied in different animal species, including man (see Gessa and Tagliamonte, 1973). However, because the majority of these studies have been carried out on adult male rats, it is appropriate to describe the effect of the drug on sexual behavior in this species.

1. PCPA induces male-to-male mounting behavior under conditions in which this does not normally occur (Sheard, 1969; Tagliamonte et al., 1969; Shillito, 1970).

2. In sexually inexperienced male rats (Tagliamonte, Tagliamonte, and Gessa,

1971), in rats with a low base line of sexual activity (Mitler, Morden, Levine, and Dement, 1972) and finally, in castrated rats treated with suboptimal doses of testosterone (Malmnäs and Meyerson, 1971; Malmnäs, 1973), PCPA increases the percentage of animals reaching ejaculation when paired with females in estrus.

3. In male rats with a high base line of sexual activity, PCPA does not further increase the number of ejaculations (Whalen and Luttge, 1970). However, it shortens the ejaculatory latency (Gessa and Tagliamonte, 1974*a*).

4. On the other hand, contradictory results have been obtained relating to the effect of the drug on other aspects of the copulatory pattern, such as intromission and mounting frequency, postejaculatory interval, etc. (Gessa and Tagliamonte, 1974*a*).

Effect on Male Sexual Behavior of Other Treatments Depleting Brain Serotonin

The hypothesis that the aphrodisiac effect of PCPA is causally related to a deficiency of brain serotonin is supported by the fact that two other treatments, having the capacity to decrease brain serotonin content, in common with PCPA, but acting through completely different mechanisms, also stimulate sexual behavior in males. One involves the intracerebral injection of 5,6-dihydroxytryptamine (5,6-DHT), which selectively destroys serotonin neurons (Baumgarten, Björklund, Lachenmayer, Nobin, and Stenevi, 1971; Björklund, Baumgarten, and Nobin, 1974). Da Prada and his colleagues (Da Prada, Carruba, O'Brien, Saner, and Pletscher, 1972) found that 5,6-DHT, injected into the lateral ventricles of rats, produces male-to-male mounting behavior. However, this effect was observed 8 hr after treatment, when levels of brain serotonin are not yet maximally depleted and 5,6-DHT is present in the central nervous system (CNS). We have injected 5,6-DHT directly into the raphe nuclei of male rats and have tested their sexual activity 15 days after treatment, when brain serotonin concentration was maximally depleted. Table 1 shows that this treatment significantly increases the percentage of animals reaching ejaculation when exposed for the first time to a female in estrus.

The second treatment consists of administering a tryptophan-free diet, which has been shown recently in our laboratory to produce a dramatic, long-lasting decrease in levels of brain tryptophan and also in brain serotonin synthesis (Biggio, Fadda, Fanni, Tagliamonte, and Gessa, 1974).

Table 2 shows that this diet produces male-to-male mounting behavior both in rats and rabbits at the time of maximal serotonin depletion.

Effect of Treatments Increasing Brain Serotonin on Male Sexual Behavior

1. L-5-hydroxytryptophan (5-HTP), the direct precursor of serotonin, suppresses male-to-male mounting behavior induced by PCPA in rats (Sheard, 1969; Tagliamonte et al., 1969; Shillito, 1970), rabbits (Gessa, 1970; Perez-Cruet et al.,

TABLE 1. Enhanced copulatory behavior in male rats after destruction of the raphe nuclei with 5,6-DHT

| Treatment | No. of animals | % of animals exhibiting (30-min observation) at least one of the following: | | | Brain[a] | |
		Mounting	Intromission	Ejaculation	5-HT (μg/g)	5-HIAA (μg/g)
Saline	29	48.27	48.27	13.74	0.64 ± 0.04	0.51 ± 0.02
5,6-DHT	23	56.52	56.52	43.43	0.25 ± 0.07	0.21 ± 0.06

Sexually inexperienced rats, weighing 300–350 g were injected with 5,6-DHT (200 μg/rat in 5 μl saline) into the raphe nuclei. Controls were injected with 5 μl of saline. Animals were tested or killed 15 days after treatment.
[a] Mean ± s.e. of six determinations.

TABLE 2. *Effect of a tryptophan-free diet on male-to-male mounting behavior and on brain 5-HT and 5-HIAA levels*

Animals	No. of animals	Diet	% of males mounting other males	Brain[a]	
				5-HT (μg/g)	5-HIAA (μg/g)
Rats	30	Basal	10	0.66 ± 0.04	0.55 ± 0.04
Rats	30	Try-free	70	0.26 ± 0.18	0.13 ± 0.02
Rabbits	8	Basal	0	0.50 ± 0.06	1.05 ± 0.12
Rabbits	8	Try-free	62.5	0.20 ± 0.03	0.43 ± 0.06

Animals received a tryptophan-free (Try-free) diet for 2 consecutive days and were observed 6 hr after the last meal for a period of 60 min. The composition of the diets is reported in Biggio, Fadda, Fanni, Tagliamonte, and Gessa (1974).

[a] Mean ± s.e. of six determinations.

1971), and cats (Ferguson et al., 1970; Hoyland et al., 1970); and also both PCPA-stimulated (Sheard, 1969; Shillito, 1969; Tagliamonte et al., 1969; Gessa and Tagliamonte, 1973) and spontaneous (Tagliamonte, Fratta, Mercuro, Biggio, Camba, and Gessa, 1972; Gessa and Tagliamonte, 1973) copulatory behavior in male rats with receptive females. We found that such 5-HTP-inhibition is potentiated by Ro 4-4602, an inhibitor of peripheral decarboxylase (Tagliamonte et al., 1972; Gessa and Tagliamonte, 1973); we have interpreted this finding as evidence for a central site of action of the serotonin precursor. It was, therefore, puzzling to learn that Ro 4-4602, at the doses used in our experiments, inhibits brain 5-HTP decarboxylase (Hyttel and Fjalland, 1972). While trying to solve this problem, we confirmed that Ro 4-4602 does indeed reduce the formation of serotonin and 5-HIAA following 5-HTP administration, but we further found that it does not affect serotonin formation following L-tryptophan administration.

These results indicate that R0 4-4602 does not inhibit the decarboxylation of 5-HTP formed within the serotoninergic neurons; therefore, we suggest that serotonin, measured in brain after the combined administration of Ro 4-4602 and 5-HTP, is mainly confined within these neurons. The rate of synthesis of the amine in these sites should even be enhanced because Ro 4-4602 favors 5-HTP penetration into the CNS (see Table 3).

2. Different monamine oxidase inhibitors, such as pargyline, phenelzine, and iproniazid, inhibit copulatory behavior in male rats (Tagliamonte et al., 1971; Gessa and Tagliamonte, 1973). We found that the time course of pargyline-induced inhibition coincides with the time of maximal accumulation of serotonin in the brain (7 to 48 hr after treatment) and that inhibition of both copulatory behavior and serotonin accumulation is prevented by PCPA (Tagliamonte et al., 1971).

3. However, in contrast to the results obtained with 5-HTP, we discovered that the administration of L-tryptophan, in single or repeated doses, fails to inhibit copulatory behavior in male rats (Tagliamonte et al., 1972; Gessa and Ta-

TABLE 3. *Effect of TRY and 5-HTP on copulatory behavior and brain serotonin metabolism of male rats*

| Treatment | % of rats ejaculating | TRY (μg/g) | Brain[a] | | |
			5-HTP (μg/g)	5-HT (μg/g)	5-HIAA (μg/g)
None	100	5.36 ± 0.07	Not detectable	0.63 ± 0.02	0.56 ± 0.06
Ro 4–4602	100	5.16 ± 0.04	Not detectable	0.59 ± 0.04	0.54 ± 0.04
5-HTP	32	5.04 ± 0.06	1.75 ± 0.21	1.63 ± 0.18	3.65 ± 0.31
Ro 4–4602 + 5-HTP	12	5.00 ± 0.07	6.08 ± 0.47	0.94 ± 0.11	2.26 ± 0.13
TRY	100	21.46 ± 0.73	Not detectable	0.74 ± 0.08	1.27 ± 0.12
Ro 4–4602 + TRY	100	20.71 ± 0.88	Not detectable	0.71 ± 0.07	1.31 ± 0.09

Drugs were given i.p.: Ro 4–4602 (50 mg/kg) 15 min prior to TRY (150 mg/kg) or 5-HTP (50 mg/kg). Animals were either tested or killed 30 min after last treatment. Mating tests were carried out on groups each containing 20 selected copulators.
[a] Mean ± s.e. of eight determinations.

gliamonte, 1973). A possible explanation for this finding is that in order to inhibit copulatory behavior brain serotonin has to reach a higher level than that which it is possible to by L-tryptophan loading. Indeed, it has been suggested that when serotonin is synthesized in excess of need, it is prevented from exerting a functional action by intraneuronal binding and deamination (Grahame-Smith, 1974); moreover, that an excess of serotonin is balanced by a decrease in spontaneous firing of central serotoninergic neurons (Aghajanian, 1972). Only when the amount of serotonin accumulated within neurons exceeds disposal or compensatory mechanisms, as might happen following a loading dose of 5-HTP but not of L-tryptophan, would a functional effect ensue. It is possible that when serotonin is released locally from nerve terminals, inhibitory concentrations might well reach the receptors concerned with mating behavior.

STIMULATORY ROLE OF BRAIN DA ON MALE SEXUAL BEHAVIOR

Our first report on the aphrodisiac effect of PCPA originally suggested that brain catecholamines may play a stimulatory role in male sexual behavior, based on the observation that the PCPA effect is greatly potentiated by pargyline, a monoamine oxidase inhibitor (Tagliamonte et al., 1969). Indeed, the inhibition of monoamine oxidase in rats with serotonin synthetic mechanisms blocked by PCPA pretreatment causes a selective accumulation of catecholamines in brain.

We were encouraged by clinical reports on the aphrodisiac effect both of L-DOPA in some parkinsonian patients (see Gessa and Tagliamonte, 1974*a*) and of amphetamines and cocaine in addicts (Snyder, 1972) to verify this hypothesis experimentally. We further took into consideration that impotence and frigidity are, in contrast, among the side effects of drugs that impair central adrenergic transmission, such as phenothiazine and butyrophenone neuroleptics (Deshaies, Richardeau, and Dechosal, 1957; Delay, and Deniker, 1961; Kamm, 1965; Haider, 1966).

Effect of L-DOPA and Apomorphine on the Sexual Behavior of the Male Rat

Benkert, Renz, and Matussek (1973) observed male--to-male mounting behavior after the administration of L-DOPA, in combination with Ro 4-4602, to rats pretreated with PCPA. This drug combination causes a selective accumulation of brain DA while serotonin levels are reduced, a condition similar to that present in rats treated with PCPA and pargyline.

Male-to-male mounting behavior has also been observed by Da Prada et al. (1972) after the administration of L-DOPA to rats pretreated with Ro 4-4602.

We studied the stimulatory effect of L-DOPA on the copulatory behavior of male rats with receptive females. In studying a potential aphrodisiac, it seemed appropriate to use animals with low basal levels of sexual activity, whereas animals with a high degree of activity were used when we wished to ascertain whether a drug inhibits copulatory behavior. We found that the combination of

L-DOPA with Ro 4-4602 markedly increased the percentage of animals reaching ejaculation (Gessa and Tagliamonte, 1974a,b; Tagliamonte, Fratta, Del Fiacco, and Gessa, 1974). On the other hand, sexual stimulation was not observed after the administration of L-DOPA alone, suggesting that dopamine (DA) concentration in brain must rise above a critical level to elicit an aphrodisiac effect. However, as the administration of L-DOPA and Ro 4-4602 not only increases brain DA content, but also decreases that of serotonin, the stimulatory effect might be ascribed to either mechanism. We therefore investigated the effect of apomorphine, which is considered to be a specific stimulator of central DA receptors (Ernst, 1967).

As shown in Table 4, a dose of apomorphine as low as 30 μg/kg s.c. markedly increased the number of rats showing mounting and intromission, and attaining ejaculation. Higher doses of apomorphine produced stereotyped behavior which prevented the occurrence of other goal-directed behavior patterns including copulation.

The dopaminergic nature of the stimulatory effect of apomorphine and L-DOPA is confirmed by the finding that it is prevented by haloperidol, a specific inhibitor of central dopamine receptors (Janssen, Niemegeers, Schellekens, and Lenaerts, 1967), in doses as low as 100 μg/kg, which are insufficient to cause overt behavioral change. This drug also suppresses the spontaneous copulatory behavior of vigorous copulators (Table 4).

Malmnäs (1973, 1974) has reported that using castrated male rats treated with suboptimal doses of testosterone, apomorphine, or L-DOPA (together with MK 486, an extracerebral decarboxylase inhibitor) the percentage of subjects displaying mounting behavior with females in estrus is increased; this percentage is reduced by pimozide, a central dopamine antagonist. Although Malmnäs' data are in good agreement with our own experiments, Hyyppä, Lehtinen, and Rinne (1971) failed to observe specific changes in copulatory behavior of adult male rats after the administration of L-DOPA and Ro 4-4602. These negative results, however, may be explained by their use of vigorous copulators and by the fact that Ro 4-4602 was in a dosage insufficient to protect L-DOPA from metabolism by peripheral decarboxylase.

RELATIONSHIP BETWEEN MONOAMINES AND OTHER AGENTS IN THE CONTROL OF SEXUAL BEHAVIOR

We have reported that in castrated male rats, PCPA causes neither male-to-male mounting behavior (Gessa, Tagliamonte, Tagliamonte, and Brodie, 1970) nor copulatory behavior with receptive females (Tagliamonte, Fratta, Mercuro, and Gessa, 1972; Del Fiacco, Fratta, Gessa, and Tagliamonte, 1974). Both effects are restored and the former greatly potentiated by testosterone. Moreover, as Table 5 shows, we found that the presence of testosterone is also essential for the stimulatory effect of apomorphine and L-DOPA on the copulatory behavior of male rats with receptive females.

Testosterone produces little or no homosexual mounting behavior in intact rats

TABLE 4. Stimulatory and inhibitory effect of apomorphine and haloperidol, respectively, on the copulatory behavior of male rats

		% of animals exhibiting within 30-min observation at least one of the following		
Basal condition	Treatment	Mounting	Intromission	Ejaculation
Noncopulators				
	None	0	0	0
	Apomorphine	76	76	50
	Haloperidol + apomorphine	0	0	0
Copulators				
	None	100	100	100
	Haloperidol	0	0	0

Values for noncopulators were obtained from 46 rats. Values for copulators were obtained from 14 rats. Haloperidol (100 µg/kg) was injected i.p., 2 hr before testing. Apomorphine (30 µg/kg) was injected s.c., 20 min before testing.

TABLE 5. *Failure of L-DOPA and apomorphine to induce copulatory behavior in castrated male rats*

	% of castrated rats showing at least one of the following		
Treatment	Mounting	Intromission	Ejaculation
None	0	0	0
L-DOPA (+ Ro 4–4602)	0	0	0
Apomorphine	0	0	0
Testosterone	100	80	70

Fifty sexually experienced rats were castrated 2 months before the present experiment. Each rat served as its own control, being tested at weekly intervals before treatments and after each treatment. Two doses of L-DOPA (100 mg/kg each) were injected i.p. 20 and 50 min, respectively, after Ro 4–4602 and the animals were tested 30 min after the last treatment. Apomorphine, 30 μg/kg, was given s.c. 20 min before the mating test. One week after the last test, castrated rats were treated with testosterone propionate (0.1 mg/kg s.c.) daily for 4 days, and tested 12 hr later.

in the presence of a normal brain serotonin content. Therefore, we might speculate that androgens act by priming a specific neuronal circuit to the stimulatory action of dopamine or a peptide factor or both; see Bertolini, Gessa, and Ferrari, *this volume)* and that, conversely, this circuit is inhibited by brain serotonin.

Malmnäs and Meyerson (1971) and Malmnäs (1973) found that suboptimal doses of testosterone are consistently effective in restoring the sexual behavior of castrated male rats following PCPA, L-DOPA, or apomorphine treatment.

Neither the pineal (Tagliamonte et al., 1969) nor the adrenal gland (Malmnäs and Meyerson, 1971; Malmnäs, 1973) seems to be essential for PCPA-induced sexual stimulation. In contrast, PCPA does not act on hypophysectomized rats (Tagliamonte et al., 1969; Gawienowski and Hodgen, 1971) even if exogenous testosterone is administered (Gawienowski and Hodgen, 1971); this suggests that an intact pituitary is required for androgen-dependent sexual stimulation.

In conclusion, there is evidence for an interrelationship of monoamines with testosterone and other hormones in controlling sexual behavior in males. However, our knowledge of this problem is still insufficient to allow a clear hypothesis to be put forward.

CONCLUSION

The data reported here support the hypothesis that sexual behavior in the male rat is inhibited by brain serotonin and is stimulated by dopamine. We are aware that drugs often have more than one action and, we should therefore, be cautious in deciding whether a given effect on behavior is causally related to a specific biochemical change. Yet we believe that we have obtained evidence in favor of such a causal relationship for different drug combinations, acting through independent mechanisms, have produced a similar behavioral effect. The relatively minute dosage of apomorphine and haloperidol, particularly, appear to argue for the specificity of the response.

Our attempt to clarify the difficult problem of the neurochemical bases of sexual behavior has involved the use of a number of different behavior patterns, such as male-to-male mounting behavior and copulatory behavior of naive, sluggish, castrated, and experienced male rats with females in estrus. Each of these models offered certain advantages and appeared to provide helpful information.

Among the important problems that remain to be solved are the identification of the monoaminergic neuronal circuits involved in the modulation of sexual behavior. It is conceivable that electrical stimulation or lesioning of specific serotoninergic or dopaminergic nuclei will help us in clarifying this problem. Another outstanding question is the extent to which the data obtained in rats can be extrapolated to other species, including man. The animal data, other than those obtained from the rat, are insufficient to answer this question. However, it may be that sexual behavior in the rat and man is modulated by a not entirely different biochemical mechanism to judge from the findings of Sicuteri, Del Bene, and Anselmi, *(this volume);* they noted that an aphrodisiac effect of L-DOPA and PCPA can be observed in both species. In addition, neuroleptics and monoamine oxidase inhibitors suppress sexual behavior in rats and produce frigidity and impotence in man.

It now seems possible that developments in the neurochemistry of sexual behavior will allow a biochemical interpretation of sexual disorders at present considered to be of psychogenic origin.

ACKNOWLEDGMENT

The authors thank H. H. Sugden for his assistance in the preparation of the manuscript.

REFERENCES

Aghajanian, G. K. (1972): LSD and CNS transmission. *Ann. Rev. Pharmacol.,* 12:157–168.

Baumgarten, H. G., Björklund, A., Lachenmayer, L., Nobin, A., and Stenevi, U. (1971): Long-lasting selective depletion of brain serotonin by 5,6-dihydroxytryptamine. *Acta Physiol. Scand.,* (Suppl.) 373:1–15.

Benkert, O., Renz, A., and Matussek, N. (1973): Dopamine, noradrenaline and 5-hydroxytryptamine in relation to motor activity, fighting and mounting behaviour. II. L-DOPA and DL-threodihydroxyphenylserine in combination with Ro 4-4602 and parachlorophenylalanine. *Neuropharmacology,* 12:187–193.

Biggio, G., Fadda, F., Fanni, P., Tagliamonte, A., and Gessa, G. L. (1974): Rapid depletion of serum tryptophan, brain tryptophan, serotonin and 5-hydroxyindoleacid by a tryptophan-free diet. *Life Sci.,* 14:1321–1329.

Björklund, A., Baumgarten, H. G., and Nobin, A. (1974): Chemical lesioning of central monoamine axons by means of 5,6-dihydroxytryptamine and 5,7-dihydroxytryptamine. In: *Advances in Biochemical Psychopharmacology, Vol. 10: Serotonin—New Vistas: Histochemistry and Pharmacology,* edited by E. Costa, G. L. Gessa, and M. Sandler, pp. 13–33. Raven Press, New York.

Da Prada, M., Carruba, M., O'Brien, R. A., Saner, A., and Pletscher, A. (1972): The effect of 5,6-dihydroxytryptamine on sexual behavior of male rats. *Eur. J. Pharmacol.,* 19:288–290.

Delay, J., and Deniker, P. (1961): *Méthodes chimiothérapiques en psychiatrie.* Masson, Paris.

Del Fiacco, M., Fratta, W., Gessa, G. L., and Tagliamonte, A. (1974): Lack of copulatory behaviour in male castrated rats after *p*-chlorophenylalanine. *Br. J. Pharmacol.,* 51:249–251.

Deshaies, G., Richardeau, N., and Dechosal, F. (1957): Chlorpromazine et réserpine en psychiatrie. *Ann. Méd. Psychiatrie,* 115:417–476.

Ernst, A. M. (1967): Mode of action of apomorphine and dexamphetamine on gnawing compulsion in rats. *Psychopharmacologia,* 10:316–323.

Ferguson, J., Henriksen, S., Cohen, H., Mitchell, G., Barchas, J., and Dement, W. (1970): "Hypersexuality" and behavioral changes in cats caused by administration of *p*-chlorophenylalanine. *Science,* 168:499–501.

Gawienowski, A. M., and Hodgen, G. D. (1971): Homosexual activity in male rats after *p*-chlorophenylalanine: Effects of hypophysectomy and testosterone. *Physiol. Behav.,* 7:551–555.

Gessa, G. L. (1970): Serotonin now: Clinical implications of inhibiting its synthesis with parachlorophenylalanine. *Ann. Int. Med.,* 73:607–629.

Gessa, G. L., and Tagliamonte, A. (1973): Role of brain monoamines in controlling sexual behavior in male animals. *Psychopharmacology, Sexual Disorders and Drug Abuse,* pp 451–462. North-Holland Publ. Co., Amsterdam.

Gessa, G. L., and Tagliamonte, A. (1974*a*): Role of brain monoamines in male sexual behavior. Mini review. *Life Sci.,* 14:425–436.

Gessa, G. L., and Tagliamonte, A. (1974*b*): Possible role of brain serotonin and dopamine in controlling male sexual behavior. In: *Advances in Biochemical Psychopharmacology, Vol. 11: Serotonin—New Vistas: Biochemistry and Behavioral and Clinical Studies,* edited by E. Costa, G. L. Gessa, and M. Sandler, pp. 217–228. Raven Press, New York.

Grahame-Smith, D. G. (1974): How important is the synthesis of brain 5-hydroxytryptamine in the physiological control of its central function? In: *Advances in Biochemical Psychopharmacology, Vol. 10: Serotonin—New Vistas: Histochemistry and Pharmacology,* edited by E. Costa, G. L. Gessa, and M. Sandler, pp. 83–91. Raven Press, New York.

Haider, I. (1966): Thioridazine and sexual dysfunctions. *Int. J. Neuropsychiatry,* 2:255–257.

Hoyland, V. J. Shillito, E. E., and Vogt, M. (1970): The effect of parachlorphenylalanine on the behaviour of cats. *Br. J Pharmacol.,* 40:659–667.

Hyttel, J., and Fjalland, B. (1972): Central 5-HTP decarboxylase inhibiting properties of Ro 4-4602 in relation to 5-HTP potentiation in mice. *Eur. J. Pharmacol.,* 19:112–114.

Hyyppä, M., Lehtinen, P., and Rinne, U. K. (1971): Effect of L-DOPA on the hypothalamic, pineal and striatal monoamines and on the sexual behavior of the rat. *Brain Res.,* 30:265–272.

Janssen, P. A. J., Niemegeers, C. J. E., Schellekens, K. H. L., and Lenaerts, F. M. (1967): Is it possible to predict the clinical effects of neuroleptic drugs (major tranquillizers) from animal data? *Arzneim. Forsch.,* 17:841–854.

Kamm, I. (1965): Control of sexual hyperactivity with thioridazine. *Am. J. Psychiatry,* 121:922–923.

Koe, K. B., and Weissman, A. (1966): *p*-Chlorophenylalanine: A specific depletor of brain serotonin. *J. Pharmacol. Exp. Ther.,* 154:499–515.

Malmnäs, C. O., and Meyerson, B. J. (1971): *p*-Chlorophenylalanine and copulatory behavior in the male rat. *Nature,* 232:398–400.

Malmnäs, C. O. (1973): Monoaminergic influence on testosterone-activated copulatory behavior in the castrated male rat. *Acta Physiol. Scand.* [Suppl.] 395.

Malmnäs, C. O. (1974): Opposite effects of serotonin and dopamine on copulatory activation in castrated male rats. In: *Advances in Biochemical Psychopharmacology, Vol. 11: Serotonin—New Vistas: Biochemistry and Behavioral and Clinical Studies,* edited by E. Costa, G. L. Gessa, and M. Sandler, pp. 243–248. Raven Press, New York.

Mitler, M. M., Morden, B., Levine. S., and Dement, W. (1972): The effects of parachlorophenylalanine on the mating behavior of male rats. *Physiol. Behav.,* 8:1147–1150.

Perez-Cruet, J., Tagliamonte, A., Tagliamonte, P., and Gessa, G. L. (1971): Differential effect of *p*-chlorophenylalanine (PCPA) on sexual behaviour and on sleep patterns of male rabbits. *Riv. Farmacol. Ter.,* 2:27–34.

Salis, P. J., and Dewsbury, D. A. (1971): *p*-Chlorophenylalanine facilitates copulatory behaviour in male rats. *Nature,* 232:400–401.

Sheard, M. H. (1969): The effect of *p*-chlorophenylalanine on behaviour in rats: Relation to brain serotonin and 5-hydroxyindoleacetic acid. *Brain Res.,* 15:524–528.

Shillito, E. E. (1970): The effect of parachlorophenylalanine on social interaction of male rats. *Br. J. Pharmacol.,* 38:305–315.

Snyder, S. H. (1972): Catecholamines in the brain as mediators of amphetamine psychosis. *Arch. Gen. Psychiatry,* 27:169–179.

Tagliamonte, A., Tagliamonte, P., Gessa, G. L., and Brodie, B. B. (1969): Compulsive sexual activity induced by *p*-chlorophenylalanine in normal and pinealectomized male rats. *Science,* 166:1433–1435.

Tagliamonte, A., Tagliamonte, P., and Gessa, G. L. (1971): Reversal of pargyline-induced inhibition of sexual behaviour in male rats by *p*-chlorophenylalanine. *Nature,* 230:244–245.

Tagliamonte, A., Fratta, W., Mercuro, G., and Gessa, G. L. (1972): Failure of *p*-chlorophenylalanine (PCPA) to restore copulatory behaviour in male castrated rats. *Riv. Farmacol. Ter.,* 3:399–403.

Tagliamonte, A., Fratta, W., Mercuro, G., Biggio, G., Camba, R. C., and Gessa, G. L. (1972): 5-Hydroxytryptophan, but not tryptophan, inhibits copulatory behaviour in male rats. *Riv. Farmacol. Ter.,* 3:405–409.

Tagliamonte, A., Fratta, W., Del Fiacco, M., and Gessa, G. L. (1974): Possible stimulatory role of brain dopamine in the copulatory behavior of male rats. *Pharmacol. Biochem. Behav.,* 2:257–260.

Whalen, R. E., and Luttge, W. G. (1970): *p*-Chlorophenylalanine methyl ester: An aphrodisiac? *Science,* 169:1000–1001.

Sexual Behavior: Pharmacology and Biochemistry, edited by M. Sandler and G. L. Gessa. Raven Press, New York © 1975.

Comparison of the Effects on Behavior of Methiothepin and Parachlorophenylalanine. I. Behavior Studies

Elizabeth E. Shillito

Institute of Animal Physiology, Babraham, Cambridge, England CB2 4AT

Behavior studies using male rats living in groups have shown that after treatment with parachlorophenylalanine (PCPA), the social interactions of the animals were increased (Shillito, 1970; Bond, Shillito, and Vogt, 1972). This change in behavior is related to changes in cerebral 5-hydroxytryptamine (5-HT) concentrations. In young animals the interactions took the form of increased chasing, which ended in one rat lying on top of another ("bundling"); in older animals male-to-male mounting was observed. Similar behavior studies with methiothepin, which is a dibenzothiapin believed to block central 5-HT receptors (Monachon, Burkard, Jalfre, and Haefely, 1972), have now shown that grouped male rats also show an increase in chasing and lying over one another.

METHODS

All the experiments were carried out on male albino rats (Tucks) as weanlings 3 weeks of age and used at 4, 5, 6, 7, and 10 weeks. The rats were kept under reversed daylight conditions for at least a week before observations started. Under these conditions, a red light was on in the room from 10:00 A.M. to 10:00 P.M. and a white light came on for the next 12 hr. At least 2 days before observation, groups of 8 or 10 rats were put into large (91 × 122 cm) observation cages. The cages contained sawdust and the area was divided up by plastic partitions. Food and water were freely available. The cages were not disturbed apart from feeding and watering, and injections were always given intraperitoneally at 11:00 A.M. after the daily observation period. The rats became active when the light changed to red at 10:00 A.M. and observations were made during 1 hr after light change. The groups were observed untreated, 24 hr after a saline injection and 24, 48, and 72 hr after treatment with PCPA or methiothepin. PCPA was given as a suspension in 1% Tween 80 at a dose of either 316 mg/kg or 100 mg/kg. Methiothepin was given as a solution in saline at a dose of 1.25, 3, or 5 mg/kg. Control groups were given saline or 1% Tween 80. All the rats could be identified individually by markings on their tails. During observations, two kinds of interactions between individuals were recorded: either mounting or bundling.

RESULTS

The effect of PCPA on cerebral concentrations of 5-HT lasts for several days and reaches its maximum depletion 3 days after treatment. The rats remained nearly immobile for 2 to 3 hr after injection before significant changes in cerebral 5-HT concentration had taken place (Koe and Weissman, 1966). Methiothepin also caused sedation for 4 hr after injection. The rats sat in a hunched posture and moved occasionally, running about jerkily and then stopping. Their eyes were half-closed and they became cold; at 10 mg/kg they showed chromodacryorrhea. During this early period changes in brain amines were maximal.

Twenty-four hr later and for 2 to 3 days postinjection, PCPA at 316 and 100 mg/kg produced an increase in chasing and lying over in young rats, but it also produced a very marked incidence of male-to-male mounting, particularly in rats older than 6 weeks. During an observation period of 1 hr the incidence of bundling increased from 15 to 75, 24 hr after injection in 5-week-old rats (Fig. 1). The incidence of mounting was increased from nil to 50 in the same time for rats of 10 weeks. The mounting behavior continued for the next 2 days. When 5-hydroxytrytophan (5-HTP) (5 mg/kg) was given before observations started, both the mounting behavior and "bundling" behavior were reduced, but this inhibition had disappeared on the next day.

An increase in chasing and lying over was seen in grouped rats treated with methiothepin (3 and 5 mg/kg) 48 hr postinjection, and in a few groups this increase was maintained for another day (Fig. 1). This increase from about 20 to 70 bundles in 1 hr was comparable to that produced with PCPA. Generally, activity returned to normal 72 hr after treatment. Injection of 5-HTP (5 mg/kg) 45 min before observations caused reduction in the original increase at 48 hr. The increase in bundling was most obvious in rats of 4 and 5 weeks, but neither in these rats nor in the older rats was male-to-male mounting observed. Several groups of rats were observed after treatment with methiothepin (1.25 mg/kg daily for 4 to 8 days). In these groups the bundling activity of the rats increased and stayed high during treatment. Activity also remained higher than in control groups for 48 hr after the last injection, as it did after single doses of methiothepin (3 and 5 mg/kg).

DISCUSSION

It has been suggested that "bundling," which involves chasing, lying over, and social grooming in young male rats, is the behavioral precursor of the adult male sexual behavior (Shillito, 1970). Treatment with PCPA produced a marked increase in these social interactions and this seemed to be related to changes in cerebral 5-HT concentrations. Although treatment with 5-HTP reduced the incidence of bundling in rats treated with methiothepin, no increase in male-to-male mounting was observed. It was possible that the methiothepin was just acting as a stimulant and the increase in bundling was the result of increased activity.

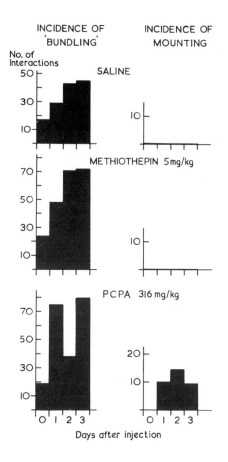

FIG. 1. Number of interactions in groups of 10 5-week-old male rats, treated with PCPA (316 mg/kg), methiothepin (5 mg/kg), or saline, and observed for 1 hr each day before injection and on 3 subsequent days.

To investigate this possibility some groups of rats were treated with a mixture of amylobarbitone sodium (7.5 mg/kg) and amphetamine sulfate (1.18 mg/kg) (Rushton and Steinberg, 1963). The rats were injected subcutaneously 35 min before observation began. The results showed that the stimulants stopped all social interactions, although the rats were active, running around the cage and eating. Therefore, it was not just an increase in activity that caused increased bundling.

A second possibility was that the sedation caused by methiothepin for up to 4 hr after injection was followed by a rebound of activity that was taking the form of bundling. This was investigated by treating some groups of rats with phenobarbital (2.5 and 5 mg/kg s.c.) 30 min before observations started. At 2.5 mg/kg, phenobarbital reduced the incidence of bundling, but it returned to control levels without any rebound on the following 2 days. At 5 mg/kg, the rats were heavily sedated during the first observation period, yet their activity returned to normal on the following day. These experiments seemed to rule out the possibility of mere postsedation excitement.

The chemical changes produced by PCPA and methiothepin are discussed by Vogt in the accompanying chapter. From a behavioral approach, the significance of this similar change in behavior after administration of the two drugs is still to be understood. It is an increase in a behavior pattern that occurs normally in young animals. The experiments with PCPA strongly suggested that bundling is a juvenile precursor of sexual activity. However, because methiothepin-treated rats never reacted with mounting, bundling may be the expression of more than one form of drive in young rats.

ACKNOWLEDGMENTS

I am grateful to Miss Christine Stride for her technical assistance, and to F. Hoffman La Roche and Company for supplies of methiothepin.

REFERENCES

Bond, V. J., Shillito, E. E. and Vogt, M. (1972): Influence of age and of testosterone on the response of male rats to parachlorophenylalanine. *Br. J. Pharmacol.,* 46:46–55.

Koe, B. K., and Weissman, A. (1966): *p*-Chlorophenylalanine: A specific depletor of brain serotonin. *J. Pharmacol. Exp. Ther.,* 154:499–516.

Monachon, M.-A., Burkard, W. P., Jalfre, M., and Haefely, W. (1972): Blockade of central 5-hydroxytryptamine receptors by methiothepin. *Arch. Pharmacol.,* 274:192–197.

Rushton, R., and Steinberg, H. (1963): Mutual potentiation of amphetamine and amylobarbitone measured by activity in rats. *Br. J. Pharmacol.,* 21:295–305.

Shillito, E. E. (1970): The effect of parachlorophenylalanine on social interaction of male rats. *Br. J. Pharmacol.,* 38:305–315.

Sexual Behavior: Pharmacology and Bio-chemistry, edited by M. Sandler and G. L. Gessa. Raven Press, New York © 1975.

Comparison of the Effects on Behavior of Methiothepin and Parachlorophenylalanine. II. Relation to Metabolism of 5-HT: Chemical Findings

Marthe Vogt

Institute of Animal Physiology, Babraham, Cambridge, England CB2 4AT

Before discussing the results we obtained with methiothepin, let me summarize the changes in cerebral monoamine metabolism that have previously been shown to accompany drug-induced mounting activity among male rats; in juvenile rats, mounting may be replaced by the interaction described as "bundling" (Shillito, preceding chapter).

First, there was a reduction in cerebral 5-hydroxytryptamine (5-HT) content, elicited either by parachlorophenylalanine (PCPA) or by 5,6-dihydroxytrypta-mine (Shillito, 1969, 1970; Tagliamonte, Tagliamonte, Gessa, and Brodie, 1969; Da Prada, Carruba, O'Brien, Saner, and Pletscher, 1972).

The effect was seen as early as 15 to 24 hr after PCPA (316 mg/kg), when no more than from one-third to two-thirds of the cerebral 5-HT had been lost (Sheard, 1969; Shillito, 1970). Furthermore, the administration of 5-hydroxytryp-tophan (5-HTP) temporarily restored normal behavior, even when only small doses (10 to 25 mg/kg) were administered, which elevated the 5-HT concentra-tion in the brain, but did not restore it to normal.

The observation of mounting after 5,6-dihydroxytryptamine (Da Prada et al., 1972) was made on rats in which the 5-HT content of whole brain was reduced to one-half. However, the total amount of 5-HT lost from the forebrain is not the only decisive factor. Sheard (1973) has compared the behavior of rats after PCPA injection and after destruction of the dorsal and medial raphe nuclei. Both procedures led to a loss of 40% of cerebral 5-HT, but only PCPA caused abnor-mal sexual behavior. In the lesioned rats the most anterior and the most posterior 5-HT-containing cell groups escaped destruction, and it is conceivable that this was responsible for the lack of abnormality in behavior.

Second, the possibility that dopamine (DA) is involved in male sexual behavior has been suggested by experiments of our Italian colleagues (Tagliamonte, Fratta, and Gessa, 1974). These authors found that lively sexual behavior was induced in sexually sluggish rats by injections of either apomorphine or of L-DOPA given together with an inhibitor of DOPA-decarboxylase. This suggests a stimulation of male sexual activity by excitation of dopamine receptors in the brain. It is not clear whether it could also lead to the misplaced sexual behavior of mounting among males.

The observation (Monachon, Burkard, Jalfre, and Haefely, 1972) that methiothepin induced so-called pontogeniculooccipital spikes and antagonized the inhibition of those spikes by 5-HTP, coupled with the observation that methiothepin increased the turnover of 5-HT, suggested that this drug was acting as a central antagonist of 5-HT. This view was confirmed (Tebecis, 1972) by iontophoretic application of 5-HT and of methiothepin to neurons of the lateral geniculate body—the inhibitory effects of 5-HT were antagonized by methiothepin. Had we found that its administration caused mounting as did that of PCPA, this would have supported the view that it acted as a central antagonist of 5-HT. However, an increase in the so-called "bundling" was found instead; estimations of forebrain 5-hydroxyindoleacetic acid (5-HIAA) were carried out to see whether this behavior could be correlated with any sign of accelerated turnover of 5-HT.

All 5-HIAA estimations were done on single forebrains from groups of injected rats killed either on the same day as their controls or 1 day earlier. Most groups contained 10 injected and 10 control rats. The method was adapted from that of Contractor (1966) as described earlier (Ahtee, Sharman, and Vogt, 1970). The term "forebrain" includes the hypothalamus but excludes the midbrain. All rats were killed at the same time of day immediately after the last observation of behavior. They were then usually 4 to 5 weeks old, but a few were between 6 and 8 weeks of age.

Table 1 shows that with doses of up to 5 mg/kg and at times ranging from 24 to 72 hr after the injection, when frequency of "bundling" was increased, there were no consistent changes in forebrain 5-HIAA concentrations. Of eight groups of rats killed 48 hr after methiothepin (3 mg/kg), only two showed an increase in 5-HIAA of about 20%. There was no correlation between increased social interaction of a group and the occasional rise in 5-HIAA concentration. The activity score and the 5-HIAA content of the forebrain were also compared in individual rats within a group, and no correlation was found. Table 1 (Groups 8 to 10) shows that rats injected with methiothepin but kept in individual cages so that social interaction could not take place had no rise in 5-HIAA. In contrast, and in confirmation of the findings by Monachon et al. (1972), there was a small but significant rise in forebrain 5-HIAA 2 hr after 5 mg/kg (Group 19), at a time when the rats are sedated, hypothermic, and do not interact.

During the last year, evidence has been obtained (Bartholini, Keller, and Pletscher, 1973; Keller, Bartholini, and Pletscher, 1973) that the action of methiothepin on brain amines is more complex than thought earlier. However, these changes, like the ones produced with 5-HIAA, have their maximum about 2 hr after the injection. In a dose of 7 mg/kg, the drug produced at this time an increase of 75% in the norepinephrine (NE) metabolite 3-methoxy-4-hydroxyphenylethyleneglycol in the rat brain, and, in a dose of 30 mg/kg, caused a 25% fall in brain NE concentration; both findings point to an increased turnover of NE. Dopamine metabolism too was accelerated by the drug. Rather higher doses are required to obtain these effects than the doses causing increased "bundling," and the effects are as evanescent as those produced on 5-HIAA.

TABLE 1. *Changes in 5-HIAA concentration in forebrain of rats given methiothepin i.p.*

Group	Dose (mg/kg)	Time elapsed since last dose (hr)	Change in 5-HIAA
1	1.25 × 4	24	None
2			None
3	3, grouped	48	None
4			18% rise*
5			22% rise*
6			None
7			16% fall
8	3, single[a]	48	None
9			None
10			None
11	3	24	21% rise*
12			None
13			20% rise*
14	5	72	26% fall
15			None
16			None
17	5	24	None
18			None
19	5	2	15% rise*

* Statistically significant.
[a] Kept in individual cages throughout the experiment.

In conclusion, the changes in social interaction exhibited 1 to 3 days after the injection of small doses of methiothepin do not coincide in time with the evanescent changes in turnover of 5-HT or of catecholamines. Whether the late effects upon behavior are in any way related to the early biochemical changes in monoamine turnover is a matter for speculation. The late behavioral change could, however, not be related to an occupancy of 5-HT receptors by methiothepin, as this would have caused an increase in 5-HIAA formation. Whether the "bundling" seen in the present work is of a different nature as that seen in juvenile rats after PCPA or 5,6-dihydroxytryptamine is another unanswered question. There is also no simple way of explaining the early sedation after 2 to 5 mg/kg by the mild changes found with these doses in turnover of all monoamines.

ACKNOWLEDGMENTS

My thanks are due to Mrs. Ariana Celis for skilled technical assistance and to F. Hoffman La Roche and Co. for a sample of methiothepin. The work was supported by a grant from the Medical Research Council.

REFERENCES

Ahtee, L., Sharman, D. F., and Vogt, M. (1970): Acid metabolites of monoamines in avian brain; Effects of probenecid and reserpine. *Br. J. Pharmacol.,* 38:72–85.

Bartholini, G., Keller, H. H., and Pletscher, A. (1973): Effect of neuroleptics on endogenous norepinephrine in rat brain. *Neuropharmacologia,* 12:751–756.

Contractor, S. F. (1966): A rapid quantitative method for the estimation of 5-hydroxyindoleacetic acid in human urine. *Biochem. Pharmacol.,* 15:1701–1706.

Da Prada, M., Carruba, M., O'Brien, R. A., Saner, A., and Pletscher, A. (1972): The effect of 5,6-dihydroxytryptamine on sexual behavior of male rats. *Eur. J. Pharmacol.,* 19:288–290.

Keller, H. H., Bartholini, G., and Pletscher, A. (1973): Increase of 3-methoxy-4-hydroxyphenylethylene glycol in rat brain by neuroleptic drugs. *Eur. J. Pharmacol.,* 23:183–186.

Monachon, M.-A., Burkard, W. P., Jalfre, M., and Haefely, W. (1972): Blockade of central 5-hydroxytryptamine receptors by methiothepin. *Arch. Pharmacol.,* 274:192–197.

Sheard, M. H. (1969): The effect of *p*-chlorophenylalanine on behaviour in rats: Relation to brain serotonin and 5-hydroxyindoleacetic acid. *Brain Res.,* 15:524–528.

Sheard, M. H. (1973): Brain serotonin depletion by *p*-chlorophenylalanine or lesions of raphe neurons in rats. *Physiol. Behav.,* 10:809–911.

Shillito, E. E. (1969): The effect of *para*chlorophenylalanine on social interaction of male rats. *Br. J. Pharmacol.,* 36:193–194P.

Shillito, E. E. (1970): The effect of *para*chlorophenylalanine on social interaction of male rats. *Br. J. Pharmacol.,* 38:305–315.

Tagliamonte, A., Fratta, W., and Gessa, G. L. (1974): Aphrodisiac effect of L-DOPA and apomorphine in male sexually sluggish rats. *Experientia,* 30:381–382.

Tagliamonte, A., Tagliamonte, P., Gessa, G., and Brodie, B. (1969): Compulsive sexual activity induced by *p*-chlorophenylalanine in normal and pinealectomized male rats. *Science,* 166:1433–1435.

Tebēcis, A. K. (1972): Antagonism of 5-hydroxytryptamine by methiothepin shown in microelectrophoretic studies on neurones in the lateral geniculate nucleus. *Nature New Biol.,* 238:63–64.

Sexual Behavior: Pharmacology and Biochemistry, edited by M. Sandler and G. L.
Gessa. Raven Press, New York © 1975.

Involvement of Monoamines in the Mediation of Lordosis Behavior

S. Ahlenius, J. Engel, H. Eriksson, K. Modigh, and P. Södersten

Departments of Pharmacology and Psychology, University of Göteborg, Göteborg, Sweden

Sexual receptivity in the female rat is strictly regulated by ovarian hormones (cf. Young, 1961). The most prominent feature of this behavior is the lordosis response; this response in combination with other signs of female receptivity is completely abolished by removal of the ovaries. Receptivity in spayed animals can be restored by appropriate treatments of estrogen alone (Davidson, Smith, Rogers, and Bloch, 1968) or, more reliably, by a single estrogen injection followed by an injection of progesterone (Boling and Blandau, 1939; Beach, 1942). It has further been shown that in the latter case the progesterone injection can be replaced by drugs known to interfere with central monoamine neurotransmission (Meyerson, 1964a,b). A major objective in the work with such neurophar-macologic agents has been to determine the relative importance of the monoamines, norepinephrine (NE), dopamine (DA), and 5-hydroxytryptamine (5-HT) in the mediation of the estrogen-drug-induced lordosis response. Studies on the effects of tetrabenazine, reserpine, and parachlorophenylalanine, drugs known to deplete brain-tissue stores of monoamines, as well as studies on the effects of a monoamine-oxidase inhibitor in combination with various monoamine precursors led to the suggestion that primarily central 5-HT has a regulatory function in the mediation of the lordosis response in the female rat (Meyerson, 1964a, Meyerson and Lewander, 1970).

Experiments performed in this laboratory on a possible additional role of the catecholamines, NE or DA or both in the mediation of estrogen-drug-induced lordosis, are reviewed, followed by a discussion of the possible mechanism by which drugs known to interfere with central monoamines may act to induce a lordosis response in estrogen-primed ovariectomized rats.

METHODS

All tests for lordosis took place in a circular (50-cm diameter) plexiglas cage, the floor of which was covered with sawdust. Each female was introduced to two cage-adapted, sexually highly experienced males. The females remained with the males until mounted 10 times. Intromissions and ejaculations were allowed to occur. If the males failed to mount, the experimental female was removed and presented to two other stimulus males, until mounted the required 10 times. Lordosis was scored as either present or absent. To be scored as displaying lordosis in response to the mounting male, the female had to arch its back to a concave position, deviate its tail laterally, and extend its neck. A lordosis-to-mount ratio (total number of lordoses displayed divided by times mounted $\times$ 100) was calculated. This quotient is known to be a sensitive index of female receptivity (Beach, 1942). Biochemical experiments were performed in parallel, using the methods of Bertler, Carlsson, and Rosengren (1958) (NE); Carlsson and Waldeck (1958) and Atack (1973) (DA), and Andén and Magnusson (1967) (5-HT).

ROLE OF CENTRAL MONOAMINES IN ESTROGEN-DRUG-INDUCED LORDOSIS

Effects of Tetrabenazine

Tetrabenazine (TBZ) is thought to act like reserpine, which has been shown to deplete brain NE, DA, and 5-HT by inhibiting the granular uptake-storage mechanism (Carlsson, 1966). The administration of TBZ, 10 mg/kg, to estrogen-pretreated ovariectomized rats results within 15 min in an increase in the number of times lordosis was displayed and a significant decrease in brain NE, DA, and 5-HT. Essentially, the same behavioral response is obtained by administering TBZ (2 mg/kg). However, this treatment only reduces brain DA and does not result in any significant effect on brain NE or 5-HT (Ahlenius, Engel, Eriksson, and Södersten, 1972b). Thus, if anything, the increase in lordosis seems to be associated with changes in brain DA. A word of caution is in order here and in the subsequent experiments to be described; whole-brain determinations of NE, DA, and 5-HT were made. Regional changes in any of these amines may occur which are concealed in a whole-brain determination.

Effects of Parachlorophenylalanine (PCPA)

The administration of PCPA is known to result in a depletion of brain monoamines, especially 5-HT (Koe and Weissman, 1966), probably as a result of inhibition of tryptophan- and tyrosine hydroxylase. We have found that injection of PCPA (150 mg/kg of the methyl ester hydrochloride, H 69/17) is followed by an increase in the number of times lordosis is displayed, together with a decrease in brain NE, DA, and 5-HT within 24 hr of injection in ovariectomized estrogen-pretreated animals. Maximal depletion of brain 5-HT was obtained 24 hr postinjection, and at this time the lordosis response was significantly reduced. With the treatment used in these experiments, brain catecholamine levels are restored within 24 hr (Ahlenius et al., 1972a). Thus, these experiments demonstrate a possible correlation between the display of lordosis and changes in brain catecholamines.

Effects of α-Methyltyrosine (α-MT)

In an attempt to evaluate more specifically the role of brain catecholamines in the mediation of estrogen-drug induced lordosis we have investigated the effects of α-MT (100 mg/kg i.p. of the methyl ester hydrochloride, H 44/68) on the display of lordosis in ovariectomized estrogen-pretreated animals. In these experiments it was found that the lordosis quotient was markedly increased 2 to 8 hr after α-MT, in parallel with a decrease in brain NE and DA (Ahlenius et al., 1972a). A qualitative observation of the behavior of these animals indicated an exaggerated lordosis, ear-wiggling, and darting in some of the α-MT-treated rats. No signs of sedation and debilitation were observed in any of these, or in the PCPA-treated animals described in the preceding paragraph.

In order to test the specificity of the effects obtained by α-MT, separate experiments were performed. As shown in Fig. 1 there was a significant increase in the number of times lordosis was displayed 2 hr after administration of α-MT, as compared with animals given NaCl. This increase in lordosis response was completely blocked by the administration of L-DOPA (50 mg/kg) 1 hr after α-MT, and concomitantly the α-MT-induced depletion of brain NE and DA was antagonized. The same dose of L-DOPA had no effect on estrogen-progesterone-activated lordosis (Fig. 2). In a second experiment, a different time schedule of drug injections was used (Fig. 3), in which there was a significant increase in the display of lordosis 4 hr after α-MT. This α-MT-induced increase in lordosis was only partially antagonized by the administration of L-DOPA, 50 mg/kg, given 3 hr after α-MT. The α-MT-induced depletion of brain catecholamines is more pronounced 4 hr after α-MT than that seen 2 hr after α-MT (cf. Fig. 1) and the L-DOPA-induced increase in brain norepinephrine is not sufficient to restore norepinephrine to normal levels. Although brain DA values are not as high in this experiment (cf. Fig. 1), the values are significantly elevated as compared with saline control levels.

Taken together, these experiments show that the α-MT-induced increase in lordosis in ovariectomized estrogen-pretreated animals is associated with changes in brain catecholamine levels. Thus, these results lend further support to the concept that the catecholamines are of importance in the mediation of lordosis behavior in the female rat.

Effects of Bis(4-Methyl-1-Homopiperazinylthiocarbonyl)disulfide (FLA-63)

In order to evaluate a possible role of brain NE in the estrogen-drug-induced increase of lordosis in ovariectomized, estrogen-pretreated animals, they were given a specific inhibitor of DA-β-hydroxylase, FLA-63 (Corrodi, Fuxe, Hamberger, and Ljungdahl, 1970). As shown in Fig. 4, there was a significant increase in the display of lordosis 4 hr, but not 2 hr, after the injection as compared with saline-vehicle-injected animals ($p = 0.019$, Mann-Whitney U-test). No biochemi-

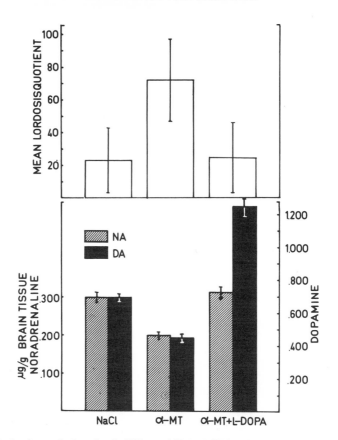

FIG. 1. Effects of α-methyltyrosine (α-MT) or α-MT + L-DOPA on lordosis behavior and on brain catecholamines in ovariectomized estrogen-pretreated rats. (Upper) Mean lordosis quotients ± SD. The methyl ester hydrochloride of α-MT, 100 mg/kg i.p. or 0.9% saline, was given 2 hr and L-DOPA or saline vehicle 1 hr before the test for lordosis or decapitation. All animals received the aromatic amino acid decarboxylase inhibitor, N^1-(DL-seryl)-N^2-(2,3,4-trihydroxybenzyl)hydrazine (Ro 4-4602), 50 mg/kg i.p. 30 min before the injection of L-DOPA or L-DOPA vehicle. The number of animals in the respective groups were NaCl (12), α-MT (13), α-MT + L-DOPA (13). Tests for statistical significance were performed by means of the Mann-Whitney U-test: α-MT-NaCl/ α-MT + L-DOPA, $p < 0.002$, NaCl $- \alpha$-MT + L-DOPA, $p > 0.05$. (Lower) Mean brain tissue levels (μg/g) of norepinephrine (NE) and dopamine (DA) ± SEM based on five determinations. Drug regimens as above. A one-way analysis of variance followed by Student's t-test revealed the following significant differences between treatments. Norepinephrine: NaCl $-$ α-MT, $p < 0.001$, α-MT $- \alpha$-MT + L-DOPA, $p < 0.001$. Dopamine: NaCl $- \alpha$-MT, $p < 0.001$, NaCl $- \alpha$-MT, + L-DOPA, $p < 0.001$, α-MT $- \alpha$-MT + L-DOPA, $p < 0.001$.

cal experiments were performed, but it is known that the administration of FLA-63 in the dose used here results in a significant decrease in rat brain NE (e.g., Ahlenius and Engel, 1971). This experiment provides further support for a role of brain NE in the mediation of lordosis in ovariectomized, estrogen-pretreated rats treated with TBZ, PCPA, α-MT, or FLA-63. The possible mode of action and physiologic implications are discussed below.

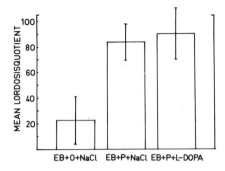

FIG. 2. Mean lordosis quotient ± SEM based on the performance of 9–10 animals. Estrogen (EB) was given in a dose of 10 μg/kg s.c. 48 hr before the test for lordosis. Progesterone (P), 0.5 mg/animal or oil vehicle (O) s.c. was given 6 hr and L-DOPA, 50 mg/kg i.p. 1 hr before the test for lordosis. All animals received the aromatic amino acid decarboxylase inhibitor Ro 4-4602, 50 mg/kg i.p., 30 min before the injection of L-DOPA or L-DOPA vehicle. Tests for statistical differences between the groups were performed by means of the Mann-Whitney U-test: $EB + 0 + NaCl − EB + P + NaCl/EB + P + L\text{-DOPA}$, $p < 0.002$. $EB + P + NaCl − EB + P + L\text{-DOPA}$, $p > 0.05$.

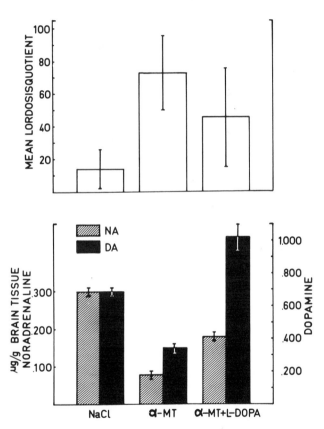

FIG. 3. α-MT, 100 mg/kg i.p. or saline vehicle, was given 4 hr and L-DOPA, 50 mg/kg i.p. or saline vehicle, 1 hr before the test for lordosis or decapitation. All animals received the aromatic amino acid decarboxylase inhibitor Ro 4-4602, 50 mg/kg i.p., 30 min before L-DOPA or L-DOPA vehicle. The following statistically significant differences were obtained. Lordosis quotient: NaCl − α-MT, $p < 0.002$, α-MT − α-MT + L-DOPA, $p < 0.05$, NaCl − α-MT + L-DOPA, $p < 0.05$. Norepinephrine and dopamine: All groups significantly different from each other at the $p < 0.001$ level. Number of subjects in the respective groups; (upper) NaCl (9), α-MT (10), α-MT + L-DOPA (10); (lower) each mean based on five determinations. For further details see Fig. 1.

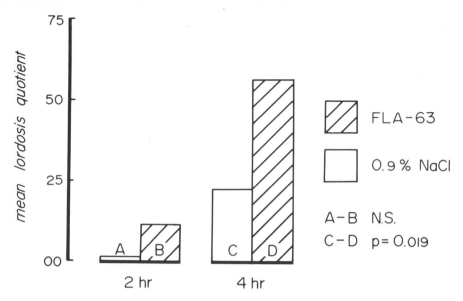

FIG. 4. Estradiol benzoate, 10 μg/kg s.c., was given 48 hr before the first test for lordosis. Thereafter the animals were randomly assigned to one of two treatments: FLA-63, 10 mg/kg i.p. or 0.9% saline, given 2 and 4 hr before tests for lordosis. Mean lordosis quotients based on the performance of eight animals in each group are shown. Statistical evaluation was performed by means of the Mann-Whitney U-test.

POSSIBLE MECHANISMS WHEREBY DRUGS INTERFERING WITH CENTRAL MONOAMINE NEUROTRANSMISSION MAY ACT TO FACILITATE THE INDUCTION OF LORDOSIS BEHAVIOR IN THE OVARIECTOMIZED ESTROGEN-PRIMED FEMALE RAT

Meyerson's (1964a) original demonstration that reserpine or tetrabenazine could replace progesterone in facilitating lordosis behavior in ovariectomized estrogen-primed female rats suggested the interesting possibility that under physiologic conditions progesterone may act to facilitate the display of lordosis by affecting central monoamine neurotransmission. However, it was also possible that reserpine and tetrabenazine did not act directly upon the neural mechanisms that mediate sexual behavior in the female rat, but acted indirectly, by stimulating ACTH secretion from the anterior pituitary, which in turn, might have activated the secretion of progesterone from the adrenals. This second possibility is supported by the well known fact that reserpine stimulates the secretion of ACTH (see review by van Loon, 1973), and by the demonstration that ACTH injections to estrogen-primed ovariectomized female rats stimulate the secretion of adrenal progesterone in sufficient quantities to enhance the display of lordosis (Feder and Ruf, 1969). However, Meyerson (1964b) presented evidence that reserpine may also stimulate lordosis in ovariectomized and adrenalectomized estrogen-primed female rats. Moreover, it was recently shown that PCPA facilitates the display of lordosis in female rats previously subjected to combined ovariectomy and adrenalectomy and primed with estrogen (Zemlan, Ward, Crowley, and Margules, 1973). At this time, therefore, there is evidence that both reserpine and PCPA may stimulate the display of sexual behavior in female rats as a result of mechanisms that are, at least in part, independent of whatever influence these drugs exert upon the hypothalamic–pituitary–adrenal axis.

That reserpine in fact can activate lordosis behavior in the ovariectomized estrogen-primed female rat as a function of pituitary–adrenal activation was convincingly demonstrated by Paris, Resko, and Goy (1971). These workers found that the injection of reserpine to ovariectomized female rats which had been pretreated with estradiol benzoate was followed by elevated levels of progesterone in the systemic plasma and was associated with the display of lordosis. Both the elevation of plasma progesterone and the facilitation of sexual behavior following reserpine treatment could be inhibited by treatment with dexamethasone, a potent corticotropin inhibitor. Similar results with mice were reported by Uphouse, Wilson, and Schlesinger (1970) and by Hansult, Uphouse, Schlesinger and Wilson (1972). Recently Larsson, Feder, and Komisaruk (1974) reported that TBZ, like reserpine, was ineffective in stimulating lordosis in adrenalectomized female rats pretreated with estrogen.

Our experiments showed that the facilitation of lordosis in estrogen-drug-treated ovariectomized female rats was correlated with a lowering of brain CA content. At the time we performed these experiments, evidence was presented that ACTH secretion in the rat may be inhibited by a central neural adrenergic mechanism (van Loon, Scapagnini, Moberg, and Ganong, 1971, and review by Ganong, 1972). We therefore suggested that catecholamine synthesis inhibitors may act to facilitate the display of lordosis in ovariectomized estrogen-primed female rats by removing a tonic inhibition of ACTH; this may activate the secretion of adrenal progesterone which may in turn advance the onset of sexual receptivity (Södersten and Ahlenius, 1972). Support for this hypothesis was provided by an experiment in which we were unable to facilitate the display of lordosis behavior in ovariectomized–adrenalectomized female rats by monoamine synthesis inhibitors (Eriksson and Södersten, 1973). Neither PCPA (150 mg/kg i.p.) nor α-MT (100 mg/kg i.p.) in doses that had previously been found to reduce the brain content of catecholamines, and in the case of PCPA of serotonin also, was effective in facilitating lordosis in these estrogen-primed (10 μg/kg EB s.c.) ovariectomized–adrenalectomized females. Females that had been ovariectomized and left with their adrenals *in situ,* however, displayed heightened levels of lordosis in response to PCPA as well as α-MT treatment, and, in addition, it was found that progesterone (0.5 mg/animal s.c.) effectively facilitated the display of lordosis in adrenalectomized as well as intact females.

It is interesting in this context to consider the evidence presented by Ganong and co-workers (see Ganong, 1972) that ACTH secretion in the rat may be inhibited by central CA, the evidence that CA (Lichtensteiger, 1971) and ACTH secretion (Critchlow, Liebelt, Bar-Sela, Mountcastle, and Lipscomb, 1963) varies during the rat estrous cylce, and the evidence that the adrenal may take part in regulating the sexual behavior of the female rat (Nequin and Schwarz, 1971). These observations suggest that CA may be involved in the control of the estrous cycle of the female rat, possibly by modulating ACTH secretion from the anterior pituitary; this may regulate the secretion of adrenal progesterone, which in turn may be of importance for the release of LH, subsequent ovulation, and the associated display of sexual behavior (Feder, Brown-Grant, and Corker, 1971).

ACKNOWLEDGMENTS

This work was supported by grants from the Swedish Council for Social Research 223/71P and 216/74P, the Swedish Medical Research Council (14X-502 and O4X-155), the Faculty of Social Sciences, University of Göteborg; J.E. is supported by the Swedish Board for Technical Development. For generous supplies of drugs we thank Hässle Ltd, Mölndal (FLA-63, H 44/68 and H 69/17). Skillful technical assistance was given by Mrs. Ingela Olsson.

REFERENCES

Ahlenius, S., and Engel, J. (1971): Behavioural and biochemical effects of L-DOPA after inhibition of dopamine-β-hydroxylase in reserpine pretreated rats. *Naunyn-Schmiedebergs Arch. Pharmacol.,* 270:349–360.

Ahlenius, S., Engel, J., Eriksson, H., Modigh, K., and Södersten, P. (1972a) Importance of catecholamines in the mediation of lordosis behaviour in ovariectomized rats treated with estrogen and inhibitors of monoamine synthesis. *J. Neural Transm.,* 33:247–255.

Ahlenius, S., Engel, J., Eriksson, H., and Södersten, P. (1972b): Effects of tetrabenazine on lordosis behaviour and on brain monoamines in the female rat. *J. Neural Transm.,* 33:155–162.

Andén, N.-E., and Magnusson, T. (1967): An improved method for the fluorimetric determination of 5-hydroxytryptamine in tissues. *Acta Physiol. Scand.,* 69:87–94.

Atack, C. V. (1973): The determination of dopamine by a modification of the dihydroxyindole fluorimetric assay. *Br. J. Pharmacol.,* 48:699–714.

Beach, F. A. (1942): Importance of progesterone to induction of sexual receptivity in spayed female rats. *Proc. Soc. Exp. Biol. Med.,* 51:367–371.

Bertler, A., Carlsson, A., and Rosengren, E. (1958): A method for the fluorimetric determination of adrenaline and noradrenaline in tissues. *Acta Physiol. Scand.,* 44:273–292.

Boling, J. L., and Blandau, R. J. (1939): The estrogen-progesterone induction of mating responses in the spayed female rat. *Endocrinology,* 25:259–264.

Carlsson, A. (1966): Drugs which block the storage of 5-hydroxytryptamine and related amines. In: *Handbook of Experimental Pharmacology, Vol. 19,* edited by O. Eichler and A. Farah, pp. 529–592. Springer, Berlin.

Carlsson, A., and Waldeck, B. (1958): A fluorimetric method for the determination of dopamine (3-hydroxytyramine). *Acta Physiol. Scand.,* 44:293–298.

Corrodi, H., Fuxe, K., Hamberger, B., and Ljungdahl, Å. (1970): Studies on central and peripheral noradrenaline neurons using a new dopamine-β-hydroxylase inhibitor. *Eur. J. Pharmacol.,* 12:145–155.

Critchlow, V., Liebelt, R. A., Bar-Sela, M., Mountcastle, W., and Lipscomb, H. S. (1963): Sex difference in resting pituitary-adrenal function in the rat. *Am. J. Physiol.,* 205:807–815.

Davidson, J. M., Smith, E. R., Rogers, C. H., and Bloch, G. J. (1968): Relative thresholds of behavioural and somatic responses to estrogen. *Physiol. Behav.,* 3:227–229.

Eriksson, H., and Södersten, P. (1973): A failure to facilitate lordosis behavior in adrenalectomized and gonadectomized estrogen-primed rats with monoamine-synthesis inhibitors. *Horm. Behav.,* 4:89–97.

Feder, H. H., Brown-Grant, K., and Corker, C. S. (1971): Pre-ovulatory progesterone, the adrenal cortex, and the "critical period" for luteinizing hormone release in rats. *J. Endocrinol.,* 50:29–39.

Feder, H. H., and Ruf, K. B. (1969): Stimulation of progesterone release and estrous behavior by ACTH in ovariectomized rodents. *Endocrinology,* 84:171–174.

Ganong, W. F. (1972): Evidence for a central noradrenergic system that inhibits ACTH secretion. In: *Brain-Endocrine Interaction,* pp. 254–266, edited by K. M. Knigge, D. E. Scott, and A. Weindl. Karger, Basel.

Hansult, C. D., Uphouse, L., Schlesinger, K., and Wilson, J. R. (1972): Induction of estrus in mice: Hypophyseal-adrenal effects. *Horm. Behav.,* 3:113–121.

Koe, B. K., and Weissman, A. (1966): *p*-Chlorophenylalanine: A specific depletor of brain serotonin. *J. Pharmacol. Exp. Ther.,* 154:499–516.

Larsson, K., Feder, H. H., and Komisaruk, B. R. (1974): Role of the adrenal glands, repeated matings, and monoamines on lordosis behavior of rats. *Pharmacol. Biochem. Behav.,* 2:685–692.

Lichtensteiger, W. (1971): Katekolaminkonzentration und Aktivität der Nervenzelle. Mikrofluometrische Untersuchungen an Tuberoinfundibulären Neuronen in verschiedenen Funktionszuständen. *Bull. Schwiz. Akad. Med. Wiss.,* 27:195–215.

Meyerson, B. J. (1964*a*): Central nervous monoamines and hormone induced estrous behaviour in the spayed rat. *Acta Physiol. Scand.,* 63: Suppl. 241.

Meyerson, B. J. (1964*b*): Estrous behaviour in spayed rats after estrogen or progesterone treatment in combination with reserpine or tetrabenazine. *Psychopharmacologia,* 6:210–218.

Meyerson, B. J. and Lewander, T. (1970): Serotonin synthesis inhibition and estrous behaviour in female rats. *Life Sci.,* 9:Part 1, 661–671.

Nequin, L. G., and Schwartz, N. B. (1971): Adrenal participation in the timing of mating behavior and LH release in the cyclic rat. *Endocrinology,* 88:325–331.

Paris, C. H., Resko, J. A., and Goy, R. W. (1971): A possible mechanism for the induction of lordosis by reserpine in spayed rats. *Biol. Reprod.,* 4:23–30.

Södersten, P., and Ahlenius, S. (1972): Female lordosis behavior in estrogen-primed male rats treated with *p*-chlorophenylalanine or α-methyl-*p*-tyrosine. *Horm. Behav.,* 3:181–189.

Uphouse, L., Wilson, J. R., and Schlesinger, K. (1970): Induction of estrus in mice: The possible role of adrenal progesterone. *Horm. Behav.,* 1:255–264.

van Loon, G. R. (1973). Brain catecholamines and ACTH secretion. In: *Frontiers in Neuroendocrinology,* pp. 209–247, edited by W. F. Ganong and L. Martini. Oxford University Press, New York.

van Loon, G. R., Scapagnini, U., Moberg, G. P., and Ganong, W. F. (1971): Evidence for central adrenergic neural inhibition of ACTH secretion in the rat. *Endocrinology,* 89:1464–1469.

Young, W. C. (1961): The hormones and mating behaviour. In: Sex and Internal Secretions, pp. 1173–1239. Williams & Wilkins, Baltimore, Maryland.

Zemlan, F. P., Ward, I. L., Crowley, W. R., and Margules, D. L. (1973): Activation of lordotic responding in female rats by suppression of serotonergic activity. *Science,* 179:1010–1011.

Sexual Behavior: Pharmacology and Biochemistry, edited by M. Sandler and G. L.
Gessa. Raven Press, New York © 1975.

Studies on the Role of Monoamines in the Hormonal Regulation of Sexual Receptivity in the Female Rat

B. J. Everitt,* K. Fuxe, T. Hökfelt, and G. Jonsson

Department of Histology, Karolinska Institutet, Stockholm, Sweden

It has been well established that sexual receptivity in the female rat is dependent on the ovarian hormones estrogen and progesterone (Young, 1961; Davidson, 1972; Davidson and Levine, 1972). Meyerson (1964a,b,c) has demonstrated that drugs interfering with monoamine neurotransmission (e.g., reserpine and tetrabenazine) can be substituted for progesterone in inducing receptivity, thereby raising the possibility that the effects of this hormone are in some way mediated by alterations in central monoaminergic neural mechanisms. It was suggested by Meyerson (1964a) that the balance of evidence pointed toward the existence of an inhibitory system of neurons in which 5-hydroxytryptamine (5-HT) is the principal transmitter, and that hormones or amine-interfering drugs facilitate estrous behavior by decreasing transmission in this inhibitory system. Whereas a number of experiments have supported this hypothesis (Hoyland, Shillito, and Vogt, 1970; Meyerson and Lewander, 1970; Zemlan, Ward, Crowley, and Margules, 1973; Everitt, Gradwell, and Herbert, *this volume*), evidence has accumulated that suggests that catecholamines (CA) also may be involved to an equal or even greater extent (Ahlenius, Engel, Eriksson, Modigh, and Södersten, 1972). Furthermore, a number of reports have implied that the behavioral effects of these drug treatments are indirect, being mediated by the release of progesterone from the adrenal cortex (Paris, Resko, and Goy, 1971; Eriksson and Södersten, 1973) although this has been refuted (Zemlan et al., 1973).

In the experiments reported here, the effects on sexual receptivity of drugs specifically affecting dopamine (DA), norepinephrine (NE), and 5-HT transmission have been investigated in both ovariectomized and adrenalectomized animals.

Although a number of studies have implied that amine metabolism or neuronal uptake mechanisms are affected by sex hormones (see Wurtman, 1971; Nixon, Janowsky, and Davis, 1974; Wirz-Justice, Hackmann, and Lichsteiner, 1974), the use of *in vitro* systems or large doses of steroids or both makes such data difficult to relate to *in vivo* effects of hormones on sexual behavior and monoaminergic neurotransmission. Thus, we have investigated the effects of *in vivo* treatments

---

* Present address: Department of Anatomy, Cambridge University, Cambridge CB2 3D4, England.

with estrogen and progesterone in doses commonly used to activate sexual receptivity on levels, turnover, and uptake of NE and 5-HT in an attempt to make the biochemical, behavioral, and pharmacologic data more comparable.

MATERIALS AND METHODS

Animals

Ovariectomized or ovariectomized/adrenalectomized Sprague-Dawley rats (250 to 300 g) were used and housed under reversed lighting (12 hr dark).

Treatments

Three categories of drugs were given to estrogen-treated ovariectomized (Part 1); ovariectomized/adrenalectomized (Part 2); or estrogen/progesterone-treated ovariectomized (Part 3) rats. These were (a) synthesis inhibitors, (b) drugs acting mainly on CA neurons, and (c) drugs acting mainly on 5-HT neurons. Full details of treatments are described under Results.

Behavioral Observations

Observations began 4 hr into the dark phase and were made by placing each female with two cage-adapted, sexually experienced males for a 5-min period. A number of components of the female's behavior were recorded, e.g., lordosis duration (in seconds), lordosis intensity, and acceptance of the male's mounting attempts, but only the proportions of mounts by the male eliciting a lordosis response by the female (L/M, or lordosis quotient LQ) is referred to here unless otherwise indicated. For fuller details see Everitt, Fuxe, Hökfelt, and Jonsson (1975). Treatment and frequency of testing for controls and experimental animals were identical except that, instead of drugs, the controls received saline injections. Statistical comparisons were made between each experimental group and its respective control group, but data from all control groups have been combined to ease presentation of the results.

Turnover of 5-HT and NE

Amine turnover was determined biochemically by studying the decline of monoamine stores after treatment with the synthesis inhibitors α-methyl-p-tyrosine (H 44/68 or AMPT, tyrosine hydroxylase) and α-propyldopacetamide (H 22/54, tryptophan hydroxylase) (for full details, see Andén, Corrodi, and Fuxe, 1969). In addition, 5-HT turnover was estimated by measuring 5-hydroxyindoleacetic acid (5-HIAA) levels in whole brain (see Korf and Volkenburgh-Sikkema, 1969; Jonsson and Lewander, 1970). Hormone treatments of ovariectomized rats were (a) estradiol monobenzoate (5 μg/rat) 48 and 24 hr before killing, either alone or (b) in combination with progesterone (500 μg/rat) 5 hr before killing.

Controls were injected with oil vehicle at the same times. H 22/54 (500 mg/kg) was injected 3 hr and H 44/68 (250 mg/kg) 4 hr before killing.

Uptake of 5-HT and NE *in vitro* after hormone treatment *in vivo*

Estrogen, progesterone, or arachis oil was given according to the above schedule. *In vitro* uptake of ^{3}H-5-HT and ^{3}H-NE was determined in cerebral cortex (slices) and anterior hypothalamus (synaptosomes). For procedural details see Results as well as Sachs and Jonsson (1972) and Lidbrink, Jonsson, and Fuxe (1971).

RESULTS

Behavioral Experiments

Part 1. Effects of Drugs on the Sexual Receptivity of Ovariectomized, Estrogen-Treated Rats

Synthesis inhibitors: AMPT (tyrosine hydroxylase inhibitor; Corrodi and Hanson, 1966) caused a significant increase in lordosis quotient (LQ) when given 2 to 4 hr before observation. Parachlorophenylalanine (PCPA, tryptophan hydroxylase inhibitor; Koe and Weissman, 1966) had a similar but slightly greater effect after the same time interval, which was still evident 26 to 28 and 50 to 52 hr later (Fig. 1). H 22/54 (tryptophan hydroxylase inhibitor; Carlsson, Corrodi, and Waldeck, 1963) caused a smaller, but significant increase in LQ (Fig. 1).

Drugs acting on CA neurons: Pimozide (a DA receptor blocker, Andén, Butcher, Corrodi, Fuxe, and Ungerstedt, 1970) caused a significant increase in LQ, which was enhanced by the addition of (+)-amphetamine (CA-releasing agent; Carlsson, Fuxe, Hamberger, and Lindqvist, 1966). Spiroperidol (DA receptor blocker; Andén et al., 1970) in combination with (+)-amphetamine produced similar results (Fig. 1). Furthermore, these three treatments resulted in significant increases in the mean duration of lordotic responses (see Everitt et al., 1975). Conversely, the DA and NE receptor-blocker chlorpromazine (Andén et al., 1970) in combination with (+)-amphetamine was without effect on the lordotic response (Fig. 1).

Thirty minutes after injection, the α-adrenergic blockers yohimbine and piperoxane (Schmitt, Schmitt, and Fenard, 1971; Bolme, Corrodi, Fuxe, Goldstein, Hökfelt, and Lidbrink, 1974) caused increases in LQ that had disappeared 1 hr after injection. In general, piperoxane was more effective than yohimbine (Fig. 1).

Drugs acting on 5-HT neurons: Cinanserin hydrochloride (a drug with 5-HT receptor-blocking properties; Dombro and Wooley, 1964) was without effect on sexual receptivity (not shown in Fig. 1), reflecting its poor 5-HT receptor-blocking properties after systemic administration (Fuxe, *unpublished*).

d-Lysergic acid diethylamide (LSD) has been reported to block release of

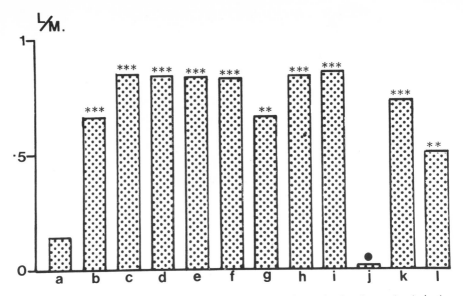

FIG. 1. The effects of drugs on the lordosis quotient of ovariectomized, estrogen-treated rats. All females received 2.0 μg/kg/day estradiol monobenzoate. Key to drug treatments: (a) Controls [saline-treated at time interval(s) appropriate to drug treatment(s)] combined for all groups, ($n = 60$); (b) AMPT, 100 mg/kg i.p. 2–4 hr before observation ($n = 10$); (c–e) PCPA methyl ester HCl, 150 mg/kg i.p. 2–4, 26–28, and 50–52 hr before observation ($n = 20$); (f) H 22/54, 500 mg/kg i.p. in two doses 2–4 hr before observation ($n = 20$); (g) pimozide 1 mg/kg i.p. 2–3 hr before observation ($n = 10$); (h) pimozide as (g) (+) d-amphetamine sulfate 3 mg/kg base i.p. 30 min before observation ($n = 10$); (i) spiroperidol 0.25 mg/kg i.p. 2–3 hr before observation + d-amphetamine, as (h) ($n = 10$); (j) chlorpromazine 5 mg/kg i.p. 90 min + d-amphetamine 30 min before observation ($n = 10$); (k) piperoxane 5 mg/kg i.p. 30 min before observation ($n = 10$); (l) yohimbine 1 mg/kg i.p. 30 min before observation ($n = 10$); L/M = lordosis quotient. Values shown are medians. ***, $p < 0.001$; **, $p < 0.01$; *, $p < 0.05$; filled circle, $p =$ ns; nd, no data. Mann-Whitney U test between each drug treatment and its saline-treated controls.

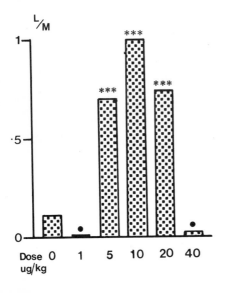

FIG. 2. The effects of d-LSD on the lordosis quotient of ovariectomized, estrogen-treated rats. All females received 2.0 μg/kg/day estradiol benzoate. All injections given 12 min before observation. In each group $n = 10$ except for 0 and 10 μg/kg where $n = 20$. Other abbreviations as in Fig. 1.

5-HT, perhaps as a result of inhibited impulse flow, if given in low dosage (Chase, Breese, and Kopin, 1967; Aghajanian, Foote, and Sheard, 1968; Aghajanian and Wells, 1968). The behavioral effects of this drug in 1, 5, 10, 20, and 40 μg/kg dosages are summarized in Fig. 2. There was no detectable effect with 1 μg/kg whereas 5 μg/kg caused a clear increase in LQ. However, 10 μg/kg, was optimal in this respect: LQ was maximal and 70% of these animals displayed the hopping and darting movements characteristic of females in estrus. There were progressively lesser effects with 20 and 40 μg/kg, with the latter even inhibiting receptivity in these estrogen-treated females (Fig. 2).

Part 2. Effects of Drugs on the Sexual Receptivity of Ovariectomized/ Adrenalectomized Estrogen-Treated Rats

It may be seen from Table 1 that adrenalectomy did not prevent the effects of AMPT, PCPA, or pimozide. There was, however, a significant and consistent

TABLE 1. Effects of pimozide, AMPT, or PCPA on components of sexual behavior in ovariectomized and ovariectomized/adrenalectomized estrogen-treated female rats

Treatment		L/M	LI	LD	AR
Pimozide	C	0.66 ± 0.05	1.94 ± 0.05	2.00 ± 0.33	0.95 ± 0.05
	CA	0.81 ± 0.05[a,c]	1.73 ± 0.18[a,c]	1.84 ± 0.25[a,c]	1.00 ± 0.02[b,c]
AMPT	C	0.68 ± 0.05	2.00 ± 0.06	1.22 ± 0.28	0.76 ± 0.09
	CA	0.74 ± 0.12[b,c]	1.50 ± 0.22[a,c]	1.00 ± 0.26[b,c]	0.90 ± 0.03[b,d]
PCPA	C	0.85 ± 0.07	1.97 ± 0.15	0.97 ± 0.09	0.83 ± 0.97
(2–4 hr)	CA	0.72 ± 0.05[a,c]	1.53 ± 0.13[a,c]	0.91 ± 0.21[b,c]	1.00 ± 0.33[a,c]
PCPA	C	0.83 ± 0.12	2.27 ± 0.20	1.23 ± 0.24	0.73 ± 0.05
(26–28 hr)	CA	0.87 ± 0.07[b,c]	1.80 ± 0.15[a,c]	1.06 ± 0.31[b,c]	0.86 ± 0.03[b,d]
Controls	C	0.14 ± 0.05	1.39 ± 0.13	0.48 ± 0.29	0.72 ± 0.07
	CA	0.29 ± 0.07[b]	1.10 ± 0.25[a]	0.47 ± 0.33[b]	0.84 ± 0.13[b]

Females received 2.0 μg/kg/day estradiol. Details of drug treatments in Results section (Fig. 1). L/M = lordosis quotient; LI = lordosis intensity; LD = lordosis duration; AR = acceptance ratio. C = ovariectomized; CA = ovariectomized/adrenalectomized. Values are medians ± semi-quartile deviation.

[a] $p < 0.05$, C versus CA for each drug treatment.
[b] p = ns, C versus CA for each drug treatment.
[c] $p < 0.05$, drug CA versus control CA.
[d] p = ns, drug CA versus control CA.

decrease in lordosis intensity (rated on a three-point scale; see Hardy and DeBold, 1971) in adrenalectomized females during each of the three treatments when compared with drug-treated castrates.

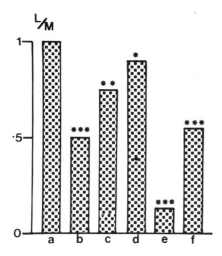

FIG. 3. The effects of drugs on the receptivity induced by estrogen/progesterone treatment of ovariectomized rats. All females received 2.0 µg/kg/day estradiol monobenzoate plus 500 µg progesterone 4 to 6 hr before testing. In addition drug treatments were as follows: (a) controls [saline-treated at time interval(s) appropriate to drug treatment(s)] combined for all groups ($n = 25$); (b) ET 495, 25 mg/kg s.c. 3½ hr after progesterone ($n = 10$); (c) fenfluramine, 5 mg/kg s.c. 3¼ hr after progesterone ($n = 10$); (d) FLA 63, 25 mg/kg s.c. given at same time as progesterone ($n = 10$); (e) ET 495 + fenfluramine — 3¼ hr after progesterone ($n = 10$); (f) ET 495 + FLA 63 as in (b) and (d) ($n = 10$). Other abbreviations as in Fig. 1.

Part 3. *Effects of Drugs on the Behavior of Ovariectomized Rats Made Receptive by Estrogen and Progesterone*

The DA receptor-stimulating agent ET 495 (Corrodi, Farnebo, Fuxe, Hamberger, and Ungerstedt, 1972) caused a significant decrease in LQ (Fig. 3). Fenfluramine, a 5-HT releasing agent (Duhault and Verdavainne, 1967; Clineschmidt, 1973), had a similar but less marked effect, whereas the DA-β-hydroxylase inhibitor FLA 63 (Svensson and Waldeck, 1969) had an even smaller, but still significant effect (Fig. 3).

The combination of ET 495 with fenfluramine caused a total inhibition of estrogen/progesterone-induced receptivity, but no such additive effects of ET 495 in combination with FLA 63 could be detected (Fig. 3).

Effects of Estrogen and Progesterone on Levels and Turnover of NE and 5-HT

Figure 4 demonstrates that levels of NE were largely unaffected by estrogen and progesterone. However, estrogen alone or in combination with progesterone significantly reduced NE turnover in brainstem (Fig. 4A). Estrogen had a similar effect on cortical NE turnover, but progesterone reversed this effect, i.e., accelerated turnover (Fig. 4B).

Alternatively, estrogen slightly elevated (7%) 5-HT levels whereas the addition of progesterone significantly reduced 5-HT levels (20%) to below oil-treated castrate levels. The data on 5-HT turnover are complicated by at least two factors—(1) the time in the day/night cycle when animals are treated with hormones and (2) the time after injection (of progesterone at least) when 5-HT or 5-HIAA levels are measured. Thus, estrogen will accelerate and progesterone

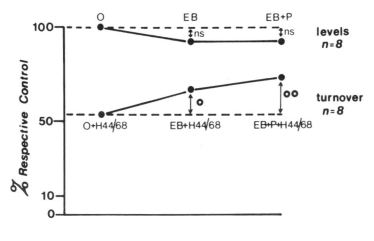

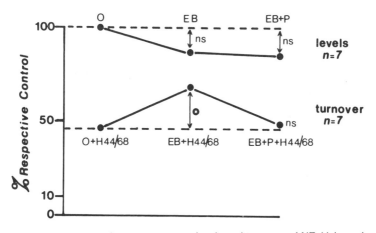

FIG. 4. Effects of estrogen and progesterone on levels and turnover of NE. Values shown are mean percentages of oil-treatment levels (levels) and of respective oil- or hormone-treatment levels (turnover). Statistical comparisons were made by a slippage test (Conover, 1971) between the three treatment conditions for both levels and turnover. O = oil vehicle; EB = estradiol benzoate; P = progesterone; H 44/68 = α-methyl-p-tyrosine, 250 mg/kg i.p. ns = not significant; encircled star ⊛ = $p < 0.05$; ⊛⊛ = $p < 0.01$.

will retard 5-HT turnover after injections at the start of the dark period whereas the opposite may occur if these hormones are given at the start of the light period. Furthermore, progesterone will retard 5-HT turnover 3 or 7 hr after injection, but will accelerate it after 5 hr. Considerably more data are necessary before the ways in which estrogen and progesterone affect 5-HT turnover become clearer.

THE EFFECTS OF ESTROGEN AND PROGESTERONE *IN VIVO* ON THE UPTAKE OF ³N-NE AND ³H-5-HT BY HYPOTHALAMUS AND CORTEX CEREBRI *IN VITRO*

Table 2 shows that uptake of ³H-5-HT was little affected by estrogen or estrogen/progesterone in either hypothalamus or cerebral cortex. Alternatively, estrogen caused a slight decrease in ³H-NE uptake in both hypothalamus and cortex, which was enhanced by the addition of progesterone, particularly in hypothalamus, where it was reduced to only 57% of the oil-treated control level.

DISCUSSION

The results of these experiments suggest that, in addition to 5-HT, DA, NE, and perhaps epinephrine (E) may have separable roles in the control by hormones of sexual receptivity.

The original suggestion that 5-HT subserves an inhibitory role (Meyerson, 1964*a*) receives varied support here. At the longer time intervals PCPA causes a large decrease in 5-HT levels (Koe et al., 1966) whereas the initially low CA levels have recovered (Ahlenius et al., 1972), indicating that the behavioral effects are mainly due to 5-HT depletion (cf. Ahlenius et al., 1972). The partial inhibition of estrogen/progesterone-induced receptivity by fenfluramine further supports Meyerson's hypothesis of 5-HT involvement, although the lack of effect of systemically injected cinanserin reported here may be overcome by placing this drug directly within 5-HT terminal-rich areas of the CNS (Zemlan et al., 1973; Ward, Crowley, and Zemlan, 1974). Although clearly implicating 5-HT-containing neurons, the effect of LSD on lordosis behavior raises the problem of its mechanism of action. In high doses it has 5-HT receptor-stimulating properties (Andén, Corrodi, Fuxe, and Hökfelt, 1968) and will inhibit sexual receptivity (Eliasson, Michanek, and Meyerson, 1972), but in low doses this drug will inhibit activity in 5-HT-containing raphe neurons (Aghajanian et al., 1968*a,b*) and it is by such a mechanism and/or by inhibiting release of 5-HT that we suggest LSD was acting in these experiments to facilitate lordosis.

The involvement of CA in the effects of drugs on receptivity, suggested by Ahlenius et al. (1972), is confirmed here by the effects of AMPT. However, a more precise interpretation now seems possible. The experiments with DA receptor blockers (pimozide and spiroperidol) and stimulators (ET 495) suggest that DA neurons play an inhibitory role in sexual behavior. Indeed, the additive effects of ET 495 and fenfluramine, causing a total inhibition of receptivity, represent strong evidence that both DA and 5-HT are inhibitory in this respect. In contrast, NE may be excitatory, since FLA 63 slightly inhibited estrogen/progesterone-activated receptivity whereas amphetamine facilitated the effects of pimozide (by enhancing NE transmission concomitant with pimozide-induced DA receptor blockade; Everitt et al., 1974). The failure of chlorpromazine to enhance receptivity, although consistent with a facilitatory role of NE, is not convincing evi-

TABLE 2. Effect of estrogen and combined estrogen–progesterone on uptake of ^{3}H-NE and ^{3}H-5-HT in hypothalamus and cerebral cortex of castrate female rats

Treatment	Hypothalamus uptake[a]				Cerebral cortex uptake[b]			
	^{3}H-NE		^{3}H-5-HT		^{3}H-NE		^{3}H-5-HT	
	cpm/mg	%	cpm/mg	%	cpm/slice	%	cpm/slice	%
Oil	31,885 ± 4,346	100	51,657 ± 11,495	100	5,540 ± 561	100	8,923 ± 982	100
Estrogen (5.0 µg × 2)	24,104 ± 2,154	76	46,598 ± 1,300	90	4,875 ± 193	88	9,517 ± 949	107
Estrogen (5.0 µg × 2) + progesterone (500 µg)	18,182 ± 2,731	57	56,758 ± 6,156	110	4,205 ± 326	76	7,500 ± 1,199	84

[a] Steroidal treatment was performed as in the text. Uptake was studied in synaptosomal fractions obtained by homogenizing hypothalamus (~50 mg) in 1.5 ml of 0.25 M sucrose and taking the supernatant after centrifuging at 3,000 rpm for 10 min. One hundred µl of NEPs was preincubated with 1.9 ml Krebs-Ringer solution for 5 min after which ^{3}H-NE (0.05 µM) or ^{3}H-5-HT (0.05 µM) was added. Incubation was continued for 5 min. After centrifuging and extraction in ethanol, toluene scintillation fluid was added and total radioactivity determined. Each homogenate was run in triplicate at 37°C, and two additional incubations were made at 0°C. An aliquot of each homogenate was taken for protein determination according to Lowry, Rosebrough, Farr, and Randall, 1951. The results are expressed as cpm/mg protein. Means ± SEM are given.

[b] After preincubation for 5 min in buffer, ^{3}H-NE (0.05 µM) and ^{3}H-5-HT (0.05 µM) were added and the incubation continued for 10 min. After rapid rinsing in fresh buffer the slices were dissolved and total radioactivity determined. Nonspecific uptake was determined by incubation at 0°C. The results are expressed as cpm/slice. Mean ± SEM. Statistical significance according to Student's t-test.

dence; Meyerson (1966) has reported that this drug has very different effects from reserpine and tetrabenazine, although all three depress CA transmission.

The surprising increase in receptivity following piperoxane and yohimbine (α-adrenergic blockers) seems inconsistent with a facilitatory role of NE. However, in the low doses used, it has been argued (Bolme et al., 1974) that these drugs preferentially block E receptors (hypothetically those on the NE cell bodies of the locus coeruleus; Hökfelt, Fuxe, Goldstein, and Johansson, 1973, 1974), while simultaneously enhancing cortical NE turnover (Bolme et al., 1974; Fuxe, Lidbrink, Hökfelt, Bolme, and Goldstein, 1974). The suggested involvement of the cerebral cortex in the behavioral effects of progesterone (Ross and Gorski, 1973; Ross, Gorski, and Sawyer, 1973) and the present finding that this hormone elevates cortical NE turnover make the effects of piperoxane and yohimbine even more interesting. Furthermore, β-adrenergic blockers also increase the lordotic response when implanted within the hypothalamus (Ward et al., 1974), which, in view of the stronger affinity of E for β-receptors (Furchgott, 1967), is additional evidence for the involvement of E. These findings taken together with the demonstration of E-containing neurons in the brainstem and hypothalamus (Hökfelt et al., 1973, 1974) suggest that E pathways may also participate in the regulation of sexual receptivity.

Failure of adrenalectomy to inhibit the effects of AMPT, PCPA, or pimozide argues against pituitary–adrenal involvement in their effects. In addition, the facts that LSD increases receptivity within 15 min, that intracerebral methysergide and cinanserin increase the lordotic response within 30 min (Ward et al., 1974), and that increased levels of 5-HT suppress hormone-induced receptivity (Meyerson, 1964a; and the present experiments) all suggest a direct effect of these drugs on the CNS (Ward et al., 1974). Furthermore, the continuing effects of PCPA 50 hr after injection seem inconsistent with adrenal progesterone involvement because behavioral refractoriness to progesterone can develop (Nadler, 1970; Barfield and Lisk, 1974); however, this may not be the case at shorter time intervals. It may also be suggested that the way in which receptivity is tested (e.g., by manual stimulation, Paris et al., 1971) could be a critical factor in the different results obtained by various workers (see also Whalen, *this volume*).

The results of the biochemical experiments reported here demonstrate the clear effects of sex hormones on uptake and turnover of 5-HT and NE. The observation that progesterone has different effects on cortical and subcortical NE turnover may indicate different roles of the NE input to these areas in the control of estrous behavior. The increase in cortical NE turnover in conjunction with the blockade of ^{3}H-NE uptake in hypothalamus (which is consistent with the reduced NE turnover here) observed during estrogen/progesterone treatment at a time when the animals could be expected to be receptive may be interpreted as support of an excitatory role of NE as discussed above. The effects of hormones on 5-HT turnover are more difficult to interpret because of the complicating factors mentioned under Results. However, the arrest of 5-HT turnover induced by progesterone in estrogen-treated rats when both hormones are given in the same schedule and at the same times of day as to induce sexual receptivity is clearly consistent with the suggested inhibitory role of 5-HT. Nevertheless, the significant differences in effects of these hormones in relationship to their times of injection and, indeed, their dosage (Everitt and Fuxe, *unpublished observations*) emphasize the need for careful standardization of the experimental conditions, particularly regarding the behavioral time course of action of the hormones. A knowledge of the mechanism of action of hormones on monoamine neurons is also essential to explain their effects on turnover of both NE and 5-HT.

In conclusion, the experiments reported in this chapter suggest that 5-HT, DA, NE, and E may have specific and separable roles in the control of sexual receptivity by estrogen and progesterone. 5-HT, DA, and E, on the basis of pharmacologic manipulations, appear to have inhibitory roles as their removal facilitates lordosis in estrogen-treated females whereas increasing DA and 5-HT activity inhibits hormone-induced receptivity. Alternatively, NE may have an excitatory role, although the evidence for this is limited by the difficulties in altering NE transmission alone in the CNS. Alterations in 5-HT and NE turnover and uptake induced by estrogen and progesterone may be interpreted as being consistent with their suggested roles in sexual behavior. However, it will remain difficult to correlate the effects of hormones on amine metabolism with the effects of drugs on behavior until the ways in which hormones modulate neuronal mechanisms are understood.

ACKNOWLEDGMENTS

B.J.E. was in receipt of a British MRC Travelling Research Fellowship. We gratefully acknowledge for financial support the Swedish Medical Research Council (Grants 04X–715; 04X–2887); the Population Council (Grant No. M73.73); Nelson Research and Development Co., and Magn, Bergvalls Stiftelse. We would also like to thank Dr. Ingeborg Ward for communicating her unpublished results to us; Professor L. Agnati for advice on statistical methods; Karin Andreasson, Ulla-Britt Finnman, Beth Hagman, and Barbro Persson for excellent technical assistance, and Birgitta Norbäck for her help in preparing this manuscript.

REFERENCES

Aghajanian, G. K., Foote, W. E., and Sheard, M. H. (1968): Lysergic acid diethylamide: Sensitive neuronal units in the midbrain raphe. *Science,* 161:706–708.

Aghajanian, G. K., and Wells, B. L. (1968): Block by LSD of the increase in brain serotonin turnover induced by elevated ambient temperature. *Nature,* 220:795–796.

Ahlenius, S., Engel, J., Eriksson, H., Modigh, K., and Södersten, P. (1972): Importance of central catecholamines in the mediation of lordosis behaviour in ovariectomized rats treated with estrogen and inhibitors of monoamine synthesis. *J. Neural. Transm.,* 33:247–255.

Andén, N.-E., Butcher, S. G., Corrodi, H., Fuxe, K., and Ungerstedt, U. (1970): Receptor activity and turnover of dopamine and noradrenaline after neuroleptics. *Eur. J. Pharmacol.,* 11:303–314.

Andén, N.-E., Corrodi, H., and Fuxe, K. (1969): Turnover studies using synthesis inhibition. In: *Metabolism of Amines in the Brain,* edited by G. Hooper. MacMillan, London.

Andén, N.-E., Corrodi, H., Fuxe, K., and Hökfelt, T. (1968): Evidence for a central 5-hydroxytrypta-mine receptor stimulation lysergic acid diethylamide. *Br. J. Pharmacol.,* 34:1–7.

Ashton Barfield, M. and Lisk, R. D. (1974): Relative contributions of ovarian and adrenal progester-one to the timing of heat in the 4-day cyclic rat. *Endocrinology,* 94:571–575.

Bolme, P., Corrodi, H., Fuxe, K., Goldstein, M., Hökfelt, T., and Lidbrink, P. (1974): Possible involvement of central adrenaline neurons in vasomotor and respiratory control. Studies on cloni-dine and its interaction with piperoxane and yohimbine. *Eur. J. Pharmacol.* 28:89–94.

Carlsson, A., Corrodi, H., and Waldeck, B. (1963): α-Substituirte Dopacetamide als Hemmer der Catechol-0-methyl-transferase und der enzymatischen Hydroxylierung aromatischer Amino-säuren. In den Catecholamin-metabolismus eingreifende Substanzen 2. *Helv. Chim. Acta,* 46: 2271–2285.

Carlsson, A., Fuxe, K., Hamberger, B., and Lindqvist, M. (1966): Biochemical and histochemical studies on the effects of imipramine-like drugs and (+)-amphetamine on central and peripheral catecholamine neurons. *Acta Physiol. Scand.,* 67:481–497.

Chase, T. N., Breese, G. R., and Kopin, I. J. (1967): Serotonin release from brain slices by electrical stimulation: Regional differences and effects of LSD. *Science,* 157:1461–1463.

Clinschmidt, B. V. (1973): 5,6-Dihydroxytryptamine: Suppression of the anorexigenic action of fenfluramine. *Eur. J. Pharmacol.,* 24:405–409.

Conover, W. J. (1971): *Practical Non-parametric Statistics.* Wiley, New York.

Corrodi, H., Farnebo, L.-O., Fuxe, K., Hamberger, B., and Ungerstedt, U. (1972): ET 495 and brain catecholamine mechanisms: Evidence for stimulation of dopamine receptors. *Eur. J. Pharmacol.,* 20:195–204.

Davidson, J. M. (1972): Hormones and reproductive behaviour. In: *Reproductive Biology,* edited by H. Balin and S. Glasser. Excerpta Medica, Amsterdam.

Davidson, J. M., and Levine, S. (1972): Endocrine regulation of behaviour. *Annu. Rev. Physiol.,* 34:375–408.

Dombro, R. S., and Wooley, D. W. (1964): Cinnamamides as structural analogs and antagonists of serotonin. *Biochem. Pharmacol.,* 13:569–576.

Duhault, J., and Verdavainne, C. (1967): Modification du taux de sérotonine cérébrale chez le rat par les trifluorométhyl-phényl-2-éthyl aminopropane (fenfluoramine 768 S). *Arch. Int. Phar-macodyn. Ther.,* 170:276–286.

Eliasson, M., Michanek, A., and Meyerson, B. J. (1972): A differential inhibitory action of LSD and amphetamine on copulatory behaviour in the female rat. *Acta Pharmacol. Toxicol. (Kbh),* 31, Suppl. 1:22.

Eriksson, H., and Södersten, P. (1973): A failure to facilitate lordosis behaviour in adrenalectomized and gonadectomized estrogen-primed rats with monoamine synthesis inhibitors. *Horm. Behav.,* 4:89–97.

Everitt, B. J., Fuxe, K., Hökfelt, T., and Jonsson, J. (1975): Pharmacological and biochemical studies on the role of monoamines in the control by hormones of sexual receptivity in the female rat. *J. Comp. Physiol. (in press).*

Furchgott, R. F. (1967): The pharmacological differentiation of adrenergic receptors. *Ann. N. Y. Acad. Sci.,* 134:553–567.

Fuxe, K., Lidbrink, P., Hökfelt, T., Bolme, P., and Goldstein, M. (1974): Effects of piperoxane on sleep and waking in the rat. Evidence for increased waking by blocking inhibitory adrenaline receptors on the locus coeruleus. *Acta Physiol. Scand.* 91:566–567.

Hardy, D. F., and DeBold, J. F. (1971): Effects of mounts without intromission upon the behaviour of female rats during the onset of estrogen-induced heat. *Physiol. Behav.,* 7:643–645.

Hökfelt, T., Fuxe, K., Goldstein, M., and Johansson, O. (1973): Evidence for adrenaline neurons in the rat brain. *Acta Physiol. Scand.,* 89:286–288.

Hökfelt, T., Fuxe, K., Goldstein, M., and Johansson, O. (1974): Immunohistochemical evidence for the existence of adrenaline neurons in the rat brain. *Brain Res.,* 66:235–251.

Hoyland, V. J., Shillito, E. E., and Vogt, M. (1970): The effect of parachlorophenylalanine (PCPA) on the behaviour of cats. *Br. J. Pharmacol.,* 40:659–667.

Jonsson, J., and Lewander, T. (1970): A method for the simultaneous determination of 5-hydroxy-3-indole acetic acid (5-HIAA) and 5-hydroxytryptamine (5-HT) in brain tissue and cerebrospinal fluid. *Acta Physiol. Scand.,* 78:43–51.

Koe, B. K., and Weissman, A. (1966): *p*-Chlorophenylalanine: A specific depletor of brain serotonin. *J. Pharmacol. Exp. Ther.,* 154:499–516.

Korf, J., and Volkenburgh-Sikkema, T. (1969): Fluorimetric determination of 5-hydroxyindoleacetic acid in human urine and cerebrospinal fluid. *Clin. Chim. Acta,* 26:301–306.

Lidbrink, P., Jonsson, G., and Fuxe, K. (1971): The effect of imipramine-like drugs and antihistamine drugs on 5-hydroxytryptamine neurons. *Neuropharmacology,* 10:521–536.

Lowry, O. H., Rosebrough, N. J., Farr, A. L., and Randall, R. J. (1951): Protein measurement with the folin phenol reagent. *J. Biol. Chem.,* 193:265–275.

Meyerson, B. J. (1964*a*): Central nervous monoamines and hormone induced estrous behaviour in the spayed rat. *Acta Physiol. Scand. Suppl.,* 63, 241:1–32.

Meyerson, B. J. (1964*b*): The effect of neuropharmacological agents on hormone activated estrous behaviour in ovariectomised rats. *Arch. Int. Pharmacodyn. Ther.,* 150:4–33.

Meyerson, B. J. (1964*c*): Estrous behaviour in spayed rats after estrogen or progesterone treatment in combination with reserpine or tetrabenazine. *Psychopharmacologia,* 6:210–218.

Meyerson, B. J. (1966): Oestrous behaviour in oestrogen treated ovariectomized rats after chlorpromazine alone or in combination with progesterone, tetrabenazine or reserpine. *Acta Pharmacol. Toxicol. (Kbh),* 24:363–376.

Meyerson, B. J., and Lewander, T. (1970): Serotonin synthesis inhibition and oestrous behaviour in female rats. *Life Sci. (I),* 9:661–671.

Nadler, R. D. (1970): A biphasic influence of progesterone on sexual receptivity of spayed female rats. *Physiol. Behav.,* 5:95–97.

Nixon, R. L., Janowsky, D. S., and Davis, J. M. (1974): Effects of progesterone, β-estradiol, and testosterone on the uptake and metabolism of ^{3}H-norepinephrine, ^{3}H-dopamine and ^{3}H-serotonin in rat brain synaptosomes. *Res. Commun. Chem. Pathol. Pharmacol.,* 7:233–236.

Paris, C. A., Resko, J. A., and Goy, R. W. (1971): A possible mechanism for the induction of lordosis by reserpine in spayed rats. *Biol. Reprod.,* 4:23–30.

Ross, J. W., and Gorski, R. A. (1973): Effects of potassium chloride on sexual behavior and the cortical EEG in the ovariectomized rat. *Physiol. Behav.,* 10:643–646.

Ross, J. W., Gorski, R. A., and Sawyer, C. H. (1973): Effects of cortical stimulation on estrous behaviour in estrogen-primed ovariectomized rats. *Endocrinology,* 93:20–25.

Sachs, C., and Jonsson, G. (1972): Degeneration of central noradrenaline neurons after 6-hydroxydopamine in newborn animals. *Res. Commun. Chem. Pathol. Pharmacol.,* 4:203–220.

Schmitt, H., Schmitt, H., and Fenard, S. (1971): Evidence for an α-sympathomimetic component in the effects of catapresan on vasomotor centres: Antagonism by piperoxane. *Eur. J. Pharmacol.,* 14:98–100.

Svensson, T. H., and Waldeck, B. (1969): On the significance of central noradrenaline for motor activity: Experiments with a new dopamine-β-hydroxylase inhibitor. *Eur. J. Pharmacol.,* 7:278–282.

Ward, I. L., Crowley, W. R., and Zemlan, F. P. (1975): Monoaminergic mediation of female sexual behaviour. *J. Comp. physiol. Psychol. (in press).*

Wirz-Justice, A., Hackmann, E., and Lichsteiner, M. (1974): The effect of estradiol diproprionate and progesterone on monoamine uptake in rat brain. *J. Neurochem.,* 22:187–189.

Wurtman, R. J. (1971): Brain monoamines and endocrine function. *Neurosciences Res. Program Bull.,* 9:251–257.

Young, W. C. (1961): The hormones and mating behaviour. In: *Sex and Internal Secretions,* edited by W. C. Young. Bailliere, London.

Zemlan, F. P., Ward, I. L., Crowley, W. R., and Margules, D. L. (1973): Activation of lordotic responding in female rats by suppression of serotoninergic activity. *Science,* 179:1010–1011.

Sexual Behavior: Pharmacology and Biochemistry, edited by M. Sandler and G. L. Gessa. Raven Press, New York © 1975.

Cholinergic Mechanisms and Sexual Behavior in the Female Rat

Leif H. Lindström

Department of Medical Pharmacology, University of Uppsala, Uppsala, Sweden

It is well established that copulatory behavior in the female rat is dependent on ovarian hormones. Although high doses of estrogen can restore the behavior in ovariectomized rats (Davidson, Smith, Rodgers, and Bloch, 1968), estrogen followed after a certain time interval by progesterone is more effective (Boling and Blandau, 1939). An antagonistic relationship between increased central nervous (CN) monoamine level and this hormone-activated response was demonstrated by Meyerson (Meyerson, 1964 *a,b;* Meyerson, Eliasson, Lindström, Michanek, and Söderlund, 1973).

Cholinergic drugs with muscarinic effects were also shown to decrease the estrogen + progesterone-activated lordosis response (Lindström and Meyerson, 1967). In this chapter, the effect of muscarinic compounds and the relationship between cholinergic and monoaminergic mechanisms with regard to lordotic behavior are reviewed and data are given on the effect of pilocarpine on sexual preference.

BEHAVIOR TECHNIQUES USED

Lordotic Behavior

Lordosis response was activated in ovariectomized Sprague-Dawley rats by estradiol benzoate (10 μg/kg) followed by progesterone (0.4 mg/rat) 48 hr later. The cholinergic or anticholinergic drugs were given either 4 to 5 hr after progesterone treatment, i.e., when lordotic behavior was fully developed, or instead of progesterone, 48 hr after estrogen treatment. When tested for lordotic behavior, the female was brought to a cage with a sexually vigorous male. Lordotic behavior was considered present if the female displayed a clear-cut lordosis response in two out of six or less mounts by the male.

Sexual Preference

The runway-choice technique used to study sexual preference recently has been described in detail [see Meyerson and Lindström, 1973; see also Meyerson *(this volume)*].

In the present study, a sexually vigorous male and an estrous female were the incentive animals. The experimental subjects were subjected to 20 consecutive trials during each test session. Estradiol benzoate was given at day 1. The results are presented as the percentage choice of the male versus the female incentive animal.

CHOLINERGIC AND ANTICHOLINERGIC DRUGS AND LORDOTIC BEHAVIOR

Atropine (1 mg/kg) and methyl atropine (5 mg/kg) had no effect on estradiol benzoate + progesterone-activated lordosis response (see Table 1). In contrast, the muscarinic compounds pilocarpine, oxotremorine, and arecolin inhibited the hormone-activated behavior (see Lindström and Meyerson, 1967). This inhibitory effect was most pronounced 30 min after administration of pilocarpine (25 mg/kg) and within 10 min after administration of oxotremorine (2 mg/kg) and arecolin (10 mg/kg). Atropine pretreatment prevented the cholinergic inhibition more effectively than did methyl atropine. This fact indicated that the inhibitory effect of the cholinergic drugs on lordosis response was of CN origin, as atropine is known to penetrate into the brain more easily than methyl atropine (Herz, Teschemacher, Hofstetter, and Kurz, 1965).

RELATIONSHIP BETWEEN CHOLINERGIC AND MONOAMINERGIC MECHANISMS

A relationship between CN cholinergic and monoaminergic mechanisms with regard to lordotic behavior was demonstrated in subsequent experiments (Lindström, 1970, 1971). The inhibitory effect of pilocarpine on lordosis response was

TABLE 1. *Effect of cholinergic and anticholinergic drugs on estradiol benzoate + progesterone-activated lordosis response in the ovariectomized female rat**

Treatment	Effect on lordosis response 10–30 min after treatment
Atropine	None
Methyl atropine	None
Pilocarpine	Decreased
Oxotremorine	Decreased
Arecoline	Decreased
MAO inhibitor + pilocarpine	Potentiated and prolonged decrease
DMI + pilocarpine	Prolonged decrease
Reserpine + pilocarpine	None
PCPA + pilocarpine	None
α-MT + pilocarpine	Decreased

Alone and after pretreatment with monoamine-oxidase (MAO) inhibitors, desmethylimipramine (DMI), reserpine and the biosynthesis inhibitors p-chlorophenylalanine (PCPA) and α-methyl-p-tyrosine (α-MT).
* For original data, see Lindström and Meyerson (1967) and Lindström (1970,1971).

TABLE 2. *Ability of pilocarpine, oxotremorine, and progesterone to activate lordosis response after pretreatment with estradiol benzoate (EB) (10 µg/kg) in ovariectomized female rats and after subsequent adrenalectomy or hypophysectomy*

Treatment	Lordosis response 4 hr after treatment
EB + pilocarpine	Effectively activated
EB + oxotremorine	Effectively activated
EB + progesterone	Effectively activated
After adrenalectomy	
EB + pilocarpine	None
EB + oxotremorine	None
EB + progesterone	Effectively activated
After hypophysectomy	
EB + pilocarpine	None
EB + progesterone	Effectively activated

For original data, see Lindström (1973).

augmented and prolonged after pretreatment with subeffective doses of the monoamine oxidase (MAO) inhibitors pargyline and nialamide (Table 1). This effect was also seen after pretreatment with the tricyclic antidepressant desmethylimipramine (DMI). The prolonged inhibitory effect was not caused by a decreased rate of metabolism of pilocarpine, as the hypothermia induced was not influenced by pretreatment with pargyline or desmethylimipramine (Lindström, 1970). The data indicate that increased CN cholinergic and monoaminergic activity have a synergistic inhibitory effect on the lordosis response.

In contrast, no inhibitory effect was seen 30 min after pilocarpine or 10 min after oxotremorine when CNS monoamines had been depleted by reserpine or tetrabenazine (see Table 1 and Lindström, 1971). This lack of effect after amine depletion indicated that the inhibition of the lordosis response by pilocarpine and oxotremorine was mediated by monoaminergic mechanisms. To investigate the relative importance of catecholamines and serotonin (5-HT), respectively, selective biosynthesis inhibitors were used. When pilocarpine was given after treatment with parachlorophenylalanine (PCPA), a selective inhibitor of 5-HT synthesis (Koe and Weissman, 1966), no inhibitory effect on the lordosis response was obtained. In contrast, pretreatment with the catecholamine synthesis inhibitor α-methyl-p-tyrosine (α-MT) did not prevent the inhibitory effect of pilocarpine. These results indicate that the inhibition of the estrogen + progesterone-induced lordosis response seen after cholinergic drugs is mediated by serotoninergic mechanisms.

THE ABILITY OF CHOLINERGIC DRUGS TO SUBSTITUTE FOR PROGESTERONE

An activating effect of pilocarpine and oxotremorine on lordotic behavior was also seen (Lindström, 1973). When given 48 hr after estradiol benzoate (10

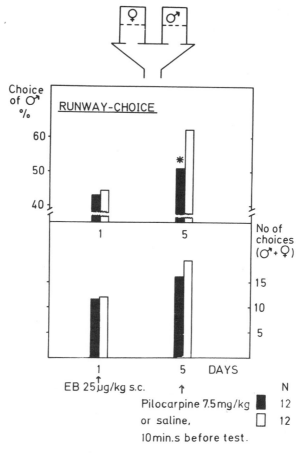

FIG. 1. Effect of pilocarpine (7.5 mg/kg) given 4 days after estradiol benzoate (25 μg/kg s.c.) on the preference for a sexually vigorous male versus an estrous female measured with the runway-choice technique. Methyl atropine (5 mg/kg) was given 30 min before pilocarpine or saline. Tests were performed 10 min after pilocarpine or saline injection. For description of the method used, see Meyerson and Lindström (1973) and Meyerson *(this volume)*.

μg/kg), both pilocarpine and oxotremorine significantly activated the lordosis response even when no progesterone was given (see Table 2). This effect was obtained in doses that were much lower than those that interfere with the overt behavior pattern. The response was not apparent until at least 3 hr after injection. This indicates a different mechanism of action compared to the inhibitory effect which was seen within half an hour and had disappeared 3 hr after the treatment. No activation of lordotic behavior by the cholinergic drugs was seen after adrenalectomy or hypophysectomy (Table 2). Therefore, the ability of pilocarpine and oxotremorine to substitute for progesterone treatment was dependent on intact pituitary–adrenal function. Release of adrenal steroids capable of activating the lordosis response is suggested.

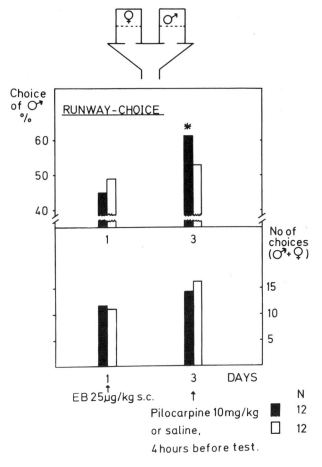

FIG. 2. Effect of pilocarpine (10 mg/kg) given 2 days after estradiol benzoate (25 μg/kg s.c.) on the preference for a sexually vigorous male versus an estrous female measured with the runway-choice technique. Tests were performed 4 hr after pilocarpine or saline injection.

PILOCARPINE AND SEXUAL PREFERENCE

Three techniques employed to study the urge of a female rat to seek contact with a sexually vigorous male were recently described (see Meyerson and Lindström, 1973). One of these, the runway-choice method, measures the preference for a male versus a female in a "run and choose" situation. This technique was used in the present study. A single injection of estradiol benzoate significantly increased the preference for the male incentive. The maximal preference was obtained 4 to 5 days after estrogen treatment (Meyerson and Lindström, 1973).

Pilocarpine (7.5 mg/kg) given 4 days after estradiol benzoate (25 μg/kg), 10 min before test, significantly decreased the preference for the male (Fig. 1). The

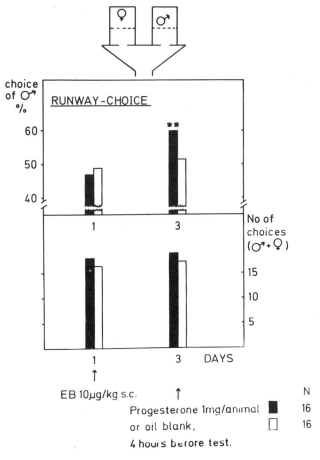

FIG. 3. Effect of progesterone (1 mg per animal) given 2 days after estradiol benzoate (10 μg/kg s.c.) on the preference for a sexually vigorous male versus an estrous female measured with the runway-choice technique. Tests were performed 4 hr after progesterone or saline injection.

total number of trials the subjects entered the goal cages was not significantly affected.

In another experiment, pilocarpine (10 mg/kg) was given 2 days after estradiol benzoate (25 μg/kg). In contrast to the previous experiment, this was before the maximal estrogen response had developed. In this experiment the test for preference was performed 4 hr after pilocarpine treatment, i.e., when muscarinic symptoms had disappeared. A significant increase in preference for the male incentive was now obtained (Fig. 2). An increased preference for the male incentive was also seen when progesterone (1 mg/rat) was given 2 days after estradiol benzoate (10 μg/kg) (Fig. 3).

As seen in the experiments on lordosis response, muscarinic compounds brought about inhibition as well as activation of the behavior pattern. This was also seen in the tests for sexual preference.

CONCLUSIONS

In the female rat, cholinergic compounds have an inhibitory effect on estrogen + progesterone-activated lordotic behavior. This effect is present at a time when muscarinic symptoms are apparent and is probably of CN origin. The inhibitory effect seems to be dependent on intact serotoninergic mechanisms. Cholinergic drugs can also activate the lordosis response when given instead of progesterone after estrogen only. This effect appears after muscarinic symptoms have disappeared; it is dependent on intact pituitary–adrenal function. Data are also presented on the effects of pilocarpine on sexual preference. The effects obtained are analogous to those seen in the experiments on lordotic behavior.

ACKNOWLEDGMENTS

This investigation was supported by grants from the Swedish Medical Research Council, B74-04x-64-10C. For generous supplies of hormones we thank Organon, the Netherlands, through Erco, Sweden.

REFERENCES

Boling, J. L., and Blandau, R. J. (1939): The estrogen-progesterone induction of mating responses in the spayed female rat. *Endocrinology,* 25:359–364.

Davidson, J. M., Smith, E. R., Rodgers, C. H., and Bloch, G. J. (1968): Relative thresholds of behavioral and somatic responses to estrogen. *Physiol. Behav.,* 3:227–229.

Herz, A., Teschemacher, H., Hofstetter, A., and Kurz, H. (1965): The importance of lipid-solubility for the central action of cholinolytic drugs. *Int. J. Neuropharmacol.,* 4:207–218.

Koe, K., and Weissman, A. (1966): *p*-Chlorophenylalanine: A specific depletor of brain serotonin. *J. Pharmacol. Exp. Ther.,* 154:499–516.

Lindström, L. H. (1970): The effect of pilocarpine in combination with monoamine oxidase inhibitors, imipramine or desmethylimipramine on oestrous behaviour in female rats. *Psychopharmacologia,* 17:160–168.

Lindström, L. H. (1971): The effect of pilocarpine and oxotremorine on oestrous behaviour in female rats after treatment with monoamine depletors or monoamine synthesis inhibitors. *Eur. J. Pharmacol.,* 15:60–65.

Lindström, L. H. (1973): Further studies on cholinergic mechanisms and hormone-activated copulatory behaviour in the female rat. *J. Endocrinol.,* 56:275–283.

Lindström, L. H., and Meyerson, B. J. (1967): The effect of pilocarpine, oxotremorine and arecolin in combination with methyl-atropine or atropine on hormone activated oestrous behaviour in ovariectomized rats. *Psychopharmacologia,* 11:405–413.

Meyerson, B. J. (1964a): Central nervous monoamines and hormone induced estrus behaviour in the spayed rat. *Acta Physiol. Scand.* [*Suppl.*], 63:241.

Meyerson, B. J. (1964b): The effect of neuropharmacological agents on hormone-activated estrus behaviour in ovariectomized rats. *Arch. Int. Pharmacodyn. Ther.,* 150:4–33.

Meyerson, B. J., and Lindström, L. H. (1973): Sexual motivation in the female rat. *Acta Physiol. Scand.* [*Suppl.*] 389:1–80.

Meyerson, B. J., Eliasson, M., Lindström, L., Michanek, A., and Söderlund, A-Ch. (1973): Monoamines and female sexual behavior. In: *Psychopharmacology, Sexual Disorders and Drug Abuse,* edited by T. A. Ban, et al. North-Holland Publ. Corp., Amsterdam.

Sexual Behavior: Pharmacology and Biochemistry, edited by M. Sandler and G. L.
Gessa. Raven Press, New York © 1975.

The Normal Heterosexual Pattern of Copulatory Behavior in Male Rats: Effects of Drugs That Alter Brain Monoamine Levels

Donald A. Dewsbury

Department of Psychology, University of Florida, Gainesville, Florida 32611

For several years my students and I have conducted a modest research program involving the effects of drugs on the copulatory behavior of male rats. The primary focus of our laboratory has been on comparative studies of copulatory behavior, and particulary on understanding adaptive significance. Then why study drugs? Besides the usual reasons, we felt, back in 1967, that there was much potential in drug–sex research and that those more experienced than we in pharmacology were not exploiting this potential fully. The literature at that time consisted of little beyond the work of M. L. Soulairac (1963) and Bignami (1966). We felt that if we could help provide some gross indication of the neurochemical control of copulatory behavior and establish a firm methodologic basis for research, we might encourage others to conduct the detailed pharmacologic analyses that were needed so badly. We now know that others had similar ideas and that ours was but one of several laboratories to be working simultaneously on the brain monoamines. We believe that our program has achieved its two goals of providing a strong methodologic base and of establishing the probable importance of brain monoamines. This chapter is a brief review of these two aspects of our program.

METHODS IN THE STUDY OF DRUGS AND COPULATORY BEHAVIOR

The validity of one's data is largely a function of the validity of one's methods. Although the ideal experiment might be conceived, rarely can it be conducted. Therefore, some compromises must be made in real-life research, but certain rules must remain inviolate. Selection of a method thus entails development of the most efficient procedures that are consistent with the essential tenets of solid methodology, with as many additional desirable features as possible considering available resources. Some of these considerations are outlined below.

The Normal Rat Pattern

It is customary to distinguish three primary classes of events in the copulatory behavior of male rats: mounts, intromissions, and ejaculations. These are labeled

M, I, and E in Fig. 1, which illustrates their temporal relationships. Mounts are scored when the male mounts the female but fails to gain vaginal penetration. Usually, only those mounts with pelvic thrusting are counted. Intromissions are scored when the male mounts and achieves intromission. Penetration lasts about 300 msec, and is indicated by a single deep thrust followed by rapid dismount. On other occasions the male attains a mount with intromission and ejaculation. Such events are termed "ejaculations," and are characterized by a longer duration of penetration followed by a distinctive stereotyped pattern of dismount.

Mounts, intromissions, and ejaculations occur in groups or "series," with each complete series terminated by an ejaculation; the postejaculatory period includes no copulations. This period is followed, in turn, by a resumption of alternating ejaculatory series and refractory periods until a satiety criterion, typically 30 min with no intromissions, is reached. Rats typically attain about seven ejaculations prior to satiety.

The following measures, illustrated in Fig. 1, have become fairly standard: mount latency (ML), latency from the start of a test to the first mount or intromission; intromission latency (IL), latency from the start of a test until the first intromission; ejaculation latency (EL), latency from the first intromission of a series to its terminal ejaculation; intromission frequency (IF), the number of intromissions in a series; mount frequency (MF), the number of mounts without intromission in a series; mean interintromission interval (MIII), mean interval separating the intromissions of a series; and postejaculatory interval (PEI), time from ejaculation to the next intromission. The series to which a measure refers can be indicated following a hyphen (e.g., IF-2). In satiety tests, it is also possible to report ejaculation frequency (EF), the number of ejaculations.

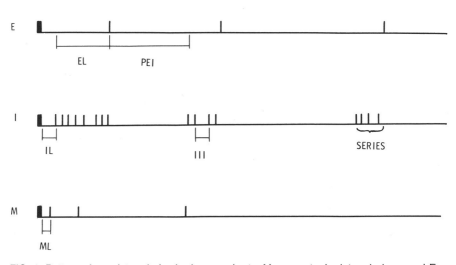

FIG. 1. Pattern of copulatory behavior in normal rats. M = mounts, I = intromissions, and E = ejaculations. Time moves from the beginning of the test at left to right.

Which Measures Are to Be Taken?

In the following discussion, it is assumed that heterosexual copulatory behavior is the behavioral pattern of interest. Research on male–male mounting has played an important role in the development of research on drugs and sexual behavior. Early studies of male–male mounting stimulated much of the interest in such research. However, male–male mounting certainly provides a different behavioral preparation from normal copulation. Results from experiments on male–male mounting are difficult to interpret because the function of such mounting is unclear and there is no substantial literature that deals with the behavior. By contrast, copulation is a biologically meaningful, much-studied behavioral pattern that is highly stereotyped and reliably elicited. It is hoped that the recent trend toward studies of the full, normal heterosexual pattern will continue.

Data are interpreted most easily if a full range of measures is reported (see Bermant, Glickman, and Davidson, 1968). A number of studies have appeared in which male–female copulation was observed, but only the total number of "mounts" (mounts + intromissions + ejaculations) was reported. With practice, observers easily can learn to differentiate mounts, intromissions, and ejaculations. To do so is critical to proper interpretation of results for several reasons. First, when only the total number of mounts is recorded, important drug effects may be missed, thereby allowing even significant changes in certain latency or frequency measures to go undetected when only mounts are scored. More important, detected changes are susceptible to gross misinterpretation. Mounts and intromissions tend to occur in bouts of one to five, which are separated from other "mount bouts" by 30 to 90 sec (Sachs and Barfield, 1970). If the first mounting of a bout results in intromission, the bout is terminated. However, if intromission is not attained on the first attempt, several additional attempts take place. Therefore, an animal that experiences difficulty in effecting intromission will display an elevated mount frequency. Let us suppose that a given drug were to interfere with the attainment of intromission. Such a drug would result in persistent mounting and would produce an increase in MF. With a full range of measures, this effect would be apparent immediately. However, if only total "mount frequency" were reported, the effect might be interpreted as a hypersexuality. Similarly, a drug that produced ejaculation after fewer insertions than normal and thus many postejaculatory refractory periods, would result in an overall decreased density of "mounts" and might be interpreted as depressing sexual behavior. In actuality, the reverse interpretation would be preferred. Proper interpretation of these and many other possible results is possible only with a full range of measures.

An additional reason for reporting a full range of measures stems from the interaction of different measures. For example, it is well known that prolongation of interintromission intervals can reduce intromission frequency (e.g., Bermant, 1964). If a drug produces both an increase in MIII and a decrease in IF, the possibility exists that the change in IF is secondary to the change in MIII. We have found exactly this result in work with both alcohol and imipramine (Dewsbury, 1967; Lovecky and Dewsbury, 1973). For cases in which just IF is reported (e.g., Butcher, Butcher, and Larsson, 1969), complete interpretation is impossible. As a further example of the interaction of measures, EL would be expected to change whenever IF or MIII changes unaccompanied by compensatory changes in the other measure.

All of the standard measures must be treated separately for different series rather than being collapsed across series (e.g., Whalen and Luttge, 1970). The changes across series within tests are among the most reliable phenomena in the study of animal behavior (e.g., Beach and Jordan, 1956; Larsson, 1956). Collapsing across series therefore entails averaging data that are known to be reliably different in different series. This obscures important effects in addition to the fact that differences that might appear in one series but not in others (e.g., Dewsbury, 1971) would be lost.

Studies in which only ejaculation frequency is reported (e.g., Tagliamonte, Tagliamonte, and Gessa, 1971) again may fail to detect drug effects in measures that could be easily calculated and reported given the effort already expended in conducting satiety tests.

Reports of the total time or percentage of time spent in sexual behavior (e.g., Sheard, 1969) are susceptible to many of the distortions discussed previously and are rather difficult to interpret.

Test Duration

Rats should be permitted a reasonable period of time to initiate copulation. Fifteen min or longer may be required in drug studies. Allowance of long intervals for initiation is particularly important in drug studies because a given drug may act to increase intromission latency. Whole tests with a complex of interesting drug effects may never be completed if a very short interval is used (e.g., the 3-min criterion of Malmnäs, 1973).

Once copulation is initiated, the problem remains of when to terminate the test. Very brief tests are inadequate because they fail to provide a full range of measures (e.g., Malmnäs, 1973). Ideally, all tests should be continued to a satiety criterion (e.g., 30 min with no intromissions). Practical considerations of observer time and efficiency often necessitate somewhat shorter tests. The density of data collected per hour of observer time decreases sharply toward the end of satiety tests.

When tests must be terminated prior to satiety, a choice must be made between a time-limited test and a series-limited test. We prefer the latter. With the time-limited procedure, tests are terminated after a specific interval, such as the 30-min interval used by Mitler, Morden, Levine, and Dement (1972). Data collected with such methods are difficult to evaluate. To report just the total frequency of mounts, intromissions, or ejaculations across all series is to risk failure to detect important drug effects as outlined previously. However, attempts to calculate the full range of standard measures contain inherent biases. This is because fewer series are completed by slower animals. Therefore, any series-limited analyses systematically eliminate data from the slowest animals in the experiment. This is done with animals showing the greatest or the least drug effect, depending upon the direction of the effect produced by the drug. This bias severely limits accurate interpretation.

In the series-limited method, tests are terminated after a given number of complete series (e.g., Ahlenius, Eriksson, Larsson, Modigh, and Södersten, 1971). This method contains an inherent inefficiency in that the duration of any given test is unpredictable. Therefore, testing is difficult to schedule when the injection-test interval is kept constant. However, the series-limited test does provide the only method, short of satiety tests, to eliminate the biases intrinsic to the time-limited procedure. Frequently, one to three complete series are observed when such a method is used.

Experimental Design

The primary decision regarding experimental design is between a within-groups design and a between-groups design. In the former, each animal receives all treatments and thus can serve as his own control. The latter design compares the performance of independent groups of animals.

Each design has its problems. The difficulty with between-groups designs stems from the large and stable individual differences that characterize rat copulatory behavior. For example, it is not uncommon for the control value for ejaculation latency of the slowest animal of a group to be 5 to 10 times as great as that of the fastest rat. With such variability and hence "error variance" in statistical tests, only very large drug effects can be detected unless the number of subjects per group is far greater than has been common in such studies.

Because of the problems created by these large individual differences and of the necessity for a stable base line, we have used the within-group designs. However, these, too, have their problems. The time permitted between successive tests of the same animal must be sufficient to permit recovery in both the behavioral and biochemical systems. Complete recovery from satiety tests in rats usually is thought to require about 2 weeks (Beach and Jordan, 1956) so that satiety tests must be scheduled at least 2 weeks apart. Recovery periods following tests with fewer ejaculations have not been well studied, thereby making the planning of intervals between such tests somewhat difficult (e.g., Mitler et al., 1972). In addition, rats often require long intervals following drug treatment for brain monoamine levels to return to base line. In work with reserpine and MAO inhibitors, for example, we have had to schedule tests up to 4 weeks apart in order to minimize carryover effects (Dewsbury and Davis, 1970; Dewsbury, Davis, and Jansen, 1972). Such long intervals increase between-test variability and hence "error variance." But there is a further problem. Copulatory behavior is known to vary as a function of both age and experience (e.g., Dewsbury, 1969). Various rebound, learning, and placebo effects can follow drug administration. For these reasons, it is critical that the order of administration of different treatments be counterbalanced for different animals when a within-groups design is used. Studies which fail to do this (e.g., Whalen and Luttge, 1970) are subject to the above-mentioned artifacts. Regardless of which design is employed, the limitations and problems inherent in the design must be considered when interpreting results.

Selection of Subjects

Most studies of the effects of a variety of independent variables upon copulatory behavior have utilized experienced rats for two reasons. First, a certain percentage of all groups of rats simply fail to copulate, even with repeated testing. The percentage varies with strain and supplier. To eliminate these animals and avoid confusing their failures to mate with experimental effects, a screening pretest is conducted. Second, behavior appears to change as a function of experience and to be less variable in experienced rats. Most experimenters therefore permit their animals 1 to 2 pretests before initiating an experiment. This procedure permits effects of various treatments to be seen against a stable base line.

Unless one is particularly interested in the initiation of copulation in naive animals, use of experienced rats appears to be the method of choice. It should be noted, however, that some drug effects may vary with experience (see Zitrin, 1973). If this is the case, the effects should be studied systematically in and of themselves.

Most studies of copulation have focused on normal, intact animals. There are some advantages to working with castrated males maintained on various androgen doses. Such a procedure eliminates the confounding effects of drug-produced alterations in hormone levels (see Malmnäs, 1973). Adrenalectomized rats may be useful in separating direct effects of drugs on brain monoamine levels from those that might involve adrenal function (e.g., Uphouse, Wilson, and Schlesinger, 1970).

It has been argued that the use of reliable, active copulators leaves no room for facilitative drug effects and that therefore sexually sluggish rats should be used (Gessa, Tagliamonte, and Tagliamonte, 1971; Tagliamonte, Fratta, Del Fiacco, and Gessa, 1973). Sexually sluggish animals may provide an interesting model for the study of drug effects. However, the neurochemical mechanisms effective in rehabilitating these abnormal rats may be quite different from the mechanisms that control behavior in normal, functioning individuals. Therefore, results may not be generalized easily between the two research areas. Furthermore, there is little evidence that maximal performance levels have been attained in control tests, particularly with respect to latency measures. For example, the study of Salis and Dewsbury (1971) involved sexually active males that were studied at an optimal time of their photoperiod. Ejaculation latencies with saline averaged 6 min. This value was halved by parachlorophenylalanine (PCPA). The argument regarding this ceiling effect was constructed largely to permit dismissal of the negative results of Whalen and Luttge (1970). However, those data are suspect on other procedural grounds. Such negative results should not be permitted to lead other researchers to utilize less than optimal designs. We would prefer to see those not specifically interested in the rehabilitation of abnormal rats study drug effects in normal populations of sexually active animals. If within-subject designs are used, correlations between control and drug performance of individual animals can be analyzed and studied easily.

Miscellaneous Procedures

The standard measures of copulatory behavior vary reliably as a function of time within the dark phase of the photoperiod (Dewsbury, 1968). Therefore, it is critical that all tests be conducted at approximately the same time of day.

Ideally, all studies should be conducted with blind procedures so that the observers lack knowledge of the treatment given to individual animals under observation. Alternatively, two observers can independently score the behavior. One of the few studies to use these ideal methods is that of Mitler et al. (1972). In practice, mounts, intromissions, and ejaculations tend to be rather clearly discriminable to experienced observers. Hence, double-blind procedures and multiple observers might not always be necessary. It would be comforting, however, to see more studies utilizing such procedures.

Animals in the control condition in any drug study should be injected with the vehicle in which the drug will be placed in the treatment condition. This permits control for possible effects of the injections themselves and of the vehicle. Studies that do not involve control injections (e.g., Whalen and Luttge, 1970) should be interpreted with great caution.

Various other procedural details (e.g., familiarization of rats with the testing arena and assurance of receptivity in females) are discussed by Dewsbury and Davis (1975).

Finally, drugs administered systemically affect a wide range of systems. Effects can be ascribed to specific neurochemical mechanisms only with great caution. Study of a variety of different drugs that produce similar and opposite alterations, preferably by means of different mechanisms, is to be encouraged.

Conclusions Regarding Methodology

The previous discussion may lead the reader to conclude that sound experiments of drug effects on copulatory behavior are difficult, if not impossible. This is not the case. Although there are many procedural problems to be encountered in such research, there are excellent examples of methodologically sound experiments in the existing literature. Duplication of these procedures can enable the student of drugs with little interest in behavior per se to conduct sound behavioral studies.

EFFECTS OF DRUGS THAT ALTER BRAIN MONOAMINE LEVELS ON COPULATORY BEHAVIOR

The effects of eight drugs that alter brain monoamine levels have been studied in our laboratory. In all studies, the above-described methodologic considerations have been utilized. All studies involved use of within-subject designs, experienced rats, and the series-limited method. We recognize that systemic administration of drugs with no biochemical assays provides a relatively crude biochemical method. However, the results suggest substantial effects of brain monoamine manipulation upon male copulatory behavior and are summarized in Table 1. Significant differences ($p < 0.05$ or better) between treated tests and the appropriate injected control tests are shown for each drug, together with information as to whether the change is an increase (I) or decrease (D) in the relevant measure.

We interpret an increase in any measure of copulatory behavior as a retardation, and a decrease as a facilitation. By this we mean simply that the animal requires fewer mounts or intromissions, or less time to attain a given behavioral criterion. No judgment with respect to adaptive significance or value is implied.

As a general rule, drugs that decrease the levels of brain monoamines, particularly serotonin, facilitate copulatory behavior, whereas drugs that increase brain

TABLE 1. *Effects of eight drugs on male copulatory behavior**

Measure	Reserpine[a]	Tetrabenazine[b]	PCPA[c]	Iproniazid[d]	Nialamide[e]	Pargyline[f]	Imipramine[g]	L-DOPA[h]
ML	—	—	—	—	—	I	—	o
IL	—	—	—	—	—	I	—	—
EL-1	—	—	D	—	I	I	—	I
EL-2	D	—	D	—	—	I	—	—
MIII-1	—	I	D	I	—	—	I	I
MIII-2	—	—	—	I	I	—	I	I
PEI-1	—	—	—	I	—	I	I	—
PEI-2	o	—	D	o	—	o	I	—
IF-1	—	D	—	—	—	I	D	—
IF-2	D	D	D	—	—	I	D	—
MF-1	—	—	D	—	—	—	—	—
MF-2	—	—	—	—	—	I	—	—

* D = significant decrease ($p < 0.05$); I = significant increase ($p < 0.05$); — = no significant change ($p > 0.05$); o = measure not reported.
[a] Reserpine, 1 mg/kg (Dewsbury and Davis, 1970).
[b] Tetrabenazine, 5 mg/kg (Dewsbury, 1972).
[c] PCPA, 4 × 100 mg/kg (Salis and Dewsbury, 1971).
[d] Iproniazid, 100 mg/kg (Dewsbury et al., 1972).
[e] Nialamide, 50 mg/kg (Dewsbury et al., 1972).
[f] Pargyline, 50 mg/kg (Dewsbury et al., 1972).
[g] Imipramine, 25 mg/kg (Lovecky and Dewsbury, 1973).
[h] L-DOPA, 200 mg/kg (+ 50 mg/kg Ro 4-4602) (Gray, Davis, and Dewsbury, 1974).

monoamine levels retard copulatory behavior. Thus, PCPA, which produces a relatively specific depletion of serotonin, has a substantial effect on a variety of measures of copulatory behavior. Reserpine and tetrabenazine, which result in depletion of all brain monoamines, generally have a more specific effect, producing primarily a decrease in intromission frequency when given in intermediate dose ranges (see also Dewsbury, 1971).

The three MAO inhibitors, iproniazid, nialamide, and pargyline, increase brain monoamine levels and produce only retardations of copulatory behavior. Imipramine, which potentiates monoamine action through interference with uptake, produces increased latencies and decreased intromission frequencies. The possibility that the latter effect is secondary to the changes in latency measures cannot be excluded. Finally, L-DOPA, which in this dose range produces a substantial increase in dopamine levels and a slight decrease in serotonin, produces a weak retardation of copulatory behavior.

All of these effects, with the possible exception of that of L-DOPA, are consistent with data based on other methods from other laboratories. The weak inhibitory effect of L-DOPA in our study and that of Hyyppä, Lehtinen, and Rinne (1971), both using normal copulating rats, contrasts with the facilitative effects reported by Tagliamonte et al. (1973) using sexually sluggish males. The choice of subjects or some other procedural difference may account for this discrepancy.

Whereas we recognize the limitations of interpretation of these data, which result from the crudeness of the biochemical manipulations, they certainly suggest a role of monoamines in the control of copulatory behavior. These findings should serve to stimulate research directed at specific behavioral effects and hopefully encourage others to examine behavioral data in a careful and detailed way.

FUTURE RESEARCH ON DRUGS AND COPULATORY BEHAVIOR

Because of the importance of copulatory behavior as a biologic phenomenon and its value as a behavioral preparation, and because of the importance of brain monoamines in the control of behavior, research on monoamine control of copulatory behavior will continue. We believe that the key to future research and interpretation will be specificity. Having established that drugs that alter brain monoamines alter copulatory behavior, the task that lies before us is to determine the specific neural mechanisms, if indeed these effects are neurally mediated.

Anatomic, physiologic, and pharmacologic specificity will be achieved through increased use of cannulation to manipulate levels in particular structures, consideration of turnover rates, use of drugs with more specific actions, and utilization of a great variety of newly developed and developing techniques. Our plea is that a concern for behavioral specificity will accompany concern for anatomic, physiologic, and pharmacologic specificity. Techniques are readily available for methodologically sound experiments with a full range of measures of copulatory behavior. These methods, in conjunction with improved anatomic, physiologic, and pharmacologic methods, should help clarify the specific modes of operation of monoamine control of copulatory behavior.

ACKNOWLEDGMENTS

This research was supported by grants from the National Science Foundation. I thank Harry Davis for help in the preparation of this manuscript.

REFERENCES

Ahlenius, S., Eriksson, H., Larsson, K., Modigh, K., and Södersten, P. (1971): Mating behavior in the male rat treated with *p*-chlorophenylalanine methyl ester alone and in combination with pargyline. *Psychopharmacologia,* 20:383–388.

Beach, F. A., and Jordan, L. (1956): Sexual exhaustion and recovery in the male rat. *Quart. J. Exp. Psychol.,* 8:121–133.

Bermant, G. (1964): Effects of single and multiple enforced intercopulatory intervals on the sexual behavior of male rats. *J. Comp. Physiol. Psychol.,* 57:398–403.

Bermant, G., Glickman, S. E., and Davidson, J. M. (1968): Effects of limbic lesions on copulatory behavior of male rats. *J. Comp. Physiol. Psychol.,* 65:118–125.

Bignami, G. (1966): Pharmacologic influences on mating behavior in the male rat: Effects of *d*-amphetamine, LSD-25, strychnine, nicotine, and various anticholinergic agents. *Psychopharmacologia,* 10:44–58.

Butcher, L. L., Butcher, S. G., and Larsson, K. (1969): Effects of apomorphine, (+)-amphetamine, and nialamide on tetrabenazine-induced suppression of sexual behavior in the male rat. *Eur. J. Pharmac.,* 7:283–288.

Dewsbury, D. A. (1967): Effects of alcohol ingestion on copulatory behavior of male rats. *Psychopharmacologia,* 11:276–281.

Dewsbury, D. A. (1968): Copulatory behavior of rats—Variations within the dark phase of the diurnal cycle. *Commun. Behav. Biol.,* 1:373–377.

Dewsbury, D. A. (1969): Copulatory behavior of rats *(Rattus norvegicus)* as a function of prior copulatory experience. *Anim. Behav.,* 17:217–223.

Dewsbury, D. A. (1971): Copulatory behavior of male rats following reserpine administration. *Psychon. Sci.,* 22:177–179.

Dewsbury, D. A. (1972): Effects of tetrabenazine on the copulatory behavior of male rats. *Eur. J. Pharmacol.,* 17:221–226.

Dewsbury, D. A., and Davis, H. N. (1970): Effects of reserpine on the copulatory behavior of male rats. *Physiol. Behav.,* 5:131–1333.

Dewsbury, D. A., and Davis, H. N. (1974): Effects of drugs on copulatory behavior of male rats. In: *Experimental Psychobiology: A Laboratory Manual,* edited by B. L. Hart. Freeman, San Francisco *(in press).*

Dewsbury, D. A., Davis, H. N., and Jansen, P. E. (1972): Effects of monoamine oxidase inhibitors on the copulatory behavior of male rats. *Phychopharmacologia,* 24:209–217.

Gessa, G. L., Tagliamonte, A., and Tagliamonte, P. (1971): Aphrodisiac effect of *p*-chlorophenylalanine. *Science,* 171:706.

Gray, G. D., Davis, H. N., and Dewsbury, D. A. (1974): Effects of L-DOPA on the heterosexual copulatory behavior of male rats. *Eur. J. Pharmacol.,* 27:367–370.

Hyyppä, M., Lehtinen, P., and Rinne, U. K. (1971): Effect of L-DOPA on the hypothalamic, pineal, and striatal monoamines and on the sexual behaviour of the rat. *Brain Res.,* 30:265–272.

Larsson, K. (1956): *Conditioning and Sexual Behavior in the Male Albino Rat.* Almqvist and Wiksell, Stockholm, Sweden.

Lovecky, D. V., and Dewsbury, D. A. (1973): Effects of imipramine on copulatory behavior of male rats. *Bull. Psychon. Soc.,* 2:237–239.

Malmnäs, C. O. (1973): Monoaminergic influence on testosterone-activated copulatory behavior in the castrated male rat. *Acta Physiol. Scand.,* Suppl. 395, pp. 1–128.

Mitler, M. M., Morden, B., Levine, S., and Dement, W. (1972): The effects of parachlorophenylalanine on the mating behavior of male rats. *Physiol. Behav.,* 8:1147–1150.

Sachs, B. D., and Barfield, R. J. (1970): Temporal patterning of sexual behavior in the male rat. *J.
Comp. Physiol. Psychol.,* 73:359–364.

Salis, P. J., and Dewsbury, D. A. (1971): *p*-Chlorophenylalanine facilitates copulatory behaviour in
male rats. *Nature,* 232:400–401.

Sheard, M. H. (1969): The effect of *p*-chlorophenylalanine on behavior in rats: Relation to brain
serotonin and 5-hydroxyindoleacetic acid. *Brain Res.,* 15:524–528.

Soulairac, M. L. (1963): Experimental study of the neurohormonal regulation of male rat sexual
behavior. (Translated by P. Salis.) *Ann. Endocrinol. (Suppl.),* 24:1–98.

Tagliamonte, A., Fratta, W., Del Fiacco, M., and Gessa, G. L. (1973): Evidence that brain dopamine
stimulates copulatory behaviour in male rats. Riv. Farmac. Terap. 4:177–181.

Tagliamonte, A., Tagliamonte, P., and Gessa, G. L. (1971): Reversal of pargyline-induced inhibition
of sexual behaviour in male rats by *p*-chlorophenylalanine. *Nature,* 230:244–245.

Uphouse, L. L., Wilson, J. R., and Schlesinger, K. (1970): Induction of estrus in mice: The possible
role of adrenal progesterone. *Horm. Behav.,* 1:255–264.

Whalen, R. E., and Luttge, W. G. (1970): *p*-Chlorophenylalanine methyl ester: An aphrodisiac?
Science, 169:1000–1001.

Zitrin, A. (1973): Changes in brain serotonin level and male sexual behavior. In: *Serotonin and
Behavior,* edited by J. Barchas and E. Usdin. Academic Press, New York.

Sexual Behavior: Pharmacology and Biochemistry, edited by M. Sandler and G. L.
Gessa. Raven Press, New York © 1975.

Humoral and Aminergic Mechanisms Regulating Sexual Receptivity in Female Rhesus Monkeys

B. J. Everitt, P. B. Gradwell,* and J. Herbert

Department of Anatomy, University of Cambridge, Cambridge, England

The sexual receptivity of female rhesus monkeys is controlled by androgens. This distinguishes them from nonprimate females in which estrogen fulfills the same function, the action of which is potentiated by progesterone in some species. Therefore, female monkeys deprived of androgens by adrenalectomy and ovariectomy become sexually unreceptive, despite being given estrogen (Everitt and Herbert, 1971). Receptivity is restored only if the monkeys receive androgens such as testosterone or androstenedione (Everitt, Herbert, and Hamer, 1972). In contrast, ovariectomized and adrenalectomized rats and rabbits require only estrogen (in conjunction with progesterone in the case of rats) without additional androgen to display normal sexual receptivity (Beyer, Cruz, and Rivaud, 1969; Zemlan, Ward, Crowley, and Margules, 1973). Do these differences between primate and nonprimate females suggest corresponding differences in the neural mechanisms upon which hormones act? It is not known whether circumscribed hormone-sensitive areas controlling sexual behavior exist in the hypothalamus of the female monkey, although this has been demonstrated in several nonprimates (Davidson, 1972). Hormones may affect sexual behavior in female rats by altering serotoninergic mechanisms (Meyerson, 1964). Is it possible that the different hormone, inducing comparable behavioral effects in primate females, does so in a similar manner?

This chapter presents evidence suggesting that androgens alter receptivity in female rhesus monkeys by acting directly on the anterior hypothalamus and may do so by modifying the action of serotonin.

BEHAVIORAL OBSERVATIONS

Sexual behavior between male–female pairs of adult rhesus monkeys was measured by methods described in detail in Everitt and Herbert (1971). Briefly, each female was paired with a male (always the same one) by being transferred to his cage for 30 min daily. A series of 10 daily observations was made on all females during each treatment. Particular attention is given here to certain components of female behavior, namely, number of presentations (i.e., invitations

---

* Present address: Department of Anatomy, University of Rhodesia, Salisbury, Rhodesia.

to the male to mount); the number of mounts initiated by the female before the first ejaculation of the male; the number of refusals (i.e., refusals to allow the male to mount when he attempted to do so). The components of the male's behavior were also recorded, but these are not considered further here.

Because females differed both with respect to their behavior levels and to which area of the brain contained hormone implants, the values for each female were treated separately. The data were first analyzed by Friedman's analysis of variance. When it was significant, comparisons were made with the pretreatment (adrenalectomized) condition using the Wilcoxon test (two-tailed).

All males were intact. All females had been bilaterally ovariectomized at least 2 months before the start of experiments and were given estradiol benzoate (either 15 or 25 μg/day s.c.) throughout all observations. Adrenalectomized females were maintained on hydrocortisone succinate (20 mg/day) and deoxycorticosterone trimethylacetate (25 mg once monthly) and remained in excellent health.

EFFECTS OF IMPLANTS IN THE HYPOTHALAMUS ON SEXUAL BEHAVIOR

Testosterone propionate was implanted intracranially through a cannula screwed into the skull under stereotactic control. The cannula consisted of a stainless steel tube (1.01 mm o.d.) down which was passed a removable inner tube (0.25 mm o.d.) bearing either testosterone or cholesterol fused to its tip. Thus, by using inner tubes of the same length either substance could be implanted successively into the same site. The inner tube projected about 5 mm beyond the outer tube. Implants were positioned 7 days before observations began and removed at the end of the series. The site of each implant was determined initially by lateral and anteroposterior radiographs and was confirmed subsequently by serially sectioning the brain.

Ten females were studied before and after adrenalectomy. Two additional females were studied only after their adrenals had been removed. Empty cannulas were implanted in six monkeys immediately after adrenalectomy, and in the other six after completion of the postadrenalectomy series of observations; implantation itself had no discernible effect on behavior.

Bilateral adrenalectomy caused females to become sexually unreceptive, even though they continued to receive estradiol, thus confirming our earlier observations (Everitt et al., 1972). All 10 females studied before and after this operation presented significantly less frequently to the males, and nine initiated a lower proportion of sexual interaction (Fig. 1a, b). In addition, nine females repeatedly refused the males' attempts to mount (Fig. 1b), whereas only two had done so infrequently before operation.

In eight adrenalectomized females, unilateral implants of testosterone propionate (mean weight 140 μg, range 105–280 μg) were made into the anterior hypothalamus/preoptic area (i.e., from the anterior border of the optic chiasm to the cranial border of the ventromedial nucleus). In seven of the adrenalectomized animals, these implants reversed the effects of adrenalectomy; females

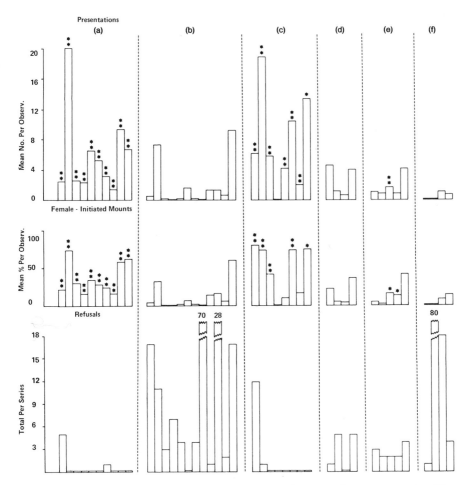

FIG. 1. Effects of intracranial implants of testosterone propionate on three components of the sexual behavior of ovariectomized, adrenalectomized, estrogen-treated female rhesus monkeys. *(Top)* Presentations; *(middle)* % mounts initiated by the female; *(bottom)* refusals to allow the male to mount. Treatments are (a) ovariectomy alone, (b) ovariectomy and adrenalectomy, (c) anterior hypothalamic/preoptic implants of testosterone, (d) anterior hypothalamic/preoptic implants of cholesterol, (e) thalamic or cortical implants of testosterone, (f) posterior hypothalamic implants of testosterone. Identity of females: 1, 1849; 2, 1886; 3, 1984; 4, 2263; 5, 2218; 6, 2219; 7, 2261; 8, 2260; 9, 2259; 10, 1887; 11, 1992; 12, 1265. Significant increases over postadrenalectomy condition shown by (*) $p < 0.05$; (**) $p < 0.01$ (Wilcoxon test). Details of hormone treatments given in text.

presented sexually to the males significantly more often, initiated more sexual interaction, and only two now refused the males' attempts to mount (Fig. 1c); thus their behavior resembled that seen before adrenalectomy. In the 8th case (female 5), the implant had been placed more laterally than in the others; in addition a large hemorrhage was discovered lying around the cannula.

In four of these seven females, testosterone was replaced by cholesterol (mean weight 226 μg, range 130–340 μg) implanted into the same area and in the other three the inner tube was replaced by one bearing no implant. Either procedure resulted in the females becoming sexually unreceptive again. Results after cholesterol implants are shown in Fig. 1d.

Five monkeys received unilateral testosterone implants (mean weight 271 μg, range 125–310 μg) into the thalamus or cerebral cortex (Fig. 1e) and another four into the posterior hypothalamus upper midbrain (i.e., the premammillary and mammillary region or pretectal area) (mean weight 195 μg, range 120–310 μg) (Fig. 1f). In general, testosterone implanted into any of these regions failed to stimulate the females' behavior and they remained sexually unreceptive (Fig. 1e, f), although one female showed a small but significant increase in receptivity after an intrathalamic implant (Fig. 1e, female 7).

Throughout this experiment, males continued to respond to a high proportion of such presentations as still occurred by attempting to mount, demonstrating that the females remained sexually attractive, presumably because they were being given estrogen (Herbert and Trimble, 1967).

The results of implanting testosterone indicate that the anterior hypothalamic region of the female monkey is sensitive to androgens and may be responsible for regulating sexual receptivity. Further work will show whether sites in the brain other than those studied here are also directly concerned with the hormonal control of the female monkey's receptivity. A similar area of the hypothalamus responds to hormones inducing receptivity in nonprimates. Estrogen implanted into the anterior hypothalamus and preoptic area of ovariectomized rats restores sexual receptivity, although those in more posterior regions of the hypothalamus of cats and rabbits are also effective (Palka and Sawyer, 1966; Davidson, 1972). Conversely, lesions in the anterior hypothalamus of female rats, cats, ewes, and guinea pigs prevent ovarian hormones from activating sexual behavior, although this finding does not necessarily establish the site of action of the hormones (Davidson, 1972).

Androgen can stimulate receptivity in nonprimate females (Whalen and Hardy, 1970). It has been suggested that this occurs because these hormones are converted to estrogen within the brain (McDonald, Beyer, Newton, Brian, Baker, Tan, Sampson, Kitching, Greenhill, and Pritchard, 1970). The observations reported here indicate that this interpretation does not apply to adrenalectomized female monkeys, for the latter became receptive only after testosterone was implanted into the hypothalamus, despite being given estradiol throughout the experiment. Sexual interaction of ovariectomized rhesus monkeys is said to be stimulated by estrogen implanted into the hypothalamus (Michael, 1969), although since cerebral cortical implants were also apparently effective it seems likely that sufficient hormone was escaping from both sites into the circulation to activate peripheral mechanisms known to alter the female's attractiveness, and hence the behavior of the male (Herbert, 1970). Female monkeys also have been found to present more frequently after large amounts of testosterone (up to 1.5 mg) were injected into various areas of the brain (Michael, 1971), with results apparently comparable to those previously reported after equivalent amounts given subcutaneously (Herbert and Trimble, 1967).

EFFECTS OF DEPLETING 5-HT ON SEXUAL RECEPTIVITY OF ADRENALECTOMIZED FEMALE MONKEYS

Ten ovariectomized, adrenalectomized, estrogen-treated females were used, nine of which had formed part of the previous experiment. When the second experiment started, seven had intracranial cannulas in position containing no hormone, whereas cannulas had been removed from the other two; all were unreceptive.

*Para*chlorophenylalanine methyl ester HCl (PCPA), a drug that inhibits tryptophan hydroxylase and hence the formation of 5-hydroxytryptamine (5-HT) (Koe and Weissman, 1966) was given by subcutaneous injection every 4 days (either 75 or 100 mg/kg) beginning 4 days before the first observation.

L-5-Hydroxytryptophan methyl ester HCl (5-HTP), the substance formed by tryptophan hydroxylase from tryptophan, was given every second day (20 mg/kg), beginning 2 days before the first observation.

PCPA administration in these females stimulated their receptivity in seven cases (Fig. 2b). Such females began presenting more frequently and thus initiated more sexual interaction with the male. Another two refused the male conspicuously less often.

Five animals in which receptivity had been stimulated by PCPA were then given this drug together with 5-HTP. This additional treatment reversed the effects of PCPA. Four females became sexually unreceptive once more, their behavior resembling that observed after adrenalectomy but before PCPA had been given (Fig. 2c).

These experiments show that depleting 5-HT can stimulate sexual receptivity of adrenalectomized female monkeys. Hitherto only androgens such as testosterone or androstenedione, have been found to have this property; other steroids, such as dehydroepiandrosterone, estrogen, progesterone, and cortisol are ineffective (Everitt and Herbert, 1971, 1972). The converse effect has also been obtained: 5-HTP given alone to ovariectomized, estrogen-treated (i.e., receptive) females causes them to become sexually unreceptive (Gradwell, Everitt, and Herbert, *in press*).

5-HIAA LEVELS AND TURNOVERS IN THE CSF

Because sampling the CSF would have interfered with the animals' behavior, treatments used during the previous experiment were replicated for this part of the study. A single sample was taken from each female (1) during estrogen treatment alone, (2) after 4, 8, and 12 days on PCPA, (3) 2 and 12 days after beginning treatment with both PCPA and 5-HTP, (4) 7 days after withdrawal of this combined treatment.

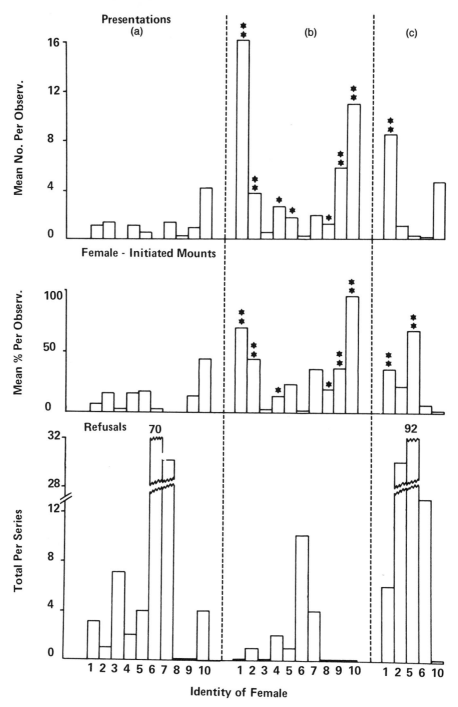

FIG. 2. Effects of altering cerebral 5-HT levels upon the sexual behavior of ovariectomized, estrogen-treated female rhesus monkeys made unreceptive by bilateral adrenalectomy. Treatments are (a) corticoid replacement therapy alone, (b) PCPA added, (c) PCPA + 5-HTP added. Components of behavior and significance levels indicated as in Fig. 1. Identity of females: 1, 1886; 2, 2259; 3, 2263; 4, 2219; 5, 2261; 6, 2260; 7, 1887; 8, 2264; 9, 1992; 10, 1265. Dosages given in text.

5-Hydroxyindoleacetic acid (5-HIAA) was measured spectrophotofluorometrically (Ashcroft and Sharman, 1962) in monkeys before and after PCPA treatment by withdrawing CSF from the cisterna magna under ketamine anesthesia between 0900 and 1100 hr BST (British standard time) on the day of the assay. Each sample consisted of about 4–6 ml and probably contained both cisternal and ventricular CSF. 5-HIAA turnover was assessed in steroid-treated animals by measuring levels immediately before, and 2 hr after, an intravenous injection of probenecid sodium (20 mg/kg) (Korf and van Praag, 1970).

Nine ovariectomized monkeys were used; seven of these were also adrenalectomized and had taken part in the preceding behavioral experiments. Table 1 shows that PCPA in the doses used reduced the level of 5-HIAA in the CSF to less than half that of the untreated condition. The addition of 5-HTP to PCPA-treated animals reversed these findings; 2 days after the first injection, 5-HIAA levels had returned almost to normal, and after 12 days levels were somewhat above this value. One week after treatment was discontinued, levels had returned again to those typical of PCPA alone, presumably because the effects of PCPA lasted longer than those of 5-HTP.

Therefore, it seems likely that the behavioral changes observed after PCPA were related to the reduced 5-HT levels rather than to alterations in catecholamines, as giving 5-HTP reversed the effects of PCPA both on behavior and 5-HIAA levels.

The area in which our testosterone implants were effective, the anterior hypothalamus, contains in both rats (Fuxe, Hökfelt, and Ungerstedt, 1969) and man (Constantinidis, Tissot, de la Torre, and Geissbuhler, 1969) high concentrations of 5-HT located principally in terminals within the suprachiasmatic nucleus. Increasing 5-HT levels in the rat inhibits the activation of estrus by hormones (Meyerson, 1964); conversely, depleting 5-HT facilitates the induction of estrous behavior or may substitute for the action of one or another of the ovarian hormones in rats (Meyerson and Lewander, 1970), cats (Hoyland, Shillito, and Vogt, 1970), and hamsters (Meyerson, 1970). Our findings in female rhesus monkeys differ from those in castrated male rats, in which PCPA activated sexual behavior only if the animals were also given testosterone (Gessa, Tagliamonte, Tagliamonte, and Brodie, 1970). However, castrated male rats showed lordotic (i.e., female-type) behavior after treatment with estrogen together with amine depletors, whereas estrogen combined with progesterone was ineffective (Södersten and Ahlenius, 1972). This finding suggests that PCPA could have had its effect on the adrenalectomized female monkey by enabling estrogen to restore sexual receptivity by a direct action on the brain, although this seems unlikely in view of the differences in hormonal control of receptivity in the two species.

5-HIAA turnover was then studied in 10 different ovariectomized monkeys under the following conditions: (1) no treatment for at least 2 months after ovariectomy, (2) estradiol (15 or 25 μg/day), (3) estradiol as before in conjunction with progesterone (15 μg/day), and (4) testosterone propionate (either 250 or 400 μg/day). Turnover was measured 10 days after each treatment had started.

TABLE 1. Levels of 5-HIAA (ng/ml) in CSF of female rhesus monkeys after treatment with PCPA and 5-HTP

	Estradiol benzoate (alone)	PCPA added			PCPA + 5-HTP		5-HTP withdrawn
		4 days	8 days	12 days	2 days	12 days	7 days
Levels (mean ± SD)	68.2 ± 9.87	31.9 ± 6.49	28.9 ± 6.99	27.2 ± 4.40	70.2 ± 13.05	107.7 ± 15.86	35.3 ± 12.79
No. of monkeys	9	9	9	9	9	5	9

Doses given in text.

A minimum period of 6 weeks elapsed between successive treatments except that progesterone was added to estrogen immediately after treatment with the latter alone had been completed. Two monkeys were given testosterone before estrogen (and estrogen plus progesterone); this change in the order of treatments had no effect upon the results.

Table 2 shows that testosterone decreased the level of 5-HIAA in the CSF somewhat, but markedly reduced the turnover of 5-HT as measured by the method used. Estradiol had a similar but lesser effect on turnover, and this was reversed by the addition of progesterone. Although these results are compatible with the interpretation that testosterone reduces 5-HIAA (and hence 5-HT) turnover, they should not be overemphasized. Steroids such as testosterone could interact in some way with probenecid directly upon the amine metabolite reabsorption mechanism (Neff, Tozer, and Brodie, 1964). Furthermore, although the effect of testosterone on 5-HT turnover is consistent with the role of the hormone in sexual receptivity, such a finding may equally reflect other actions of steroids, including those on the hypothalamopituitary system.

Perhaps the increased 5-HT turnover in progesterone-treated monkeys is related to the sexual unreceptivity observed in such animals (Everitt and Herbert, 1971). Some women have also reported loss of libido after taking oral contraceptive preparations containing relatively high amounts of progestin (Grant and Mears, 1967), although progesterone may also induce unreceptivity by lowering plasma androgen levels in both female monkeys (Hess and Resko, 1973) and women (Bulbrook, Hayward, Hevian, Swain, Tang, and Wang, 1973).

The experiments reported here cannot be taken as conclusive evidence that androgens regulate sexual receptivity by a specific action on a serotoninergic neural system. An alternative interpretation is possible: lowering 5-HT levels may render animals generally more responsive to sensory stimuli (e.g., olfactory or visual) eliciting behavior. Other categories of behavior, such as eating, aggression, and sleep, also have been reported as altered by depleting 5-HT (Weissman and Harbert, 1972), although changes in one mode of behavior (sexual) was not

TABLE 2. Levels (ng/ml) and turnovers (levels 2 hr after probenecid as % initial value) in CSF of 10 ovariectomized rhesus monkeys given steroid hormones

	No treatment	Estradiol benzoate (15 or 25 μg/day)	Estradiol + progesterone (15 μg + 15 mg/day)	Testosterone propionate (250 or 400 μg/day)
Levels				
Mean	76.1	72.2	78.4	67.4[a]
Range	57.1–113.7	57.2–94.6	60.4–118.4	52.1–97.9
Turnover				
Mean	207.1	149.8[a]	177.4	130.6[a]
Range	174.4–236.4	127.1–185.4	133.9–226.6	102.1–169.3

[a] $p < 0.01$ (Wilcoxon test, two-tailed) compared to values in untreated monkeys.

predictably correlated with those in another (motor activity) in male rats (Malmnas, 1973). Electric shock, which presumably has a nonspecific effect, can facilitate either aggressive or sexual behavior in rats under appropriate conditions (Caggiula, 1972). Because the conditions used in our experiments encourage primarily sexual stimuli, changes in this behavior would be the most likely to occur.

The two interpretations are not necessarily mutually exclusive. The specific role of estrogen in regulating the receptivity of nonprimate females is hardly to be doubted, yet the same hormone alters a variety of other behaviors, e.g., aggression (Mugford and Nowell, 1971) and food intake (Drewett, 1973), and lowers sensory thresholds (Vernikos-Danellis, 1973).

Taken together, the work reported here suggests that there is a hormone-sensitive area in the anterior hypothalamus that controls sexual receptivity in primate as well as in nonprimate females, but that, in primates this region responds to androgens rather than estrogens. The possibility further exists that androgens regulate receptivity in monkeys by altering the activity of a serotonin-containing system in this part of the brain. Similar systems are probably involved in other neuroendocrine functions, e.g., ovulation (Kordon and Glowinski, 1972), so that a major problem is to understand the way that a specific hormone (e.g., androgens in female monkeys) causes a change in a certain behavior (e.g., receptivity) by acting on a particular part of the serotoninergic pathways.

ACKNOWLEDGMENTS

Supported, in part, by the Medical Research Council. PBG was in receipt of a British Council scholarship. We thank Dr. F. Long (Roche) for supplying some of the PCPA, J. D. Hamer for help with adrenalectomies, Miss P. Stacey for technical assistance, and Dr. G. Horn and Dr. E. B. Keverne for commenting on the manuscript.

REFERENCES

Ashcroft, G. W., and Sharman, D. F. (1962): Drug induced changes in the concentration of 5-OR indolyl compounds in CSF and caudate nucleus. *Br. J. Pharmacol.,* 19:153–160.

Beyer, C., Cruz, M. L., and Rivaud, A. V. (1969): Persistence of sexual behavior in ovariectomized–adrenalectomized rabbits treated with cortisol. *Endocrinology,* 85:790–793.

Bulbrook, R. D., Hayward, J. L., Hevian, M., Swain, M. C., Tang, D., and Wang, D. Y. (1973): Effect of steroidal contraceptives on levels of plasma androgen sulphates and cortisol. *Lancet,* 1:628–631.

Caggiula, A. R. (1972): Shock-elicited copulation and aggression in male rats. *J. Comp. Physiol. Psychol.,* 80:393–397.

Constantinidis, J., Tissot, R., de la Torre, J-C., and Geissbuhler, F. (1969): Essai de localisation des monoamines dans l'hypothalamus humain. *Pathol. Biol.,* 17:361–363.

Davidson, J. M. (1972): Hormones and reproductive behavior. In: *Hormones and Behavior,* edited by S. Levine, pp 64–104. Academic Press, New York.

Drewett, R. F. (1973): Estrous and diestrous components of the ovarian inhibition on hunger in the rat. *Anim. Behav.,* 21:772–780.

Everitt, B. J., and Herbert, J. (1971): The effects of dexamethasone and androgens on sexual receptivity of female rhesus monkeys. *J. Endocrinol.,* 51:575–588.

Everitt, B. J., and Herbert, J. (1972): Hormonal correlates of sexual behaviour in subhuman primates. *Dan. Med. Bull.,* 19:246–258.

Everitt, B. J., Herbert, J., and Hamer, J. D. (1972): Sexual receptivity of bilaterally adrenalectomised rhesus monkeys. *Physiol. Behav.,* 8:409–415.

Fuxe, K., Hökfelt, T., and Ungerstedt, U. (1969): Distribution of monoamines in the mammalian central nervous system by histochemical studies. In: *Metabolism of Amines in the Brain,* edited by G. Harper. Macmillan, London.

Gessa, G. L., Taliamonte, A., Tagliamonte, P., Brodie, B. B. (1970): Essential role of testosterone in the sexual stimulation induced by *p*-chlorophenylalanine in male animals. *Nature,* 227:616–617.

Grant, E. C. G., and Mears, E. (1967): Mental effects of oral contraceptives. *Lancet,* 2:945.

Herbert, J. (1970): Hormones and reproductive behaviour in rhesus and talapoin monkeys. *J. Reprod. Fert. Suppl.,* II:119–140.

Herbert, J., and Trimble, M. R. (1967): Effect of oestradiol and testosterone on the sexual receptivity and attractiveness of the female rhesus monkey. *Nature,* 216:165–166.

Hess, D. L., and Resko, J. A. (1973): The effects of progesterone on the patterns of testosterone and estradiol concentration in the systemic plasma of the female rhesus monkey during the intermenstrual period. *Endocrinology,* 92:446–453.

Hoyland, V. J., Shillito, E. E., and Vogt, M. (1970): The effect of parachlorophenylalanine (PCPA) on the behaviour of cats. *Br. J. Pharmacol.,* 40:659–667.

Koe, B. K., and Weissman, A. (1966): *p*-Chlorophenylalanine: A specific depletor of brain serotonin. *J. Pharmacol., Exp. Ther.,* 154:499–516.

Kordon, C., and Glowinski, J. (1972): Role of hypothalamic monoaminergic neurons in the gonadotrophic release-regulating mechanisms. *Neuropharmacology,* 11:153–142.

Korf, J., and Van Praag, H. M. (1970): The intravenous probenecid test: A possible aid in evaluation of the serotonin hypothesis on the pathogenesis of depression. *Psychopharmacologia,* 18:129–132.

Malmnas, C. O. (1973): Monoaminergic influence on testosterone-activated copulating behavior in the castrated male rat. *Acta Physiol. Scand. Suppl.,* 395:5–128.

McDonald, P. G., Beyer, C., Newton, F., Brian, B., Barker, R., Tan, H. S., Sampson, C., Kitching, P., Greenhill, R., and Pritchard, D. (1970): Failure of 5, α-dihydrotestosterone to initiate sexual behaviour in the castrated male rat. *Nature,* 227:964–965.

Meyerson, B. J. (1964): Central nervous monoamines and hormone induced estrus behaviour in the spayed rat. *Acta Physiol. Scand. Suppl.,* 63:241:1–32.

Meyerson, B. J. (1970): Monoamines and hormone activated oestrous behaviour in the ovariectomised hamster. *Psychopharmacologia,* 18:50–57.

Meyerson, B. J., and Lewander, T. (1970): Serotonin synthesis inhibition and oestrous behaviour in female rats. *Life Sci.,* 9:661–671.

Michael, R. P. (1969): Neural and non-neural mechanisms in the reproductive behaviour of primates. *Proc. 3rd Int. Congr. Endocrinol. Exc. Med. Int. Congr. Ser.,* 184:302–309.

Michael, R. P. (1971): Neuroendocrine factors regulating primate behavior. In: *Frontiers in Neuroendocrinology,* edited by L. Martini and W. J. Ganong, pp. 359–398. Oxford Univ. Press, England.

Mugford, R. A., and Nowell, N. W. (1971): Endocrine control over production and activity of the anti-aggression pheromone from female mice. *J. Endocrinol.,* 49:225–232.

Neff, N. H., Tozer, T. N., and Brodie, B. B. (1964): A specialised transport system to transfer 5-HIAA directly from brain to blood. *Pharmacologia,* 6:162.

Palka, Y. S., and Sawyer, C. H. (1966): Effects of hypothalamic implants of ovarian steroids on oestrous behaviour in rabbits. *J. Physiol.,* 185:25–1269.

Södersten, P., and Ahlenius, S. (1972): Female lordosis behaviour in oestrogen-primed male rats treated with *p*-chlorophenylalanine or α-methyl-*p*-tyrosine. *Horm. Behav.,* 3:181–189.

Vernikos-Danellis, J. (1973): Effects of hormones on the central nervous system. In: *Hormones and Behavior,* edited by S. Levine, pp. 11–63. Academic Press, New York.

Weissman, A., and Harbert, C. A. (1972): Recent developments relating serotonin and behaviour. *Ann. Rep. Med. Chem.,* 7:47–58.

Whalen, R. E., and Hardy, D. F. (1970): Induction of receptivity in female rats and cats with oestrogen and testosterone. *Physiol. Behav.,* 5:529–533.

Zemlan, F. P., Ward, I. L. L., Crowley, W. R., and Margules, D. L. (1973): Activation of lordotic responding in female rats by suppression of serotonergic activity. *Science,* 179:1010–1011.

Sexual Behavior: Pharmacology and Biochemistry, edited by M. Sandler and G. L.
Gessa. Raven Press, New York © 1975.

Major Tranquilizers and Sexual Function

A. Dotti and M. Reda

Psychiatric Institute, University of Rome, Rome, Italy

ENDOCRINE EFFECTS

Animal experimentation has established an inhibitory effect of neuroleptics on pituitary luteinizing hormone (LH) with consequent suppression of both estrous and menstrual cycles, delay of the onset of puberty, and absence of corpora lutea in female rats. In male rats the same drugs induce atrophy of the testes, regression of the epithelium of the seminal vesicle, atrophy of the prostate, and reduction of spermatogenesis (Psychoyos, 1968).

In women treated with neuroleptics, alterations of the menstrual cycle with amenorrhea is not an uncommon side effect, especially with high doses of phenothiazines given over considerable periods of time. The occurrence of menstrual irregularities in women with neuropsychiatric disorders makes it difficult to establish the mechanism involved and the frequency with which amenorrhea occurs (Shader, 1970). Compared with the phenothiazines, we have noticed a very high incidence of amenorrhea in women of child-bearing age treated with Sulpiride®, a relatively new psychotropic drug the use of which is spreading rapidly in Italy.

Causally related to inhibition of pituitary LH function by tranquilizers is the effect on hypothalamic control of pituitary prolactin function: when gonadotropic secretion is depressed, production of prolactin is markedly increased and vice versa. The major tranquilizers decrease the secretion of prolactin inhibitory factor (PIF) in the hypothalamus, an effect probably mediated by catecholamine receptor blockade. It is not known, however, whether the endocrine effects are caused by blockade of norepinephrine or dopamine receptors. Furthermore, direct action on the pituitary gland is quite possible because neuroleptic drugs such as haloperidol and pimozide are strongly taken up by the pituitary gland. Therefore, the effects obtained using these drugs have to be interpreted with caution (Fuxe and Hökfelt, 1970).

A syndrome of isolated prolactin deficiency has been identified by using chlorpromazine stimulation as a test for prolactin reserve (Turkington, 1972).

Both in males and females the increase of prolactin secretion, induced by major tranquilizers causes gynecomastia and galactorrhea, the incidence of which varies, depending on the potency of the drug itself, to its dosage, to the duration of drug administration and, finally, to host factors (Shader, 1970).

Sawyer (1965) demonstrated that the higher centers of the brain are involved in the effects of major tranquilizers on sexual function: electroencephalogram (EEG) thresholds are modified after direct electrical stimulation of the hypothalamus and of two closely related systems: the reticular activating system (RAS) and the limbic system. A sleepy EEG record, suggesting inhibition of the RAS, was observed after administration of chlorpromazine.

NONENDOCRINE EFFECTS

From a clinical point of view, nonendocrine side effects on sexual behavior undoubtedly have a greater degree of importance and frequency than do endocrine ones.

Neuroleptics have an action not only on the hypothalamus but also on the RAS, the limbic system, and other higher centers, thereby reducing the intensity of both internal and external stimuli. To a great extent, the therapeutic effects of neuroleptics must be attributed to these actions. A reduction of the sensory input and emotional impulse reduces interest in the external world, thereby inhibiting sex-related drives.

There are two primary problems in evaluating the side effects of neuroleptics on human sexual function. The first centers on the definition of human sexual behavior. This is not an easy question to answer; certainly, the definition cannot be restricted to copulatory activity. Physiologic factors in humans are conditioned to such an extent by psychologic and cultural influences that to reduce our considerations of human sexual behavior merely to heterosexual copulation is obviously an oversimplification (Beach, 1970).

The second problem originates in the presence of disturbed sexual behavior prior to treatment in nearly all psychiatric patients. One may say that disturbances in sexual behavior are parallel and in proportion to the degree of psychologic alteration.

We must add to this the peculiar elaboration that the side effects of neuroleptics may undergo in the individual patient. Consequently, loss of libido can be experienced as persecution by the doctor or as a hypochondriacal complaint set in a depressive symptomatology pattern, etc.

Major tranquilizers facilitate social adjustment of the individual by reducing mental symptoms and behavioral deviations, but they also inhibit his natural drives. At the same time the clinical problem seems to be without solution in that the more we control psychotic symptoms with drugs the more the expressive capacity of the individual is impaired. In selecting and administering a drug, too much stress is placed on the target symptoms, and too little to the target functions of behavior including sexual function (Irwin, 1974). The aim of the therapy should be improvement of the overall state of the patient rather than mere suppression of hallucinations and delusions.

Very little attention is paid to sexual behavior by the majority of psychiatrists in clinical practice, probably because of the strong cultural attitude against the patient's sexual activities inside an institution. Within an institution, loss of libido can be considered a therapeutic side effect of neuroleptics, but in dealing with ambulatory patients, to ignore the disabling effect of drugs on sexual function must be harmful. Based on our experience, frigidity, impotence, and loss of libido are often causes of depression or of an arbitrary interruption of the treatment, even when sexual behavior is so disturbed that it is confined to masturbation.

Until now attention to this aspect of treatment has been scanty. The purpose of this brief note is to advocate suitable consideration of the problem based on careful and objective observation.

REFERENCES

Beach, F. A. (1970): Some effects of gonadal hormones on sexual behavior. In: *The Hypothalamus* edited by L. Martini, M. Motta, and F. Fraschini. Academic Press, New York.

Fuxe, K., and Hökfelt, T. (1970): Central monoaminergic system and hypothalamic function. In: *The Hypothalamus,* edited by L. Martini, M. Motta, and F. Fraschini. Academic Press, New York.

Irwin, S. (1974): How to prescribe psychoactive drugs. *Bull. Menninger Clin.,* 38:1–13.

Psychoyos, A. (1968): The effects of reserpine and chlorpromazine on sexual function. *J. Reprod. Fertil.* (Suppl. 4), 47–60.

Sawyer, C. H. (1965): Blockade of the release of gonadotrophic hormones by pharmacologic agents. *Proc. 2nd Int. Cong. Endocrinol.,* London, Excerpta Medica Foundation, Se. 83:629–634.

Shader, R. I. (1970): Endocrine, metabolic, and genitourinary effects of psychotropic drugs. In: *Clinical Handbook of Psychopharmacology,* edited by A. Di Mascio and R. I. Shader, pp. 205–212. Science House, New York.

Turkington, R. W. (1972): Phenothiazine stimulation test for prolactin reserve: The syndrome of isolated prolactin deficiency. *J. Clin. Endocrinol.,* 34:247–249.

Sexual Behavior: Pharmacology and Biochemistry, edited by M. Sandler and G. L.
Gessa. Raven Press, New York © 1975.

Antiandrogen Treatment in Sexually Abnormal Subjects with Neuropsychiatric Disorders

P. Saba, F. Salvadorini, F. Galeone, C. Pellicanò, and E. Rainer

Psychiatric Hospital of Volterra, Pisa, Italy

Hypersexual symptoms have often been noted in neuropsychiatric disorders (Laschet and Laschet, 1967; Apostolakis and Schmidt, 1968; Hoffet, 1968; Mothes, Lehnert, Samimi, and Ufer, 1972). These symptoms, particularly in psychotic subjects, traditionally have been believed to be psychogenic in origin (Giese, Krause, and Schmidt, 1968; Petri, 1969). However, hormonal factors have also been suggested as a factor in their genesis, and indeed, impaired androgen activity has been found in many sexual deviations (Apostolakis and Schmidt, 1968; Loraine, Ismail, Adamopoulos, and Dove, 1970). It is well recognized that at the central nervous system level, androgens can promote many behavioral traits connected with sexuality, e.g., sexual aggressiveness, libido, and sexual drive (Neumann, von Berswordt-Wallrabe, Elger, Steinbeck, Hahn, and Kramer, 1970; Neumann, Steinbeck, and Hahn, 1970). On this basis, the positive effect of antiandrogen treatment has been explained, both in patients with sexual deviations occurring in isolation and in mentally disturbed patients (Laschet and Laschet, 1967; Seebandt, 1968; Horn, 1971).

In previous studies information about basal androgen status has been lacking. We now present data on basal plasma testosterone levels and the effect on them of antiandrogen treatment by cyproterone acetate in subjects having neurologic or psychiatric disorders or both, with prominent hypersexual features.

MATERIAL AND METHODS

The present investigation was carried out on 24 subjects (20 men and four women), aged 16 to 67 years, grouped as follows:

Group I: Eleven male subjects suffering from subnormal mental development (I.Q. < 60), due to congenital or early acquired brain lesions. Most of these patients were hospitalized mainly on account of abnormal sexual behavior—they either masturbated or exhibited themselves or both, several times a day, and had aggressive tendencies.

Group II: Five male patients (three with mental retardation and two with depressive illness) identified as passive homosexuals, with obsessive "partner research."

Group III: Eight subjects (four men and four women) with a diagnosis of schizophrenia, whose prominent psychiatric symptoms were sexual delusions and erotic aggressiveness. Two of the women presented with homosexual drive.

Table 1 shows, for each patient, age, neurologic or psychiatric diagnosis or both, in addition to primary symptoms in the sexual field.

In all patients, basal plasma testosterone (TS) concentration was measured by radioimmunoassay (Luisi, Franchi, Menchini, Barletta, Fassorra, Ciardella, and

TABLE 1. *Characteristics of study population*

Cases	Age (years)	Neurologic or psychiatric disorder	Main symptoms in the sexual field
Group I			
J.S.	20	Congenital mental deficiency	Masturbation–exhibitionism
P.F.	26		
V.S.	16		
H.J.	45	Postencephalitic mental deficiency	Erotic aggressiveness
L.P.	34	Postencephalitic mental deficiency	Masturbation–exhibitionism
P.V.	32		
P.A.	35		
C.C.	35	Postencephalitic mental deficiency	Masturbation–aggressiveness
B.C.	29		
M.F.	64	Cerebral sclerosis	Masturbation–aggressiveness
F.D.	66	Cerebral sclerosis	Exhibitionism–paedophily
Group II			
M.P.	67	Postencephalitic mental deficiency	Passive homosexuality
C.A.	42		
G.T.	57		
M.V.	58	Reactive depressive illness	Passive homosexuality
B.C.	28		
Group III			
Men			
G.C.	46	Schizophrenia	Masturbation–erotic delusions
B.P.	21	Schizophrenia	Exhibitionism–erotic delusions
P.M.	22	Schizophrenia	Aggressiveness–erotic delusions
O.C.	21		
Women			
S.R.	40	Schizophrenia	Aggressiveness–erotic delusions
F.M.	58		
P.C.	33	Schizophrenia	Homosexuality–erotic delusions
C.R.	46		

Gagliardi, 1973) in blood samples obtained at 8 A.M., on 3 nonconsecutive days. The same blood samples from Group II patients were also used to measure 5-α-dihydrotestosterone (5-DHT) by a protein-binding method (Luisi, Franchi, Levanti, and Santoni, 1973). The results were analyzed statistically by Student's *t*-test.

In the two homosexual women whose clinical picture was indicative of high androgen activity (Group III), further investigations were performed as follows: (1) evaluation of diurnal pattern of plasma cortisol level; (2) effect of synthetic corticotropin (tetracosactide–Synacthen® (CIBA), 0.25 mg) stimulation on plasma cortisol level; (3) effect on plasma cortisol, TS, and 5-DHT levels of suppression by dexamethasone (2 mg daily for 3 days) and stimulation by HCG (5,000 I.U. per day), during the last 3 days of a 5-day period of dexamethasone administration (2 mg/day). Plasma cortisol was measured by a protein-binding method (Malvano, Dotti, and Grosso, 1973).

In all patients, other laboratory investigations were carried out, both base line and during treatment, including a full blood count, blood glucose, urea nitrogen, alkaline phosphatase, total serum bilirubin and serum glutamic oxalacetic transaminase assay. In most male patients seminal analysis was also performed.

The treatment in all male patients and in the one postmenopausal woman was a daily administration of cyproterone acetate 100 to 200 mg, in two divided doses, in eight cycles of 40 to 60 days each interrupted by a 20 to 40-day period. The other three women received, for eight cycles, a combined treatment of cyproterone acetate (50 mg twice a day) for the first 10 days after menstruation and ethyniloestradiol (0.05 mg/day) for the first 20 days of the menstrual cycle. In all patients therapy with psychotropic drugs was not altered.

During the clinical trial, the mental state and behavior of each patient were monitored by continuous observation and psychiatric assessment, including, whenever possible, the Rorschach test.

RESULTS

Basal Hormone Assay

Group I patients had blood testosterone levels (mean ± S.E.=613 ± 45.8 ng/100 ml) within normal range (Table 2). In Group II, blood testosterone level was slightly reduced in one case (422 ng/100 ml) and low in the other four patients, although the difference in this group (300.4 ± 38.4 ng/100 ml) from the normal level (527.3 ± 138.4 ng/100 ml) was not statistically significant (Table 2). In Group II subjects, mean 5-DHT level (26 ± 1.6 ng/100 ml) was significantly lower ($p < 0.001$) than that in normal men (51 ± 6.5). In Group III, male patients had a normal level of TS (647 ± 82.3 ng/100 ml). Of the four women, the two with mild hirsutism had TS and 5-DHT concentrations higher than in normal women (see Table 3). In these two patients further endocrine investigations (Table 3) pointed to the adrenals as the main androgen source.

TABLE 2. *Hormonal findings in pretreatment conditions (plasma values)*

Patients	Testosterone (ng/100 ml)	5-α-Dihydro-testosterone (ng/100 ml)
Group I (two subjects)	613 ± 45.8[a]	—
Group II (five subjects)	300.4 ± 38.4[b]	26 ± 1.6[c]
Group III		
Men (four subjects)	647 ± 82.3[b]	—[c]
Women (four subjects)	78.5 ± 28.7[b]	—[c]
Normal men	527.3 ± 138.4[b]	51 ± 6.5[c]
Normal women	48 ± 9.8	20 ± 3.0

[a] Mean ± SEM
[b] Not significant.
[c] $p < 0.001$.

TABLE 3. *Effect of drugs on plasma steroid concentrations in two homosexual women (Group III)*

	Plasma TS (ng/100) (ml)		Plasma 5-DHT (ng/100)(ml)		Plasma cortisol (μg/100 ml)		
	C.R.	P.C.	C.R.	P.C.	C.R.	P.C.	Time
Basal	76	149	31	36.5	14	12	8 A.M.
					12	11	12 A.M.
					10	14	4 P.M.
					10	11	11 P.M.
"Synacthen" (0.25 mg after 30 min)					25	22	—
"Synacthen" (0.25 mg after 60 min)					17	18	—
Dexamethasone (2 mg × 3 days)	50	106	24	24	2	3	—
Dexamethasone (2 mg × 5 days) + HCG (5000 I.U. × 3 days)	50	108	—	—	2.5	3	—

Therapeutic Effects

In all patients, a sedative effect was observed.

The first effect on the sexual behavior of Group I patients to become evident was a decrease of spontaneous erections, which disappeared completely 7 to 10 days after the beginning of the treatment. After 15 to 22 days of therapy, masturbatory activity was no longer observed; exhibitionism also disappeared. All reappeared 15 to 20 days after stopping treatment.

In Group II patients, a satisfactory reduction of libido and consequently of "partner research" was obtained after about 15 days of treatment. Moreover, in the two cases with depressive illness, a good improvement of mood was also obtained. The homosexual tendency was not altered.

After a 30-day period of treatment, Group III female patients showed significant improvement in the psychological symptoms of hypersexuality in three cases. In these patients, a nearly normal mental state was obtained toward the end of the third treatment cycle so that two of them were discharged. Moreover, hirsutism, seborrhoea, and acne, which had previously been evident in two patients, showed favorable response to treatment. No significant improvement in mental state was obtained in the only patients in whom psychologic factors were prominent.

In two male patients in the same group, a disappearance of erotic delusions was observed toward the end of the first cycle of therapy. In the meantime, masturbation and sexual aggressiveness were reduced. The other male patients who had pronounced psychologic factors affecting their inner lives showed a decrease in manifestations without any observable change in mental state.

Even in patients in whom no great difference in psychiatric status was observed, because of the sedative effect of the drug, psychologic rapport was more easily established.

Other Observations

Weight changes during the entire course of treatment were minimal; the drug was well tolerated in all patients although five showed an increase in sweating and a decrease in appetite during the first week. No significant alteration in any of the other blood tests was detected. In male patients, azoospermia was observed for a period of up to 90 to 110 days after the end of treatment.

DISCUSSION

Even if it be accepted that plasma androgen level gives a rough indication of androgenicity (Vermeulen, 1968), the hormonal findings in Group I and III patients show that in such cases of hypersexuality, absolute hyperandrogenism is rarely encountered. Elevated levels of TS and 5-DHT were only found in the two psychotic women with adrenal hirsutism in the third group. In agreement with the suggestion of Laschet and Laschet (1968a) hypersensitive state of the sexual hypothalamic center to androgens cannot be excluded so that even with normal blood levels of TS and 5-DHT, androgen-induced hypersexuality may be observed.

In male homosexual patients (Group II), the role played by androgens in the genesis of the homosexual state has yet to be demonstrated. Loraine et al. (1970) suggest that the homosexual tendency in men is due to insufficient induction of the central nervous system by androgens, in early (perinatal) life. This view receives confirmation from the low androgen level met with in true male homosexuality (Loraine et al., 1970; Saba, Salvadorini, Galeone, and Luisi, 1973). The presence of such androgens is only able to stimulate the homosexual libido (Dörner and Hinz, 1968). The opposite has been suggested to explain female homosexuality (Dörner, 1968). In this sexual deviation, the possible occurrence of early abnormal androgen induction in the central nervous system is supported by the finding of high plasma androgen values (Loraine et al., 1970).

In the present investigation, even though normal plasma TS levels were generally found, the possibility that hypersexual symptoms in subjects with neuropsychiatric diseases are related to androgenicity is confirmed by the positive effect obtained with the administration of cyproterone acetate. Indeed, this drug is known to prevent all androgen-dependent events (Neumann et al., 1970) by a competitive action at both peripheral (Chandra, Orii, and Wacker, 1967) and hypothalamic receptor sites (Saba, Marescotti, and Tronchetti, 1972). The therapeutic effect was more evident in hypersexual subjects with brain damage (Group I) and in homosexuals (Group II). However, in this second group of patients, only the sexual urge was depressed, the direction of the drive being entirely unaffected. In our psychotic subjects, when psychogenic factors were not evident in their inner life, the drug was highly effective. In the other subjects, improvement was barely detectable. This finding indicated that in psychoses with hypersexual symptoms, androgens do not always have a determinant role. Even in the absence of specific effect, cyproterone acetate therapy was a considerable aid for psychotherapy by virtue of its sedative action.

In conclusion, our findings agree with those of others (Laschet and Laschet, 1968a,b; Hoffet, 1968; Ott, 1968; Horn, 1971), i.e., that cyproterone acetate is effective in the management of patients with abnormally increased or aberrant sexuality occurring in association with mental retardation. Furthermore, the present work suggests that in psychoses linked directly or indirectly with hypersexuality, but unconnected with any abnormality of androgen production, the possibility of a therapeutic approach appears to be more useful than psychopharmacotherapy.

As the cyproterone acetate effect is related, in time, to treatment, in order to sustain the benefit and avoid recurrence, continuous drug administration or a not unduly long gap between successive treatment cycles is necessary.

SUMMARY

In 24 sexually abnormal subjects with neurologic or psychiatric disorders or both, basal evaluation of blood testosterone levels was followed up by a study of the effect of cyproterone acetate treatment.

High TS levels were found in only two psychotic women. The drug was effective in hypersexual subjects with brain damage, in homosexual patients, and in hypersexual psychotic subjects in whom psychogenic factors were not evident.

The results obtained indicate that androgens, independent of their absolute values, are important in the genesis of many sexual deviations associated with neuropsychiatric disorders.

ACKNOWLEDGMENT

The authors are grateful to Schering, A. G., Berlin, for supplying the cyproterone acetate used in this investigation.

REFERENCES

Apostolakis, M., and Schmidt, H. (1968): Testosterone excretion in psychiatric and organic sexual disorders. In: *Testosterone,* (Proc. Workship Conf. Tremsbuttel, 1967.), edited by J. Tamm, pp. 197–201. Thieme, Stuttgart.

Chandra, P., Orii, H., and Wacker, A. (1967): Effect of an antiandrogenic steroid on the testosterone stimulated activity of aggregate polymerase in the prostate nuclei of rats. *Hoppe Seyler's Z. Physiol. Chem.,* 348:1085–1086.

Dörner, G. (1968): Hormonal induction and prevention of female homosexuality. *J. Endocrinol.,* 42:163–164.

Dörner, G., and Hinz, G. (1968): Induction and prevention of male homosexuality by androgen. *J. Endocrinol.,* 40:387.

Giese, H., Krause, W. F. J., and Schmidt, H. (1968): Sexualhormone in Beziehung zur Sexualität. *Forum Psychiatr.,* 20:189–200.

Hoffet, H. (1968): Über die Anwendung des Testosteronblockers Cyproteronacetat (SH 714) bei Sexualdelinquenten und psychiatrischen Anstaltpazienten. *Praxis,* 57:221–230.

Horn, H. J. (1971): Behandlung mit Cyproteronacetat hebt bei Sexualdelinquenten erotische Reizschwelle. *Med. Trib.* 6:26.

Laschet, U., and Laschet, L. (1967): Antiandrogentherapie der pathologisch gesteigerten und abartigen Sexualität des Mannes. *Klin. Wochenschr.,* 45:324–325.

Laschet, U. and Laschet, L. (1968a): Die Behandlung der pathologisch gesteigerten und abartigen Sexualität des Mannes mit dem Antiandrogen Cyproteronacetat. In: *Das Testosteron—Die Struma,* pp. 116–119. Springer, Berlin, Heidelberg, New York.

Laschet, U., and Laschet, L. (1968b): Antiandrogen treatment of hypersexuality or abnormal sexuality in men. Simp. Esteroides Sexuales, edited by F. Albrecht, J. Sanchez, and H. Willomitzer, pp. 194–197. Saladruck, Berlin.

Loraine, J. A., Ismail, A. A. A., Adamopoulos, D. A., and Dove, G. A. (1970): Endocrine function in male and female homosexuals. *Br. Med. J.,* 4:406–408.

Luisi, M., Franchi, F., Menchini, F., Barletta, D., Fassorra, C., Ciardella, F., and Gagliardi, G. (1973): Radioimmunoassay for plasma testosterone. *Steroids Lipids Res.,* 4:213–223.

Luisi, M., Franchi, F., Levanti, C., and Santoni, R. (1973): The measurement of the dihydrotestosterone in humans. *Steroids (in press).*

Malvano, R., Dotti, C., and Grosso, P. (1973): ^{125}I-labelled cortisol TME for competitive protein binding. *Clin. Chim. Acta,* 47:167–173.

Mothes, C., Lehnert, J., Samimi, F., and Ufer, J. (1972): Klinische Prüfung von Cyproteronacetat bei Sexualdeviationen-Gesamtauswertung. In: Schering Symp. über Sexualdeviationen und ihre Medikamentöse Behandlung, Berlin 17–18 Mai, Monographs 2, 1971, Life Sciences, edited by G. Raspe, pp. 65–87. Pergamon Press, Vieweg, Oxford, Edinburgh, and New York.

Neumann, F., Steinbeck, H., and Hahn, J. D. (1970): Hormones and brain differentiation. In: *The Hypothalamus,* pp. 569–603, edited by L. Martini, M. Motta, and F. Fraschini. Academic Press, New York, London.

Neumann, F., von Berswordt-Wallrabe, R., Elger, W., Steinbeck, H., Hahn, J. D., and Kramer, M. (1970): Aspects of androgen-dependent events as studied by antiandrogens. *Rec. Progr. Horm. Res.,* 26:337–410.

Ott, F. (1968): Hypersexualität, antiandrogen und Hodenfunktion. *Praxis,* 57:218–220.

Petri, H. (1969): Exhibitionismus: Theoretische und Soziale Aspekte und die Behandlung mit Antiandrogenen. *Nervenarzt,* 40:220–228.

Saba, P., Marescotti, V., and Tronchetti, F. (1972): Effect of testosterone and of anti-androgens on the behaviour of hypothalamic neurons in male rats. IV Internat. Congr. Endocr., Washington, June 18-24, 1972. Excerpta Med. Internat. Congr. Ser., 256:3.

Saba, P., Salvadorini, F., Galeone, F., and Luisi, M. (1973): Hormonal findings in male homosexuals. *IRCS Med. Sci.,* 3:15.

Seebandt, G. (1968): Gedanken und Uberlegungen zur Behandlung Sexualtriebartiger Psychopathen mit Antiandrogenen. *Otheff. Gesundheit wes.,* 30:60–71.

Vermeulen, A. (1968): Testosterone excretion, plasma testosterone levels and testosterone production rates in health and disease. In: *Testosterone,* edited by J. Tamm, pp. 170–175. G. Thieme, Stuttgart.

Sexual Behavior: Pharmacology and Biochemistry, edited by M. Sandler and G. L.
Gessa. Raven Press, New York © 1975.

Technical and Legal Aspects in the Pharmacologic Treatment of Sex Offenders

F. Ferracuti and R. Bartilotti[1]

University of Rome, Medical School and Rebibbia Prison Center,[1] Rome, Italy

The pharmacologic treatment of sex offenders with psychoactive drugs, although currently the object of a great deal of interest, is beyond the scope of this chapter. The present focus of interest is on antiandrogens; it is to this group of substances that we draw our attention, although not to their pharmacologic and therapeutic characteristics, which have been dealt with elsewhere (Hoffet, 1968, 1969; Seebandt, 1968; Anon., 1969; Field and Williams, 1970; Bauer, 1970; Neumann, 1971, 1973; Laschet and Laschet, 1972; Money, 1972; Rainer, 1972; Saba, Pariante, Marescotti, Biasci, and Della Valle, 1972; Laschet, 1973).

Interest in these substances has been stimulated by several favorable reports. Although the antiandrogens appear to have no effect on the direction (normal or abnormal) of the sex drive, they effectively control libido, sex drive, sex behavior, and performance, reducing or eliminating sexual behavior in the human male. Furthermore, the effects are reversible, and harmful side effects (such as general feminization, obesity, etc.) appear to be minimal. Several clinical trials have been performed or are in progress. Such a therapeutic approach, particularly when compared with irreversible practices, such as castration (Stürup, 1972) or stereotactic electrocoagulation of hypothalamic "sex centers" (Roeder, Müller, and Orthner, 1971), stands a good chance of being favorably accepted and of being used, or at least proposed for use, in an increasing fashion.

It is our purpose here to discuss briefly some methodologic and legal problems that, in our view, must be solved before the utilization of antiandrogens for the treatment of SO can be broadly accepted.

On the methodologic side, some of our observations are drawn from the recent paper of Mohr (1972). Sex offenders are relatively rare, and most sex offenses are not very dangerous. Most such offenses are definitional in nature, and their incidence tends to vary with the variations of public opinion on which sexual behaviors should be the object of legal action. Proof of this can be found in the drastic changes in the rate of offenses that has followed, e.g., the liberalization of pornography in Denmark. The delimitation of the offenders on whom antiandrogens should be used is rather difficult. Most sex offenses are episodic, and these offenders exhibit a very low recidivism rate. Are we justified in utilizing such deeply modifying agents in, for example, a one-time offender of statutory rape, or must we limit antiandrogens to multiple recidivists? If so, where do we draw the line? Can criteria be found (legal, in conjunction with meaningful clinical parameters) to identify those offenders for whom antiandrogen therapy is needed, and to separate them from those for whom a short prison term is necessary, or better? Do we propose to use antiandrogens as a total substitute for penalty, or as a partial substitute? If we advocate antiandrogen treatment rather than penalty, will public opinion tolerate a total renunciation of prison terms? Will victims (and their relatives) accept a total medical model, with little or no retributory aspects, as a general policy for SO? The offense–illness equation may be unacceptable to the general public.

Sex offenses are acts that must be defined by the characteristics of the offender, of the victim, and of the total situation in which they occur—to base our intervention only on the psychologic characteristics of the offender is erroneous. Antiandrogens will do nothing for the consenting victim or for the crime-generating situation, nor is it very clear as to how long the use of these substances is proposed. What will be the time limits of the therapy? Presumably, it will be determined by the point at which the danger of recidivism disappears, and, hopefully, until other therapeutic techniques, such as psychotherapy, have eliminated or compensated for the abnormality underlying the legally proscribed behavior. However, it is well known to workers in this field how fallacious it is to try to establish absolute, clear-cut criteria for a behavior that presents so many individually different patterns that are also likely to change within the individual's life experience, according to his environmental circumstances.

Even were these methodologic obstacles to be overcome, and the subject to agree to antiandrogen therapy, what would be the practical modalities of carrying out such a program?

1. Daily or weekly administration presupposes a tight control system and access to an external, probation-like structure, which is presently nonexistent or malfunctioning in many countries.

2. Administration by implant would facilitate treatment, but how much do we really know about the rate of absorption? Would the administration of androgens compensate the implant? What will happen at the termination of the implant? The rather exact quantitative criteria that we use in animal experimentation generally are not feasible in man, particularly in an unwilling, or only partially willing, legally restrained convict. The round-the-clock observation that we carry out in our animal laboratories is precluded by real-life outpatient situations.

Next, we move to the more specific legal problems involved in this type of treatment; the following remarks appear in order. In general, the problem of valid consent remains doubtful. Given the climate of noncooperation and radicalism that prevails in most of our institutions, any depriving intervention, even if medically sound and temporary, is likely to evoke emotionally charged reactions, which will overflow the medical model and trespass into politically based objections.

On the other hand, total acceptance of the medical model with antiandrogen therapy, even for nonmentally ill inmates, would pave the way to medical treatment with psychoactive drugs of other behavioral antisocial manifestations. The control of aggression would be passed on to physicians, with possible overuse of sedatives. The issues concerning the legality and morality of such an approach are far from being solved.

The consent of the convict poses the usual dilemma of validity in the case of the mentally ill subject, and of moral coercion and bargaining in the case of the nonmentally ill subject. The right to cure can only be invoked partially in cases in which mental illness is absent or ill-defined. Sexual offenders are rarely psychotic, and psychopathy in most legislations is not sufficient grounds for a declaration of insanity. The acceptance of a medical model, with the inherent "right to treatment," would seem to imply recognition of psychopathy as grounds for the defense of insanity.

Obviously, the progress in treatment techniques calls for new legislation, for which the pioneering research reported in this volume provides the needed doctrinal foundations. Specifically, in Italy, article 552[1] of the penal code prohibits treatments that can stop generative power. This article, with the accompanying article 553,[2] which prohibits public advertising of practices against generation, is the expression of legislation, which recognized generative powers as non-renounceable. The Italian Constitutional Court, in 1971, has declared article 553 unconstitutional, but has not dealt with article 552. The articles in question make no distinction between temporary and permanent "impotence to generate." A bill is currently in the House to modify article 552, which proposes the elimination of temporary impotence, and excludes sanctions for the person and the physician. At present, however, only a "condition of necessity," such as, for example, a seminoma, will permit medical intervention.

To sum up the preceding notes, the following points are open for discussion and would benefit from further study and consideration.

1. Which sex offenders should be subjected to antiandrogen therapy? How do we define them?
2. How do we intend to institutionalize and legislate treatment? Which control agency should carry it out, or supervise or monitor it?
3. What concurrent treatments should be proposed? Sex offenders are individuals. Standard patterns of treatment are not likely to succeed. How do we propose to individualize the "therapy-mix" which is likely to be most effective in a given case?

---

[1] Art. 552 Italian penal code: *Procurata impotenza alla procreazione.* Chiunque compie, su persona dell'uno o dell'altro sesso, col consenso di questa, atti diretti a renderla impotente alla procreazione, è punito con la reclusione da sei mesi a due anni e con la multa da lire mille a cinquemila. Alla stessa pena soggiace chi ha consentito al compimento di tali atti sulla propria persona.

[2] Art. 553 Italian penal code: *Incitamento a pratiche contro la procreazione.* Chiunque pubblicamente incita a pratiche contro la procreazione o fa propaganda a favore di esse è punito con la reclusione fino a un anno o con la multa fino a lire diecimila. Tali pene si applicano congiuntamente se il fatto è commesso a scopo di lucro.

4. What about termination of treatment and aftercare? When and how do we stop?

5. From a legal standpoint, how do we define valid consent in a nonmentally ill subject? And how do we deal with the unclear definitions of mental illness, of sexual psychopathy, in a legal framework?

6. Specifically, in Italy, abrogation or modification of article 552 of the penal code appears to be necessary before such treatments can be used in any large-scale approach.

7. Individualization and multiple therapeutic approaches appear to be the most valid path of progress. In this context, antiandrogens are a powerful new tool at our disposal and further study of their properties and characteristics is a high priority in medicolegal and criminologic research.

REFERENCES

Anon. (1969): Eine "Pille' für den Mann. Neuartige Behandlungsmöglichkeit bei Sexualdelinquenten. *Kriminalistic,* 23:257–258.

Bauer, G. (1970): Aktuelle Probleme in der Kriminologie. (Ein Bericht über die Kriminologentagung in Saarbrücken, 2–5 Oktober, 1969.) *Prax. Kinderpsychol. Kinderpsychiatr.,* 19:151–156.

Field, L. H., and Williams M. (1970): The hormonal treatment of sexual offenders. *Med. Sci. Law,* 10:27–34.

Hoffet, H. (1968): On the application of the testosterone blocker cyproterone acetate (SH 714) in sex deviants and psychiatric patients in institutions. *Praxis,* 7:221.

Hoffet, H. (1969): Neue Wege in der Behandlung von Sexualdelinquenten. *Kriminalistik,* 23:405–508; 23:484–488.

Laschet, U. (1973): Antiandrogens in the treatment of sex offenders: Mode of action and therapeutic outcome. In: *Contemporary Sexual Behavior: Critical Issues in the 1970s,* edited by J. Zubin and J. Money. Johns Hopkins University Press, Baltimore, Maryland.

Laschet, U., and Laschet, L. (1972): *Antiandrogens in Sexual Disorders: Influence of Cyproterone Acetate on the Human Neuroendocrine System (mimeographed edition).*

Mohr, J. W. (1972): Evaluation of treatment. In: *Sexual Behaviors. Social, Clinical and Legal Aspects,* edited by H. L. P. Resnik and M. E. Wolfgang. Little, Brown, Boston, Massachusetts.

Money, J. (1972): The therapeutic use of androgen-depleting hormone. In: *Sexual Behaviors. Social, Clinical and Legal Aspects,* edited by H. L. P. Resnik and M. E. Wolfgang. Little, Brown, Boston, Massachusetts.

Neumann, F. (1971): Use of cyproterone acetate in animal and clinical trials. *Gynecol. Invest.,* 2: 150–179.

Neumann, F. (1973): Antiandrogens. *Med. Klin.,* 68:329–333.

Rainer, E. (1972): I ciproterone acetato nel trattamento medico dei delinquenti sessuali (Castrazione ormonale). *Sessuologia,* 13:89–95.

Roeder, F., Müller, D., and Orthner, H. (1971): Weitere Erfahrungen mit der stereotaktischen Behandlung sexualler Perversionen. *J. Neuro-Visceral Relations [Suppl.],* 10:317–324.

Saba, P., Pariante, F., Marescotti, V., Biasci, G., and Della Valle, M. (1972): Effetti indotti dal trattamento con ciproterone acetato in pazienti cerebropatici gravi, con manifestazioni di sessualità esaltata. *Sessuologia,* 13:139–143.

Seebandt, G. (1968): Thoughts and reflections on the treatment of sex-deviant psychopaths with antiandrogens. *Mschr. Gesundheits. Sozial- hyg.,* 30:66.

Stürup, G. K. (1972): Castration: The total treatment. In: *Sexual Behaviors. Social, Clinical and Legal Aspects,* edited by H. L. P. Resnik and M. E. Wolfgang. Little, Brown, Boston, Massachusetts.

Sexual Behavior: Pharmacology and Biochemistry, edited by M. Sandler and G. L. Gessa. Raven Press, New York © 1975.

Physiologic and Pharmacologic Actions of Hormonal Steroids in Sexual Behavior

William G. Luttge, Nicholas R. Hall, and Cleatus J. Wallis

Department of Neuroscience and Center for Neurobiologic Sciences, University of Florida College of Medicine, Gainesville, Florida 32610

In recent years considerable progress has been made in the elucidation of the stimulatory actions of androgens in both neural and peripheral target tissues. In rats and mice castration results in the loss, and exogenous androgen therapy the restoration, of sexual and agonistic behavior, perinatal neural and peripheral sexual differentiation, normal suppression of gonadotropin secretion, and maintenance and growth of sex accessory tissues (e.g., Pfeiffer, 1936; Beeman, 1947; Beach, 1948; Davidson, 1969a; Luttge and Whalen, 1970; Edwards, 1971; Gorski, 1971; Bronson, Whitsett, and Hamilton, 1972). Prior to 1968 it was generally believed that testosterone (4-androsten-17β-ol-3-one) was the major naturally occurring hormone responsible for these androgen effects. However, with the discovery that dihydrotestosterone (5α-androstan-17β-ol-3-one) was more potent than testosterone in stimulating growth of the prostate, and with the additional discovery that testosterone can be metabolically converted intracellularly in both neural and peripheral tissues to dihydrotestosterone and other 5α-reduced metabolites (Fig. 1), the hypothesis was raised that testosterone metabolites (including estrogens) may be the active agents in androgen target tissues (e.g., Baulieu, Lasnitzki, and Robel, 1968; Bruchovsky and Wilson, 1968; Jaffe, 1969; Beyer, Morali, and Cruz, 1971; Stern and Eisenfeld, 1971; Beyer, Gay, and Jaffe, 1972; Buric, Becker, Peterson, and Voigt, 1972; Massa, Stupnicka, Kniewald, and Martini, 1972; Whalen and Rezek, 1972; Baum and Vreeburg, 1973; Becker, Grabosch, Hoffman, and Voigt, 1973; Larsson, Sodersten, and Beyer, 1973; Schmidt, Giba-Tziampiri, Rotteck, and Voigt, 1973; Feder, Naftolin, and Ryan, 1974). These revelations have stimulated numerous studies in which the potency or neuroanatomic localization or both of naturally occurring hormones have been assessed. But the question of whether or not these findings reflect reasonable physiologic mechanisms or simply pharmacologic demonstrations has seldom been considered. In this chapter we discuss this possibility in the course of reviewing recent findings concerning male sexual behavior in the rat and mouse.

ANDROSTEN VERSUS ANDROSTAN ANDROGENS

Rats

In our early studies with rats, we found that testosterone and androstenedione (4-androsten-3,17-dione) were equipotent in restoring sexual behavior in long-

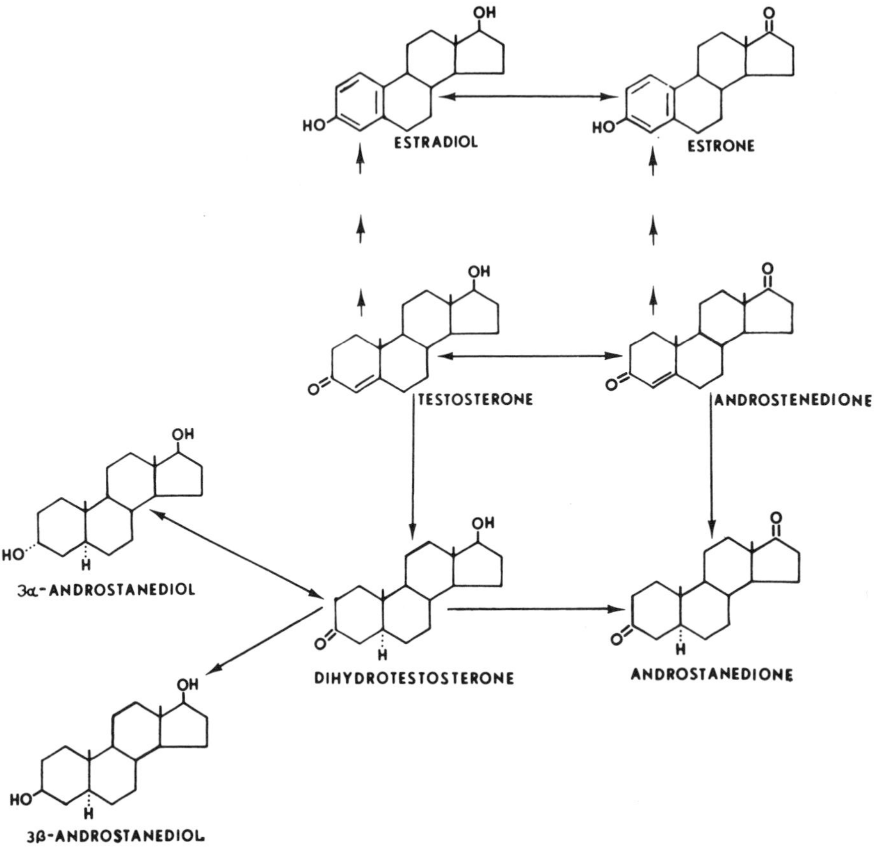

FIG. 1. Schematic representation of androgen metabolism in neural and peripheral target tissues.

term castrate males and in stimulating the male-like pattern of sexual differentiation of the neural control of gonadotropin secretion in perinatal females whereas dihydrotestosterone was found to be completely ineffective (Luttge and Whalen, 1969, 1970; Whalen and Luttge, 1971a). Although most of these findings have been independently demonstrated in a number of other laboratories (Brown-Grant, Munck, Naftolin, and Sherwood, 1971; Feder, 1971; McDonald and Doughty, 1972; McDonald, Beyer, Newton, Brien, Baker, Tan, Sampson, Kitching, Greenhill, and Pritchard, 1970; Ulrich, Yuwiler, and Geller, 1972; Beyer, Larsson, Perez-Palacios, and Morali, 1973); Morali, Larsson, Perez-Palacios, and Beyer (1974) have reported that testosterone and androstenediol (5-androsten-3, 17-diol) were both more potent than androstenedione in stimulating copulation in sexually inexperienced castrate male rats. Beyer et al. (1973) have further shown that, like dihydrotestosterone, 3α-androstanediol (5α-androstan-3α,

17β-diol) is also totally ineffective in restoring sexual behavior in castrate male rats.

An analysis of the effectiveness of various androgens to maintain sexual behavior after castration showed that testosterone and androstenedione were both active, whereas dihydrotestosterone treatment was no more effective than oil (Whalen and Luttge, 1971b). Therefore, in rats dihydrotestosterone and other 5α-reduced androgens are ineffective in the stimulation and maintenance of male sexual behavior whereas testosterone, androstenedione, and other androsten androgens are capable of stimulating copulation. Because only this latter group of androgens can be aromatized in the brain to form estrogens (Naftolin, Ryan, and Petro, 1971), the hypothesis has been raised that estrogens may play a role in androgen-induced male sexual behavior. This possibility is further discussed later.

Mice

In our first studies with castrate mice, we found that in the CD-1 strain testosterone effectively stimulated isolation-induced intermale fighting with untreated castrate males whereas neither androstenedione nor dihydrotestosterone exhibited this ability (Luttge, 1972). In the Swiss-Webster strain, we again found that testosterone was effective and androstenedione ineffective in stimulating intermale fighting, but unlike our findings with the CD-1 strain, dihydrotestosterone was also found to stimulate fighting in Swiss-Webster males (Luttge and Hall, 1973a).

In addition, strain differences were found in the modulation of sexual behavior. In a direct strain comparison, we found that in CD-1 mice only testosterone effectively stimulated sexual behavior in adult male castrates whereas in Swiss-Webster mice dihydrotestosterone was found to be nearly as effective as testosterone (Luttge and Hall, 1973b). The effectiveness of two other 5α-reduced androgens, 3α- and 3β-androstanediol, in the induction of sexual behavior in castrate Swiss-Webster males has also been tested (Luttge, Hall, and Wallis, 1974). Testosterone was again found to be the most potent stimulator of male-like sexual behavior, followed by 3β-androstanediol and finally by 3α-androstanediol. Dihydrotestosterone failed to stimulate sexual behavior when dissolved in the propylene glycol vehicle used in this study; however, in a separate study in which the hormones were dissolved in the oily vehicle used in our previous studies with dihydrotestosterone, this 5α-reduced androgen was again found to be a potent stimulator of male sexual behavior.

Closer examination of these data reveals that testosterone has a lower threshold and a shorter latency to induction of copulatory behavior than does dihydrotestosterone. Therefore, it is unlikely even in the Swiss-Webster mouse that testosterone secreted by the testis stimulates male sexual behavior through its metabolic conversion to dihydrotestosterone or its metabolities 3α-and 3β-androstanediol or both. However, the fact that these 5α-reduced androgens did stimulate copulation provides an argument against the contention that testosterone stimulates male sexual behavior in the Swiss-Webster mouse solely through its metabolic aromatization to an estrogen.

Recent studies in the hamster (Whalen and DeBold, 1974), rabbit (Beyer and Rivaud, 1973), guinea pig (Alsum and Goy, 1974), and rhesus monkey (Phoenix, 1974) have also shown that dihydrotestosterone treatment can result in display of male sexual behavior in castrated animals. These findings together with ours for the Swiss-Webster mouse challenge the generality of the hypothesis that in the male rat testosterone stimulates sexual behavior by its aromatization to estradiol.

AROMATIZATION AND ANTIESTROGENS

In experiments specifically designed to test the aromatization hypothesis, we studied the induction of female sexual behavior in the ovariectomized rat. When given prior to progesterone priming the aromatizable androgens, testosterone and androstenedione were both found to stimulate the display of the lordosis posture indicative of sexual receptivity (Whalen, Battie, and Luttge, 1971). In a similar study Beyer and Komisaruk (1971) reported that treatment with the nonaromatizable androgen dihydrotestosterone did not stimulate lordosis behavior as did similar treatment with testosterone. When treatment with an antiestrogen (CI-628; Parke, Davis) was combined with testosterone propionate treatment, the display of lordosis behavior following progesterone priming was found to be reduced dramatically (Whalen, Battie, and Luttge, 1972). Because CI-628 was shown to lack antiandrogenic properties (on seminal vesicle wet weight) we concluded that the inhibition of female sexual behavior was due to the inhibition of the effects of the aromatization-produced estrogens.

To test the possibility that this antiestrogen might also block androgen-induced male sexual behavior, four castrate male rats previously shown to display consistent copulatory behavior under testosterone propionate therapy were given additional daily injections of CI-628 (Whalen et al., 1972). Even after 8 weeks of antiestrogen treatment no consistent changes in the display of male sexual behavior were observed, although the dose of CI-628 should have been sufficient to block lordosis behavior caused by aromatization-produced estrogens in similarly treated females. These data strongly suggest that aromatization-produced estrogens do not play a significant role in testosterone-induced male sexual behavior in the rat.

AROMATIZATION, 5α REDUCTION, AND ANTIANDROGENS

As described earlier, several groups of investigators have hypothesized that testosterone may stimulate sexual arousal through its aromatization to estradiol in the brain, while it stimulates the peripheral tissues necessary for the performance of male sexual behavior through its 5α reduction to dihydrotestosterone. This hypothesis stems mainly from the observation that although long-term treatment with high doses of estrogens stimulated the display of mounts and even occasional intromissions in castrate male rats (Davidson, 1969b; Sodersten, 1973), mounts, intromissions, and ejaculations were readily induced in castrate rats with low doses of estradiol benzoate combined with dihydrotestosterone (Baum and Vreeburg, 1973; Larsson et al., 1973; Feder et al., 1974).

To test specifically this challenging hypothesis of androgen action, we have recently completed an experiment in which the effects of the antiandrogen cyproterone acetate (Schering AG) on estradiol benzoate + dihydrotestosterone-induced male sexual behavior were assessed (Luttge, Hall, Wallis, and Campbell, 1975). In this study long-term castrate sexually naive male rats were placed into one of eight groups and injected daily with either oil–benzyl benzoate vehicle (V), cyproterone acetate (C), estradiol benzoate (E), dihydrotestosterone (D), E + C (EC), E + D (ED), D + C (DC), or E + D plus C (EDC). Replicating earlier studies, we found that ED treatment successfully stimulated the display of mounts, intromissions, and ejaculations (Fig. 2). No other group displayed ejaculations. Although mounts and intromissions were displayed by several males in the EDC and EC groups, the frequency of the display of these behaviors even in these groups was far below that displayed by the males in the ED group. Other behavioral indices, including latency to first display of each behavior and number of tests in which each behavior was displayed, were likewise dramatically reduced in all groups compared to the ED group.

Therefore, it is clear that treatment with the antiandrogen cyproterone acetate can effectively block the induction of male sexual behavior in rats stimulated by injections of estrogen plus dihydrotestosterone. The question remains as to the mechanism of this inhibitory action. Because it is well known that cyproterone acetate can block the peripheral effects of androgens (e.g., Neumann, von Berswordt-Wallrabe, Elger, Steinbeck, Hahn, and Kramer, 1970), we examined the seminal vesicles and penises of all males at the conclusion of the behavioral tests. Only those groups receiving dihydrotestosterone (i.e., D, ED, DC, and EDC) had significantly heavier seminal vesicles and penises than vehicle-treated controls. These males also had significantly longer penises. In each case the addition of cyproterone acetate reduced these androgen-dependent parameters, but with the exception of penis lengths for the EDC group this reduction was not to the level of the vehicle-injected controls.

The most obvious conclusion from this study is support for the hypothesis that dihydrotestosterone treatment stimulates sexual behavior in estrogen-treated castrate males because it stimulates the peripheral tissues required for the display of the complete pattern of copulation (i.e., a well-developed penis is presumably required for the display of ejaculatory behavior). Although this conclusion may be valid, the extension of the general hypothesis to include the concept that testosterone stimulates male sexual behavior solely through its conversion to estrogen and dihydrotestosterone remains to be proved. One major problem with this expanded theory is the fact that whereas cyproterone acetate treatment may be able to block male sexual behavior stimulated by injections of estrogen plus

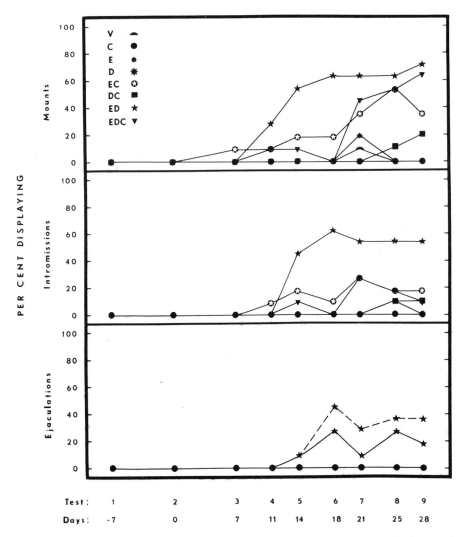

FIG. 2. Percentage of castrate male rats in each group displaying mounts, intromissions, and ejaculations on two tests prior (tests 1 and 2) and seven tests after (tests 3–9) initiation of a daily s.c. hormone injection regime. Males were injected with benzyl benzoate–oil vehicle (V), cyproterone acetate (C) (10 mg/day), estradiol benzoate (E) (1 μg/day), dihydrotestosterone (D) (1 mg/day), E + C (EC) (1 μg + 10 mg/day), E + D (ED) (1 μg + 1 mg/day), D + C (DC) (1 mg + 10 mg/day), or E + D + C (EDC) (1 μg + 1 mg + 10 mg/day). All tests were terminated at 15 min except those in which males exhibited five or more intromissions (dashed line). In these cases tests were extended an additional 5 min to allow the male the opportunity to achieve ejaculation. (From Luttge et al., 1975.)

dihydrotestosterone, this antiandrogen does not block male sexual behavior stimulated by injections of testosterone propionate (Beach and Westbrook, 1968; Whalen and Edwards, 1969). Figure 3 illustrates this apparent discrepancy.

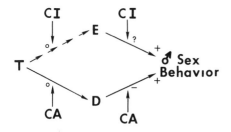

FIG. 3. Summary scheme for the observed and expected actions of testosterone (T), estradiol (E), dihydrotestosterone (D), cyproterone acetate (CA), and CI-628 (CI) on the display of male sexual behavior. Behavioral facilitation (+), inhibition (−), and no effect (o). ? = effect not directly tested.

CONCLUDING ARGUMENTS

If testosterone is working as a result of its conversion to estrogen and dihydrotestosterone, then an injection of testosterone ought to be essentially the same as an injection of estrogen plus dihydrotestosterone. If this mechanism is correct, then both cyproterone acetate treatment and CI-628 treatment should block male sexual behavior in rats injected with testosterone. Because neither of these antihormones blocks testosterone-stimulated behavior, and because nonaromatizable 5α-reduced androgens can stimulate male sexual behavior in mice, hamsters, rabbits, guinea pigs, and rhesus monkeys *(vide supra),* it seems highly improbable that the aromatization of testosterone plays a major physiologic role in the induction of male sexual behavior. Therefore, the demonstration that estrogen plus dihydrotestosterone can stimulate the complete pattern of male sexual behavior in the rat is considered to be a pharmacologic and not a physiologic demonstration.

ACKNOWLEDGMENTS

The research from the authors' laboratory described in this chapter was supported by Grant HD-07049-01 from the National Institute of Child Health and Human Development and by Grant MH-25191-01 from the National Institute of Mental Health of the U.S. Public Health Service. Additional funds were provided by Project No. 726 of the National Institutes of Health General Research Grant RR-5362-11 awarded to the University of Florida College of Medicine. N.R.H. and C.J.W. were supported by predoctoral fellowships provided by National Institute of Mental Health Training Grant MH–10320–09 awarded to the University of Florida Center for Neurobiological Sciences. The excellent technical assistance of James C. Campbell and Judith G. Vogel is also gratefully acknowledged.

REFERENCES

Alsum, P., and Goy, R. W. (1974): Actions of esters of testosterone, dihydrotestosterone or estradiol on sexual behavior in castrated male guinea pigs. *Horm. Behav.,* 5:207–217.
Baulieu, E. E., Lasnitzki, I., and Robel, P. (1968): Metabolism of testosterone and action of metabolites on prostate glands grown in organ culture. *Nature,* 219:1155–1156.

Baum, M. J., and Vreeburg, J. T. M. (1973): Copulation in castrated male rats following combined treatment with estradiol and dihydrotestosterone. *Science,* 182:283–285.

Beach, F. A. (1948): *Hormones and Behavior.* Hoeber-Harper, New York.

Beach, F. A., and Westbrook, W. H. (1968): Morphological and behavioral effects of an anti-androgen in male rats. *J. Endocrinol.,* 42:379–382.

Becker, H., Grabosch, E., Hoffmann, C., and Voigt, K. D. (1973): Metabolism and mode of action of androgens in target tissues of male rats. III. Metabolism of 5α-androstane-3,17-dione, of 5α-androstane-3α,17β-diol and of 5α-androstane-3β,17β-diol in target organs and peripheral tissues. *Acta Endocrinol.,* 73:407–416.

Beeman, E. A. (1947): The effect of male hormone on aggressive behavior in mice. *Physiol. Zool.,* 20:373–405.

Beyer, C., Gay, V., and Jaffe, R. B. (1972): Testosterone metabolism in target tissues: Effects of testosterone and dihydrotestosterone injection and hypothalamic implantation on serum LH in ovariectomized rats. *Endocrinology,* 91:1372–1375.

Beyer, C., and Komisaruk, B. (1971): Effects of diverse androgens on estrous behavior, lordosis reflex, and genital tract morphology in the rat. *Horm. Behav.,* 2:217–225.

Beyer, C., Larsson, K., Perez-Palacios, G., and Morali, G. (1973): Androgen structure and male sexual behavior in the castrated rat. *Horm. Behav.,* 4:99–108.

Beyer, C., and Rivaud, N. (1973): Differential effect of testosterone and dihydrotestosterone on the sexual behavior of prepuberally castrated male rabbits. *Horm. Behav.,* 4:175–180.

Bronson, F. H., Whitsett, J. M., and Hamilton, T. H. (1972): Responsiveness of accessory glands of adult mice to testosterone: Priming with neonatal injections. *Endocrinology,* 90:10–16.

Brown-Grant, K., Munck, A., Naftolin, F., and Sherwood, M. R. (1971): The effects of the administration of testosterone propionate alone or with phenobarbitone and of testosterone metabolites to neonatal female rats. *Horm. Behav.,* 2:173–182.

Bruchovsky, N., and Wilson, J. D. (1968): The conversion of testosterone to 5α-androstan-17β-ol-3-one by rat prostate *in vivo* and *in vitro. J. Biol. Chem.,* 243:2012–2021.

Buric, L., Becker, H., Petersen, C., and Voigt, K. D. (1972): Metabolism and mode of action of androgens in target tissues of male rats. I. Metabolism of testosterone and 5α-dihydrotestosterone in target organs and peripheral tissues. *Acta Endocrinol.,* 69:153–164.

Davidson, J. M. (1969a): Feedback control of gonadotropin secretion. In: *Frontiers in Neuroendocrinology,* edited by W. F. Ganong and L. Martini. Oxford Univ. Press, New York.

Davidson, J. M. (1969b): Effects of estrogen on the sexual behavior of male rats. *Endocrinology,* 84:1365–1372.

Edwards, D. A. (1971): Neonatal administration of androstenedione, testosterone, or testosterone propionate: Effects on ovulation, sexual receptivity and aggressive behavior in female mice. *Physiol. Behav.,* 6:223–228.

Feder, H. H. (1971): The comparative actions of testosterone propionate and 5α-androstan-17β-ol-3-one propionate on the reproductive behavior, physiology and morphology of male rats. *J. Endocrinol.,* 51:241–252.

Feder, H. H., Naftolin, F., and Ryan, K. J. (1974): Male and female sexual responses in male rats given estradiol benzoate and 5α-androstan-17β-ol-3-one propionate. *Endocrinology,* 94:136–141.

Gorski, R. (1971): Gonadal hormones and the perinatal development of neuroendocrine function. In: *Frontiers in Neuroendocrinology,* edited by L. Martini and W. F. Ganong. Oxford Univ. Press, New York.

Jaffe, R. B. (1969): Testosterone metabolism in target tissues: Hypothalamic and pituitary tissues of adult rat and human fetus, and the immature rat epiphysis. *Steroids,* 114:483–498.

Larsson, K., Sodersten, P., and Beyer, C. (1973): Sexual behavior in male rats treated with estrogen in combination with dihydrotestosterone. *Horm. Behav.,* 4:289–299.

Luttge, W. G. (1972): Activation and inhibition of isolation induced inter-male fighting behavior in castrate male CD-1 mice treated with steroidal hormones. *Horm. Behav.,* 3:71–81.

Luttge, W. G., and Hall, N. R. (1973a): Androgen-induced agonistic behavior in castrate male Swiss-Webster mice: Comparison of four naturally occurring androgens. *Behav. Biol.,* 8:725–732.

Luttge, W. G., and Hall, N. R. (1973b): Differential effectiveness of testosterone and its metabolites in the induction of male sexual behavior in two strains of albino mice. *Horm. Behav.,* 4:31–43.

Luttge, W. G., Hall, N. R., and Wallis, C. J. (1974): Studies on the neuroendocrine, somatic and behavioral effectiveness of testosterone and its 5α reduced metabolites in Swiss-Webster mice. *Physiol. Behav.,* 13:553–561.

Luttge, W. G., Hall, N. R., Wallis, C. J., and Campbell, J. C. (1975): Stimulation of male and female sexual behavior in gonadectomized rats with estrogen and androgen therapy and its inhibition with concurrent anti-hormone therapy. *Physiol. Behav.,* 14 *(in press).*

Luttge, W. G., and Whalen, R. E. (1969): Partial defeminization by administration of androstenedione to neonatal female rats. *Life Sci.* (I), 8:1003–1008.

Luttge, W. G., and Whalen, R. E. (1970): Dihydrotestosterone, androstenedione, testosterone: Comparative effectiveness in masculinizing and defeminizing reproductive systems in male and female rats. *Horm. Behav.,* 1:265–281.

Massa, R., Stupnicka, E., Kniewald, Z., and Martini, L. (1972): The transformation of testosterone into dihydrotestosterone by the brain and the anterior pituitary. *J. Steroid Biochem.,* 3:383–399.

McDonald, P. G., and Doughty, C. (1972): Comparison of the effects of neonatal administration of testosterone and dihydrotestosterone in the female rat. *J. Reprod. Fertil.,* 30:55–62.

McDonald, P. G., Beyer, C., Newton, F., Brien, B., Baker, R., Tan, H. S., Sampson, C., Kitching, P., Greenhill, R., and Pritchard, D. (1970): Failure of 5α-dihydrotestosterone to initiate sexual behavior in the castrated male rat. *Nature,* 227:964–965.

Morali, G., Larsson, K., Perez-Palacios, G., and Beyer, C. (1972): Testosterone, androstenedione, and androstenediol: Effects on the initiation of mating behavior of inexperienced castrated male rats. *Horm. Behav.,* 5:103–110.

Naftolin, F., Ryan, K. J., and Petro, Z. (1974): Aromatization of androstenedione by the anterior hypothalamus of adult male and female rats. *Endocrinology,* 90:295–298.

Neumann, F., von Berswordt-Wallrabe, R., Elger, W., Steinbeck, H., Hahn, J. D., and Kramer, M. (1970): Aspects of androgen-dependent events as studied by antiandrogens. *Rec. Prog. Horm. Res.,* 26:337–410.

Pfeiffer, C. A. (1936): Sexual differences of the hypophyses and their determination by the gonads. *Am. J. Anat.,* 58:195–225.

Phoenix, C. (1974): Effects of dihydrotestosterone on sexual behavior of castrated male rhesus monkeys. *Physiol. Behav.,* 12:1045–1055.

Schmidt, H., Noack, I., and Voigt, K. D. (1972): Metabolism and mode of action of androgens in target tissues of male rats. II. Mode of action of testosterone and 5α-dihydrotestosterone at a cellular level on seminal vesicles and prostates of rats. *Acta Endocrinol.,* 69:165–173.

Schmidt, H., Giba-Tziampiri, O., von Rotteck, G., and Voigt, K. D. (1973): Metabolism and mode of action of androgens in target tissues of male rats. IV. Mode of action of 5α-androstane-3,17-dione, 5α-androstane-3α,17β-diol and of 5α-androstane-3β,17β-diol at a cellular level on seminal vesicles and prostates of rats. *Acta Endocrinol.,* 73:599–611.

Sodersten, P. (1973): Estrogen-activated sexual behavior in male rats. *Horm. Behav.,* 4:247–256.

Stern, J. M., and Eisenfeld, A. J. (1971): Distribution and metabolism of ^{3}H-testosterone in castrated male rats; Effects of cyproterone, progesterone and unlabeled testosterone. *Endocrinology,* 88: 1117–1125.

Ulrich, R., Yuwiler, A., and Geller, E. (1972): Failure of 5α-dihydrotestosterone to block androgen sterilization in the female rat. *Proc. Soc. Exp. Biol. Med.,* 139:411–413.

Whalen, R. E., Battie, C., and Luttge, W. G. (1971): Androgen-induced receptivity. *Horm. Behav.,* 2:355–356.

Whalen, R. E., Battie, C., and Luttge, W. G. (1972): Anti-estrogen inhibition of androgen induced sexual receptivity in rats. *Behav. Biol.,* 7:311–320.

Whalen, R. E., and DeBold, J. F. (1974): Comparative effectiveness of testosterone, androstenedione and dihydrotestosterone in maintaining mating behavior in the castrated male hamster. *Endocrinology,* 95:1674–1679.

Whalen, R. E., and Edwards, D. A. (1969): Effects of the anti-androgen cyproterone acetate on mating behavior and seminal vesicle tissue in male rats. *Endocrinology,* 84:155–156.

Whalen, R. E., and Luttge, W. G. (1971a): Perinatal administration of dihydrotestosterone to female rats and the development of reproductive function. *Endocrinology,* 89:1320–1322.

Whalen, R. E., and Luttge, W. G. (1971b): Testosterone, androstenedione, and dihydrotestosterone: Effects on mating behavior of male rats. *Horm. Behav.,* 2:117–125.

Whalen, R. E., and Rezek, D. L. (1972): Localization of androgenic metabolites in the brain of rats administered testosterone or dihydrotestosterone. *Steroids,* 20:717–725.

Sexual Behavior: Pharmacology and Biochemistry, edited by M. Sandler and G. L.
Gessa. Raven Press, New York © 1975.

Sexual Differentiation and Patterns of Sexual and Maternal Behavior in the Rat: Role of Neonatal Gonadotropins and Gonadal Steroids

B. D. Goldman, R. S. Bridges, and D. N. Quadagno*

*Department of Biobehavioral Sciences, University of Connecticut, Storrs, Connecticut 06268
and *Department of Physiology and Cell Biology, University of Kansas, Lawrence, Kansas
66044*

It has long been recognized that testicular hormones produced during early life have a profound role in "masculinizing" several physiologic systems. Sexual behavior has been the most studied of the behavioral parameters so affected; however, it has more recently been observed that agonistic and maternal behaviors are also influenced by the developmental effects of testicular hormones. This review deals with (a) recent findings on the role of pituitary gonadotropins in the process of neonatal sexual differentiation in rodents and (b) the role of neonatal testicular hormone in the development of mechanisms that regulate maternal behavior in the rat.

SEXUAL BEHAVIOR

Neonatal Testicular Hormone and "Masculinization" of Sexual Behavior

Several investigators have reported that castration of the neonatal rat results in the development of an animal that is unable to display the normal repertoire of masculine sexual behavior in adulthood, but is capable of showing a high level of feminine behavior following treatment with estrogen and progesterone (Gorski, 1971). Because male laboratory rats of most strains display only very low levels of female sexual behavior following castration in adulthood, the results after neonatal castration represent a marked increase in the ability of the animal to respond behaviorally to "female" sex steroids. It is generally believed that the alteration in this case is primarily at the level of the central nervous system (CNS), as lordotic behavior appears to be regulated by changes in CNS "sensitivity." However, one must consider some recent findings that indicate an increase in the sensitivity of tactile receptors in the genital area following estrogen treatment in the adult female rat (Komisaruk, Adler, and Hutchinson, 1972).

The decrease in the capacity to display masculine sexual behavior following neonatal castration may be due to peripheral or central effects, or to both. Penis size is reduced in such animals and cannot be fully restored by treatment with androgen in adulthood. Because sexual behavior is reduced in male rats by application of a local anesthetic to the penis, it appears possible that any treatment that might reduce genital sensitivity could alter masculine sexual behavior (Beach, 1968). Nevertheless, complete copulatory-like behavior (excluding ejaculation) has been induced in female rats by long-term estrogen implants (Emery and Sachs, *personal communication*), suggesting that the presence of normal male genitalia need not always be a limiting factor.

Neonatal Pituitary Gonadotropins and Sexual Differentiation

Because the adult testis is largely under pituitary control, it was of interest to determine whether this was also true for the neonatal testis, especially with respect to the masculinizing effects of the testis (see above). It was found that both LH and FSH were present only in very low concentrations in the blood of neonatal male rats; however, both gonadotropins were present in markedly in-

TABLE 1. *Inhibition of gonadotropin secretion by testosterone propionate (TP) in castrated neonatal male rats*

Treatment	No. rats	LH (ng/ml serum)	FSH (ng/ml serum)
Intact, untreated, day 6	4	0.9	—
Castrated, day 5			
Oil, day 6	6	3.4	667
3 μg TP, day 6	11	0.9	500
Oil, day 6	5; 5[a]	4.0; 7.5	600; 1,000
30 μg TP, day 6	6; 6[a]	0.9; 0.9	407; 383
Oil, days 6 and 7	6	7.8	793
3 μg TP, days 6 and 7	9	0.9	253
Oil, days 6 and 7	3	8.8	867
30 μg TP, days 6 and 7	6	0.9	280

[a] Two groups of controls and corresponding experimental groups are summarized here. The first group of oil-treated animals were littermates of the first group of TP-treated rats, and the second group of controls were littermates of the second group of experimentals.
From Goldman and Gorski (1971).

creased concentrations one day after castration. The rapid response to castration in the neonatal male was similar to that observed in the adult (Goldman, Grazia, Kamberi, and Porter, 1970), and Goldman and Gorski (1971) were able to reverse the castration response by the administration of androgen (Table 1). The neonatal female showed higher blood levels of both LH and FSH as compared to littermate males. It was suggested that this might result from a failure of the neonatal ovary to produce sufficient steroids to inhibit gonadotropin secretion (Goldman et al., 1970).

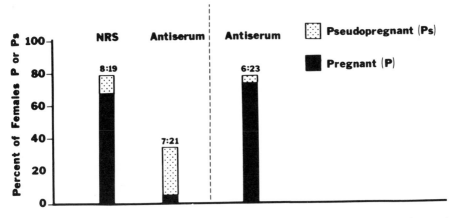

FIG. 1. Percentages of pregnancies and pseudopregnancies resulting from pairings of normal females with adult males that had received normal rabbit serum (NRS) or gonadotropin antiserum (GTH/AS) during neonatal life. (Left) Treated on days 1, 3, and 5; (right) treated on days 7, 9, and 11. The first number above each bar denotes the number of males used; the second number indicates the total number of females used. Each male was used in at least two separate tests. (From Goldman and Mahesh, 1970.)

The administration of gonadotropin antiserum (GTH/AS)[1] to newborn male rats (aged 1 to 5 days) resulted in the development of males that failed to impregnate females in adulthood, even though their testes appeared normal at the time of testing (Fig. 1). When the antiserum treatment was delayed until 7 to 11 days of age, this effect was not observed (Goldman and Mahesh, 1970). In a further study this result was repeated in a second strain of rats. Furthermore, it was found that the antiserum-treated males obtained very few intromissions when paired with estrous females in behavioral tests (Fig. 2). As male rats require several intromissions before achieving an ejaculation, it seems likely that the ability to gain only infrequent intromissions would severely limit the ability of the antiserum-treated males to impregnate females (Goldman, Quadagno, Shryne, and Gorski, 1972).

In further behavioral tests it was found that male rats treated neonatally with GTH/AS were able to display high levels of feminine sexual behavior following treatment with estrogen and progesterone in adulthood (Fig. 2); indeed, their level of performance (lordosis quotient) was not statistically different from that of normal female rats (Goldman et al., 1972). The reduced capacity for masculine sexual behavior and increased ability to display feminine behavior after neonatal treatment with GTH/AS was again demonstrated in a later study (McCullough, Quadagno, and Goldman, 1974).

We interpret the above-described results as follows: neonatal gonadotropins

---

[1] The antiserum cross-reacted with both LH and FSH of rat origin; therefore, the relative importance of these two hormones could not be determined.

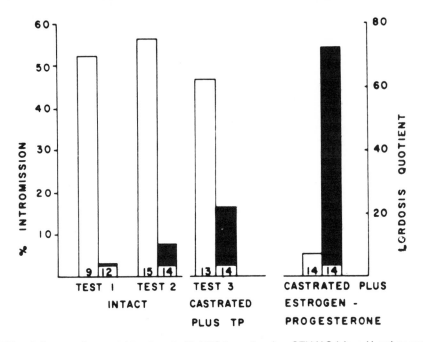

FIG. 2. Influence of neonatal treatment with NRS (open bars) or GTH/AS (closed bars) on male and female sexual behavior of adult male rats. Numbers at the base of each bar indicate the number of animals tested. In each case the behavior of antiserum-treated males was significantly different from that of control males ($p < 0.001$, Mann–Whitney U-test). (From Goldman et al., 1972.)

(LH and/or FSH) are required to stimulate the rat testis to produce sufficient hormone (probably androgen) for masculinization of the systems that regulate patterns of sexual behavior in adulthood. Thus, neonatal antiserum treatment is somewhat similar in effect to neonatal castration. It should be noted that this hypothesis does not explain one additional observation that was made in three of the four studies listed above, i.e., it was found that neonatal treatment with GTH/AS failed to "demasculinize" the systems that regulate cyclic release of GTH, or males that received GTH/AS neonatally failed to show formation of corpora lutea when castrated and implanted with ovarian tissue in adulthood (Fig. 3). Rats castrated at birth are able to support a sufficiently cyclic pattern of GTH release to allow for corpora lutea formation. It may be that some androgen is produced during neonatal life even when GTH is blocked, and this small amount of steroid may be sufficient to masculinize the system that regulates the release of GTH, but not the systems that regulate sexual behavior.

The role of neonatal GTH may be absent or reduced in the mouse as treatment with GTH/AS failed to reduce the capacity for display of masculine sexual behavior in adulthood in this species. However, neonatal castration did decrease male sex behavior as tested following treatment with androgen in adulthood (Quadagno, Wolfe, Ho, and Goldman, *unpublished data*).

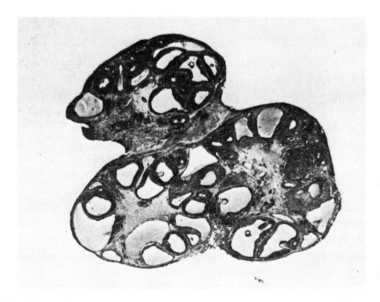

FIG. 3. Typical histologic appearance of an ovarian graft removed 1 month after SC transplantation into male rats treated neonatally with GTH/AS. This particular male rat had achieved a lordosis quotient of 93.3 when tested after priming with ovarian hormones. (From Goldman et al., 1972.)

MATERNAL BEHAVIOR

Hormonal Control in Adulthood

Maternal behavior, like sexual behavior, appears to be at least partly under hormonal control (Noirot, 1972). The administration of combinations of estrogen, progesterone, and prolactin has elicited maternal behavior in virgin rats (Moltz, Lubin, Leon, and Numan, 1970; Zarrow, Gandleman, and Denenberg, 1971). However, it is not clear whether all three hormones are required, which hormone is most important, or whether, in fact, any of these hormones is really essential in the postpartum female rat. For example, it has been reported that 24-day-old rats of both sexes exhibit a shorter latency for "sensitization" to pups than do adult rats, even though the blood levels of gonadal steroids would be expected to be low in the 24-day-old animals (Bridges, Zarrow, Goldman, and Denenberg, 1974). Also, Leon, Numan, and Moltz (1973) observed that virgin rats respond to pups more rapidly 8 weeks after ovariectomy as compared to intact virgins. Rats ovariectomized during late pregnancy showed a more rapid onset of maternal behavior than did intact pregnant females, although serum prolactin remained low (i.e., failed to show the rise characteristic of parturient females) during the period of behavioral testing (Bridges, Goldman, and Bryant, 1974).

Sexual Dimorphism of Maternal Behavior

Virgin female rats will begin to display some elements of maternal behavior (e.g., pup retrieval, licking of pups, crouching, and nest building) after several consecutive days of exposure to rat pups even when no other treatment is administered. This process of development of maternal behavior through exposure to pups has been called "sensitization." Male rats of the Long-Evans strain usually failed to display all the above-mentioned aspects of maternal behavior even after 7 consecutive days of exposure to pups whereas both intact and ovariectomized females usually showed all behaviors after an average latency of 4 to 5 days (Table 2). These observations suggest a sexual dimorphism in the behaviors, possibly with an endocrinologic basis. This is further confirmed by the finding that six of eight males castrated at birth displayed all four aspects of maternal behavior with an average latency of 5 days exposure to pups. Males treated with GTH/AS in infancy also showed considerably more maternal behavior than untreated or NRS-treated males and were not significantly different from virgin females in this respect (Table 2). Thus, in the Long-Evans strain, maternal behavior, like sexual behavior, appears to be sexually dimorphic and is probably suppressed by testicular hormones secreted during neonatal life under the influence of gonadotropins.

The findings in the Purdue-Wistar rat were somewhat different in that adult males and females did not differ significantly in the time required for sensitization to pups. In fact, 24-day-old male rats became sensitized with a latency of only 1.3 ± 0.5 days whereas older males (30 to 54 days) required 4.1 to 7.5 days for

TABLE 2. *Percentage and latency in days for each group to show the four aspects of maternal behavior: Retrieval, licking, crouching, and nest building*

Group	Percentage to show all behaviors	Latency to show all behaviors (days)	Range (days)
Intact females (N=11)	72.72[a,e; b,e]	5.4	4–7
Ovariectomized females (N=11)	54.54[a,d; b,c]	4.5	3–7
Intact males (N=15)	6.67	5.0	5 (1 animal)
GTH/AS males (N=14)	50.00[a,c; b,c]	4.7	3–7
Males castrated at birth (N=8)	75.00[a,d; b,c]	5.0	4–7
NRS males (N=14)	14.28	6.0	5–7 (2 animals)

[a] Significantly different from intact males
[b] Significantly different from NRS males.
Analyzed with χ^2: [c] $p < 0.05$, [d] $p < 0.01$, and [e] $p < 0.001$.
From McCullough et al. (1974).

sensitization. Females showed a similar "developmental" pattern. However, when another behavioral test was used, the Purdue-Wistar rats also demonstrated some degree of sexual dimorphism with respect to maternal behavior. Specifically, when adult rats were treated with a "maternal" hormone regimen (estradiol benzoate and progesterone for 20 days followed by prolactin on the morning of the 21st day) females showed a greater tendency to retrieve pups from one arm of a T-maze than did males (Table 3). Because similar sex differences were not observed following hormone treatment when pups were placed in the home cage, it may be that dimorphism in maternal behavior in this strain appears only when the testing procedure is such as to require strong motivational factors. In the same study neonatally castrated males responded like control females and neonatally androgenized females behaved like control males (Table 3). Therefore, the findings suggest that the sexual dimorphism in maternal responsiveness is mediated by the presence or absence of androgen neonatally; neonatal androgen apparently inhibits the full development of maternal responsiveness in adulthood (Bridges, Zarrow, and Denenberg, 1973).

This chapter deals exclusively with the rat and with only two of the several physiologic systems that may be modified by exposure to testicular hormones in early life. It is already clear that species differences occur in the extent to which developmental aspects of various parameters are under hormonal control. For example, the male hamster, unlike the male rat, is easily induced to display the lordotic response (although this can be inhibited by a large dose of exogenous androgen administered in early life). Nevertheless, the general pattern of "masculinization" by early exposure to testicular hormone appears to be a general feature among mammals with differences occurring mainly with respect to the specific list of parameters that undergo hormonal modification in each respective species.

TABLE 3. *Percentage of animals retrieving in the T-maze: Numbers in parentheses are N*

Genetic sex	Neonatal treatment	Adult treatment	
		Vehicle	Hormone
Male	Sham castrate	0.0 (11)	11.6 (17)
	Castrate	0.0 (11)	42.9 (14)
Female	None	5.9 (17)	48.0 (25)
	Oil	12.5 (16)	42.9 (14)
	TP	25.0 (12)	5.6 (18)

From Bridges et al. (1973).

ACKNOWLEDGMENTS

This work was supported in part by PHS Grant No. HD 05481 and by a grant from the University of Connecticut Research Foundation.

REFERENCES

Beach, F. A. (1968): Factors involved in the control of mounting behavior by female mammals. In: *Perspectives in Reproduction and Sexual Behavior,* pp. 83–131, edited by M. Diamond. Indiana University Press, Bloomington.

Bridges, R. S., Goldman, B. D., and Bryant, L. P. (1974): Serum prolactin concentrations and the initiation of maternal behavior in the rat. *Horm. Behav.,* 5:219–226.

Bridges, R. S., Zarrow, M. X., Goldman, B. D., and Denenberg, V. H. (1974): A developmental study of maternal responsiveness in the rat. *Physiol. Behav.,* 12:149–151.

Bridges, R. S., Zarrow, M. X., and Denenberg, V. H. (1973): The role of neonatal androgen in the expression of hormonally induced maternal responsiveness in the adult rat. *Horm. Behav.,* 4: 315–322.

Goldman, B. D., and Gorski, R. A. (1971): Effects of gonadal steroids on the secretion of LH and FSH in neonatal rats. *Endocrinology,* 89:112–115.

Goldman, B. D., Grazia, Y. R., Kamberi, I. A., and Porter, J. C. (1970): Serum gonadotropin concentrations in intact and castrated neonatal rats. *Endocrinology,* 88:771–776.

Goldman, B. D., and Mahesh, V. B. (1970): Induction of infertility in male rats by treatment with gonadotropin antiserum during neonatal life. *Biol. Reprod.,* 2:444–451.

Goldman, B. D., Quadagno, D. M., Shryne, J., and Gorski, R. A. (1972): Modification of phallus development and sexual behavior in rats treated with gonadotropin antiserum neonatally. *Endocrinology,* 90:1025–1031.

Gorski, R. A. (1971): Gonadal hormones and the perinatal development of neuroendocrine function. In: *Frontiers of Neuroendocrinology,* pp. 237–290, edited by L. Martini and W. F. Ganong. Oxford Univ. Press, New York.

Komisaruk, B. R., Adler, N. T., and Hutchinson, J. (1972): Genital sensory field: Enlargement by estrogen treatment in female rats. *Science,* 178:1295–1298.

Leon, M., Numan, M., and Moltz, H. (1973): Maternal behavior in the rat: Facilitation through gonadectomy. *Science,* 179:1018–1019.

McCullough, J., Quadagno, D. M., and Goldman, B. D. (1974): Neonatal gonadal hormones: Effect on maternal and sexual behavior in the male rat. *Physiol. Behav.,* 12:183–188.

Moltz, H., Lubin, M., Leon, M., and Numan, M. (1970): Hormonal induction of maternal behavior in the ovariectomized nulliparous rat. *Physiol. Behav.,* 5:1373–1377.

Noirot, E. (1972): The onset of maternal behavior in rats, hamsters, and mice: A selective review. In: *Advances in the Study of Behavior,* Vol. 4, pp. 107–145, edited by D. S. Lehrman, R. A. Hinde, and E. Shaw. Academic Press, New York.

Zarrow, M. X., Gandleman, R., and Denenberg, V. H. (1971): Prolactin: Is it an essential hormone for maternal behavior in the mammal? *Horm. Behav.,* 2:343–354.

Sexual Behavior: Pharmacology and Biochemistry, edited by M. Sandler and G. L. Gessa. Raven Press, New York © 1975.

Behavioral Effects of 19-Hydroxytestosterone

J. O. Johnston, J. F. Grunwell, H. D. Benson, A. Kandel, and V. Petrow

Merrell-National Laboratories, Division of Richardson-Merrell Inc., Cincinnati, Ohio 45215

Physiologic and behavioral parameters are mediated by changing levels of gonadal steroids, as orchiectomy inhibits sexual behavior and maintenance of secondary sex glands. The rate at which these parameters fade varies among various species (Young, 1961). The onset of copulatory behavior in maturing rats parallels a marked increase in circulating levels of testosterone (Stone, 1924; Resko, Feder, and Goy, 1968). Similar data for adolescent boys suggest that rising testosterone levels (August, Grumbach, and Kaplan, 1972) are related to the onset of masturbation, nocturnal emission (Ramsey, 1943), and heterosexual infatuation (Kephart, 1973). These data would imply that sex-oriented activities are correlated with rising plasma testosterone levels, although this conclusion should await the evaluation of testosterone and its metabolites for their effect on copulatory related target tissues.

TESTOSTERONE METABOLISM IN SOMATIC TARGET TISSUES

Evidence accumulating over several years has now established that trophic responses of secondary sex glands previously credited to the action of testosterone are caused by its local metabolism. In rat prostatic tissue cultures, 5α-dihydrotestosterone (5α-DHT) increases hyperplasia of epithelial cells, whereas 3β-androstenediol promotes hypertrophy and fluid secretion (Baulieu, Lasnitzki, and Robel, 1968; Baulieu, 1970). Testosterone is converted to its 5α-metabolite *in vivo* (Bruchovsky and Wilson, 1968) and a specific cytosol receptor has been isolated (Mainwaring, 1969), which is responsible for the translocation of the 5α-DHT molecule to the nucleus where DNA-regulated processes are activated. These data support the concept that testosterone is a "prohormone" and its 5α-metabolite(s) is an active principle in initiation of hormonal action in androgen-dependent cells, such as the prostate (Fig. 1).

This concept raises the question of the role of testosterone metabolites in another major activity attributed to this testicular steroid: its influence on male behavior. Castration causes disappearance of copulatory behavior and atrophy and loss of secretory function of accessory glands. Replacement therapy with testosterone in castrated rats has revealed different sensitivities to this steroid in somatic and behavioral responses. Minimal levels of testosterone, which normalized accessory sex gland weights, did not restore sexual behavior even after 2 months of therapy (Davidson, 1972). Treatment of castrated rats with a potent synthetic androgen, or an antiandrogen, had predictable diverse effects on the accessory sexual structures, but were without effect on "androgen-dependent" mating behavior (Beach and Westbrook, 1968; Whalen and Edwards, 1969). The active somatic testosterone metabolite, 5α-DHT, failed to maintain copulatory behavior in castrated rats (McDonald, Beyer, Newton, Brien, Baker, Tan, Sampson, Kitching, Greenhill, and Pritchard, 1970). These observations were confirmed by Whalen and Luttge (1971); Feder (1971); Davidson, Johnston, Block, Smith, and Weick (1971); and Beyer, Larsson, Pérez-Palacios, and Morali (1973).

These latter authors have evaluated 10 natural androgens in castrated rats for their effect on inducing sexual behavior and development of sexual accessory structures. Besides testosterone, only androstenedione and androstenediol were effective in stimulating copulatory behavior. These data suggested that 5α-reduction of androgens promotes androgenic effects in peripheral tissues, but does not play a role in the action of androgens on the brain. Only androgens that could be aromatized to estrogens elicited full copulatory behavior in the castrated rat.

ESTROGEN-STIMULATED MALE SEXUAL BEHAVIOR

Pharmacologic dosages, 2 to 200 μg/rat/day of estradiol benzoate (EB) did produce some "androgenic-like" effects of homotypical behavior in castrated rats (Ball, 1937, 1939; Beach, 1942; Lisk and Suydam, 1967; Davidson, 1969; Pfaff, 1970; Södersten, 1973; Larsson, Södersten, and Beyer, 1973a,b). Copulatory behavior patterns displayed by EB-treated prepubertally castrated rats consist of stimulated mounting and thrusting with limited intromission and an absence of ejaculation (Pfaff, 1970; Södersten, 1973). Sexually experienced castrated rats treated with 100 μg/day of EB for 24 days will exhibit the complete repertoire of copulatory behavior characterized by longer latencies, more mounts, and intromissions before culminating in ejaculation. Similar treatment of intact rats with EB induces testicular atrophy presumably through gonadotropin inhibition with marginal to significant effects on copulatory behavior (Davidson, 1969; Södersten, 1973).

This difference in copulatory patterns between testosterone-treated and EB-treated castrated rats may reflect the lack of adequate stimulation by EB of peripheral tissues, particularly the cornified papilla of the glans penis. Combination therapy in castrated rats with EB and 5α-DHT induced copulatory behavioral patterns comparable to testosterone-treated castrates or intact males (Baum and Vreeburg, 1973; Larsson, Södersten, and Beyer, 1973a,b; Feder, Naftolin, and Ryan, 1974). These observations suggest that the behavioral effects of testosterone are caused by the central action of estradiol and the peripheral activity of the 5α-dihydro metabolite.

The minimum reported dosage of EB that will activate mounting behavior with or without 5α-DHT is 2 μg/day (Baum and Vreeburg, 1973). This dosage also induces lordosis in castrated males, a heterotypical behavioral phenomenon seldom observed among intact males (Stone, 1924). The low levels of circulating estradiol in normal male rats (de Jong, Hey, and van der Molen, 1973) would appear to be inadequate to activate these behavioral responses, but the estrogenic levels resulting from metabolites formed from androgens present in the rat brain at testosterone-activated copulatory centers may be the responsible factors (Lisk, 1967). In addition, enzymes necessary to aromatize androgens to estrogens are present in the rat brain (Ryan, Naftolin, Reddy, Flores, and Petro, 1972).

Aromatization of testosterone to estradiol involves initially the hydroxylation at the C-10 methyl position. Considering the possibility that hydroxylated metabolites of testosterone could impart behavioral responses, we undertook chemical synthesis and biologic evaluation for behavioral and endocrine activities of the 19-hydroxy analogues of testosterone (Fig. 2).

MATERIALS AND METHODS

Behavioral Studies

Animals: Mature, sexually experienced male Sprague-Dawley rats were utilized after being used for breeding from 2 to 8 months of age. A reversed photoperiod of 14 hr of artificial daylight illumination (2130 to 0930 hr) was imposed with 24 hr of constant dim red light. Following at least 2 weeks of acclimation, these intact rats were individually screened for copulatory behavior with an estrous

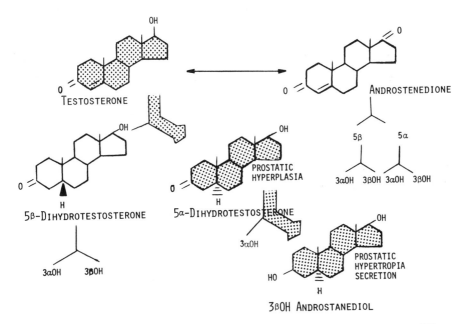

FIG. 1. Prostatic metabolism of testosterone and active metabolites. From Baulieu, 1970.

female. Only animals with high levels of copulatory performance, 15 to 20 intromissions and two or more ejaculations per 10 min, were used. These animals were assigned as intact (I), surgically castrated (C), adrenalectomized (A), or castrated/adrenalectomized (C/A). All adrenalectomized rats were maintained *ad libitum* on 1% sucrose and 0.9% NaCl water solution. Males were reevaluated for copulatory performance following a postoperative period of at least 4 weeks. Mature Sprague-Dawley rats were bilaterally ovariectomized and were administered 20 µg/rat EB subcutaneously, followed 72 hr later with 1.6 mg/rat progesterone once per week. Sexual receptivity was observed about 4 hr following the progesterone administration at which time the most responsive females were selected as stimulus animals.

Behavioral Observations: Behavioral observations were made in Plexiglas chambers under red light illumination, starting 5 to 5½ hr after the onset of room darkness and during 1330 to 1600 hr. Males were selected at random from the total study population and each male was allowed a 5-to-10 min acclimation period prior to placement of an estrous female in the chamber. Numbers of posterior-oriented mounts, intromissions with pelvic thrusting, and ejaculations were recorded.

Copulatory events were recorded for 10 min for each animal using the following schedule: (a) once prior to assignment to groups (I, C, A, C/A, above); (b) once during period following surgery as indicated and preceding drug treatment; (c) on days 2, 8, 12, and 15 during a 14-day drug treatment period.

Following drug treatment, the rats were sexually rested for at least 4 weeks before being reevaluated and were assigned to another drug treatment. In a preliminary evaluation, ultrasonic rat vocalizations which are associated with copulatory behavior were monitored by a ¼-in. condenser microphone, oscilloscope, and magnetic tape recorder.

Endocrine Activities

Mouse Uterotrophic Assay: Immature female CF_1 mice, 9 to 11 g, were identified, weighed, and randomly assigned to treatment groups of six animals. Control groups containing 12 animals each were either not treated or given olive oil vehicle (5 ml/kg). Estradiol-17β was used as a standard at 0.1, 0.3, 0.5, 1.0, and 3.0 µg/kg/day for 3 days in treatment groups. The test steroid was administered in six to nine different concentrations (5 ml/kg) over at least a 3-log dose-response range. On the fourth day, the uterus was removed, trimmed of extraneous tissue, cleared of intraluminal fluid, and then weighed to the nearest 0.1 mg. Uterine weights were calculated on the basis of wet tissue weight as milligrams per 10 g final body weight.

Rat Androgenic Assay: Immature Sprague-Dawley rats, 35 to 50 g, were bilaterally castrated at 21 days of age, identified, weighed, and randomly assigned to treatment groups of eight animals. Control groups received either no treatment or olive oil vehicle (0.1 ml/rat). Testosterone administered at 0.06, 0.24, 0.48, and 1.92 mg/rat/day was used as a reference standard. Test steroids in a volume of 0.1 ml/rat were administered subcutaneously in comparable concentrations to testosterone. The day after a 10-day treatment period, levator ani muscle, seminal vesicles, and ventral prostate were removed, trimmed of extraneous tissue, and weighed to the nearest 0.1 mg. Organ weights were expressed as milligrams wet tissue per 100 g final body weight.

Steroid Preparation: All steroids used in these studies except known standards were synthesized by Dr. Grunwell and Dr. Benson. Crystalline steroidal compounds were prepared for subcutaneous administration by mechanical grinding in olive oil. For initial screening of a compound in behavioral studies, a dose of 500 µg/kg was administered to a treatment group of five animals. After a positive response at this dose, active compounds were confirmed in a dose-response evaluation.

Compounds evaluated for copulatory behavior were: testosterone propionate (TP); 19-hydroxytestosterone (17β, 19-dihydroxyandrost-4-en-3-one) (19-OH-T); 19-hydroxy-5α-dihydrotestosterone diacetate (17β, 19-dihydroxy-5α-androstan-3-one diacetate) (19-OH-5α-DHTA); 19-hydroxy-5β-dihydrotestosterone diacetate (17β-19-dihydroxy-5β-androstan-3-onediacetate)(19-OH-5β-DHTA); 5α-DHT; and estradiol-17β (estra-1,3,5(10)-triene-3,17β-diol).

RESULTS

Mouse Uterotrophic: Estradiol-17β, the assay standard, significantly ($p \leq 0.05$) increased uterine weight at 0.3 to 0.5 µg/kg. Similar uterotrophic responses were obtained for testosterone at 30 mg/kg; 19-OH-T at 3 to 10 mg/kg; 5α-DHT at 10 mg/kg. No significant ($p = 0.05$) changes in uterine weight occurred after administration of as much as 100 mg/kg of 19-OH-5α-DHTA. Of these androgens, only 19-OH-T had a dose-response curve that was parallel with estradiol. Testosterone and 5α-DHT exhibited dose-related effects characteristic of their anabolic/androgenic activity (Fig. 3).

Rat Androgenic Assay: Treatment of immature castrated rats with testosterone at dosages as low as 0.015 mg/rat/day induced significant ($p \leq 0.05$) increases in ventral prostate weight. Marked androgenic dose responses were observed for 5α-DHT, testosterone, and its propionated ester. At the highest dosage of 19-OH-T evaluated (1.92 mg/rat/day), there were significant ($p \leq 0.01$) increases in ventral prostate weight; however, the resulting dose-response curve was relatively flat and was not parallel to testosterone. Estradiol or 19-OH-5α-DHTA did not cause any increases in prostate weight at dosages as high as 1.92 or 0.48 mg/rat/day, respectively (Fig. 4).

Behavioral Responses: Copulatory behavioral tests were conducted using adult intact rats as controls and comparisons were made among A, C, and A/C animals treated with 500 µg/kg of 5α-DHT, TP, 19-OH-T, or vehicle control. The same C- and A/C-prepared animals were reassigned to the same steroids for a second evaluation 4 weeks after completion of the first study. Data were pooled to obtain

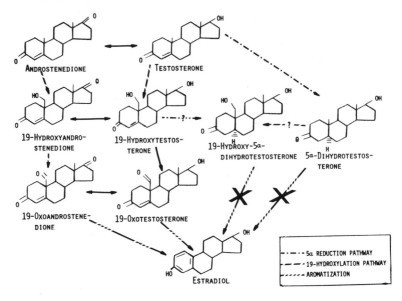

FIG. 2. Partial metabolism of testosterone.

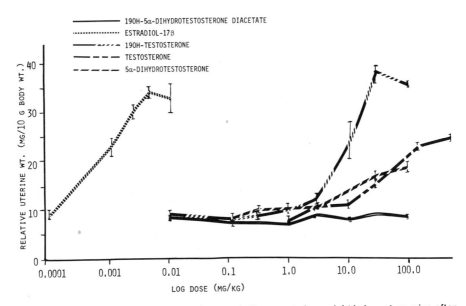

FIG. 3. The effects of various testosterone metabolites on uterine weight in immature mice after 3 days of treatment.

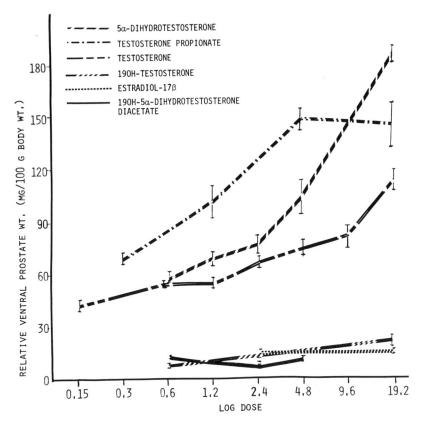

FIG. 4. The effects of testosterone metabolites (mg/rat/10 days) on ventral prostate weight of immature castrated rats after 10 days of treatment.

treatment groups of 10 animals per treatment (Fig. 5). Regardless of steroid treatment, all adrenalectomized rats had copulatory parameters that approached those of the intact controls. Only testosterone and 19-OH-T, but not 5α-DHT, established near-normal copulatory patterns by day 15 in C- or C/A-prepared rats. However, the C/A-prepared rats were more responsive to treatment with 19-OH-T than animals that had only been castrated. On the second day of treatment, copulatory responses were observed for C/A rats administered 19-OH-T, whereas the onset of sexual behavior in castrated animals treated with this steroid occurred on day 15 after the 14-day treatment period. Therefore, C/A-prepared rats have been used in further studies because of this apparent increase in animal copulatory responsiveness over the castrated rats treated with 19-OH-T. This unexplained insensitivity may be caused by increased metabolism of exogenous steroids by the adrenals in castrated rats or by inhibitory effects of the adrenals or both (Fig. 4).

A dose-response evaluation of 19-OH-T using 10 to 500 μg/kg s.c. showed that treatment with 100 µg/kg or greater elicited normal copulatory patterns in C/A rats. At lower doses, the number of mounts and intromissions increased, but not the number of ejaculations. Oral administration produced normal copulatory patterns with a dose of 50 mg/kg but not 5 mg/kg of 19-OH-T in C/A rats (Figs. 6, 7).

Additional behavioral evaluations were undertaken to further elucidate the role of the 19-hydroxylation enzymes in imparting behavioral activity to C_{19} androgens. Compounds selected were estradiol-17β, the end product of the aromatization of testosterone, and the 5α/β-position isomers of 19-OH-DHTA. Estradiol was evaluated at doses of 500, 10, and 1 µg/kg for induction of copulatory responses in C/A-prepared rats. After 14 days of estrogen treatment, most estrogen-treated rats were mounting with pelvic thrusting, but only approximately half the groups achieved ejaculations. Only the 5α-isomer of 19-OH-DHTA was able to induce copulatory behavior in C/A rats. These animals exhibited a marked increase in copulatory activity on day 2 of treatment (Figs. 6, 7).

The C/A animals receiving 500 µg/kg of either TP, 19-OH-T, or 19-OH-5α-DHTA would vocalize as did the intact rats at approximately 22 kHz during their postejaculatory refractory period. Some of these animals also emitted a 50-kHz whistle prior to and during a mounting episode.

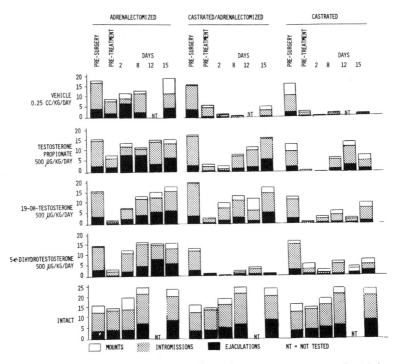

FIG. 5. Copulatory profiles for A-, C-, and C/A-prepared male rats treated s.c. for 14 days with 500 µg/kg of either TP, 19-OH-T, or 5α-DHT.

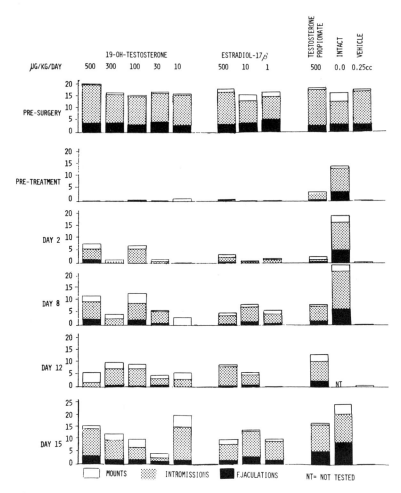

FIG. 6. Copulatory profiles for C/A-prepared rats treated s.c. for 14 days with various doses of 19-OH-TP and estradiol-17β.

DISCUSSION

The role of circulating steroids of testicular origin appears to be multifaceted in regulation of peripheral somatic and central psychic components in expression of copulatory behavior. In most species, the requirements for adequate penile and secondary sex gland development are obtained by local conversion of secreted levels of testosterone to its 5α-dihydrotestosterone metabolite. Because copulatory behavior in the rat cannot be maintained by the administration of 5α-DHT, McDonald et al. (1970) suggested that extragonadal aromatization of androgens may be an obligatory pathway for copulatory behavior. This was demonstrated for sexual behavior in the female rat (Beyer and Komisaruk, 1971) and in the rabbit (Beyer, Vidal, and Mijares, 1970). Species and strain differences occur in the copulatory behavioral responses following the administration of these steroids. Luttge and Hall (1973) reported that 5α-DHT is effective in inducing copulatory activity when administered to castrated Swiss-Webster mice but not to CD-1 mice.

Castrated guinea pigs (Feder et al., 1974) and rhesus monkeys (Phoenix, 1973) exhibit copulatory behavior when administered 5α-DHT. However, castrated hamsters (Christensen, Coniglio, Paup, and Clemens, 1973) and rabbits (Beyer and Rivaud, 1973) failed to maintain male behavioral parameters after treatment with 5α-DHT. These exceptions would suggest that separate metabolic pathways or active intermediates or both may be involved in the expression of copulatory behavior. Our studies suggest that the same enzyme(s), 19-hydroxylase, could convert both an aromatizable androgen, testosterone, or a nonaromatizable androgen, 5α-DHT, into probable behaviorally active compounds.

The first step in conversion of testosterone to an estrogen introduces a hydroxyl group on the C-10 methyl position. This metabolite, 19-OH-T, has an endocrine profile of activities which differs from testosterone. The molecule has a marginal androgenicity, and increased estrogenicity because the uterine-weight responses are parallel to those of estradiol but not of testosterone. A more pronounced loss of endocrine activity occurred for the 19-OH-5α-DHTA, as the dose-response curves of this compound did not parallel either estradiol or testosterone. This hydroxylation imparted behavioral activity to the 5α- but not to the 5β-isomer of DHT (Table 1).

The behavioral activity of 19-OH-T is in agreement with recent data reported by Parrott (1974). In his study, 19-OH-TP [ester position(s) not specified] treatment of castrated rats that achieved ejaculation had postejaculatory refractory intervals comparable to testosterone-treated castrates or intact rats, but their level of copulatory performance was lower than testosterone controls. During this

TABLE 1. *Endocrine and behavioral parameters of testosterone and metabolites*

	Endocrine effects (minimal dose for response)		Behavioral effects on C/A rats* relative to testosterone (% response, day 15, 14-day treatment)		
Structure	Uterine weight (mg/kg)	Ventral prostate weight (mg/day)	Mounts	Intro-missions	Ejacu-lations
Testosterone	30.0	0.015	100	100	100
Dihydrotestosterone	10.0	<0.06	5	4	4
19-Hydroxytestosterone	10.0	>1.92	109	93	96
19-Hydroxy-5α-dihydro-testosterone diacetate	>100.0	>0.48	50	43	36
Estradiol	0.0003	>1.92	58	46	20

* Castrated/adrenalectomized rats.

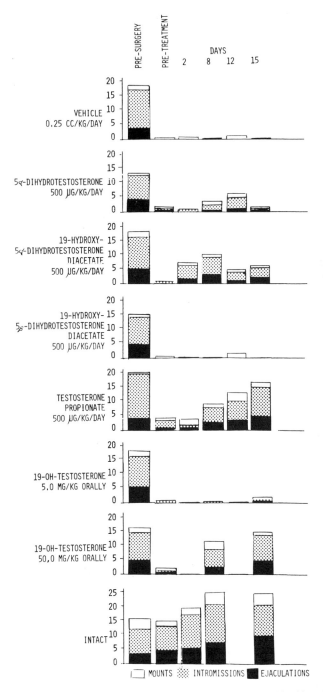

FIG. 7. Copulatory profiles for C/A-prepared rats treated for 14 days with either 19-OH-T, 5.0 or 50.0 mg/kg orally, or 500 μg/kg s.c. of 19-OH-5α-DHTA or 19-OH-5β-DHTA.

refractory period, the rat will emit an ultrasonic 22-kHz vocalization prior to its return to mounting activity (Barfield and Geyer, 1972). It is significant that in our study, C/A rats treated with either 19-OH-T or 19-OH-5α-DHTA will vocalize at the same frequencies as do intact males (Johnston and Willson, 1974). Hypothalamic implants of 19-OH-TP promoted behavioral activity in castrated rats, which is indicative of a central action. In these studies, estradiol was also effective but did not exceed the responses induced by implantation of 19-OH-TP. Both of these compounds were more effective after systemic 5α-DHT was administered concurrently to maintain peripheral copulatory-dependent structures (Parrott and McDonald, 1974). Therefore, the endocrine-behavioral components of sexual behavior of the male rat appear to require somatic support from androgenic metabolites and central activation from other metabolites with apparently marginal inherent somatic activity. The facilitatory role of estrogens is unclear, since an antiestrogen will not inhibit testosterone-induced behavioral activity in the castrated male rat (Whalen, Battie, and Luttge, 1972), but will inhibit testosterone-induced lordosis in the female (McDonald and Doughty, 1972). Brain steroid metabolite levels and localization will be required to confirm a physiologic role of 19-hydroxylase in conversion of somatic to behaviorally active compounds.

SUMMARY

Increased gonadal secretion of testosterone occurs concurrently with the onset of male sexually oriented behavior. Extragonadal androgen metabolism appears to be responsible for copulatory behavior in the male rat. The first-step metabolism of testosterone, an apparent "prohormone," can induce significant separations between peripheral somatic and central actions. The somatic effects were associated with a 5α-reductase pathway, whereas hydroxylation of the C-10 methyl position appeared to be the pivotal point in the transition from somatic to behavioral responses. The expression and maintenance of copulatory activity in the male rat probably results from the combined effect of these two metabolic pathways.

ACKNOWLEDGMENTS

The authors are indebted to Ms. D. Stephens, Ms. T. Lockwood, and Ms. K. Dowdy for excellent technical assistance in conducting the endocrine bioassays, and to C. L. Wright for behavioral observations. We also thank Ms. M. Newton for manuscript and graphic preparations with assistance from Ms. L. Johnson.

REFERENCES

August, C. P., Grumbach, M. M., and Kaplan, S. L. (1972): Hormonal changes in puberty. III. Correlation of plasma testosterone, LH, FSH, testicular size, and bone age with male pubertal development. *J. Clin. Endocrinol. Metab.*, 34:319–326.

Ball, J. (1937): Sex activity of castrated male rats increased by estrin administration. *Endocrinology,* 23:197–199.

Ball, J. (1939): Male and female mating behavior in prepubertally castrated male rats receiving estrogens. *J. Comp. Psychol.,* 28:273–284.

Barfield, R. J., and Geyer, L. A. (1972): Sexual behavior: Ultrasonic postejaculatory song of male rats. *Science,* 176:1349–1350.

Baulieu, E. E. (1970): The action of hormone metabolites: A new concept in endocrinology. *Ann. Clin. Res.,* 2:246–250.

Baulieu, E. E., Lasnitzki, I., and Robel, P. (1968): Metabolism of testosterone and action of metabolites on prostate glands grown in organ culture. *Nature,* 219:1155–1156.

Baum, M. J., and Vreeburg, J. T. M. (1973): Copulation in castrated male rats following combined treatment with estradiol and dihydrotestosterone. *Science,* 182:283–285.

Beach, F. A. (1942): Copulatory behavior in prepubertally castrated male rats and its modification by estrogen administration. *Endocrinology,* 31:679–683.

Beach, F. A., and Westbrook, W. H. (1968): Dissociation of androgenic effects on sexual morphology and behavior in male rats. *Endocrinology,* 83:395–398.

Beyer, C., and Komisaruk, B. (1971): Effects of diverse androgens on estrous behavior, lordosis reflex, and genital tract morphology in the rat. *Horm. Behav.,* 2:217–225.

Beyer, C., Larsson, K., Pérez-Palacios, G., and Morali, G. (1973): Androgen structure and male sexual behavior in the castrated rat. *Horm. Behav.,* 4:99–108.

Beyer, C., and Rivaud, N. (1973): Differential effects of testosterone and dihydrotestosterone on the sexual behavior of prepubertally castrated male rabbits. *Horm. Behav.,* 4:175–180.

Beyer, C., Vidal, N., and Mijares, A. (1970): Probable role of aromatization in the induction of estrous behavior by androgens in the ovariectomized rabbit. *Endocrinology,* 87:1386–1389.

Bruchovsky, N., and Wilson, J. D. (1968): The conversion of testosterone to 5α-androstan-17β-ol-3-one by rat prostate *in vivo* and *in vitro. J. Biol. Chem.,* 243:2012–2021.

Christensen, L. W., Coniglio, L. P., Paup, D. C., and Clemens, L. G. (1973): Sexual behavior of male golden hamsters receiving diverse androgen treatments. *Horm. Behav.,* 4:223–229.

Davidson, J. M. (1969): Effects of estrogen on the sexual behavior of male rats. *Endocrinology,* 84:1365–1372.

Davidson, J. M. (1972): Hormones and reproductive behavior. In: *Reproductive Biology,* edited by H. Balin and S. Glasser, p. 877. Excerpta Medica, Amsterdam.

Davidson, J. M., Johnston, P., Bloch, G. J., Smith, E. R., and Weick, R. F. (1971): Comparative responses to androgen of androgenic, behavioral and other parameters. In: *Proceedings of the III International Congress of Hormonal Steroids,* edited by V. H. T. James and L. Martini, p. 727. Excerpta Medica, Amsterdam.

de Jong, F. H., Hey, A. H., and van der Molen, H. J. (1973): Effect of gonadotropins on the secretion of oestradiol-17β and testosterone by the rat testis. *J. Endocrinol.,* 57:277–284.

Feder, H. H. (1971): The comparative actions of testosterone propionate and 5α-androstan-17β-ol-3-one propionate on the reproductive behavior, physiology and morphology of male rats. *J. Endocrinol.,* 51:241–252.

Feder, H. H., Naftolin, F., and Ryan, K. J. (1974): Male and female responses in male rats given estradiol benzoate and 5α-androstan-17β-ol-3-one propionate. *Endocrinology,* 94:136–141.

Johnston, J. O., and Willson, R. D. (1974): Unpublished data.

Kephart, W. M. (1973): Evaluation of romantic love. *Med. Aspects Human Sex.,* 7:92–108.

Larsson, K., Södersten, P., and Beyer, C. (1973a): Induction of male sexual behavior by oestradiol benzoate in combination with dihydrotestosterone. *J. Endocrinol.,* 57:563–564.

Larsson, K., Södersten, P., and Beyer, C. (1973b): Sexual behavior in male rats treated with estrogen in combination with dihydrotestosterone. *Horm. Behav.,* 4:289–299.

Lisk, R. D. (1967): Neural localization for androgen activation of copulatory behavior in the male rat. *Endocrinology,* 80:754–761.

Lisk, R. D., and Suydam, A. J. (1967): Sexual behavior patterns in the prepubertally castrated rat. *Anat. Rec.,* 157:181–190.

Luttge, W. G., and Hall, N. R. (1973): Differential effectiveness of testosterone and its metabolites in the induction of male sexual behavior in two strains of albino mice. *Horm. Behavior,* 4:31–43.

Mainwaring, W. I. P. (1969): A soluble androgen receptor in the cytoplasm of the rat prostate. *J. Endocrinol.,* 45:531–541.

McDonald, P. G., Beyer, C., Newton, F., Brien, B., Baker, R., Tan, H. S., Sampson, C., Kitching,

P., Greenhill, R., and Pritchard, D. (1970): Failure of 5α-dihydrotestosterone to initiate sexual behavior in castrated male rats. *Nature,* 227:964–965.

McDonald, P. G., and Doughty, C. (1972): Inhibition of androgen-sterilization in the female rat by administration of an antioestrogen. *J. Endocrinol.,* 55:455–456.

Parrott, R. F. (1974): Effects of 17β-hydroxy-4-androsten-19-ol-3-one (19-hydroxytestosterone) and 5α-androstan-17β-ol-3-one (dihydrotestosterone) on aspects of sexual behavior in castrated male rats. *J. Endocrinol.,* 61:105–115.

Parrott, R. F., and McDonald, P. G. (1975): Sexual behavior of male rats implanted in the brain with either 19-hydroxytestosterone, testosterone, oestradiol or cholesterol and treated with dihydrotestosterone propionate subcutaneously *(in press.)*

Pfaff, D. W. (1970): Nature of sex hormone effects on rat sex behavior: Specificity of effects and individual patterns of response. *J. Comp. Physiol. Psychol.,* 73:349–358.

Ramsey, G. V. (1943): The sexual development of boys. *Am. J. Phsychol.,* 56:217–234.

Resko, J. A., Feder, H. H., and Goy, R. W. (1968): Androgen concentrations in plasma and testes of developing rats. *J. Endocrinol.,* 40:485–491.

Ryan, K. J., Naftolin, F., Reddy, V., Flores, F., and Petro, Z. (1972); Estrogen formation in the brain. *Am. J. Obstet. Gynecol.,* 114:454–460.

Södersten, P. (1973): Estrogen activated sexual behavior in male rats. *Horm. Behav.,* 4:247–256.

Stone, C. P. (1924): The awakening of copulatory ability in the male albino rat. *Am. J. Physiol.,* 68:407–424.

Whalen, R. E., Battie, C., and Luttge, W. G. (1972): Anti-estrogen inhibition of androgen induced sexual receptivity in rats. *Behav. Biol.,* 7:311–320.

Whalen, R. E., and Edwards, D. A. (1969): Effects of the antiandrogen cyproterone acetate on mating behavior and seminal vesicle tissue in male rats. *Endocrinology,* 84:155–156.

Whalen, R. E., and Luttge, W. G. (1971): Testosterone, androstenedione and dihydrotestosterone: Effects on mating behavior of male rats. *Horm. Behav.,* 2:117–125.

Young, W. C. (1961): The hormones and mating behavior. In: *Sex and Internal Secretions,* edited by W. C. Young, p. 1173. Williams and Wilkins, Baltimore, Maryland.

Sexual Behavior: Pharmacology and Biochemistry, edited by M. Sandler and G. L.
Gessa. Raven Press, New York © 1975.

Sexual Modification of Cardiovascular Regulation

Christopher Bell

Department of Physiology, University of Melbourne, Parkville, Australia

Tonic cardiovascular control is mediated in two ways: by the activity of vasomotor nerves and circulating hormones. The vasomotor nerves are predominantly constrictor in effect, although in certain situations such as the pregnant uterus dilator influences may also be important. The major circulating hormonal system is the renin–angiotensin system, which both produces direct vasoconstriction through the effect of angiotensin II (AII) on vasomotor transmitter release and on the vascular muscles and stimulates water and Na^+ retention through provocation of release of aldosterone. As well as producing physiologic regulation of the cardiovascular system, these two control pathways appear to be involved in the pathogenesis of hypertension, and their significance in this context is accented by recent experimental evidence that hypertension of both renal and nonrenal origin is due primarily to active vasoconstriction (Smirk, 1972; Poyser, Shorter, and Whiting, 1974). There is increasing evidence that circulating sex hormones exert profound influences on the mechanisms of cardiovascular control, and that these influences may be related to the development of cardiovascular disease. It is the purpose of this chapter briefly to examine this evidence.

The most dramatic effects of sex steroids on the cardiovascular system are seen during pregnancy. In man and other species studied, blood pressure tends to fall during pregnancy (Grollman, 1947; Fregly, 1957; MacGillivray, Rose, and Rowe, 1969), and this seems to be associated with decreased sensitivity of the vasculature to constrictor agonists (Mackaness and Dodson, 1957; Chesley, Talledo, Bohler and Zuspan, 1965; Hettiaratchi and Pickford, 1968; Teeuw and Jong, 1973). Hettiaratchi and Pickford (1968) produced a similar desensitization with progesterone, but could not mimic the effect of pregnancy by estrogen administration. Teeuw and Jong (1973) observed that the greatest desensitization occurred at the period of maximum progesterone production, but at other times they were unable to draw any correlation between hormone levels and vascular sensitivity. During pregnancy the adrenergic fluorescence associated with both the uterine muscle innervation and that of the uterine blood vessels declines markedly (Nakanishi, McLean, Wood, and Burnstock, 1968; Rosengren and Sjöberg, 1968; Sjöberg, 1968a). Within the uterine wall this decline is paralleled by a fall in the measurable norepinephrine (NE) stores (Sjöberg, 1968a; Owman and Sjöberg, 1973). However, in the external uterine vessels, although fluroescence is reduced, the NE stores are not depleted (Bell, *unpublished observation*). Therefore, the absence of fluorescence may represent resequestration rather than depletion of the

NE within the axons. In view of the correlation of adrenergic fluorescence seen with that portion of transmitter that is releasable (Malmfors, 1965), it is not surprising that the vasomotor nerves supplying the uterine vessels have been reported to release much less NE during late pregnancy than at other times (Bell and Vogt, 1971). The decline in uterine NE can be mimicked by oöphorectomy or chorionic gonadotropin administration (Owman and Sjöberg, 1973). However, neither treatment mimics the effect of pregnancy on the external uterine arteries (Bell, *unpublished observation*). The reduced constrictor capacity of the uterine vasculature during pregnancy could be regarded as a safeguard against uterine flow reduction in the face of generalized cardiovascular stress (Bell, 1974). However, testing such a proposal presents many difficulties, and the teleologic significance of the changes seen remains to be elucidated.

In addition to this generalized cardiovascular depression, pregnancy involves a large selective increase in blood flow through the uterus to provide for adequate fetal nourishment. Considerable evidence now exists to indicate that the uterine hyperemia in pregnancy is related to circulating estrogens; this evidence has been reviewed recently elsewhere (Bell, 1974). In certain species, such as sheep, estrogens appear to increase uterine blood flow by a direct action on the uterine vasculature (Greiss, Gobble, Anderson, and McGuirt, 1967; Bell, 1974). In other species, such as the guinea pig, estrogens act by sensitization of the uterine vessels to the dilator effect of acetylcholine (ACh) released from vasomotor nerves. This latter mechanism is likely to be involved during pregnancy in the human (Bell, 1974). Thus, low estrogen production during pregnancy, which is recognized as an indication of fetoplacental insufficiency (Macnaughton, 1967; Beisher, Bhargava, Brown, and Smith, 1968; Klopper, 1968) may be a cause as well as an effect of reduced placental perfusion.

Both androgens and estrogens can affect the reactivity of the cardiovascular system under nonpregnant conditions. Briggs and Briggs (1972) observed that plasma monoamine oxidase (MAO) levels in men were inversely proportional to the rate of testosterone production whereas in women they varied inversely with estrogen production. Castration of male rats causes an increase in plasma MAO; administration of estrogen to females or testosterone to males produces a fall in the enzyme level (Billewicz-Stankiewicz and Ambroziak, 1965). In amenorrheic women the plasma MAO is higher than normal; it is reduced by estrogen therapy and this effect is antagonized by progestins (Vogel, Broverman, and Klaiber, 1971). Tryding, Tufvesson, and Nilsson (1972) reported that serum MAO falls sharply at puberty, and rises again at the age of about 50 in women and 65 in men, also suggesting an influence of circulating sex hormones. In addition to their inhibitory effect on circulating MAO, both androgens and estrogens inhibit extraneuronal tissue uptake mechanisms for catecholamines (CA) (Iversen and Salt, 1970; Nicol and Rae, 1972). It might therefore be expected that high blood levels of these hormones would increase cardiovascular reactivity to CA. In line with this, Greenberg, George, Kadowitz, and Wilson (1973) observed that testosterone treatment enhanced cardiovascular responses of both male and female dogs to NE and to tyramine but did not affect responses to AII or nitroglycerine. Andro-gen-induced sensitization to the cardiovascular effects of CA also has been re-ported for the cat (Burn, Finney, and Goodwin, 1950; Bhargava, Dhawan, and Saxena, 1967). In the rat, by comparison, femaleness or estrogen treatment of males causes enhancement of vascular reactivity to constrictors (Altura, 1972, 1973; Lloyd, 1959). Such species differences probably reflect variability in male and female hormone balance. Estrogen sensitization in the rat may not be related to changes in CA metabolism, as constrictor responses to posterior pituitary hormones as well as to NE and epinephrine (E) are potentiated. However, re-sponses to AII and 5-hydroxytryptamine (5-HT) are not affected (Altura, 1973).

The capacity of vasomotor nerves to release transmitter as well as to affect the blood vessels is modified by estrogens. Estrogen treatment of female rabbits leads to increased fluorescence in the adrenergic nerves of the uterus and its blood vessels and increased tissue levels of NE (Sjöberg, 1968b). This effect is antago-nized by progesterone administration (Falck, Owman, Rosengren, and Sjöberg, 1969). Adham and Schenk (1969) observed that the amount of CA fluorescence in the vasomotor nerves of the rat uterus was much greater at estrus than at diestrus. However, in this species, Rudzik and Miller (1962) reported no rise in uterine NE stores at estrus. It is possible that the situation observed by Adham and Shenk (1969) is similar to that described earlier in this report as occurring in the guinea pig during pregnancy.

The effects of female sex hormones on the renin–angiotensin–aldosterone axis have received much attention recently because of the widespread interest in estrogen–progestin mixtures as oral contraceptives, and in their possible side effects. The modification by such compounds of angiotensin production and aldosterone secretion is thought to be attributable to their estrogen component Carey, 1971; Laragh, 1971). Estrogens are known to increase the ability of the renin–renin substrate system to produce AII (Helmer and Griffith, 1952; Haas and Goldblatt, 1967; Menard, Malmejac, and Milliez, 1970), with consequent stimulation of aldosterone production and sodium retention. This property of estrogens has been thought to be due to increased synthesis of renin substrate (Carey, 1971; Laragh, 1971). However, other steps in the renin–aldosterone axis may also be affected. Laragh (1971) reported that some patients taking oral contraceptives exhibited an enhanced ability to form AII, which could not be fully accounted for by their increased renin substrate levels; we have found recently that rats receiving oral contraceptive treatment show an increased capac-ity to convert the biologically inactive product of renin substrate breakdown (angiotensin I) to AII (Bell and Bakhle, *unpublished observation*). A small per-centage of women taking oral contraceptives develop hypertension that shows remission on cessation of therapy (Laragh, Sealey, Ledingham, and Newton, 1967; Skinner, Lumbers, and Symonds, 1969; Tapia, Johnson, and Strong, 1973).

It seems likely that this hypertension is due to excessive stimulation of AII and aldosterone production by the steroids ingested, in the absence of adequate compensatory mechanisms. Possible factors that have been suggested to be involved in these patients are inadequate feedback inhibition of renin release (Skinner et al., 1969) and inadequate inactivation of AII (Tapia et al., 1973).

Progesterone also causes increased AII production and aldosterone secretion. However, unlike the results with estrogens, this is not due to direct stimulation of the system, but to the fact that progesterone antagonizes the Na^+ reabsorptive action of aldosterone in the renal tubules (Landau and Lugibihl, 1961). This natriuretic effect led to progesterone being administered to renal hypertensive animals and to both essential and renal hypertensive patients (Armstrong, 1959; Genest, Nowaczynski, Koiw, Sandor, and Biron, 1960), and it was found to cause reduction of the elevated blood pressure in some cases. More recently, raised plasma progesterone levels have been recorded in benign essential hypertensives, and the suggestion has been made that hypertension in such patients may result from an inability to produce sufficient progesterone to counteract the deleterious effects of excessive aldosterone activity (Genest, Nowaczynski, Kuchel, and Sasaki, 1972).

There is ample epidemiologic evidence to indicate that premenopausal women exhibit relative resistance to hypertension (Stamler, Stamler, and Pullman, 1967) and to atherosclerosis and myocardial infarction (Haas, Hemker, and Snellen, 1970). The comparative susceptibility of men to these diseases may be attributable partly to their androgen production, and Nowaczynski, Fraygehan, Silah, Millette, and Genest (1968) have shown that some essential hypertensives have low urinary excretion of the testosterone metabolite dehydroepiandrosterone, suggesting possible impairment of androgen excretion. However, a beneficial effect of female hormones is likely to be at least as important in determining the sex difference. The factor of greatest significance in this regard has been widely suggested to be estrogens, but the evidence to support such a contention is far from conclusive. Although estrogens can reverse the gross arterial damage produced by cholesterol-feeding in rabbits (Mohri and Numano, 1973), their prophylactic and therapeutic effects in clinical atheroma are not dramatic (Furman, 1969). Furthermore, the evidence presented in this report indicates that estrogens tend to cause stimulation of AII production, water and Na^+ retention and, like androgens, enhance vascular reactivity to constrictor stimuli. It would seem unlikely that these characteristics are associated with resistance to hypertension. In contrast, the antagonistic effect of progesterone on aldosterone and its apparent capacity to desensitize the vasculature to constrictor stimuli would make it well fitted to such a role. Perhaps the active corpus luteum of fertility rather than the Graafian follicle of feminism is the key to female cardiovascular health.

ACKNOWLEDGMENT

This work has been supported by the National Heart Foundation of Australia.

REFERENCES

Adham, N., and Schenk, E. A. (1969): Autonomic innervation of the rat vagina, cervix and uterus and its cyclic variation. *Am. J. Obstet. Gynecol.,* 104:508–516.

Altura, B. M. (1972): Sex as a factor influencing the responsiveness of arterioles to catecholamines. *Eur. J. Pharmacol.,* 20:261–265.

Altura, B. M. (1973): Influence of sex and estrogens on responsiveness of arterioles to catecholamines and neurohypophyseal hormones. *Circulation,* 48:IV–137.

Armstrong, J. G. (1959): Hypotensive action of progesterone in experimental and human hypertension. *Proc. Soc. Exp. Biol.,* 102:452–455.

Beischer, N. A., Bhargava, V. L., Brown, J. B., and Smith, M. A. (1968): The incidence and significance of low oestriol excretion in an obstetric population. *J. Obstet. Gynaecol. Br. Commonw.,* 75:1024–1033.

Bell, C. (1974): Control of uterine blood flow in pregnancy. *Med. Biol.,* 52:219–228.

Bell, C., and Vogt, M. (1971): Release of endogenous noradrenaline from an isolated muscular artery. *J. Physiol. (Lond.),* 215:509–520.

Bhargava, K. P., Dhawan, K. N., and Saxena, R. C. (1967): Enhancement of noradrenaline pressor responses in testosterone treated cats. *Br. J. Pharmacol.,* 31:26–31.

Billewicz-Stankiewicz, J., and Ambroziak, T. (1965): Badania nad "adrenalinooksydaza" osocza Krwi. *Acta Physiol. Polon.* 16:689–694.

Briggs, M., and Briggs, M. (1972): Relationship between monoamine oxidase activity and sex hormone concentration in human blood plasma. *J. Reprod. Fertil.,* 29:447–450.

Burn, J. H., Finney, D. J., and Goodwin, L. G. (1950): *Biological Standardization.* Oxford Univ. Press, Oxford.

Carey, H. M. (1971): Principles of oral contraception. 2. Side effects of oral contraceptives. *Med. J. Aust.,* 2:1242–1250.

Chesley, L. C., Talledo, E., Bohler, C. S., and Zuspan, F. P. (1965): Vascular reactivity to angiotensin II and norepinephrine in pregnant and non-pregnant women. *Am. J. Obstet. Gynecol.,* 91:837–842.

Falck, B., Owman, C., Rosengren, E., and Sjöberg, N.-O. (1969): Reduction by progesterone of the estrogen-induced increase in transmitter level of the short adrenergic neurons innervating the uterus. *Endocrinology.,* 84:958–959.

Fregley, M. J. (1957): The interaction of pregnancy and hypertension. *Acta Physiol. Pharmacol. Ned.* 5:278–291.

Furman, R. H. (1969): Endocrine factors in atherogenosis. In: *Atherosclerosis,* edited by F. G. Schettler and G. S. Boyd. Elsevier, Amsterdam.

Genest, J., Nowaczynski, W., Koiw, E., Sandor, T., and Biron, P. (1960): Adrenocortical function in essential hypertension. In: *Essential Hypertension. An International Symposium,* edited by K. D. Block and P. T. Cottier. Springer-Verlag, Berlin.

Genest, J., Nowaczynski, W., Kuchel, D., and Sasaki, C. (1972): Plasma progesterone levels and 18-hydroxydeoxycorticosterone secretion rate in benign essential hypertension in humans. In: *Hypertension '72,* edited by J. Genest and E. Koiw. Springer-Verlag, Berlin.

Greenberg, S., George, W. R., Kadowitz, P. J., and Wilson, W. R. (1973): Androgen-induced enhancement of vascular reactivity. *Can. J. Physiol. Pharmacol.,* 52:14–22.

Greiss, F. C., Jr., Gobble, F. L., Jr., Anderson, S. G., and McGuirt, W. F. (1967): Effect of acetylcholine on the uterine vascular bed. *Am. J. Obstet. Gynecol.,* 99:1073–1077.

Grollman, A. (1947): Effect of pregnancy on the course of experimental hypertension. *Am. J. Physiol.,* 151:373–379.

Haas, E., and Goldblatt, J. (1967): Kinetic constants of the human renin and human angiotensinogen reaction. *Circ. Res.,* 20:45–55.

Haas, J. D. de, Hemker, H. C., and Snellen, H. A. (Eds.) (1970): *Ischaemic Heart Disease.* Leiden Univ. Press, Leiden.

Helmer, O. M., and Griffith, R. S. (1952): The effect of the administration of estrogens on the renin-substrate (Hypertensinogen) content of rat plasma. *Endocrinology,* 51:421–426.

Hettiaratchi, E. S. G., and Pickford, M. (1968): The effect of oestrogen and progesterone on the pressor action of angiotensin in the rat. *J. Physiol.,* 196:447–451.

Iversen, L. L., and Salt, P. J. (1970): Inhibition of catecholamine uptake by steroids in the isolated rat heart. *Br. J. Pharmacol.,* 40:528–530.

Klopper, A. (1968): The assessment of feto-placental function by oestriol assay. *Obstet. Gynecol. Surv.,* 23:813–838.

Landau, R. L., and Lugibihl, K. (1961): The catabolic and natriuretic effects of progesterone in man. *Rec. Progr. Horm. Res.* 17:249–292.

Laragh, J. H. (1971): The pill, hypertension and the toxemias of pregnancy. *Am. J. Obstet. Gynecol.,* 109:210–213.

Laragh, J. H., Sealey, J. E., Ledingham, J. G. G., and Newton, M. A. (1967): Oral contraceptives. Renin, aldosterone, and high blood pressure. *JAMA,* 201:918–922.

Lloyd, S. (1959): The vascular responses of the rat during the reproductive cycle. *J. Physiol.,* 148: 625–632.

MacGillivray, I., Rose, G. A., and Rowe, B. (1969): Blood pressure survey in pregnancy. *Clin. Sci.,* 37:395–407.

Mackaness, G. B., and Dodson, L. F. (1957): The pressor response to renin during pregnancy in the rat. *Br. J. Exp. Pathol.,* 38:628–634.

Macnaughton, M. C. (1967): Hormone excretion as a measurement of fetal growth and development. *Am. J. Obstet. Gynecol.,* 97:998–1019.

Malmfors, T. (1965): Studies on adrenergic nerves. *Acta Physiol. Scand.,* 64:S 248.

Menard, J., Malmejac, A., and Milliez, P. (1970): Influence of diethylstilboestrol on the renin–angiotensin system of male rats. *Endocrinology,* 86:774–780.

Mohri, K., and Numano, F. (1973): Histochemical analysis of tissue catecholamine in the arteries of cholesterol-fed rabbits treated with pyridinolcarbamate, estrogen and progesterone. In: *Atherogenesis,* edited by T. Shimamoto, F. Numano, and C. M. Addison. *Excerpta Medica,* Amsterdam.

Nakanishi, H., McLean, J., Wood, C., and Burnstock, G. (1968): The role of sympathetic nerves in control of the non-pregnant and pregnant uterus. *J. Reprod. Med.,* 2:20–33.

Nicol, C. J. M., and Rae, R. M. (1972): Inhibition of accumulation of adrenaline and noradrenaline in arterial smooth muscle by steroids. *Br. J. Pharmacol.,* 44:361P-362P.

Nowaczynski, W., Fraygehan, F., Silah, J., Millette, B., and Genest, J. (1968): Further evidence of altered adrenal cortical function in hypertension: dehydroepiandrosterone excretion rate. *Can. J. Biochem.,* 46:1031–1038.

Owman, C., and Sjöberg, N.-O. (1973): Effect of sex hormones on neuronal norepinephrine in reproductive tract. *Proc. Third Int. Catecholamine Symp.* Strasbourg, May 1973.

Poyser, R. H., Shorter, J. H., and Whiting, R. L. (1974): The production of hypertension and the effects of some antihypertensive agents in the conscious unrestrained cat. *Br. J. Pharmacol.,* 51:149.

Rosengren, E., and Sjöberg, N.-O. (1968): Changes in the amount of adrenergic transmitter in the female genital tract of rabbit during pregnancy. *Acta Physiol. Scand.,* 72:412–424.

Rudzik, A. D., and Miller, J. W. (1962): The effect of altering the catecholamine content of the uterus on the rate of contractions and the sensitivity of the myometrium to relaxin. *J. Pharmacol. Exp. Ther.,* 138:88–95.

Sjöberg, N.-O. (1968a): Considerations on the cause of disappearance of the adrenergic transmitter in uterine nerves during pregnancy. *Acta Physiol. Scand.,* 72:501:517.

Sjöberg, N.-O. (1968b): Increase in transmitter content of adrenergic nerves in the reproductive tract of female rabbits after oestrogen. *Acta Endocrinol.,* 57:405–413.

Skinner, S. L., Lumbers, E. R., and Symonds, E. M. (1969): Alteration by oral contraceptives of normal menstrual changes in plasma renin activity, concentration and substrate. *Clin. Sci.,* 36: 67–76.

Smirk, F. H. (1972): Characteristics of the New Zealand strain of genetically hypertensive rats considered in relation to essential hypertension. In: *Spontaneous Hypertension: Its Pathogenesis and Complications,* edited by K. Okamoto. Igaku Shoin, Tokyo, Japan.

Stamler, J., Stamler, R., and Pullman, T. N. (Eds.) (1967): *The Epidemiology of Hypertension.* Grune & Stratton, New York.

Tapia, H.R., Johnson, C. E., and Strong, G. G. (1973): Effect of oral contraceptive therapy on the renin–angiotensin system in normotensive and hypertensive women. *Obstet. Gynecol.,* 41:643–649.

Teeuw, A. H., and de Jong, W. (1973): Time course of decrease in blood pressure and in blood pressure response to vasopressor agents during pregnancy in the rat. *Pfluegers Arch.,* 341:197–208.

Tryding, N., Tufvesson, G., and Nilsson, S. (1972): Ageing, monoamines and monoamine oxidase levels. *Lancet.,* 1489.

Vogel, W., Broverman, D. M., and Klaiber, E. L. (1971): EEG responses in regularly menstruating women and in amenorrheic women treated with ovarian hormones. *Science,* 172:388–391.

Sexual Behavior: Pharmacology and Biochemistry, edited by M. Sandler and G. L. Gessa. Raven Press, New York © 1975.

Penile Erection and Ejaculation: A Central Effect of ACTH-Like Peptides in Mammals

A. Bertolini, G. L. Gessa, and W. Ferrari

Institutes of Pharmacology, Universities of Modena and Cagliari, Italy

This chapter describes a peculiar sexual stimulant effect of ACTH and related peptides and also presents our attempts (1) to define the amino acid sequence optimal for eliciting this effect, (2) to clarify the role of testosterone in this response, and (3) to identify the site of action of ACTH-like peptides in brain. Finally, the possible physiologic significance of the central action of these peptides is discussed.

To give an over-all picture of the central effects of ACTH in brain, this chapter is prefaced by a brief description of two other original effects of ACTH, its capacity to induce stretching and yawning movements and to give rise to EEG changes.

STRETCHING–YAWNING SYNDROME AND EEG CHANGES INDUCED BY ACTH AND MSH

Previous studies from our laboratories have shown that the injection of ACTH or melanophore-stimulating hormone (MSH) into the cerebrospinal fluid (CSF) of mammals induces a peculiar syndrome, characterized principally by the frequent repetition of stretching and yawning movements. This effect we have named the "stretching–yawning syndrome" (SYS) (see Ferrari, Gessa, and Vargiu, 1963).

Rabbits and rats exhibit both stretching and yawning movements, monkeys mostly yawning, whereas in cats and dogs stretching prevails (see Fig. 1).

The SYS begins 30 to 60 min after the injection of a few micrograms of ACTH, α- or β-MSH into the cisterna magna. The animal stretches or yawns in the way it usually does when it awakens from sleep; however, it reiterates these movements repeatedly at intervals of a few minutes for many hours (in dogs for as long as 72 hr). The onset of the SYS is more rapid when the peptides are injected into the third ventricle or into those hypothalamic areas that are close to the hypophysis. The latter were found to be the most sensitive brain region to this action of ACTH (Gessa, Pisano, Vargiu, Crabai, and Ferrari, 1967).

The SYS is an exaggeration of what normally occurs at the time of arousal from sleep or when the body feels tired and prone to sleep; it is our opinion that stretchings and yawnings might be considered an evolutionary vestige of an adaptive mechanism to aid arousal after sleep or to counter the urge to sleep when

FIG. 1. Stretching, yawning, and penile erection (rabbits) induced by ACTH injected into the CSF.

it is imminent and conditions are unsuitable. (For a more detailed description of the SYS and a discussion of its physiologic significance, see Gessa et al., 1967, 1973.) In cats with chronically implanted electrodes, we consistently observed that each stretching or yawning movement induced by ACTH is associated with cortical activation (Gessa et al., 1973).

However, such EEG arousal does not appear to be merely a consequence of proprioceptive input originating from the stretching or yawning acts, for these events begin together, and at times cortical desynchronization precedes the behavioral change. It seems likely that ACTH is responsible both for the cortical activation and for the stretching–yawning act; this, in turn, might serve as a means for reinforcing the state of wakefulness. These findings support the idea that stretchings and yawnings have an arousal significance.

SEXUAL STIMULATION BY INTRACEREBRAL OR INTRATHECAL INJECTION OF ACTH OR MSH

We have observed recently that ACTH-like peptides, when injected into the CSF of different animal species, often cause recurrent episodes of penile erection and ejaculation. This effect has been observed in our laboratories in rats, rabbits, cats, and dogs; and it has been confirmed by Baldwin in rabbits (Baldwin, Haun, and Sawyer, 1974) and Kinnard (reported by MacLean, 1973) in squirrel monkeys.

In adult male rabbits, in which this effect can be more consistently evoked, the sexual response begins at approximately the same time as the SYS, i.e., 15 to 60 min after the injection of ACTH or MSH into the lateral ventricle; the sexual response accompanies the SYS for the first 2 to 5 hr. The sexual stimulant effect of ACTH is characterized by recurrent episodes of penile erection accompanied by copulatory movements, each episode often culminating in ejaculation. Sexual stimulation may be so intense that, during the first 2 or 3 hr following treatment, the animals may ejaculate up to a dozen times. Subsequently, ejaculation does not terminate penile erection and the animals look exhausted. During an episode of sexual excitement, the rabbit frequently yawns and stretches, although the two phenomena may also occur separately. Moreover, the SYS outlasts the sexual response by several hours. Finally, as reported below, ACTH produces no sexual effect in castrated animals, although it does elicit the SYS. It is important to point out that ACTH-like peptides, unlike drugs acting on brain monoamines such as parachlorophenylalanine or apomorphine (see Gessa and Tagliamonte, 1974), do not enhance social interaction; this is particularly evident in the male rabbit, which, during episodes of sexual stimulation, does not seek to copulate with either male or female partners. In addition, the administration of β-ACTH$^{1-24}$ into the lateral ventricle of rats does not increase the percentage of males copulating with receptive females. However, in sexually experienced male rats, the hormone markedly shortens the ejaculation latency and also decreases the number of mounts and intromissions prior to ejaculation (Table 1). These findings indicate that erection and ejaculation or copulatory behavior can be influenced differentially.

AMINO ACID SEQUENCE ESSENTIAL FOR ELICITING THE SEXUAL RESPONSE

This study was carried out on adult male New Zealand rabbits, with stainless steel cannulas chronically implanted into the lateral ventricle.

TABLE 1. *Effect of β-ACTH$^{1-24}$, injected into the lateral ventricle, on the copulatory pattern of sexually experienced male rats*

Treatment (no. animals)	μg or μl injected	Latency to 1st ejaculation (min)	No. mounts prior to ejaculation (mount frequency)	No. intromissions prior to ejaculation (intromission frequency)
None (18)	—	13.07 ± 3.45	3.0 ± 2.4 (0.23)	9.0 ± 5.0 (0.70)
Saline (10)	10 μl	12.32 ± 4.05	2.8 ± 2.3 (0.22)	7.6 ± 2.3 (0.60)
β-ACTH$^{1-24}$ (8)	5 μg in 10 μl saline	7.80 ± 1.73[a]	2.6 ± 2.1 (0.38)	6.0 ± 2.6 (0.75)

Rats were paired with females in estrus.
[a] $p < 0.01$ with respect to saline-treated or untreated rats.
β-ACTH$^{1-24}$ or saline was injected 30 min prior to mating test, through chronically implanted cannulas.

TABLE 2. *Peptides capable of inducing penile erection and the stretching–yawning syndrome after injection into the lateral ventricle of rabbits*

Peptide[a]	Dose (μg or I.U.)	No. rats with erections/ treated rats[b]	No. rats with SYS/treated rats
β_p-ACTH	10	10/10	10/10
	5	10/10	10/10
	1	6/10	8/10
β-ACTH[1-24]	5	30/30	30/30
	2.5	7/8	8/8
	1	4/10	6/10
Alkali-treated β-ACTH[1-24]	5	8/8	8/8
DW-75	2.5	8/8	8/8
	1	8/8	8/8
α_p-MSH	5	5/5	5/5
β_p-MSH	5	5/5	5/5
β_h-MSH[8-22]	10	2/4	3/4
β_s-LPH	50	5/5	5/5
	10	6/10	10/10
STH	20	0/5	0/5
LYS-vasopressin	10 I.U.	0/10	0/10
Oxytocin	0.2 I.U.	0/10	0/10
Bradykinin	30	0/20	0/20

Experimental details are reported in Bertolini, Gessa, Vergoni, and Ferrari (1968).
* p = pig; h = human; s = sheep.
[a] Structure of the active peptides is reported in Table 3.
[b] At least three episodes of penile erection during the 3-hr observation.

The results, summarized in Table 2, show that among the various peptides tested, only those possessing direct adrenocorticotropic or melanophore-stimulating activities or both induce both erection and SYS, the effective doses being roughly equal for inducing either effect. Indeed, these behavioral changes are induced by natural and synthetic ACTH-like peptides as well as by α- and β-MSH and by β-lipotropic hormone (β-LPH).

Table 3 correlates the amino acid sequence necessary for producing the behavioral changes with that essential for adrenal and melanophore stimulation. It appears that the amino acid sequence required for producing behavioral changes is smaller than that essential for adrenal stimulation. ACTH fully retains the capability of inducing stretchings, yawnings, and penile erections after having been boiled in 0.1 N NaOH, a procedure that degrades the ACTH molecule and destroys its adrenocorticotropic but not its intrinsic MSH activity (Pickering and Li, 1964).

Consistently, little or no adrenocorticotropic activity is exerted by α-MSH,

TABLE 3. *Amino acid sequence essential for inducing the SYS and penile erection in rabbits*

Peptide	ACTH activity IU/mg	MSH activity U/g	Amino acid sequence	Reference
β_p-ACTH	95–117	1.1×10^8	H–Ser–Tyr–Ser–MET–GLU–HIS–PHE–ARG–TRY–GLY–Lys–Pro . . . Phe–OH^{39}	Li (1972)
β_s^1-ACTH$^{1-24}$	100–120	1.2×10^8	H–Ser–Tyr–Ser–MET–GLU–HIS–PHE–ARG–TRY–GLY–Lys–Pro . . . Pro–OH^{24}	Hofmann and Yajima (1962)
DW-75	275	—	dH–Ser–Tyr–Ser–NLE–GLU–HIS–PHE–ARG–TRY–GLY–Lys–Pro . . . Val–NH$_2$^{25}	Doepfner (1966)
α_p-MSH	3.5	2×10^{10}	CH$_3$CO–Ser–Tyr–Ser–MET–GLU–HIS–PHE–ARG–TRY–GLY–Lys–Pro–Val–NH$_2$^{13}	Steelman and Guillemin (1959)
β_p-MSH	< 0.1	2.5×10^9	Asp . . . Pro–Tyr–Lys–MET–GLU–HIS–PHE–ARG–TRY–GLY–Ser–Pro . . . Asp^{18}	Li (1959)
β_h-MSH$^{8-22}$	—	2.2×10^{12}	H–Pro–Tyr–Arg–MET–GLU–HIS–PHE–ARG–TRY–GLY–Ser–Pro . . . Asp–OH^{15}	Yajima et al. (1968)
β_s-LPH	1.1	2.9×10^7	H–Glu . . . Pro–Tyr–Lys–MET–GLU–HIS–PHE–ARG–TRY–GLY–Ser–Pro . . . Glu–NH$_2$^{90}	Lohmar and Li (1968); Chrétien and Li (1967)

"Active core"

β-MSH or β-LPH, all of which are highly potent in producing the behavioral changes under discussion. The β-LPH molecule consists of 90 amino acids and contains, in position 41–58, the complete sequence of bovine β-MSH. Because of this structural feature, it is not surprising that β-LPH exhibits certain biologic properties characteristic of β-MSH (Lohmar and Li, 1968), including the ability to produce sexual stimulation and the SYS. Nonetheless, although all the active peptides possess MSH activity, there is no correlation between their MSH potency and their ability to induce behavioral changes.

From the structures recorded in Table 3, it will be seen that the "core sequence" essential for inducing the SYS and sexual stimulation is the esapeptide Gll–Hist–Phel–Arginyl–Tryl–Glycine. The core sequence might also include the methionine residue (preceding glutamic acid), present in all active peptides except the pentacosapeptide DW-75. In the latter, the readily oxidizable methionine is substituted by its isologous norleucine residue; this substitution is considered to be at least partially responsible for the great potency of this peptide as an adrenal stimulant (Doepfner, 1966). Interestingly, it proved to be the most potent in producing both the SYS and sexual stimulation.

PERMISSIVE ROLE OF TESTOSTERONE IN THE SEXUAL RESPONSE TO ACTH

The results of these studies are summarized in Table 4: (1) Castration eliminates the sexual response to ACTH in rats and rabbits, even when carried out a few days prior to treatment. (2) The sexual response to ACTH in intact rabbits is also prevented by cyproterone acetate, a substance that antagonizes the effects

TABLE 4. *Permissive role of testosterone in the sexual response to β-ACTH[1-24] or DW-75*

Animal species	Pretreatment	Peptide	μg/g into lateral ventricle	Animals with erection/treated animals	Animals with SYS/treated animals
Rabbits	None	DW-75	10	15/15	15/15
	Castration	DW-75	10	0/5	4/5
	Castration + testosterone	DW-75	10	5/5	5/5
	Cyproterone acetate	DW-75	10	2/6	6/6
Rats	None	β-ACTH[1-24]	1	15/15	15/15
	Castration	β-ACTH[1-24]	1	0/15	15/15
	Castration + testosterone	β-ACTH[1-24]	1	15/15	15/15

Castration was carried out 4–15 days prior to treatment. Testosterone propionate was given subcutaneously at the dose of 3 mg/kg in rabbits and 0.5 mg/kg in rats, daily for 3 days; last injection 12 hr before experiment. Cyproterone acetate was given at the dose of 20 mg/kg i.p. daily for 3 days; last injection 12 hr before experiment. In addition, 4 mg of the steroid was injected into the lateral ventricle 1 hr before DW-75.

TABLE 5. *Anabolic steroids can substitute for testosterone in permitting the sexual response to β-ACTH$^{1-24}$ in castrated rats*

Pretreatment	Animals with erection/ treated animals	Animals with SYS/ treated animals
—	0/10	10/10
Testosterone	9/10	10/10
Norboletone	8/10	10/10
4-Chlorotestosterone	8/10	10/10

Experimental condition: adult male rats castrated 40 days prior to experiment. The steroids were given subcutaneously at a dose of 0.5 mg/kg daily for 4 days; last treatment 12 hr before the intraventricular administration of 1 μg of β-ACTH$^{1-24}$.

of testosterone. It would be of interest to study whether cyproterone acetate inhibits the ACTH response in male rats as well, for it fails to inhibit spontaneous sexual behavior in this species (Davidson and Levine, 1972). (3) In castrated rabbits and rats, ACTH still produces stretching and yawning movements, indicating that the stimulatory effect of ACTH on sexual behavior requires the presence of testosterone, which is not necessary to SYS. (4) The response to ACTH is fully restored by treating the castrated rats and rabbits with testosterone propionate. However, it is intriguing to note that testosterone can be replaced both in rabbits and rats, by two potent anabolic steroids, norboletone and 4-chlorotestosterone (Table 5), both of which are considered to be weakly androgenic using the Hershberger test in rats (Hershberger, Shipley, and Meyer, 1953), but as potent as testosterone in promoting the growth of the clitoris in female rabbits (Bertolini and Mucci, 1969).

The foregoing results suggest that the capacity of restoring the sexual response to ACTH in castrated animals may be a sensitive test for revealing the central androgenic activity of a steroid. Conversely, the antiandrogenic properties of a substance may be disclosed by its capacity to abolish the sexual stimulatory effect of ACTH in intact rabbits.

PRESENCE IN THE HYPOTHALAMUS OF MATERIAL ACTIVE IN INDUCING THE SYS AND SEXUAL STIMULATION

An important question with regard to the physiologic significance of our finding is whether peptides, which are capable of stimulating sexual behavior, are normally present in the CNS of animals.

Different studies have shown the presence of material with adrenocorticotropic and melanophore-stimulating activity in the hypothalamus of different animal species (Guillemin, Hearn, Cheek, and Housholder, 1957; Royce and Sayers, 1958; Farrell, 1959; Guillemin, Schally, Lipscomb, Andersen, and Long, 1962). However, it is unclear whether this material is conveyed from the hypothalamus or is actually synthesized *in situ*. The latter possibility is suggested by the findings

TABLE 6. *Penile erection and the SYS induced in rabbits by ACTH-like peptides isolated from the hypothalamus of intact and hypophysectomized–adrenalectomized male rats*

Source of active peptide	Dose injected into lateral ventricle. Material contained in:	Rabbits with erection/treated rabbits	Rabbits with SYS/treated rabbits
β-ACTH[1-24]	1 μg	5/5	5/5
Rat pituitary	1 hypophysis	6/7	7/7
Hypothalamus from intact rats	4 hypothalami	3/6	3/6
Hypothalamus from hypophysectomized– adrenalectomized rats	1 hypothalamus	2/4	3/4

Extraction and isolation procedures for the peptide material and other technical details are reported in Bertolini et al. (1971).

of Winnick, Hussa, and Winnick (1969), who showed that slices of bovine hypothalamus actively synthesize a peptide that resembles ACTH in certain physicochemical properties, e.g., molecular size and pattern of labeled leucine incorporation.

We have isolated from hog and rat hypothalamus an ACTH-like peptide that produced sexual excitement and the SYS in male rabbits after intraventricular injection (Bertolini, Gentile, Greggia, Sternieri, and Ferrari, 1971). The material obtained from the hypothalamus of a single rat exhibited roughly one-eighth of the activity of the ACTH present in the hypophysis of one rat. The amount of this hypothalamic material was roughly doubled in hypophysectomized rats and quadrupled in rats both hypophysectomized and adrenalectomized. These findings, reported in Table 6, indicate that the ACTH-like peptide is synthesized in the hypothalamus, and that its concentration is increased under conditions known to increase the concentration of corticotropin-releasing-factor (CRF). Consistently, the active hypothalamic peptide behaved more like CRF than ACTH, in that it enhanced blood corticosterone levels in intact rats, although it was incapable of doing so in hypophysectomized rats. These results suggest that the CRF molecule contains the peptide sequence required for eliciting stretching, yawning, and sexual stimulation, and that when these behavior patterns occur under physiological conditions, they might be elicited by an endogenous peptide closely related to CRF.

LOCALIZATION IN THE CNS OF THE "BEHAVIORAL RECEPTORS" FOR ACTH PEPTIDES

To identify the site of action of ACTH in producing the stretching and yawning behavior pattern, the hormone has been microinjected into different brain areas of cats through chronically implanted cannulas. These experiments revealed that the hypothalamic areas lining the third ventricle are the most sensitive brain regions for the stretching effect of ACTH (Gessa et al., 1967). In contrast, a lesion placed in the preoptic area, destroying the structures that take up ^{3}H-testosterone, was found to destroy the capacity of ACTH to induce erections and ejaculations, but not stretching-yawning behavior (Bertolini, Vergoni, and Bernardi, 1969).

The results of these experiments, plus the fact that testosterone is not needed for the stretching-yawning response to ACTH, indicate that the receptors responsible for the latter effect are different from those responsible for sexual excitement. However, the lesion data do not provide complete evidence that the preoptic area is the ACTH target for sexual response, because the lesion might merely have removed a brain area essential for the behavior pattern to occur. It is hoped that further information with regard to site of sexual action of ACTH peptides will be provided by the microinjection technique.

PHYSIOLOGIC SIGNIFICANCE

Our findings are of great interest, for they indicate that ACTH-like peptides, in addition to androgens, can directly influence sexual behavior in males. A pointer to the physiologic significance of this finding is provided by the fact that the active peptides are normally present in the hypothalamus, the active doses are very small, and the behavioral changes induced are an exaggeration of physiologic response.

One corollary of these considerations is that erection and ejaculation might be physiologically elicited by ACTH-like peptides, either synthesized in the hypothalamus or released by the hypophysis, to reach the hypothalamus by means of an inverted portal flow (Torok, 1964) or by some other route. The validity of this hypothesis is sustained by the fact that ACTH-like peptides are the only known substances capable of producing erection and ejaculation when applied to the CNS.

A further corollary is that the central physiologic role of testosterone, which is essential for the sexual response to ACTH, might be to sensitize the central receptors to the action of the active peptides.

The fact that sexual excitement, stretching–yawning behavior, and cortical desynchronization are elicited by the action of the same peptides in brain raises the question of the interrelationship of these effects. Normally, stretching is associated with orgasm in different animal species, and yawning is displayed by male rhesus monkeys during coitus (see Goy and Resko, 1972).

At the present time, we may only speculate that ACTH or related peptides have the potential ability to activate a variety of neural circuits responsible for different patterns of behavior. The activation of one or another circuit would depend upon whether other factors, such as hormones or monoamines, have sensitized or desensitized that circuit to the active peptide. The common denominator of these behavior patterns seems to be arousal. It is pertinent to recall that a close relationship exists between stretching–yawning behavior and cortical activation, that in lower species MSH subserves camouflage purposes and, finally, that ACTH is released peripherally in response to stress.

Among the important points to be clarified are (1) the reason for the time lag before the onset of ACTH effects (is the latency due to the time required for the peptide to reach the target receptor, or to some indirect mechanism?), and (2) the nature of the reiterative occurrence of the ACTH effects. These problems are linked to that of what biochemical mechanism is involved in the central effect of ACTH peptides. Further work is continuing in our laboratories in an effort to resolve these problems.

ACKNOWLEDGMENT

We thank H. H. Sugden for his help in the preparation of this manuscript.

REFERENCES

Baldwin, D. M., Haun, C. K., and Sawyer, C. H. (1974): Effects of intraventricular infusion of ACTH$^{1-24}$ and ACTH$^{4-10}$ in LH release, ovulation, and behavior in the rabbit. *Brain Res. (in press)*.

Bertolini, A., Gentile, G., Greggia, A., Sternieri, E., and Ferrari, W. (1971): Possible role of hypothalamic corticotropin-releasing factor in the induction of sexual excitement in adult male rats. *Riv. Farmacol. Ter.,* 2:243–249.

Bertolini, A., Gessa, G. L., Vergoni, W., and Ferrari, W. (1968): Induction of sexual excitement with intraventricular ACTH: Permissive role of testosterone in the male rabbit. *Life Sci.,* 7:1203–1206.

Bertolini, A., and Mucci, P. (1969): High androgenicity in the rabbit of some anabolic steroids. *Riv. Farmacol. Ter.,* 1:45–55.

Bertolini, A., Vergoni, W., and Bernardi, M. (1969): Perdita della capacità dell'ACTH d'indurre eccitazione sessuale per lesione delle zone cerebrali accumulanti testosterone. *Boll. Soc. Ital. Biol. Sper.,* 45:1139–1140.

Chrétien, M., and Li, C. H. (1967): Isolation, purification, and characterization of γ-lipotropic hormone from sheep pituitary glands. *Can. J. Biochem.,* 45:1163–1174.

Davidson, J. M., and Levine, S. (1972): Endocrine regulation of behavior. *Annu. Rev. Physiol.,* 34:375–407.

Doepfner, W. (1966): Biological characterization of a new and highly potent synthetic analogue of corticotrophin. *Experientia,* 22:527–528.

Farrell, G. (1959): Steroidogenic properties of extracts of beef diencephalon. *Endocrinology,* 65:29–33.

Ferrari, W., Gessa, G. L., and Vargiu, L. (1963): Behavioral effects induced by intracisternally injected ACTH and MSH. *Ann. N.Y. Acad. Sci.,* 104:330–343.

Gessa, G. L., Concu, A., Demontis, G., Mereu, G. P., Olianas, M., and Tagliamonte A. (1973): Effetto dell'iniezione intraliquorale di ACTH sull'EEG del gatto. *Riv. Farmacol. Ter.,* 4:55a–64a.

Gessa, G. L., Pisano, M., Vargiu, L., Crabai, F., and Ferrari, W. (1967): Stretching and yawning movements after intracerebral injection of ACTH. *Rev. Can. Biol.,* 26:229–236.

Gessa, G. L., and Tagliamonte, A. (1974): Role of brain monoamines in male sexual behavior. *Life Sci.,* 14:425–436.

Goy, R. W., and Resko, J. A. (1972): Gonadal hormones and behavior of normal and pseudohermaphroditic nonhuman female primates. In: *Recent Progress in Hormone Research (Proc. 1971 Laurentian Hormone Conf.),* Vol. 28, edited by E. B. Astwood. Academic Press, New York and London.

Guillemin, R., Hearn, W. R., Cheek, W. R., and Housholder, D. E. (1957): Control of corticotrophin release: Further studies with in vitro methods. *Endocrinology,* 60:488–506.

Guillemin, R., Schally, A. V., Lipscomb, H. S., Andersen, R. N., and Long, J. M. (1962): On the presence in hog hypothalamus of β-corticotropin releasing factor, α- and β-melanocyte stimulating hormones, adrenocorticotropin, lysine-vasopressin and oxytocin. *Endocrinology*, 70: 471-480.

Hershberger, L. G., Shipley, E. G., and Meyer, R. K. (1953): Myotrophic activity of 19-nortestosterone and other steroids determined by modified levator and muscle method. *Proc. Soc. Exp. Biol. Med.*, 83:175–180.

Hofmann, K., and Yajima, H. (1962): Synthetic pituitary hormones. *Rec. Prog. Horm. Res.*, 18:41–88.

Li, C. H. (1959): The relation of chemical structure to the biologic activity of pituitary hormones. *Lab. Invest.*, 8:574–587.

Li, C. H. (1972): Hormones of the adenohypophysis. *Proc. Am. Philo. Soc.*, 116:365–382.

Lohmar, P., and Li, C. H. (1968): Biological properties of ovine β-lipotropic hormone. *Endocrinology*, 82:898–904.

MacLean, P. D. (1973): An evolutionary approach to the investigation of psychoneuroendocrine functions. *Horm. Brain Func., Budapest*, 1971:379–389.

Pickering, B. T., and Li, C. H. (1964): Adrenocorticotropins XXIX. The action of sodium hydroxide on adrenocorticotropin. *Arch. Biochem. Biophys.*, 104:119–127.

Royce, P. C., and Sayers, G. (1958): Corticotropin releasing activity of a pepsin labile factor in the hypothalamus. *Proc. Soc. Exp. Biol. Med.*, 98:677–680.

Steelman, S. L., and Guillemin, R. (1959): Adrenocorticotropic activity of alpha melanocyte stimulating hormone (α-MSH). *Proc. Soc. Exp. Biol. Med.*, 101:600–601.

Torok, B. (1964): Structure of the vascular connections of the hypothalamo-hypophysial region. *Acta Anat.*, 59:84–99.

Winnick, M., Hussa, R. O., and Winnick, T. (1969): Synthesis of corticotrophin-like polypeptides and protein by bovine hypothalamus, median eminence and pituitary tissue slices. *J. Endocrinol.*, 44:537–544.

Yajima, H., Okada, Y., Kinomura, Y., and Minami, H. (1968): Studies on peptides. XX. Synthesis of the octadecapeptide corresponding to the entire aminoacid sequence of monkey β-melanocyte-stimulating hormone. *J. Am. Chem. Soc.*, 90:527–528.

Sexual Behavior: Pharmacology and Biochemistry, edited by M. Sandler and G. L. Gessa. Raven Press, New York © 1975.

Effects of Intraventricular Injections of Corticotropins on Hypothalamopituitary Ovarian Function and Behavior in the Female Rabbit

Charles H. Sawyer, David M. Baldwin, and Charles K. Haun

Departments of Anatomy, University of California and University of Southern California Medical Schools and UCLA Brain Research Institute, Los Angeles, California 90024

A peculiar stretching and yawning syndrome (SYS) has been described in various mammals following injection of peptides with ACTH or MSH activity into the cerebrospinal fluid (Ferrari, Gessa, and Vargiu, 1963; Gessa, Pisano, Vargiu, Crabai, and Ferrari, 1967). More recently, Bertolini and co-workers (1968, 1969) observed a dramatic display of sexual excitement following similar treatments in male rats and rabbits. It was thought that the primary sites of action of the peptides were hypothalamic structures close to the wall of the third ventricle. In preliminary unpublished studies Haun and Haltmeyer have noted that intraventricular injections of ACTH[1-24] can stimulate LH release and gonadal steroid secretion as well as sexual excitement in male and female rabbits. The buck displays copulatory movements and ejaculates repeatedly following ACTH[1-24] treatment, even in the absence of the female.

The rabbit doe is a reflex ovulator, i.e., rupture of ovarian follicles ordinarily occurs only after mating, thereby assuring the expelled ova a maximal opportunity of fertilization. The doe's acceptance of the buck and the triggered release of her pituitary ovulating hormone involve discrete areas of her hypothalamus, as revealed by stereotactic electrical stimulation, placement of lesions, and implantation of sex steroids (Sawyer, 1959, 1967). Palka and Sawyer (1966) showed that estrogen implants localized in the ventromedial nucleus evoked behavioral estrus whereas basal midline median eminence–arcuate nucleus implants influenced pituitary–gonadal function (Kanematsu and Sawyer, 1963).

Temporal and quantitative aspects of LH release leading to ovulation now can be studied by measuring blood levels of LH with radioimmunoassay (RIA) methods, and a heterologous RIA system for rabbit LH has been developed in our laboratory (Scaramuzzi, Blake, Papkoff, Hilliard, and Sawyer, 1972). With this method, patterns of LH release have been traced after coitus, electrical stimulation of the amygdala, and the injection of the releasing factor (LRH) (Kanematsu, Scaramuzzi, Hilliard, and Sawyer, 1974) as well as following intraventricular infusions of norepinephrine (NE) (Sawyer, Hilliard, Kanematsu, Scaramuzzi, and Blake, 1974). These curves are illustrated in Fig. 1. With this

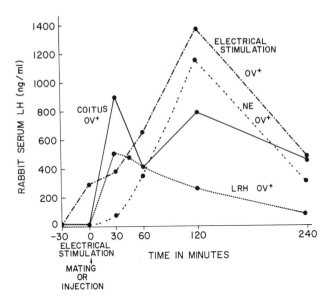

FIG. 1. Patterns of serum LH content in estrogen-primed female rabbits following coitus, electrical stimulation of the amygdala, and i.v. infusion of LRH (from Kanematsu et al., 1974) and intraventricular infusion of norepinephrine (NE) (from Sawyer et al., 1974). Ovulation was induced (OV+) by each of these treatments.

information as background it seemed desirable to reexamine the effects of intraventricular ACTH on behavior and to correlate changes in serum LH levels with behavioral observations. In addition, electrophysiologic correlates of the changes have been recorded with chronically implanted electrodes. Many of the data to be reported here as well as details of the methods employed have been published recently (Baldwin, Haun, and Sawyer, 1974).

EFFECTS OF ACTH$^{1-24}$ and ACTH$^{4-10}$ ON BEHAVIOR AND OVULATION

The results are summarized in Table 1. In the first group of six animals with permanently implanted electrodes, 10 μg ACTH$^{1-24}$ (Tetracosactide®, Organon) was injected 1 hr after a control injection of saline. To avoid disturbing the animals while electrical recordings were being made, bleedings for LH assay were omitted and behavioral observations were too limited to score accurately. Changes in electrical activity of the brain are reported below; five of these six rabbits ovulated in response to the treatment. Animals in the second group were bled by cardiac puncture and were injected intraventricularly with 10 μg ACTH$^{1-24}$ within minutes of the first bleeding. Of seven rabbits so treated six exhibited the stretching and yawning syndrome (SYS), five showed sexual excitement (lordosis and tail deviation), and five ovulated. Similar treatment with ACTH$^{4-10}$ (Group 3) resulted in two animals showing SYS and one showing

TABLE 1. *Effects of intraventricular infusions of ACTH and LRH on stretching and yawning behavior (SYS), sexual behavior, and ovulation*

Group	Treatment	Bled	No. animals treated	SYS	Sex behavior	No. animals ovulating
1	Saline–ACTH$^{1-24}$ [a]	—	6	—	—	5
2	ACTH$^{1-24}$	+	7	6	5	5
3	ACTH$^{4-10}$	+	4	2	1	0
4	Saline	+	9	1	1	0
5	Saline–ACTH$^{1-24}$	+	5	2	2	0
6	Saline–ACTH$^{4-10}$	+	3	0	0	0
7	LRH	+	4	0	0	0

[a] Electrical recordings were made in these animals. They were not subjected to bleeding.

sexual excitement, but none ovulated. Saline alone (Group 4) given under this schedule did not induce ovulation but curiously one animal of the nine displayed the SYS and sexual excitement. When ACTH$^{1-24}$ injection was preceded by three bleedings and saline injection over a 2-hr period (Group 5) it was no longer effective in inducing ovulation and only two of the five rabbits revealed the SYS and sex behavior. Group 6 showed that three animals receiving ACTH$^{4-10}$ in this sequence failed to display even the behavioral changes. Synthetic LRH was injected intraventricularly at a dosage of 10 μg to each of four animals in Group 7. None showed SYS or sexual excitement during the next 4 hr, but all ovulated. In Table 1 the time of onset of the observed behavioral changes was about 30 min, and they persisted in some animals for as long as 4 hr. The latency was the same whether injection was made into a lateral ventricle or the third ventricle.

EFFECTS OF ACTH AND LRH ON LH RELEASE

When the ACTH$^{1-24}$ was injected intraventricularly immediately after the first bleeding, a very dramatic rise in serum LH occurred, usually within 30 min (Fig. 2) with levels dropping again to preinjection values in all animals by 6 hr. In every instance but one, regardless of whether ovulation was to follow, a rise in LH (range 200 to 900 ng/ml) was observed—at 0.5 hr in six animals, 1.5 hr in one animal, and a second peak in another at 3 hr after administration of ACTH$^{1-24}$. If, however, blood was withdrawn and intraventricular saline given 2 hr prior to the ACTH$^{1-24}$, there was little or no elevation in serum LH (Fig. 3).

Saline injection had little effect on serum LH levels as indicated in Fig. 3. Among 11 cases, not illustrated, in which LH levels were measured at multiple intervals for 6 hr after treatment with saline, only two animals showed a slight elevation of 50 ng/ml 30 min after injection, and they returned to control values throughout the remainder of the experimental period. Of three animals bled and injected with saline followed by ACTH$^{4-10}$, one showed elevated serum LH (160 ng/ml) 3 hr post-ACTH$^{4-10}$, but this was insufficient to induce ovulation. When

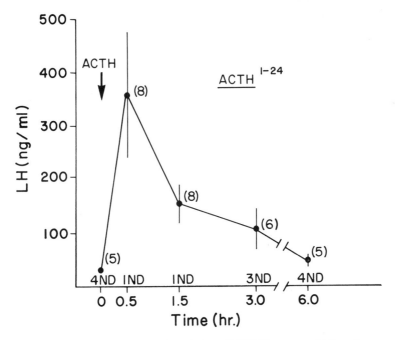

FIG. 2. Effect of an intraventricular injection of 10 μg ACTH$^{1-24}$ on serum LH in estrogen-primed female rabbits. Number of cases in parentheses. Vertical lines limit S.E.M. ND = Nondetectable levels.

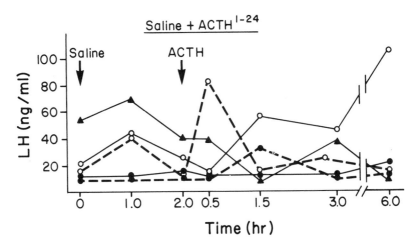

FIG. 3. Serum LH in female rabbits after intraventricular injection of saline and removal of blood by cardiac puncture, followed 2 hr later with 10 μg ACTH$^{1-24}$. The animals were bled three times prior to the ACTH infusion, with 4 ml of blood taken each time. (From Baldwin, Haun, and Sawyer, 1974, courtesy of *Brain Res.*)

ACTH[4-10] was given alone, two of six animals were observed to have a nonovulatory rise in serum LH whereas the other four animals showed essentially no change.

Intraventricular injection of LRH produced a dramatic elevation in serum LH with a temporal relationship similar to that following injection of ACTH[1-24], i.e., peaking at 30 min, but the amount of LH released after LRH was considerably greater, with peaks ranging from 900 to 1,700 ng/ml.

EFFECTS OF ACTH[1-24] ON MULTIUNIT ELECTRICAL ACTIVITY OF THE PREOPTIC REGION

Changes in multiple unit activity (MUA) following intraventricular infusions were observed in all six animals in which electrical records were taken. However, in one case, later found to be hydrocephalic as a result of a cannula-induced infection, elevated MUA in the periventricular preoptic area (PPO) followed infusion of saline as well as ACTH solution. In the other five animals MUA showed elevations of varying amplitude and duration in the lateral preoptic (LPO)–diagonal band area and PPO following infusion of ACTH[1-24]. Prior infusion of saline had no effect on the electrical activity in these animals.

In two rabbits, in each of which clear-cut elevations in MUA in the LPO–diagonal band were observed on three separate occasions at about monthly intervals, the rise started within 10 to 20 min, reached a peak at 60 to 90 min and returned to preinfusion levels by 2 to 2.5 hr (Fig. 4). Other areas tested (amygdala, dorsomedial hypothalamus, fornix, premammillary area, septum, and lateral hypothalamic area) showed no response attributable to ACTH[1-24] infusion. No changes in cortical (frontal or limbic), olfactory bulb, or hippocampal EEG could be correlated with MUA elevations induced by ACTH[1-24].

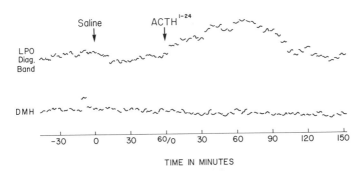

FIG. 4. A typical example of the changes in multiunit activity in the LPO–diagonal band area after intraventricular infusion of 10 μg ACTH[1-24]. A simultaneous recording in the dorsomedial hypothalamic area (DMH) was typical of areas showing no response. This figure was prepared by extracting 4-sec segments during high-amplitude–slow-wave EEG patterns from each 5 min of a continuous recording.

DISCUSSION

The induction of SYS reported here in female rabbits is similar to that described earlier in males (Ferrari et al., 1963; Gessa et al., 1967) indicating that there is little or no sex difference in this behavioral response to $ACTH^{1-24}$. In contrast, noticeable sexual excitement in the female rabbit was much less dramatic than that described for the male (Bertolini et al., 1968, 1969). This may reflect a real sex difference in response to $ACTH^{1-24}$, or it may mean merely that sexual excitement in singly caged females is more difficult to assess than in males. Because LRH has been shown to stimulate sexual behavior in estrogen-primed ovariectomized rats (Moss and McCann, 1973), it seemed possible that the sexual behavior we were observing might be due to release of LRH and therefore not a direct effect of $ACTH^{1-24}$ on behavior. Because infusion of large quantities of LRH caused a substantial release of LH without a noticeable effect on behavior, this explanation was not supported by our data. Bertolini, Gentile, Greggia, Sternieri, and Ferrari, (1971) proposed a similar role for corticotropin releasing factor (CRF) and suggested that CRF might be contained in the $ACTH^{1-24}$ peptide sequence.

It is of interest that compounds with structural relationships similar to the naturally occurring ACTH molecule, e.g., $ACTH^{1-24}$, and α-MSH (Li, 1972), also exert similar effects on the induction of SYS and sexual excitement (Ferrari et al., 1963; Gessa et al., 1967; Bertolini et al., 1969). Natural ACTH, $ACTH^{1-24}$, and α-MSH as well as a smaller fragment of ACTH, e.g., $ACTH^{4-10}$, can also influence the extinction of conditioned avoidance response in rats (De Weid, 1969). However, intraventricular infusions of 10 μg $ACTH^{4-10}$ (approximately three times the amount of $ACTH^{1-24}$ on a molar basis) failed to induce ovulation and were much less effective in causing LH release or inducing SYS and sexual excitement. This suggests that although some stimulating activity may be retained on the shorter molecule, the additional amino acid residues on the $ACTH^{1-24}$ are necessary for maximum hormonal and behavioral responses.

Correlated with these effects on behavior, intraventricular injection of $ACTH^{1-24}$ given alone or preceded 1 hr earlier by infusion of saline-induced ovulation or LH release or both in a majority of animals were tested (Table 1; Fig. 2). In contrast, when $ACTH^{1-24}$ injection was preceded by cardiac puncture bleedings at 0, 1, and 2 hr in conjunction with injection of saline, ovulation and LH release were inhibited (Table 1; Fig. 3). Under these conditions, the ability of $ACTH^{1-24}$ to promote SYS and sexual excitement was also suppressed. Thus, it would appear that the nonspecific stress of bleeding prior to the $ACTH^{1-24}$ infusion resulted in an increased threshold of responsiveness to intraventricular ACTH. Recently, Sawyer (1972) referred to earlier unpublished studies with Saul in which electrical stimulation of the amygdala under acute stereotactic conditions was ineffective in inducing ovulation whereas such stimulation in the unstressed chronically implanted rabbit was highly successful (Saul and Sawyer, 1961). Furthermore, Ellendorff, Colombo, Blake, Whitmoyer, and Sawyer (1973) reported that surgical stress in combination with amygdala stimulation in the proestrous rat would block cyclic ovulation, but in chronically implanted rats under otherwise similar conditions ovulation was not inhibited. The above results as well as those reported in this study suggest that a central nervous response to a particular stimulus may be altered by nonspecific stress. Whether these effects are due to direct changes in neural responsiveness, or indirectly through the feedback of adrenal secretions remains to be determined. Glucocorticoids have been reported to alter brain electrical activity (Sawyer, Kawakami, Meyerson, Whitmoyer, and Lilley, 1968), oppose the effects of ACTH on conditioned avoidance behavior (De Weid, 1969), and inhibit LH release (Baldwin and Sawyer, 1974).

Any suggestions at this time as to how $ACTH^{1-24}$ might cause release of LH must be quite speculative. Nevertheless, because catecholamines are in general stimulatory to LH release (Ganong, 1972) and, in particular, norepinephrine infused into the third ventricle of rabbits activates LH release (Sawyer et al., 1974), it might be suggested that $ACTH^{1-24}$ stimulates central adrenergic pathways responsible for LH release. Similarly, sex behavior appears to be stimulated by elevating the catecholamine (CA)/serotonin balance, which can be achieved by treating with CA precursors such as DOPA or inhibitors of serotonin synthesis such as p-chlorophenylalanine (PCPA). PCPA has been reported to induce compulsive sexual activity in rats by Tagliamonte, Tagliamonte, Gessa, and Brodie, (1969) and in rabbits by Bertolini (1970c) and Perez-Cruet, Tagliamonte, Tagliamonte, and Gessa (1971). Intraventricular serotonin prevents the sexual excitement but not the SYS evoked in male rabbits by intraventricular $ACTH^{1-24}$ (Bertolini and Casalgrandi, 1970). The sexual excitement is also blocked by intraventricular injection of 6-OH-dopamine 48 hr prior to $ACTH^{1-24}$ (Bertolini, 1970a). The work of Bertolini has also suggested that the intraventricular $ACTH^{1-24}$ effects on the brain may be mediated by a mobilization of K^+ ions (Bertolini, 1970b) and/or by an activation of adenyl cyclase which can be blocked by prostaglandin E_1 (Bertolini, 1971). Recently, Jacobowitz (1973) has described a molecular configurational similarity between the end serine–tyrosine amino acids of ACTH and norepinephrine, and he suggests that a competitive mechanism may exist between the catecholamine molecule and binding sites of such peptides as ACTH, α-MSH, and CRF.

Although saline infusion was essentially without effect on LH release, a few animals showed a slight rise in serum LH levels 30 min after infusion. Because ventricular expansion has been reported to elevate plasma LH in the rat (Porter, Mical and Cramer, 1971–1972) it may be that these animals experienced acute ventricular expansion at the time of infusion. Similarly, the SYS and sex behavior seen in one of the nine animals infused with saline may have been induced by physical stimulation.

The sites of action of these peptide hormones are unknown. Areas adjacent to the third ventricle have immunoreactive ACTH concentrations much greater than those found in plasma (Kendall, McGilvra, and Lamorena, 1973). In addition, hypothalamic areas lining the third ventricle were, with the exception of the caudate nucleus, the most sensitive for induction of SYS in the cat (Gessa et al., 1967). These investigators proposed that these hypothalamic areas were connected with the reticular system to maintain an aroused state (as determined by cortical EEG patterns) as drugs known to block the reticular system suppressed the SYS. In the present study, no definite changes in sleep–wake EEG patterns were observed following ACTH infusion. However, electrode sites in the LPO–diagonal band and PPO areas were found to respond to intraventricular ACTH$^{1-24}$ with elevated MUA activity. Whether these changes are related to behavior, hormone release, or to some other CNS response is not known. Obviously more detailed studies will be needed before anything conclusive can be said about the site(s) of action of these peptide molecules on the CNS.

SUMMARY

The effects of intraventricular (lateral and third ventricles) injection of ACTH$^{1-24}$, ACTH$^{4-10}$, and LRH on behavior, LH release (radioimmunoassay), and ovulation were studied in estrogen-primed female rabbits. In addition, electrical recordings were made of EEG and multiple unit activity (MUA) in various areas of the brain in six animals. In the first study, in which only limited behavioral observations were made due to the electrical recording procedures, ACTH$^{1-24}$ was given 1 hr after a control injection of saline, a sequence followed by ovulation in five of six rabbits. In eight trials involving seven animals given ACTH$^{1-24}$ alone and subjected thereafter to multiple bleedings, five displayed sexual excitement, six demonstrated the stretching and yawning syndrome (SYS), and six had elevations of serum LH with a peak at 0.5 to 1.5 hr after infusion, of which five ovulated. Another group of five animals was bled several times by cardiac puncture and infused intraventricularly with saline 2 hr before the ACTH$^{1-24}$. None of these five animals showed appreciable elevations in serum LH or ovulation, but two of five exhibited the SYS and sexual behavior. Treatment with saline alone in nine rabbits had essentially no effect on these responses. ACTH$^{4-10}$ did not induce ovulation in any of the animals tested, but when given without prior bleeding to four animals, two showed the SYS and one, sexual excitement. A nonovulatory rise in serum LH was observed in two of five animals receiving ACTH$^{4-10}$ alone. LRH caused an elevation in LH with subsequent ovulation in four of four rabbits tested, but no behavioral changes were noted. Increased electrical activity was observed in rabbits with electrode placements in the area of the lateral preoptic (LPO)–diagonal band of Broca and the periventricular preoptic area. Other areas showed little or no change in MUA. These results demonstrate that, when administered under appropriate conditions, intraventricular infusions of ACTH$^{1-24}$ are highly effective in initiating SYS, sexual excitement, LH release, and ovulation. These responses are suppressed when preceded by the nonspecific stress of bleeding. The results are consistent with the hypothesis that intraventricular ACTH may exert its effects by interacting with adrenergic nerve pathways or endings in the brain.

ACKNOWLEDGMENTS

This work was supported by grants from NIH NS 01162 and the Ford Foundaton. D.M.B. was supported as a postdoctoral trainee in neuroanatomy by Grant 5 T01 NS 5464.

REFERENCES

Baldwin, D. M., Haun, C. K., and Sawyer, C. H. (1974): Effects of intraventricular infusion of ACTH$^{1-24}$ and ACTH$^{4-10}$ in LH release, ovulation and behavior in the rabbit. *Brain Res.,* 80:291–301.

Baldwin, D. M., and Sawyer, C. H. (1974): Effects of dexamethasone on LH release and ovulation in the cyclic rat. *Endocrinology* 94:1397–1403.

Bertolini, A. (1970a): Inhibition of sexual excitement after intraventricular β^{1-24}-ACTH in male rabbits treated with 6-OH-dopamine. *Riv. Farmacol. Terap.* 1:493–497.

Bertolini, A. (1970b): Possible role played by cerebral K$^+$ in β^{1-24}-ACTH induced sexual excitement in the male rabbit. *Riv. Farmacol. Terap.* 1:499–506.

Bertolini, A. (1970c): Stretching and yawning induced in rats and rabbits with *p*-chlorophenyalanine and *p*-chloromethylamphetamine. *Riv. Farmacol. Terap.* 1:507–512.

Bertolini, A. (1971): Inhibition of the action of ACTH on CNS by Prostaglandin E$_1$. *Riv. Farmacol. Terap.* 11:XVII–XX.

Bertolini, A., and Casalgrandi, L. (1970): Serotonin as the possible mediator of the sexual excitement produced in male animals by intraventricular ACTH. I. Blockade with serotonin of the sexual excitement induced in rats with ACTH. *Riv. Farmacol. Terap.* I:229–233.

Bertolini, A., Gentile, G., Greggia, A., Sternieri, E., and Ferrari, W. (1971): Possible role of hypothalamic corticotropin-releasing factor in the induction of sexual excitation in adult male rats. *Riv. Farmacol. Terap.* 11:243–249.

Bertolini, A., Gessa, G. L., Vergoni, W., and Ferrari, W. (1968): Induction of sexual excitement with intraventricular ACTH; Permissive role of testosterone in the male rabbit. *Life Sci.,* 7(II):1203–1206.

Bertolini, A., Vergoni, W., Gessa, G. L., and Ferrari, W. (1969): Induction of sexual excitement by the action of adrenocorticotrophic hormone in brain. *Nature,* 221:667–669.

De Weid, D. (1969): Effects of peptide hormones on behavior. In: *Frontiers in Neuroendocrinology,* edited by W. F. Ganong and L. Martini, pp. 97–140. Oxford Univ. Press, New York.

Ellendorff, F., Colombo, J. A., Blake, C. A., Whitmoyer, D. I., and Sawyer, C. H. (1973): Effects of electrical stimulation of the amygdala on gonadotropin release and ovulation in the rat. *Proc. Soc. Exp. Biol. Med.,* 142:417–420.

Ferrari, W., Gessa, G. L., and Vargiu, L. (1963): Behavioral effects induced by intracisternally injected ACTH and MSH. *Ann. N.Y. Acad. Sci.,* 104:330–345.

Ganong, W. F. (1972): Pharmacological aspects of neuroendocrine integration, *Prog. Brain Res.,* 38:41–57.

Gessa, G. L., Pisano, M., Vargiu, L., Crabai, F., and Ferrari, W. (1967): Stretching and yawning movements after intracerebral injection of ACTH. *Rev. Canad. Biol.* 26:229–236.

Jacobowitz, D. M. (1973): Distribution of biogenic amines in the pituitary gland. *Prog. Brain Res.,* 39:199–209.

Kanematsu, S., and Sawyer, C. H. (1963): Effects of intrahypothalamic and intrahypophysial estrogen implants on pituitary prolactin and lactation in the rabbit. *Endocrinology* 72:243–252.

Kanematsu, S., Scaramuzzi, R. J., Hilliard, J., and Sawyer, C. H. (1974): Patterns of ovulation-inducing LH release following coitus, electrical stimulation and exogenous LH-RH in the rabbit. *Endocrinology (in press).*

Kendall, J. W., McGilvra, R., and Lamorena, T. L. (1973): ACTH in cerebrospinal fluid and brain. *Program 55th Annual Meeting, The Endocrine Society,* A–78, Abstract.

Li, C. H. (1972): Hormones of the adenohypophysis. *Proc. Am. Phil. Soc.,* 116:365–382.

Moss, R. L., and McCann, S. M. (1973): Induction of mating behavior in rats by luteinizing hormone-releasing factor. *Science,* 181:177–179.

Palka, Y. S., and Sawyer, C. H. (1966): The effects of hypothalamic implants of ovarian steroids on oestrous behavior in rabbits. *J. Physiol. (Lond.)* 185:251–269.

Perez-Cruet, J., Tagliamonte, A., Tagliamonte, P., and Gessa, G. L. (1971): Differential effect of *p*-chlorophenylalanine (PCPA) on sexual behavior and on sleep patterns of male rabbits. *Riv. Pharmacol. Terap.,* 11:27–34.

Porter, J. C., Mical, R. S., and Cramer, O. M. (1971–1972): Effect of serotonin and other indoles on the release of LH, FSH, and prolactin. *Horm. Antagonist Gynecol. Invest.,* 2:13–22.

Saul, G. D., and Sawyer, C. H. (1961): EEG-monitored activation of the hypothalamohypophysial system by amygdala stimulation and its pharmacological blockade. *EEG Clin. Neurophysiol.,* 13:307.

Sawyer, C. H. (1959): Nervous control of ovulation. In: *Recent Progress in the Endocrinology of Reproduction,* edited by C. W. Lloyd, pp. 1–20. Academic Press, New York.

Sawyer, C. H. (1967): Effects of hormonal steroids on certain mechanisms in the adult brain. In: *Proceedings of the Second International Symposium on Hormonal Steroids.* Excerpta Medica, Int. Congr. Ser. 132, pp. 763–775.

Sawyer, C. H. (1972): Functions of the amygdala related to the feedback actions of gonadal steroid hormones. In: *Neurobiology of the Amygdala,* edited by B. Eleftheriou, pp. 745–762. Plenum, New York.

Sawyer, C. H., Hilliard, J., Kanematsu, S., Scaramuzzi, R., and Blake, C. A. (1974): Effects of intraventricular infusions of norepinephrine and dopamine on LH release and ovulation in the rabbit. *Neuroendocrinology,* 15:328–337.

Sawyer, C. H., Kawakami, M., Meyerson, B., Whitmoyer, D. I., and Lilley, J. J. (1968): Effects of ACTH, dexamethasone and asphyxia on electrical activity of the rat hypothalamus. *Brain Res.,* 10:213–226.

Scaramuzzi, R. J., Blake, C. A., Papkoff, H., Hilliard, J., and Sawyer, C. H. (1972): Radioimmunoassay of rabbit luteinizing hormone: Serum levels during various reproductive states. *Endocrinology,* 90:1285–1291.

Tagliamonte, A., Tagliamonte, P., Gessa, G. L., and Brodie, B. B. (1969): Compulsive sexual activity induced by *p*-chlorophenylalanine in normal and pinealectomized rats. *Science,* 166:1433–1435.

Sexual Behavior: Pharmacology and Bio-chemistry, edited by M. Sandler and G. L. Gessa. Raven Press, New York © 1975.

Effect of ACTH$^{4\text{-}10}$ on Copulatory and Sexually Motivated Approach Behavior in the Male Rat

B. Bohus, H. H. L. Hendrickx, A. A. van Kolfschoten, and T. G. Krediet

Rudolf Magnus Institute for Pharmacology, Medical Faculty, University of Utrecht, Vondellaan 6, Utrecht, The Netherlands

The concept that the brain serves as a target organ of testicular and ovarian hormones that enables them to organize and activate male and female sexual behavior enjoys a long history. However, the idea is more recent that the release of pituitary hormones, whether of anterior, intermediate, or posterior lobe origin (ACTH, MSH, vasopressin), accompanies adaptive behavior and that, in turn, changes in the levels of these hormones modulate behavior. A profound influence of adrenocorticotrophic hormone (ACTH) on extinction behavior of rats in avoidance (Levine and Jones, 1965; de Wied, 1966; Bohus, Nyakas, and Endröczi, 1968) and approach situation (Gray, Mayes, and Wilson, 1971; Guth, Levine, and Seward, 1971) has been well established. In addition, ACTH-induced changes in aggressive behavior have also been reported (Brain, Nowell, and Wouters, 1971; Leshner, Walker, Johnson, Kelling, Kreisler, and Svare, 1973).

An important feature of the behavioral effects of ACTH is that they are independent of its action on the adrenal cortex; the peptide shares its effect with α- and β-MSH (Kastin, Miller, Nockton, Sandman, Schally, and Stratton, 1973) and with even smaller fragments of the ACTH molecule (de Wied, 1966; Garrud, Gray, and de Weid, 1974). Although a considerable number of observations on the influence of pituitary peptide hormones on behavioral responses relating to self-preservation are available, relatively little is known about the effect of ACTH on reproductive behavioral processes. Inhibition of copulatory activity in the male rabbit by intravenously administered ACTH was reported by Korányi, Endröczi, and Tárnok (1965, 1966). In contrast with this observation, sexual excitation was observed in the same species by Bertolini, Vergoni, Gessa, and Ferrari (1969) after intraventricular administration of ACTH$^{1\text{-}24}$ and α-MSH even in the absence of the female.

Although the influence of ACTH and ACTH-like peptides on adaptive responses motivated by fear or hunger is obvious, observations relating to their effects on sexual behavior tend to be inconclusive. Therefore, in order to investigate further the role and mechanisms of action of ACTH-like peptides on behavioral adaptation, the influence of ACTH$^{4\text{-}10}$ on copulatory behavior and on a sexually motivated approach response of the male rat was studied. ACTH$^{4\text{-}10}$ is practically devoid of adrenocorticotrophic activity but possesses the behaviorally active sequence of ACTH (de Wied, 1969).

THE EFFECT OF ACTH[4-10] ON COPULATORY BEHAVIOR
OF CASTRATED MALE RATS WITH AND WITHOUT TESTOSTERONE
REPLACEMENT

In order to investigate the influence of ACTH[4-10] on male behavioral patterns, sexually experienced rats were castrated; their copulatory behavior then was studied with highly receptive, estrogen-primed stimulus female rats. Castrated animals, with and without testosterone replacement, were used for the following reasons: (1) the gradual decrease of copulatory activity following castration in the absence of testosterone made it possible to investigate whether ACTH[4-10], with its influence on avoidance behavior, would be able to prevent the effect of castration; and (2) the administration of testosterone to castrated rats provided a stringent control of copulatory behavior and excluded the possibility of an effect of ACTH[4-10] on the gonads.

Administration of ACTH[4-10] before each exposure failed to influence the gradual decline in copulatory activity that followed castration in the sexually experienced male rat. The percentage of rats showing ejaculation or displaying intromission or mounting or both were of the same order of magnitude for each test in ACTH[4-10] treated and control groups. It is of interest that mild electric shock to the skin, which probably releases ACTH from the anterior pituitary, also failed to prevent the disappearance of copulatory behavior in castrated male rats (Barfield and Sachs, 1970). It would seem, therefore, that increasing arousal by nonspecific stimuli and, perhaps, also by ACTH-like peptides, as indicated by other behavioral studies (Weiss, McEwen, Silva, and Kalkut, 1970; Bohus, 1973; de Wied, 1974) cannot replace androgen-induced sexual arousal. A dose of 50 μg of testosterone propionate, administered daily, appeared to be the threshold amount of androgen to restore full copulatory behavior in all castrated rats of our inbred Wistar strain. ACTH[4-10] administration before each session did not affect the occurrence of full copulatory behavior in castrated rats treated with this threshold amount or a higher dose (200 μg/rat) of testosterone propionate.

Analysis of the quantitative indices of male copulatory behavior, however, did point to an effect of ACTH[4-10] in castrated rats treated with the threshold dose of testosterone. As shown in Table 1, administration of ACTH[4-10] in a dose of 20 μg before each session resulted in an increase in intromission and ejaculation latencies, whereas ejaculation was followed by a longer postejaculatory interval in rats treated with 50 μg of testosterone. ACTH[4-10] failed to influence these quantitative measures of copulatory behavior either in castrated rats without replacement therapy or in those treated with the higher dose of testosterone.

These observations indicate that rats treated with ACTH[4-10] tend to be "sluggish" copulators after the initial mounts. The effect of the peptide appeared to be testosterone-dependent. One might therefore suggest that ACTH[4-10] modifies testosterone-induced copulatory mechanisms. In addition, the dose of testosterone seemed to be a crucial factor. Although no substantial quantitative differences were observed between the effects of these two doses of testosterone, it is

TABLE 1. *Effect of ACTH[4-10] on postcastration copulatory behavior of sexually experienced male rats with or without replacement therapy with testosterone propionate (TP)*

Treatment	Mount		Intromission		Ejaculation latency (sec)	Postejaculatory interval (sec)
	Latency (sec)	Frequency	Latency (sec)	Frequency		
Placebo + saline	78.5 ± 15.6[a]	11.3 ± 1.9	135.5 ± 24.2	3.2 ± 0.3	165.3 ± 34.7	562.1 ± 49.4
Placebo + ACTH4-10	67.7 ± 17.3	8.2 ± 0.9	173.7 ± 51.2	2.3 ± 0.3	129.4 ± 40.2	537.4 ± 53.6
TP 50 μg + saline	13.6 ± 3.1	5.1 ± 2.0	22.0 ± 2.5 }[b]	3.5 ± 0.5	58.0 ± 12.9 }[c]	259.0 ± 10.6 }[b]
TP 50 μg + ACTH4-10	26.0 ± 5.2	8.7 ± 1.5	45.6 ± 8.1	5.1 ± 0.7	175.5 ± 24.7	286.9 ± 7.2
TP 200 μg + saline	11.3 ± 3.4	8.3 ± 1.6	14.5 ± 3.4	4.6 ± 0.4	111.6 ± 16.4	278.9 ± 22.8
TP 200 μg + ACTH4-10	20.1 ± 6.7	6.4 ± 0.7	20.8 ± 3.9	5.3 ± 0.5	128.0 ± 16.7	272.6 ± 12.7

[a] Mean ± SE was calculated from the medians of eight observations in each rat. Each group consisted of seven rats.

[b] $p < 0.05$; [c] $p < 0.01$.

probable that androgen-activated mechanisms of rats treated with the higher dose of testosterone were more resistant to the modifying effect of ACTH$^{4-10}$. Observations on the relationship between fear motivation and the effect of ACTH or ACTH-like peptides on the behavior pattern suggested that facilitation of avoidance behavior by peptides is absent if the motivation level is too low or too high (Weiss et al., 1970; Lissák and Bohus, 1972). Therefore, it is possible that the threshold dose of testosterone induced a sexual arousal state highly sensitive to modifying influences. The low arousal level in castrated rats without supplementary therapy and the high arousal state in rats treated with the higher dose of testosterone might then explain the lack of effect of ACTH$^{4-10}$ on copulatory behavior. It is of interest to note that the inhibitory effect of ACTH on sexual behavior in the intact rabbit can also be prevented by pretreatment with testosterone (Korányi et al., 1965, 1966).

The mechanism of action of ACTH$^{4-10}$ on copulatory behavior in the male rat is not clear. It seems likely that ACTH$^{4-10}$, while increasing nonsexual arousal to environmental stimuli, decreases the responsiveness of the male to the female. This assumption corresponds with the notion that ACTH or ACTH-like peptides facilitate the motivational property of environmental and internal stimuli probably through increasing specific arousal within the limbic–midbrain circuit (Bohus, 1973). Furthermore, this hypothesis assumes that increased release of these peptides in response to environmental stimuli is accompanied by diminished copulatory activity. Indeed, Szechtman, Lambrou, Caggiula, and Redgate (1974) recently reported that sexual arousal or copulatory performance does not activate pituitary-adrenal system function per se. However, some males showing activation of the pituitary–adrenal system were also somewhat "sluggish" copulators. These authors suggested that pituitary activation might indicate insufficient habituation to the receptive females.

Our suggestion concerning the possible mode of action of ACTH$^{4-10}$ on intromission-ejaculatory mechanisms presupposes that systemically administered peptide influences specific central nervous system functions. Observations on extinction of avoidance behavior showed that intracerebral administration of ACTH$^{1-10}$ peptide simulates the behavioral effect of systemically given peptide (van Wimersma Greidanus and de Wied, 1971). However, Bertolini et al. (1969) reported that the intraventricular administration of ACTH$^{1-24}$ or α-MSH results in sexual excitation in the rabbit. Recent observations by Sawyer, Baldwin, and Haun (this volume) show, on the other hand, that intraventricular administration of ACTH$^{1-24}$ but not of ACTH$^{4-10}$ is followed by lordotic behavior and ovulation in the female rabbit. Accordingly, it is questionable whether ACTH$^{4-10}$ is the moiety responsible for sexual excitation brought about by ACTH$^{1-24}$ or α-MSH.

EFFECT OF ACTH$^{4-10}$ ON THE EXTINCTION OF A SEXUALLY MOTIVATED RUNWAY RESPONSE IN THE MALE RAT

According to Beach (1956), male sexual behavior depends upon at least two partially independent mechanisms. A sexual-arousal mechanism increases the male's sexual excitement above a copulatory threshold and results in mounting and intromission. The initial intromission then activates a second process (or processes) designated as the intromission and ejaculatory mechanism which brings the male to the ejaculatory threshold and results in ejaculation. Previous experiments indicate that ACTH$^{4-10}$ affects intromission and ejaculatory mechanism but fails to modify sexual arousal. However, several observations suggest that mildly painful stimuli, which probably lead to ACTH release from the pituitary gland, elicit copulation in naive males (Caggiula and Eibergen, 1969) and prepubertal males (Goldfoot and Baum, 1972). Because one cannot exclude that the lack of effect of ACTH$^{4-10}$ on sexual arousal is caused by insensitivity of the testing procedure or inappropriate stimulus conditions, it was considered of interest to study the influence of this peptide on extinction of a sexually motivated approach response in a straight runway. The observations of Beach and Jordan (1956) indicate that alley speed can be employed as a measure of sexual motivation in the male rat. Extinction behavior was chosen in order to eliminate interactions with copulatory behavior.

Naive male rats were trained to reach an estrogen-primed female in the goal box of the runway. Twenty acquisition trials were spaced over eight sessions in a period of 4 weeks. On reaching the goal box, members of one group of rats were allowed to contact the female and achieve a full ejaculation pattern after each trial. Rats in another group could never contact the female because of a wiremesh partition in the goal box. During extinction training (three trials per session), the female was removed from the goal box. ACTH$^{4-10}$ administration prior to each extinction session resulted in a delay of extinction of the runway response in rats that were allowed to copulate during the acquisition period

TABLE 2. *Effect of ACTH*$^{4-10}$ *on extinction of a sexually motivated runway response in the male rat*

Acquisition conditions[a]	Treatment[b]	Session					
		1	2	3	4	5	6
Copulation experience	ACTH$^{4-10}$	25 ± 4[c, d]	26 ± 4	31 ± 7	35 ± 10	46 ± 5	49 ± 9[e]
	Saline	31 ± 6	38 ± 7	46 ± 8	60 ± 15	76 ± 15	69 ± 7
No contact with the female	ACTH$^{4-10}$	50 ± 12	40 ± 6	42 ± 14	49 ± 14	32 ± 6	45 ± 8
	Saline	40 ± 20	44 ± 11	49 ± 12	45 ± 6	70 ± 23	37 ± 10

[a] The animals of the copulation experience group could contact the receptive female in the goal box and full copulation was allowed. The other group could never contact the female because of the partition in the goal box. The female was not present in the goal box during the extinction period.

[b] ACTH$^{4-10}$ (20 µg/rat) or saline was given 1 hr prior to each extinction session.

[c] Mean latencies of three trials per session expressed in sec.

[d] Mean ± SE of 10 rats.

[e] Two-way analysis of variance indicates a significant treatment × session interaction ($p < 0.01$).

(Table 2). Whereas the running latencies increased as extinction training progressed, ACTH$^{4\text{-}10}$-treated rats ran faster than control animals. ACTH$^{4\text{-}10}$, however, failed to affect running behavior in those rats that could not contact the female during the training period.

These observations indicate that ACTH$^{4\text{-}10}$ affects motivation of male rats in their efforts to reach a receptive female. However, the fact that the urge to seek contact with the female was preserved by the peptide only in rats that were rewarded during the acquisition period raises some doubt about whether there exists a direct effect of the peptide on sexual arousal per se. Similarities between the effects of ACTH analogues on extinction of differently motivated behavioral responses seem to suggest that the peptide preserves an arousal state which is related to learning rather than to any specific motivation (fear, hunger, or sex).

SUMMARY AND CONCLUSIONS

ACTH4$^{\text{-}}$10, a behaviorally active analogue of ACTH, affects various mechanisms involved in sexual behavior in the male rat. The peptide appears to influence innate copulatory patterns by affecting intromission and ejaculatory mechanisms in a negative manner. These effects depend upon the presence of threshold amounts of testosterone in castrated rats. The urge to seek contact with the female was preserved by the peptide even if the female was removed from the goal box of a runway. However, this effect could be observed only in males that had had copulatory experience during acquisition of the approach response. These and other observations on the behavioral effects of ACTH analogues support the conclusion that these neuropeptides do not influence sexual arousal or copulatory mechanisms directly but modify sexual behavior by affecting nonsexual behavioral mechanisms related to adaptation to environmental stimuli.

ACKNOWLEDGMENTS

ACTH$^{4\text{-}10}$ peptide was supplied by Organon BV, Oss, The Netherlands. H.H.L.H. was supported by the Scrinerius Stichting.

REFERENCES

Barfield, R. J., and Sachs, B. D. (1970): Effect of shock on copulatory behavior in castrate male rats. *Horm. Behav.,* 1:247–253.
Beach, F. A. (1956): Characteristics of masculine "sex drive." In: *Nebraska Symposium on Motivation,* edited by M. R. Jones, pp. 1–32. Univ. of Nebraska Press, Lincoln, Nebraska.
Beach, F. A., and Jordan, L. (1956): Effects of sexual reinforcement upon the performance of male rats in a straight runway. *J. Comp. Physiol. Psychol.,* 49:105–110.
Bertolini, A., Vergoni, W., Gessa, G. L., and Ferrari, W. (1969): Induction of sexual excitement by the action of adrenocorticotrophic hormone in brain. *Nature,* 221:667–669.
Bohus, B. (1973): Pituitary–adrenal influences on avoidance and approach behavior of the rat. In: *Drug Effects on Neuroendocrine Regulation,* edited by E. Zimmermann, W. H. Gispen, B. H. Marks, and D. de Wied. Vol. 39: *Progress in Brain Research,* pp. 407–420. Elsevier, Amsterdam.

Bohus, B., Nyakas, C., and Endröczi, E. (1968): Effects of adrenocorticotropic hormone on avoidance behaviour of intact and adrenalectomized rats. *Int. J. Neuropharmacol.,* 7:307–314.

Brain, P. F., Nowell, N. W., and Wouters, A. (1971): Some relationships between adrenal function and the effectiveness of a period of isolation in inducing intermale aggression in albino mice. *Physiol. Behav.,* 6:27–29.

Caggiula, A. R., and Eibergen, R. (1969): Copulation of virgin male rats evoked by painful peripheral stimulation. *J. Comp. Physiol. Psychol.,* 69:414–419.

Garrud, P., Gray, J. A., and de Wied, D. (1974): Pituitary–adrenal hormones and extinction of rewarded behaviour in the rat. *Physiol. Behav.,* 12:109–119.

Goldfoot, D. A., and Baum, M. (1972): Initiation of mating behavior in developing male rats following peripheral electric shock. *Physiol. Behav.,* 8:857–863.

Gray, J. A., Mayes, A. R., and Wilson, M. (1971): A barbiturate-like effect of adrenocorticotropic hormone on the partial reinforcement acquisition and extinction effects. *Neuropharmacology,* 10: 223–230.

Guth, S., Levine, S., and Seward, J. P. (1971): Appetitive acquisition and extinction effects with exogenous ACTH. *Physiol. Behav.,* 7:195–200.

Kastin, A. J., Miller, L. M., Nockton, R., Sandman, C. A., Schally, A. V., and Stratton, L. O. (1973): Behavioral aspects of melanocyte-stimulating hormone (MSH). In: *Drug Effects on Neuroendocrine Regulation,* edited by E. Zimmermann, W. H. Gispen, B. H. Marks, and D. de Wied. Vol. 39: *Progress in Brain Research,* pp. 461–470. Elsevier, Amsterdam.

Korányi, L., Endröczi, E., and Tárnok, F. (1965/66): Sexual behavior in the course of avoidance conditioning in male rabbits. *Neuroendocrinology,* 1:144–157.

Leshner, A. I., Walker, W. A., Johnson, A. E., Kelling, J. S., Kreisler, S. J., and Svare, B. B. (1973): Pituitary adrenocortical activity and intermale aggressiveness in isolated mice. *Physiol. Behav.,* 11:705–711.

Levine, S., and Jones, L. E. (1965): Adrenocorticotropic hormone (ACTH) and passive avoidance learning. *J. Comp. Physiol. Psychol.,* 59:357–360.

Lissák, K., and Bohus, B. (1972): Pituitary hormones and avoidance behavior of the rat. *Int. J. Psychobiol.,* 2:103–115.

Szechtman, H., Lambrou, P. J., Caggiula, A. R., and Redgate, E. S. (1974): Plasma corticosterone levels during sexual behavior in male rats. *Horm. Behav.,* 5:191–200.

Weiss, J. M., McEwen, B. S., Silva, M. T., and Kalkut, M. (1970): Pituitary-adrenal alterations and fear responding. *Am. J. Physiol.,* 218:864–868.

Wied, D. de (1966): Inhibitory effect of ACTH and related peptides on extinction of conditioned avoidance behavior. *Proc. Soc. Exp. Biol. Med.,* 122:28–32.

Wied, D. de (1969): Effects of peptide hormones on behavior. In: *Frontiers in Neuroendocrinology 1969,* edited by W. F. Ganong and L. Martini, pp. 97–140. Oxford University Press, New York.

Wied, D. de (1974): Pituitary–adrenal system hormones and behavior. In: *The Neurosciences 3rd Study Program,* edited by F. O. Schmitt and F. G. Worden, pp. 653–666. MIT Press, Cambridge, Massachusetts.

Wimersma Greidanus, T. B. van, and de Wied, D. (1971): Effects of systemic and intracerebral administration of two opposite acting ACTH-related peptides on extinction of conditioned avoidance behavior. *Neuroendocrinology,* 7:291–301.

Sexual Behavior: Pharmacology and Biochemistry, edited by M. Sandler and G. L. Gessa. Raven Press, New York © 1975.

Sexual Problems of the Schizophrenic and Preschizophrenics

Silvano Arieti

125 East 84th Street, New York, New York 10028

The sexual life of the schizophrenic and the schizophrenic-to-be is paradoxical. Although intimately related to the present or future psychosis, there is nothing specific in it that could not be repeated for the nonpsychotic (Arieti, 1967).

This chapter begins with a brief description of the manifest sexual life of the patient and proceeds to a discussion of the sexual conflicts that are frequently found prior to or during schizophrenic disorders.

A striking change in the sexual behavior of the schizophrenic has been noticed lately in the United States; I am not in a position to say whether similar change has been observed in other countries (Arieti, 1974). Whereas until approximately 15 years ago sexual activity and acting out were relatively rare in schizophrenics, recently they have become a common occurrence both in hospitalized and non-hospitalized patients. Sexual activity of the schizophrenic used to be so limited compared to that of normal people as to induce even psychiatrists of such high caliber as Sandor Rado to believe that the schizophrenic was not interested in sexual pleasure or in any pleasure at all; he was suffering from anhedonia. Other psychiatrists interpreted this lack of sexual activity to be part of the schizophrenic withdrawal, and, in prepsychotic states, to be part of the schizoid personality, which seriously limited interpersonal contacts of any kind. Other psychiatrists of the Freudian school interpreted this lack of interest as part of decathexis or withdrawal of libido. Eventually both the theory of anhedonia and of withdrawal of cathexis proved wrong. Now, at least in the United States, the beginning of a schizophrenic episode is often characterized by increased sexual behavior. Even patients who, by their profession, education, and training, are considered less likely to do so, such people as priests, ministers, rabbis, or seminary students, give vent at the onset of the psychosis to unrestrained heterosexual and homosexual behavior. Some male patients reported that they had an irresistible impulse to touch or bump into girls who were passing by on the street. When the patients were hospitalized, they had the urge to touch with sexual intentions female patients and nurses. Some patients in the initial stage of the illness do not refrain from masturbating or exhibiting in public places or on the wards of the hospital. Rape is rare; but promiscuity is relatively frequent in both sexes. Obvious seduction on the part of female patients has become very common. Therefore, the change probably has nothing or little to do with sexual function per se, but rather with control.

What I have said in reference to patients in the initial stage of the illness could be repeated for chronic patients. In the years 1941–1945, while I was working in Pilgrim State Hospital, sexual activities among chronic patients were very rare. Later years in psychiatric hospitals have shown these activities to occur with decidedly more frequency. It might be that this difference is only the result of cultural and administrative changes. Probably the difference in cultural climate goes through not only the schizophrenic barrier but also, what may be even more surprising, that barrier which, like a Chinese wall, separates the traditional state hospital from the world. Less restrictiveness and more permissiveness have become common practice. In addition, in recent years it has become a usual procedure in many hospitals to have patients of both sexes reside in the same wards. This increased sexual activity in the schizophrenic has to be interpreted as a method, on the part of the patient, for maintaining some contacts with the world and for using whatever human possibilities are left to him.

In addition to increased difficulty in controlling sexual urges, desire to defy or to seek power are reasons for increased sexual activity. The eventual marked decline in sexuality in patients who continue to regress indefinitely must be considered, in addition to the schizophrenic process, as partially due to hospitalization, lack of stimulation, detachment, and so on. Contrasted with the decreased activity in overt sexual life, however, is the persistent and occasionally even increasing role of sexual symbolism in the delusions and ideas of reference of some chronic patients. These cases, which often express sex symbols in unusual and bizarre ways, refer to life in general and not only to sexual activity.

Some schizophrenics who recover completely and who, during their psychosis, had interrupted their sexual life, may reacquire normal sexual functions. I have treated female patients who could achieve only clitoral orgasm before the psychosis, and yet were able to achieve vaginal orgasm after recovery.

On the other hand, a patient of mine who had achieved only clitoral orgasm before, became acutely psychotic while she was experiencing her first vaginal orgasm. At the very moment that she was experiencing a pleasure that she had never experienced before, she received telepathic messages from her sexual partner. After the sexual act she began to receive telepathic messages from many people, most of them from potential lovers or men to whom she felt attracted.

What I have so far reported discloses that there is nothing specific in the sexual behavior of the schizophrenic. However, for most people sexual life transcends sex itself, and is connected with problems of identity, value, self-worthiness; therefore, it is natural that the fragile personality of the patient may be affected deeply by it. It is also easy to understand how the psychosis, which produces a disorganization of the personality, may produce an alteration of sexual life.

In a psychodynamic frame of reference, the psychosexual conflicts that precede the psychosis are more important than sexual life per se. Again, I must say that although we do not find anything specific, the evaluation of the sexual conflicts of the preschizophrenic throws additional light on the psychodynamics of the disorder.

Psychologic difficulties connected with the boy's first ejaculations and the young girl's menarche as a rule are not directly involved with the psychodynamics of schizophrenia. To be more specific, the possible revival in girls of an archaic fear of being castrated and the fear of eventually becoming castrated in boys who masturbate or who have wet dreams does not play an important role in the development of the disorder. Sexual deprivations, anomalies, or lack of sexual control may facilitate the occurrence of a psychosis only when they affect the self-image injuriously.

The most common sexual difficulty on the part of the future schizophrenic consists of the inability to establish a definite and stable sex identity. Although the occurrence of this difficulty cannot be evaluated statistically with accuracy, I would roughly estimate that it is quite frequent. But again in most cases the difficulty could be better defined as one of gender identity rather than sex identity. As many authors have described, the child who is going to become schizophrenic in adulthood has some indecision as to what his sex is going to be later in life. Children who know that they are boys or girls are not sure that they will maintain their sexual identity throughout their lives. Boys may lose a penis; girls may grow one. Although many children have these thoughts, in the preschizophrenics they assume the form of serious uncertainty for several reasons. To the usual reluctance to have frank discussions about sex, which is determined by our cultural mores, is added the fear or anxiety of bringing up such explosive matters with parents who are remote or are likely to misunderstand the child. In many cases the uncertainty about sex identity stems from the fact that to some extent children connect the uneasy and disturbed atmosphere around them with their belonging to a given sex. If they were girls instead of boys or boys instead of girls, they think, their parents would give them affection and approval. If the most disturbing parent is of the opposite sex, the child would like to be of the same sex as this parent so that he might resist him or her better. In my opinion the most common cause of uncertainty in sex identification is the fact that the preschizophrenic child who feels rejected by both parents also tends to reject them; therefore the child has difficulties in identifying with either one of them. This lack of definite sex identity hinders the patient throughout his prepsychotic life, increases his difficulties in the act of living, and undermines his defenses.

In the later stages of childhood the young individual succeeds in hiding the sexual uncertainty transmitted from early childhood and reaches some kind of sexual identity; but this identity is not deeply grounded and is easily shaken later by the events of life. The unfavorable dealings with the world reinforce in the patient the feeling that he or she is not really a man or a woman. He sees himself in an ambiguous position. After the onset of the psychosis, this lack of definite sexual identity becomes manifest in the overt schizophrenic symptomatology. The different gender identity that the patient may assume and his drawings of human figures with characteristics of both sexes are expressions of this psychosexual conflict.

Next in frequency among the sexual difficulties of the preschizophrenic is homosexuality, both in its latent and overt forms. Until not too long ago in psychoanalytic theory latent homosexuality was considered the major etiologic factor of paranoia, paranoid states, and paranoid types of schizophrenia. This conception was first expressed by Freud in his report on the Schreber case (Freud, 1911).

Some confusion still exists about the meaning of "latent homosexuality." This term does not only mean that homosexuality is not practiced. It means that the patient is not fully aware of his own homosexual tendency. A patient may have a manifest but unpracticed form of homosexuality. The latent homosexual has become aware since early life of the hostility or at least lack of acceptance to which this type of sexuality has been subjected on the part of the society in which he lives. Homosexuality thus becomes unacceptable to him, too. The patient consequently makes strong efforts to repress his own wishes or to divert them into other areas. To a large extent this repression is successful. Sooner or later, however, the patient can no longer repress these wishes.

According to my experiences, as well as those of many other psychiatrists, the importance of homosexuality in the etiology of all paranoid disorders has been exaggerated. There is nothing specific in latent homosexuality per se as a cause of psychosis. Homosexuality in some cases leads to psychologic decompensation only because it engenders a great deal of anxiety to the patient who is no longer able to repress this "unacceptable" sexual orientation. In a hypothetical homosexual society, or in a society which did not discriminate against homosexuality, this psychosexual conflict would not have the power to lead to a psychosis.

I must also stress that, according to my clinical findings, not only latent but also overt homosexuality has a role in the psychodynamics of some cases of schizophrenia. Here again social ostracism rather than homosexuality per se is the pathogenetic factor. I could not obtain relevant data for comparing the incidence of overt homosexuality between schizophrenics and the general population, and therefore I am not in a position to say whether a difference exists. In the cases of overt homosexuality the psychologic difficulty emerges not from the effort to repress the sexual urge, but from the effort to suppress it. The patient eventually succumbs to the desire, although according to my findings, somewhat later in life than nonschizophrenic homosexuals. The patient may become an impulsive or compulsive homosexual, and consequently enter into constant conflict with society.

Most probably the early identity difficulties that predispose the patient to homosexuality are related to those that predispose him to schizophrenia. In contrast, there is some justification for the belief that homosexuality, as an organization involving the whole personality, preceded the formation of a definite self or self-image. In late childhood and adolescence the patient realizes the social implications of homosexuality, and the self-image may be unfavorably affected.

A third common cause of psychosexual conflict in the prepsychotic is the feeling of inadequacy as a sexual performer, which is usually part of a general feeling of inadequacy. However, it is reinforced by the concept of the self as sexually inadequate, culminating in a vicious circle.

These feelings of sexual inadequacy in the preschizophrenic do not appear to originate from castration threats or from brooding over the size or shape of one's genitals. These preoccupations are generally a pretext, or a particular channeling of a previously existing feeling of inadequacy.

Sexual indifference or lack of concern about sexual life is also found in a certain number of preschizophrenics. This detachment from what pertains to sex is generally part of the schizoid type of relating. It originates as a defense against the anxiety-provoking environment, but subsequently it becomes part of one's life pattern. On the other hand, some schizoid persons retain strong interest in sexual matters and repeatedly masturbate. At times indifference toward sexual matters occurs at the onset of the psychosis.

If the prepsychotic feels inadequate as a sexual performer, he feels even more inadequate as a sexual partner and as a love object. Feeling sexually undesired and unloved is an experience injurious to the self, but feeling unlovable and undesirable is even more devastating emotionally. In other words, what is particularly damaging is not the idea that the patient does not obtain love or sexual gratification now. It is the idea that he is so constituted or has such a personality as to never be able to elicit love or sexual desire.

These unbearable feelings at times compel these patients to impulsive behavior aimed at proving at least a minimum of sexual adequacy. Patients become promiscuous in order to reassure themselves that they can be accepted as sexual partners.

Another psychosexual conflict of the preschizophrenic, which was common in the past, is now rather rare. It consists of the patient's fear of succumbing to his or her own heterosexual desires with undesirable partners, with partners objected to by the families, or in ways not sanctioned by society. This conflict occurs in adolescents or young adults brought up in puritanical, Victorian, or very religious cultures. A greater acceptance of sexuality or even of masturbation as a sexual relief has caused an almost complete disappearance of this conflict, even in the preschizophrenic.

Summarizing, we can make the following statements about sexual conflicts in the preschizophrenic.

1. These conflicts are not specific and may also occur in persons who never become psychotic. Only uncertainty about sexual or gender identification seems to be considerably more common in the preschizophrenic.

2. In relationship to the psychodynamics of schizophrenia, sexual life is not important in itself but only insofar as it may affect injuriously the self-image. Either because the patient perceives himself as a sexually inadequate person, or as a homosexual, or as an undesirable sexual partner, or as lacking sexual self-control, or as having no definite sexual identity, he may develop a devastating concept of himself. Moreover, in the case of lack of definite sexual or gender

identity, there is a continuous draining of the resources of the person who strives toward self-identity.

REFERENCES

Arieti, S. (1967): Sexual conflict in psychotic disorders. In: *Sexual Problems. Diagnosis and Treatment in Medical Practice,* edited by Charles William Wahl. Free Press, New York.

Arieti, S. (1974): *Interpretation of Schizophrenia.* Basic Books, New York.

Freud, S. (1911): Psycho-analytic notes upon an autobiographical account of a case of paranoia (Dementia Paranoides). *Jahrbuch für psychoanalytische und psychopathologische Forschungen,* Vol. 3. (Reprinted in *Collected Papers,* Vol. 3, p. 387–470.)

Sexual Behavior: Pharmacology and Biochemistry, edited by M. Sandler and G. L.
Gessa. Raven Press, New York © 1975.

Authentic Feminine Erotic Response

Natalie Shainess

*Columbia University, College of Physicians and Surgeons, and William Alanson White
Institute of Psychiatry, Psychoanalysis and Psychology, New York, New York 10028*

Views of the nature of feminine sexual expression and its derivative sources
have been both confused and confusing. Among the questions asked have been
whether woman experiences libidinal drive, and, if so, at what period in her
monthly cycle? Is she capable of orgasm or not? What is the major area of genital
sensation?

Psychoanalytic theories have varied from the apparently sensible to the aston-
ishing. Some psychoanalysts have compared feminine sexual activity to doll play,
or to the early sucking experience of the infant, terming it a "regressive" phenomenon; some insist that the female sexual act is not completed until the birth
of a child; labor and delivery are described in orgastic terms, and the infant
appears comparable to the male end product of orgasm—the ejaculate! Today
there has been a tendency to equate the clitoris with the penis, with insistence
on clitoral orgasm as the only valid response, perhaps supported by recent research.

Freud, who has been criticized—and not unfairly—for his theories of feminine
psychology, nonetheless had many profound insights into femininity. These insights still have great validity in the sexual area, but perhaps they need redefini-
tion. Freud did not fail to recognize the occurrence of feminine orgasm, nor was
he misled by feminine anatomy. In *Transformation of Puberty* (Freud, 1938) he
made the following statement about feminine orgasm:

> The role (of the clitoris) is to conduct the excitement to the adjacent genital parts; it acts
> like a chip of pinewood which is utilized to set fire to the harder wood. It often takes
> some time before this transference is accomplished. . . . This anaesthesia (vaginal) may
> become permanent if the clitoris refuses to give up its excitability. . . . If the transference
> of the erogenous excitability from the clitoris to the vagina succeeds, the woman then
> changes her leading zone for the future sexual activity.

I do not believe he meant that the clitoris gave up its *total* excitability, but rather,
its major role—its role beyond the initiator in genital experience. For reasons
I will attempt to clarify, I would prefer the term "authentic orgasm" to "vaginal."
I would like to add that whatever we may learn or discover through laboratory
research, there will remain interpersonal elements that cannot be explained—for
example, the postcoital tristesse or tears that are sometimes triggered immediately
following orgasm (I do not exclude men from this response, but it appears to be
less prevalent and dramatic in them).

This leads me to ask: Can sex be separated completely from the sociocultural matrix? Having evolved as humans over the millennia, and no longer bound by the immutable rhythmic mating patterns of lower animal forms (presumably leading to satisfaction in *both* sexes), can our sexuality return to the primitive and simple? The geneticist Theodosius Dobzhansky has stated that the cultural has taken primacy over the biologic for the last 10,000 years—so this appears to be most unlikely.

SEXUAL SELF-AWARENESS

Turning to some of the confusions previously suggested, why has feminine response been so difficult to understand? Perhaps, in some measure, because men have done the studying and interpreting, their vision is often blurred by the paradoxical clash between women's needs and responses and their own view of women as need-servers and satisfiers. The notion that women were also equipped to be potent was of lesser concern. Many find it hard to visualize the sexual response as similar in both sexes, tumescence being an essential condition for both, and leading to increasing sensation and function.

An existential dilemma has been posed to women particularly by transition from the "primitive" to the "civilized" state, seriously handicapping her. De Beauvoir (1953) has said that in the sexual act, man transcends himself (in orgasm) and then returns to himself. But woman, first violated (that is, her body integrity is penetrated), then becomes alienated (in pregnancy she is other than herself). The sexual act for "man in society" is not very different from that of "man in the primordial state." But for woman it is quite changed, because the social consequences of sexual participation, and even more so when pregnancy results, are not in harmony with the simple biologic. As man set the conditions and confines within which woman was to live, her life circumstances often depended upon her desirability and sexual use of this for other ends. Her capacity to collaborate sexually without necessarily being an active participant reinforced the male thesis that service to him was more significant, and thereby blunted awareness of her own sexual needs. She accepted this, but I should add also rebelled, for the frequent frigidity she experienced was not only a consequence of her passive acceptance, but also of her anxiety, fear, rage, or defiance, or need in some way to control, or to defeat—in short, to gain an empty victory over her partner, who may not even have been of her own choosing. Whatever its root, her unresponsiveness was a retroflexed destructiveness directed primarily against herself.

SPECTRUM OF FEMININE RESPONSES

I have visualized the range of feminine responses as a spectrum (Shainess, 1968), reflecting the view that the sexual response is a distillate of the total personality, although constitutional and physiologic factors make their contribu-

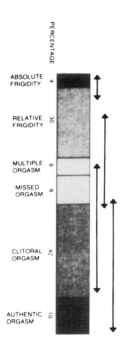

FIG. 1. Spectrum of feminine erotic response. Arrows indicate the range of possible shift, either spontaneously, or with treatment. There is a range of responses within each woman, depending on the processing of the variables for each sexual engagement. But as indicated, there is a limit to the range of shift.

tion. Activity is an important component of the authentic response whereas passivity, both physically and in personality structure, lead to frigidity (see Fig.1). Starting at the left, absolute frigidity (under any conditions), about 4%, shifts to relative frigidity, approximately 30%, on to multiple orgasm, about 6%, and not a sign of supercapacity but a fantasy misinterpretation of multiple erotic sensations never quite summing up to total satisfaction and orgastic release—and equivalent in the male to gain and loss of erection in a given sexual interaction, if he persists. Then, on to missed orgasm, 8%, an "almost" response in which further interest is lost, and central nervous system changes have apparently occurred, in the absence of genital sensation, then to clitoral orgasm, about 42% of the spectrum, and the prevalent response of our time (representing to a considerable extent both alienated and mechanical sexual activity), and finally, the authentic "vaginal" orgasm, possibly as high as 10%, and indicating a free and total involvement. The arrows indicate a range of shift within the woman, which may occur with treatment, or growth, or regression. The demands of the society also affect the response; and in Freud's time, because of sexual codes, woman's more dependent position and lack of adequate means of birth control with its related fear and anger (at the need to comply sexually with the threat of unwanted pregnancy an ever-present specter) probably caused more women to experience relative frigidity. There is a comparable spectrum for male responses (Shainess, 1973a).

FEMININE EROTIC DRIVE

Libidinal awareness is crucial for optimal sexual experience, yet this has been a confused and confusing issue for women. Some women never seem to be aware of a bodily or genital sensation impelling them toward sexual activity. Some claim it, but close examination reveals that they are talking about social and interpersonal factors, or a need for physical closeness or intimacy. In other women, it has been noted, but has been found to be evanescent and not persisting in comparison with men. Perhaps this is so because in men the presence of fluid in the seminal vesicles adds its insistence to endocrine stimulation. Studies in the past have not been conclusive. Psychoanalyst Benedek (1960), correlating libidinal interest with studies of the cytologic state of the vaginal mucosa throughout the menstrual cycle, believed that maximum libidinal intensity coincided with ovulation, seemingly to serve survival of the species. Yet in spite of her findings, she suggested that libidinal interest is under psychic control—and surely Dobzhansky would agree with this. Yet it has been the clinical finding of a number of psychoanalysts, including myself, that libidinal awareness seems to peak shortly following the sudden drop in estrogen, on the day preceding or on the first day of menstruation.

I believe help is at hand in solving this problem by researchers of the pharmacology of sex. Hembree (1974) has noted the confusion in studies of the relationship between peak estrogen and peak sexual interest in the human female. He disputes the role of testosterone as a factor in libidinal drive, observing that it is a prehormone that can be changed into estrogens. Hembree points out that because gonadotropic hormone is released in bursts, no one measurement can mean very much.

Continuing from this base, the work of Pfaff (1974) in studies on bound labeled estradiol in the hypothalamic and limbic structures, seems to offer much promise. There was a similarity of structures binding hormones in all animals studied. In the monkey, 2 hr after intravenous perfusion with labeled hormone, he was able to observe the appearance and extent of bound hormone in the brain by his autoradiographic technic. Sexual activity began to appear after 2 hr, but the maximum activity appeared after 15 hr, leading him to ask what occurred in the lapsed 13 hr. I believe that when these studies are applied to the human female, the question of peak monthly drive will be answered. If, in fact, it occurs shortly premenstrual in timing, it could again be explained as a survival mechanism —nature's last-ditch effort to ensure impregnation, with a lapse of time after the sudden fall in estrogen level. This information could be very helpful in sorting out components of the feminine erotic response.

ORGASTIC SITE

Recently there has been considerable debate over the question of the site of major stimulation and response in the female—of so-called clitoral as opposed

FIG. 2. Sagittal section showing comparable genital areas of male and female.

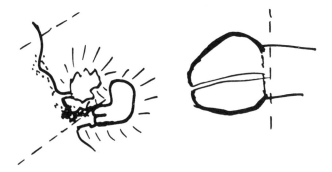

FIG. 3. Sagittal section showing genital areas of male and female, similar to those in Fig. 2. Dots indicate end organs responding to touch and light pressure. Crosses indicate end organs responding to deep pressure.

to vaginal orgasm—both misnomers, because orgasm is a complex central nervous system function involving alterations in consciousness as well as diffuse bodily sensations, and accompanied by vaginal contractions and a feeling of euphoria.

Studies of masturbating women in the laboratory (Masters and Johnson, 1966) not necessarily responding to drive or need, and using at times mechanical vibratory equipment, are not in my view normal conditions for the study of sexual response. They have tended to produce artificial and pathophysiological results. Furthermore, a period of "plateau" is not a normal finding in the progressive sexual interaction leading to orgasm.

Comparable sections of genital anatomy for male and female show that the clitoris is only a small part of the equivalent male area. Kinsey's (1953) excellent neuroanatomic description of the different specialized sensory nerve endings show that the clitoris is heavily endowed with endings responding to light touch. These continue in considerable numbers to the vaginal introitus—the site of major sensibility—and a bit beyond in the anterior wall; endings responding to deep pressure predominate in the vagina. The radial markings on the sketch surrounding the uterus, bladder, and vagina suggest the stretch on ligaments and other organs, and pressure, when the vagina is expanded by the penis, indicating that somaesthetic sensation through stimulation of autonomic nerves is also involved, especially just prior to orgasm, when women are often more aware of the need to be deeply penetrated (Shainess, 1973b).

This indicates perhaps more clearly from a neuroanatomic vantage point what I have tried to demonstrate before: that the clitoral response is only a partial response (to stimulation of only part of the pudendal nerve which serves the entire genital area) in which persistent—and therefore irritant and pathologic—overstimulation of the easily accessible clitoris finally triggers an orgasm. But this orgasm, coming from an organ intended primarily for arousal, is less satisfying than the more total response. In support of this thesis, it is well to remember that women who have undergone clitoridectomy have been able to experience orgasm.

As a subjective differentiation—and this seems to be borne out by Fisher's (1973) reports—the clitoral sensation triggering orgasm seems to be sharper, yet lacking in depth and less satisfying than the so-called vaginal orgasm, when described by women who have experienced both. The "vaginal response" seems to be arrived at more rapidly, and leads to a more automatic rhythmical movement as orgasm impends, and is accompanied by a conscious need to be deeply penetrated. Whereas clitoral sensation can be achieved passively, activity is essential for the vaginal or, more accurately, authentic orgasm. Women who have experienced both report it virtually impossible to return to the clitoral, when unfortunate circumstances may call for this.

SUMMATION OF FACTORS FOR AUTHENTIC RESPONSE

In considering feminine erotic response, I previously (Shainess, 1966) listed a number of conditions that must summate to trigger authentic response. To round out the picture these conditions are summarized here. First, I suggest that no two sexual experiences are ever identical. It is impossible to enumerate the quantity of energy (I do not use this term in the literal sense, but lack a better one) contributed by each of the conditions I enumerate, and some may outweigh others in importance. Included among the physiologic are the previously discussed endocrine influences and awareness of libidinal drive, the site of stimulation, the extent of free activity, the degree of wakefulness in the diurnal sleep–wakefulness pattern, the constitutional vitality—and most important of all, a potent male partner.

Among psychologic factors are the degree of interest in the partner, active choice of partner and the sexual activity, a durable relationship in which the sexual interaction can be part of a progressive learning experience (sex is rarely gratifying initially for a woman with a new partner). As far as the woman herself is concerned, successful psychosexual growth and mastery are important, accompanied by a positive sense of self or self-esteem, freedom from anxiety or guilt, or from narcissistic self-preoccupation, or anger, or the need to control others. The willingness to take risks and the presence of creative resources also affect the experience, as do cultural expectations of the feminine sexual role.

If several of these factors are present in sufficient degree, or all to some degree, then an authentic response is likely to result. Notice, I have said nothing of love; but when it exists, it cannot fail to enhance the experience. Nor have I mentioned the role of the male partner psychologically, which obviously makes major contributions.

In concluding, let me say that the woman who experiences authentic orgastic response needs no reassurance, has no doubts about her sexual participation. Actively involved in a "dialogue" she has evoked or willingly engaged in, but not apart or intellectualizing, nor obsessively ruminating, nor fantasizing special conditions, nor anxiety- or fear-ridden, nor narcissistically "on stage," nor competing with her partner—she feels her passion grow, dares to respond in a way that answers her need and heightens her sensations, becomes aware of a time when she can no longer maintain control—and then experiences the full flood of release, with its alterations of consciousness; and then, the stillness in the wake of the storm, with its backwash of gratitude to and appreciation of the partner, suggesting that men, too, will gain something from women's greater sexual self-awareness and authenticity.

REFERENCES

Benedek, T. (1960): Organization of the reproductive drive. *Int. J. Psychoanal.,* 61:1–15.

De Beauvoir, S. (1953): *The Second Sex.* Knopf, New York.

Fisher, S. (1973): *The Female Orgasm.* Basic Books, New York.

Freud, S. (1938): The transformation of puberty: Three contributions to the theory of sex. In: *Basic Writings of Sigmund Freud.* Random House, New York.

Hembree, W. (1974): Endocrine physiology of human sexuality. Presented at the Eighth Biennial Meetings of the New York District Branches, Amer. Psych. Assoc.

Kinsey, A. C., Pomeroy, W. B., Martin, C. E., and Gebhard, P. H. (1953): *Sexual Behavior in the Human Female.* Saunders, Philadelphia, Pennsylvania.

Masters, W. H., and Johnson, V. E. (1966): *Human Sexual Response.* Little, Brown, Boston, Massachusetts.

Pfaff, D. (1974): Hormone binding neurons and the neurophysiology of sex behavior. Presented at the Eighth Biennial Divisional Meetings of the New York District Branches, Amer. Psych. Assoc.

Shainess, N. (1966): A re-assessment of feminine sexuality and erotic experience. In: *Science and Psychoanalysis, Vol. X,* edited by J. Masserman. Grune & Stratton, New York.

Shainess, N. (1968): The therapy of frigidity. In: *Current Psychiatric Therapies, Vol. 8,* edited by J. Masserman. Grune & Stratton, New York.

Shainess, N. (1973): The distaff side of impotence. *Med. Insight,* 5:34–42.

Shainess, N. (1975): Authentic feminine orgastic response. *Sexuality and Psychoanalysis,* Brunner/ Mazel, New York.

Sexual Behavior: Pharmacology and Biochemistry, edited by M. Sandler and G. L.
Gessa. Raven Press, New York © 1975.

Sexual Arousal Mechanisms in Male Homosexuals

Irving Bieber

132 East 72nd Street, New York, New York 10021

From the point of arousal to the point of satisfaction in a sexual act, heterosexual impulses have relatively few intervening variables as compared to homosexuality. Homosexuality is not a mere heterosexual counterpart whereby the subject simply prefers a same-sex partner as one prefers a southern to a northern climate. Myriad intervening variables, rooted in psychopathology, complicate the expression of homosexuality from the point of arousal to that of termination in the homosexual act. I have been able to delineate several categories of stimuli and conditions that evoke sexual arousal in male homosexuals; to use the current American vernacular, this chapter is a discussion of what "turns on" the homosexual.

DISPLACEMENT OF THE HETEROSEXUAL STIMULUS

In many instances, the homosexual is aroused by stimuli that he identifies, consciously or unconsciously, as feminine. Frequently, the homosexual is aroused by a man who possesses certain significant features, usually resembling those of his mother or a sister. These physical features particularly involve the eyes—their color, the shape of the palpebral fissure, the expression around the eyes, and even the eyebrows. During the course of his analysis, one of my patients became aware that he was being "turned on" by women who had eyebrows similar to his mother's. Other physical features that homosexuals identify as feminine include skin texture and color, and fat distribution, especially in areas of the breasts, abdomen, hips, buttocks, and thighs. Any feature perceived as feminine that cues an arousal is a heterosexual stimulus. The true heterosexual nature of homosexual arousal cues are located in homosexual objects and, in this way, fears and inhibitions about heterosexual activity and gratification are circumvented.

Homosexuals are latent heterosexuals. All homosexuals go through a phase of heterosexual development before the homosexual organization takes place. Homosexuality evolves as an adaptation to disturbances in heterosexual development. Such disturbances are the consequences of a disordered parent–child relationship that not only creates heterosexual dysfunction, but also produces profound disturbances in interpersonal relationships with other males. The most frequently occurring pathologic parent–child pattern is the close-binding inappropriately intimate mother and the detached and/or hostile father (Bieber et al., 1962). As the child who becomes a homosexual develops, he experiences a continuity of traumatic attitudes and behavior in his encounters with other boys through childhood into midadolescence. This sort of boy is usually identified as the "sissy" by his peer mates and it is an easy matter for any intelligent grade school teacher to identify such a youngster as a prehomosexual. His maladaptive socialization serves to entrench his fears of other males, particularly those perceived as having power, either physical or social. At the same time, such an individual continues to have a profound yearning for affection and acceptance by other males.

The homosexual adaptation serves three major functions: (1) a substitute for heterosexual activity and gratification; (2) a defense against expectations of injury from other males; and (3) a reparative function organized to strengthen damaged self-esteem and to repair defective interpersonal relationships, particularly with males.

The following dream illustrates an experience in which a homosexual is aroused by a displaced heterosexual stimulus; it demonstrates how the homosexual adaptation serves primarily as a substitute for heterosexuality, replacing inhibited heterosexual gratification.

> I see my mother naked to the waist. She is putting on a tube brassiere and I am getting sexually aroused, although I am not moving toward her. All of a sudden, my father appears at her side. As he sees me, he starts to frown. Of course, I immediately start to lose my erection. But then I think to myself, "Why should he stop you from having sexual feelings toward Mother?" And I try to continue being aroused by her.

> Then a man, a cab driver, brings me to my destination. I am sexually aroused by him as he is handsome and well-built. He leads me up to a dance studio. There are a multitude of girls in Danskins (tights), but I go for the man's paunch which suddenly is uncovered. It is odd because it lacks hair and is fat, characteristics that I did not observe in him before. I allow myself this impulsive gesture by saying to myself, "Well, these women must know that men that associate themselves with dance are homosexuals, so I might as well act accordingly."

EROTICIZING THE FEARED OBJECT

Homosexuals are frequently aroused by a man who possesses characteristics that they identify either as symbols of masculine power, which they fear, or who has characteristics of men in their past history whom they feared. This mechanism is clearly demonstrated by a patient who was aroused by men whose hands resembled his father's. The patient's father was a burly worker with enormous hands, a man who was unremittingly hostile to my patient and who often beat him. His father's hands, which he consciously feared all through his childhood, became an erotic stimulus in his homosexual adult life.

Another illustration of the sexualization of the feared object is exemplified by a young man of 25 who was exclusively homosexual at the time I saw him in a psychiatric interview. When I asked him what in particular "turned him on," he responded, "Hair." In the course of the interview, he reported a dream: he was in bed with an attractive young lady, when a large, hairy arm, bearing a knife in hand, emerged from under the bed and attempted to kill him. This dream demonstrates several elements commonly found in the dreams of homosexuals that clearly illuminate the operant psychodynamics. The dream begins with an explicit heterosexual scene. Heterosexual scenes often appear in the dreams of homosexuals and document the latent heterosexuality. A heterosexual scene will be followed by one in which the subject is attacked by another male—and this occurs in this dream. Generally, there is a third segment in which homosexual behavior is depicted. Of especial significance in this dream is the arm of the attacker. It is hairy. The arm, which threatens to kill the subject, contains the very physical feature, hair, which, for this individual, is an arousal cue that particularly "turns him on." Homosexuals are commonly aroused by symbols of masculine power such as the large penis and muscular physique. In my clinical experience, I have found that homosexuals who are voyeuristic are especially aroused by the sight of a large penis, which they identify with masculine power. The identification of the large penis with power generally represents a cluster of attitudes toward the large penis: admiration, envy, hostility. One of my patients, after fellating a partner who was chosen for his large penis, dreamed that night that he had blood on his teeth.

Eroticizing the feared object is a mechanism closely related if not identical to the psychodynamics operant in masochism and sadism. Central to the understanding of masochism and sadism is the recognition that each is primarily an adaptation to the fear of power. In masochism, the individual is sexually aroused by a powerful object or by the symbol of power; in sadism, the individual becomes sexually aroused when he thinks he can overpower a partner who, in some significant way, is associated with a feared object. One of my patients is a bisexual who becomes sexually aroused by a man or woman he feels he can overpower. He is very fearful of attack by men especially when engaged in heterosexual activity; at the same time, he is fearful of sexual rejection by women. The fantasy of overpowering a man or a woman physically, combined with treating him or her overprotectively, evokes a sense of power that sets off sexual arousal.

SEXUAL AROUSAL IN RESPONSE TO MANIFESTATIONS OF AFFECTION FROM MALES

Homosexuals are frequently aroused sexually by expressions of affection, warmth, or interest from other men. These warmly related men may not necessarily be the type, physically or psychologically, who would ordinarily arouse homosexual interest. It is clearly the affectionate affect itself that is arousing. Homosexual patients have reported that they cannot resist responding to masculine warmth—so much is their yearning for affection and acceptance by other men. Once having succeeded in evoking warmth or interest in another male, the homosexual tends rapidly to lose interest especially if warmth has been the major or sole reason for a liaison. He then seeks warmth from another man and still another as if compelled to persuade the entire male population to love him. Much of the compulsive cruising so frequently engaged in represents an unconscious attempt to achieve this end.

SEXUAL AROUSAL BY PHYSICAL CONTACT WITH ANOTHER MALE

Closely related, but not identical with being sexually aroused by an affectionate male, is the arousal that occurs when being held. According to the descriptions of homosexual patients, in some of their homosexual contacts and relationships, their primary wish is to lie in bed with another man and to be held by him. Although sexual arousal usually occurs, the basic aim is contact. The sexual behavior occurring in this context is reported as not very exciting; the orgasms that terminate the contact are not very intense. The patients themselves are aware that the gratification seems much more associated with the contact than with the sexual activities. These men have histories of inadequate physical contact with both parents who tended not to touch or hold their child and, in general, avoided tactile relatedness. Dr. Mark Hollender, professor and chairman of the Department of Psychiatry at Vanderbilt Medical College, has written on the wish, in women, to be held. He pointed out that many of the sexual experiences of such women grow out of a wish of this type. In some, the wish to be held by a man excites them sexually and leads to a sexual experience that becomes incorporated in contact gratification. Many of the women Hollender describes are consciously aware of their contactual desires and that they are only interested in having sexual intercourse in order to satisfy their need to be held.

SITUATIONS POTENTIATING HOMOSEXUAL AROUSAL

Certain significant life situations facilitate arousal in homosexuals and in the bisexual subgroup. Significant situations may also precipitate a homosexual type of syndrome in heterosexuals with homosexual tendencies, which has been described in detail (Bieber, 1972). The potentiating situations for heterosexuals include falling in love, getting married, becoming a parent, occupational successes, and other meaningful achievements. Homosexuals may step up their homosexual activities as a response to a high point in their lives. The psychodynamic common denominator is the belief that their success or fulfillment in the areas of sexuality or work will antagonize powerful males and that these fearsome men will be motivated to act out dangerously hostile, even lethal, behavior. The meaning of the homosexual phenomena and of the obsessions, fantasies, and dreams of heterosexuals with homosexual problems is that of placating the irrationally perceived, threatening males. The homosexual acts or fantasies serve as a medium through which to magically communicate submission in masochistic acts to the feared men, or, conversely, domination in sadistic homosexual acts.

Finally, homosexuality serves to appease males who are giving them pleasure. The appeasement and submission are defensive attempts to stave off potential attack.

For some men, homosexuality serves as a magical way of restoring damaged self-esteem, or of overcoming feelings of helplessness, or of ensuring a pathologic dependency on powerful men. The wish to interiorize symbols of masculine power, particularly the large penis, as referred to earlier, becomes integrated with the homosexual activity such as in fellatio or insertee anal intercourse, thus producing a spurious sense of masculinity and effectiveness.

Heterosexual men in whom a pathologically dependent adaptation represents a major constellation in coping with helplessness, frequently symbolize this type of relatedness with other males in homosexual terms. They will have fantasies and dreams of fellatio and they will have impulses to act out such fantasies. Such experiences are common sources of homosexual panic states. In homosexuals who are pathologically dependent on a partner, usually an older man, or one who is fulfilling a paternal role, much of the sexual arousal is related to perpetuating the dependent relationship. In such cases, sexual arousal occurs in the context of security operations.

One may ask, are not the mechanisms I have described in the sexual arousal of homosexuals also operant in heterosexual arousal? The answer is yes. Some of the mechanisms are operant in heterosexual arousal; for example, the eroticizing of power can be observed in both sexes, although more frequently in women. For women who are attracted to power, masculine power is an important erotic stimulus, whether perceived in physical or in intellectual terms, or as wealth, status, and so forth. Also, there are men who are "turned on" by powerful women, however her power is perceived, whether by physical, psychologic, or social characteristics. In the classic paper on masochism by Krafft-Ebing (1965), for whom the syndrome is named, men are described who were sexually aroused by the fantasy of powerful women. Contact satisfactions through sexuality are found in both sexes and in hetero- and homosexuals, as mentioned by Hollender (1970), who wrote on women who wish to be held. Several of the mechanisms I have described for the homosexual can also be identified among heterosexuals. Yet, there is this profound difference—homosexual arousal is always associated with psychopathology, whereas in most instances, heterosexual arousal is the derivate of inborn biologic mechanisms that guarantee heterosexual arousal. Individuals of every species in which reproduction results from heterosexual mating are born with biologic mechanisms that guarantee heterosexual arousal. Space will not permit me to dilate on my observations, which have convinced me that olfaction is the sensory modality in man that initially evokes heterosexual arousal. The other sensory modalities are rapidly integrated into early sexual organization so that in the normal adult, vision, touch, and hearing, in addition to olfaction, are active in heterosexual arousal. Most heterosexual arousal is a direct experience and the derivate of biologic processes.

REFERENCES

Bieber, I. (1972): Homosexual dynamics in psychiatric crises. *Am. J. Psychiatry,* 128:10.

Bieber, I., Dain, H. J., Dince, P. R., Drellick, M. G., Grand, H. G., Gundlach, R. H., Kremer, M. W., Rifkin, A. H., Wilbur, C. B., and Bieker, T. B. (1962): *Homosexuality—A Psychoanalytic Study of Male Homosexuals.* Basic Books, New York.

Hollender, M. H. (1970): The need or wish to be held. *Arch. Gen. Psychiatry,* 22:445.

Krafft-Ebing, R. (1965): *Psychopathia Sexualis,* translated from the 12th ed. by F. S. Klaf, p. 86. Bell, New York.

Sexual Behavior: Pharmacology and Biochemistry, edited by M. Sandler and G. L. Gessa. Raven Press, New York © 1975.

Clinical Studies on the Effects of Neurohormones on Sexual Behavior

O. Benkert

Psychiatrische Klinik der Universität München, München, Germany

The experiments described in this chapter are designed to examine whether it is possible to approach sexual impotence from a perspective of biologic psychiatry. Studies are reported on: the hypothalamopituitary axis in impotent patients; therapeutic trials with thyrotropin-releasing hormone (TRH), luteinizing hormone-releasing hormone (LHRH) and L-parachlorophenylalanine (L-PCPA) in impotent patients; the effect of L-PCPA on pituitary hormone and testosterone concentrations in healthy volunteers; and the effect of L-5-hydroxytryptophan (L-5-HTP) in patients with increased sexual behavior and healthy volunteers.

The syndrome of sexual impotence as used for patient selection in this chapter must first be defined (Benkert, 1973*a*). Patients with obvious endocrine and physical disturbances have been excluded from the series. All patients were between 30 and 65 years of age.

The main clinical feature was a diminished or nonexistent capacity of erection prior to sexual intercourse, together with a retained, reduced, or nonexistent sexual drive. In addition ejaculation was sometimes premature or delayed. The inability to obtain an erection must have existed for at least 1 year and there had to be a regular partner. With these criteria of selection, the group of patients was necessarily small. Methodologic problems, particularly those concerned in identifying a therapeutic effect of drugs in patients with sexual impotence, are discussed in subsequent sections.

HYPOTHALAMOPITUITARY AXIS IN IMPOTENT PATIENTS

The possibility of drug-regulated sexual impotence raises the question of whether disturbances exist in the hypothalamopituitary axis of affected patients and whether hormone concentrations, regulated by this axis, lie within a normal range of values.

Hypothalamopituitary–Gonadal Axis

A decrease of urinary testosterone (Ismail, Davidson, Loraine, Cullen, Irvine, Cooper, and Smith, 1970) and a slight decrease of plasma testosterone (Legros, Servais, and Franchimont, 1973; Vermeulen, 1973) have been reported in impo-

TABLE 1. *Testosterone and LH response in impotent patients*

Testosterone		LH response (25 μg LHRH i.v.)	
(*n* = 12)	(*n* = 11)	(*n* = 12)	
age < 48	age > 48	0 min	30 min
670 ± 219	658 ± 238	2.3 ± 0.6	9.2 ± 3.8
		Δ30: 6.9 ± 3.7	
Controls: 400–900 ng/100 ml		Controls: Δ30 > 2.0 ng/ml	

tent patients without endocrine disorders. In addition, the blood level of luteinizing hormone (LH) seemed to be normal in impotent patients but the LH response was higher in those patients who had higher basic levels (Legros et al., 1973).

Plasma testosterone level was measured in 23 impotent patients who were divided into two groups, over and less than 48 years of age. The concentration did not differ from healthy controls in either group (Table 1).

In 12 of these 23 patients, plasma LH concentration was measured and was within the normal range (see values at time 0 min in Table 1). To determine whether there might be a dysfunction in the hypothalamopituitary axis the LH response was measured in these 12 patients after intravenous injection of 25 μg LHRH. Even then, the LH response, measured as the difference between LH plasma levels at times 0 and 30 min, showed no difference compared with controls (Table1).

Hypothalamopituitary Thyroid Axis

From clinical experience, a connection between thyroid disorders and changes in sexual behavior is well known (see review by Zitrin, 1974). A study of the hypothalamopituitary–thyroid axis in impotent patients thus seemed to be indicated.

In 12 affected subjects, plasma levels of thyroid stimulating hormone (TSH), L-triidothyronine (T_3) and thyroxine (T_4) were within the normal range (Table 2). The TSH response too, expressed as the difference between plasma TSH levels at zero time and 30 min, showed no significant difference compared with controls.

TABLE 2. T_3, T_4, *and TSH response in impotent patients* (n = 12)

T_3	T_4	TSH response (200 μg TRH i.v.)	
		0 min	30 min
111.6 ± 21.8	6.2 ± 1.9	2.0 ± 0.8	10.1 ± 3.6
		Δ30: 8.1 ± 3.0	
Controls:	Controls:	Controls: Δ30: 2.7–23.6 μE/ml	
87–177 ng/100 ml	4.5–10.0 μg/100 ml		

The methods of estimation are described elsewhere (Benkert, Horn, Pickardt, and Schmid, *in preparation*).

THERAPEUTIC TRIALS IN IMPOTENT PATIENTS

TRH

Although no impairment of the hypothalamopituitary–thyroid axis could be detected, at least by the methods employed, TRH was given to impotent patients empirically to determine whether there was any therapeutic effect. Some stimulatory effect on the hypothalamic centers seemed conceivable because of the neurotropic action of TRH which has been demonstrated in animal experiments (Plotnikoff, Prange, Breese, Anderson, and Wilson, 1974; Kruse, 1974); the thyroid stimulating effect of TRH might also be helpful.

TRH was given orally to 12 impotent patients in a dose of 40 mg/daily for 4 weeks in a double-blind crossover technique compared with placebo. They were selected, in randomized order, either to receive placebo in the first 4 weeks and then TRH for a further 4 weeks or vice versa. The patients were asked about their daily sexual feelings and behavior in a questionnaire. Every 2 weeks questionnaires were examined and a subjective assessment of the effect of the drug took place. A therapeutic effect during either placebo or TRH period was marked as a plus (Table 3). A review of daily questionnaires and subjective evaluation by the doctor showed no beneficial effect of TRH over placebo. Oral TRH did have a similar effect on the hypothalamo pituitary-thyroid axis as intravenous TRH, however (Benkert et al., *in preparation*).

One potential problem in this experiment was the double-blind with crossover design. It was sometimes difficult to estimate the therapeutic effect in the second 4 weeks, because of the possibility of a hangover effect. In succeeding studies, therefore, a double-blind design without crossover was favored.

TABLE 3. *Effect of TRH and placebo in impotent patients* (n = 12)

Placebo (4 wk)	TRH (4 wk)	Group 1 ($n = 6$)	TRH (4 wk)	Placebo (4 wk)	Group 2 ($n = 6$)
0	0	1	0	0	0
+	0	1	+	0	3
0	+	2	0	+	2
+	+	2	+	+	1

TRH was given daily (morning) in a dosage of 40 mg over a period of 4 weeks. + is the beneficial effect within the mentioned period; 0 represents no beneficial effect within the mentioned period.

LHRH

Recent animal experiments have shown that LHRH may play a role in induction of mating behavior (Moss and McCann, 1973) and facilitate the lordosis response in female rats (Pfaff, 1973). In addition, certain sleep research data in the human point to a possible connection between LH and sexual function: a slight increase in circulating LH activity during REM sleep has been observed (Rubin, Kales, and Odell, 1973); REM sleep-associated increases in testosterone concentration, stimulated perhaps by LH, have been reported (Evans, MacLean, and Ismail, 1971); penile erections are known to occur during REM sleep (Fisher, Gross, and Zuch, 1965). These results prompted us to give LHRH, now available as a nasal spray, to impotent patients.

In a double-blind study, six patients have been treated so far. All were given placebo spray for 2 weeks; thereafter three received LHRH spray (1 mg/day) for 4 weeks and three placebo spray for 4 weeks. After this, a 2-week course of placebo spray treatment followed for all patients. When the trial had finished, patients were asked to fill out the questionnaires for a further 2-month period.

Two patients in the placebo group reported no effect; one patient noted some improvement during placebo administration which lasted only until the end of the treatment. One of the patients taking LHRH found a good increase in penile erection during the LHRH period, an effect that persisted after the spray had been discontinued. The second patient in the LHRH group had a strong increase in penile erection after changing from LHRH to placebo spray. The third reported an unpleasant sensitivity of penis and testis and showed seminal emission during urination until the end of the placebo period; after discontinuing LHRH, he observed an increase of penile erection during intercourse which persisted during the drug-free period until the end of the sixth week.

Because only six patients have been treated thus far, no final result can be given. However, compared with other drug studies in impotent patients with TRH, L-DOPA, PCPA, and antiserotonergic substances, initial results with LHRH, particularly after its discontinuation, seem to be promising.

L-PCPA

The sexual stimulating effect of PCPA in rats has been well documented (Gessa and Tagliamonte, 1974). In pilot studies, PCPA and serotonin antagonists (in combination with mesterolone) seemed to have a beneficial effect in some sexually impotent patients (Benkert, 1973*b*). In these studies, DL-PCPA in a dose of 3 g per day has resulted in side effects; 1.0 g per day was used in the present experiments. D- and L-PCPA are known from animal experiments to be equally potent in producing depletion of brain serotonin and 5-hydroxyindoleacetic acid (5-HIAA) (Fratta, Biggio, Mercuro, Di Vittorio, Tagliamonte, and Gessa, 1973).

In a double-blind study 10 patients were given placebo for 2 weeks. Then five received placebo for the next 4 weeks; the other five were treated with L-PCPA.

TABLE 4. *Effect of L-PCPA and placebo in impotent patients* (n = 10)

Plac. (2 wk)	*Plac.* (4 wk)	Plac. (2 wk)	Plac. (2 wk)	*n* (5)	Pat. no.
0	0	0	/	1	1
+	+	0	0	1	10
0	+	0	0	2	6, 7
0	+	+	0	1	8

Plac. (2 wk)	L-*PCPA* (4 wk)	Plac. (2 wk)	L-PCPA (2 wk)	*n* (5)	Pat. no.
0	0	0	/	3	2 (*), 9 (*), −3 (†)
+	0	0	/	1	5
0	+	0	+	1	4 (†)

L-PCPA was given daily in a dosage of 1.0 g (0.25–0.5 g) over a period of 4 weeks. Asterisk (*) after patient number means strong side effects; (†) means slight side effects. See Table 3 for abbreviations.

Placebo was again administered to all in the 7th and 8th weeks. Those patients who noted an effect during the middle 4-week period again received placebo or L-PCPA for a further 2 weeks (Table 4). Placebo appeared to have a significantly better therapeutic effect over L-PCPA after the 6th week. In the L-PCPA group, only patient No. 4 showed a beneficial effect, i.e., a strong increase in penile erection during intercourse. As this occurred only when he was on L-PCPA therapy, this patient can be classified as an L-PCPA responder (Table 4).

Four patients complained of side effects, including periods of mental dullness, headache, and vertigo when they were under L-PCPA medication. These were so pronounced in two (Nos. 2 and 9) that they would have obscured any beneficial effect which might have resulted from the treatment.

The overall result of this study is that L-PCPA in a dosage of 1.0 g per day over 4 weeks has no therapeutic effect when compared with placebo. The reasons for the lack of effectiveness may be several: severe side effects, inadequate dosage, or perhaps that activity is only present when the drug is combined with testosterone. As one of the five patients might be classified as a responder, it seems worthwhile at present to continue these studies. But it is obvious that in the investigation of a condition with such a high placebo response, methodologic considerations become more prominent. Large double-blind studies, double-blind crossover studies and, indeed, controlled single case studies all must play their part in its elucidation.

In addition to the questionnaires, respiration rate, pulse rate, and penis plethysmography were assessed before and at the end of the drug period (6th week) during the presentation of pornographic slides. However, only detailed daily questionnaires turned out to be suitable for assessing any drug effect on impotence.

EFFECT OF L-PCPA ON PITUITARY HORMONES AND TESTOSTERONE IN HEALTHY VOLUNTEERS

It is of interest to determine whether PCPA has any effect on pituitary hormones in the human as animal experiments provide evidence that the secretion of hypothalamic releasing hormones is controlled by biogenic amines in the basal hypothalamus (Fuxe and Hökfelt, 1969). Contradictionary results on the effect of PCPA on gonadotropins, ovulation, and testicular function in animals have been reported (Donoso, Bishop, Fawcett, Krulich, and McCann, 1971; Brown and Fawke, 1972; Kordon and Glowinski, 1972; Bliss, Frischat, and Samuels, 1972; Gawienowski, Merker, and Damon, 1973).

In six healthy male volunteers the effect of 1.5 g L-PCPA per day given over

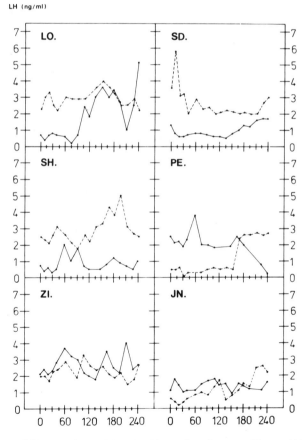

FIG. 1. Effect of L-PCPA on plasma-LH in healthy male volunteers. Plasma-LH was measured in six subjects over 240 min at 15-min intervals before (solid line) and after (dotted line) intake of 1.5 g L-PCPA daily over a period of 12 days.

FSH (ng/ml)

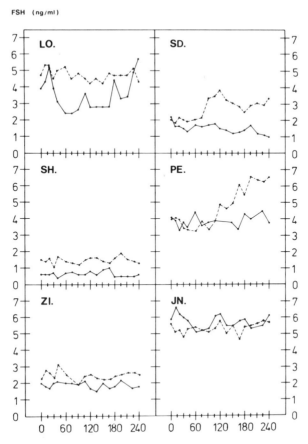

FIG. 2. Effect of L-PCPA on plasma FSH in healthy male volunteers. Plasma-FSH was measured in six subjects over 240 min at 15-min intervals before (solid line) and after (dotted line) intake of 1.5 g L-PCPA daily over 12 days.

a period of 12 days on plasma concentrations of the following hormones was measured: LH, follicle stimulating hormone (FSH); growth hormone (GH); TSH, testosterone, estrone, estradiol—17β, 17-α-hydroxyprogesterone and cortisol. Urinary 5-HTAA decreased significantly ($p < 0.025$), from 6.06 ± 2.8 μg/ml to 1.75 ± 0.96 μg/ml after L-PCPA treatment.

A slight increase in plasma FSH level compared to base line values, which did not reach significance, was seen in five subjects after L-PCPA administration. Individual values remained within the normal range, however (Fig. 1). No influence of L-PCPA on LH level could be recorded (Fig. 2); nor was there an effect on testosterone or the other hormones mentioned previously. These results and assay procedures will be reported in greater detail elsewhere (Benkert, Bender, Bidlingmaier, and Butenandt, 1974).

EFFECT OF L-5-HTP IN PATIENTS WITH INCREASED SEXUAL BEHAVIOR AND HEALTHY VOLUNTEERS

It seemed of interest to study whether L-5-HTP can attenuate sexual behavior in man as it appears to do in animals (Gessa and Tagliamonte, 1974).

L-5-HTP in Healthy Volunteers

Four healthy subjects, aged 24 to 30 years, received placebo for 4 weeks. For 4 weeks thereafter they ingested the decarboxylase inhibitor Ro 4–4602 (3 X 125 mg daily), combined with 300 mg L-5-HTP for 1 week and 600 mg L-5-HTP for the remaining 3 weeks. The subjects were asked to fill out daily questionnaires similar to those used for the impotent patients; they were told that they would receive a drug that might influence sexual behavior in either direction. There was indeed some slight decrease of sexual behavior in two subjects, but this decrease tends to correlate with such side effects as diarrhea. The other two subjects showed neither side effect nor behavior change. Two additional subjects developed brief psychotic episodes during the medication and had to be excluded from the experiment.

L-5-HTP in Patients

The treatment with L-5-HTP of five patients with exhibitionism or increased sexual behavior was more difficult than in the healthy controls because their reliability in filling out questionnaires and taking drugs was not always guaranteed. They had been told they would get a drug to help their condition. They were asked to fill out daily questionnaires concerning their sexual behavior. Perhaps the most objective criterion of their sexual behavior was the daily statement of ejaculation frequency. Placebo, L-5-HTP alone or in combination with Ro 4–4602 (3 X 125 mg daily) was given in different drug schedules (maximal 600 mg L-5-HTP), over a period of 2 to 6 months.

Although transient periods of lower ejaculation frequency were observed, there was no significant difference between test and control periods. Therefore, L-5-HTP does not appear to be an effective drug for the treatment of increased sexual behavior. These data are reported in detail elsewhere (Benkert, Matal, and Wiederholt, 1974).

SUMMARY

No pathologic changes were found in the hypothalamopituitary–gonadal axis and in the hypothalamopituitary-thyroid axis in impotent patients. TRH and L-PCPA administration has no beneficial effect on this condition, whereas LHRH seems to have an effect only after drug discontinuation. Only by filling out daily questionnaires is it possible to assess drug effects in impotent patients. L-PCPA did not influence plasma levels of pituitary hormones and testosterone in healthy male subjects. L-5-HTP had no effect on sexual behavior in patients manifesting an increase and in healthy volunteers.

REFERENCES

Benkert, O. (1973*a*): Wirkung von Serotonin-Antagonisten bei sexueller Impotenz. *Pharmakopsychiatry,* 6:218–223.

Benkert, O. (1973*b*): Pharmacological experiments to stimulate human sexual behavior. In: *Psychopharmacology, Sexual Disorders and Drug Abuse,* (edited by: T. A. Ban et al.), pp. 489–495. North-Holland Pub. Co., Amsterdam and London.

Bliss, E. L., Frischat, A., and Samuels, L. (1972): Brain and testicular function. *Life Sci. I,* 11: 231–238.

Brown, P. S., and Fawke, L. (1972): Effects of reserpine, *p*-chlorophenylalanine, α-methyltyrosine, thymoxamine or methallibure on pituitary FSH in male rats. *J. Reprod. Fertil.,* 28:167–175.

Donoso, A. O., Bishop, W., Fawcett, C. P., Krulich, L., and McCann, S. M. (1971): Effects of drugs that modify brain monoamine concentrations on plasma gonadotropin and prolactin levels in the rat. *Endocrinology,* 89:774–784.

Evans, J. I., MacLean, A. W., and Ismail, A. A. A. (1971): Concentration of plasma testosterone in normal men during sleep. *Nature,* 229:261–262.

Fisher, C., Gross, J., and Zuch, J. (1965): Cycle of penile erection synchronous with dreaming (REM) sleep: Preliminary report. *Arch. Genet. Psychiatry,* 12:29–45.

Fratta, W., Biggio, G., Mercuro, G., Di Vittorio, P., Tagliamonte, A., and Gessa, G. L. (1973): The effect of D- and L-*p*-chlorophenylalanine on the metabolism of 5-hydroxytryptamine in brain. *J. Pharmacol. Pharmacol.,* 25:908–909.

Fuxe, K., and Hökfelt, T. (1969): Catecholamines in the hypothalamus and the pituitary gland. In: *Frontiers in Neuroendocrinology,* edited by W. F. Ganong, and Martini L., pp. 47–96. Oxford University Press, New York.

Gawienowski, A. M., Merker, J. W., and Damon, R. A. (1973): Alteration of sexual behavior and sex accessory glands by *p*-chlorophenylalanine and testosterone. *Life Sci.,* 12:307–315.

Gessa, G. L., and Tagliamonte, A. (1974): Role of brain monoamines in male sexual behavior. *Life Sci.,* 14:425–436.

Ismail, A. A. A., Davidson, D. W., Loraine, J. A., Cullen, D. R., Irvine, W. J., Cooper, A. J., and Smith, C. C. (1970): In: *Reproduction Endocrinology,* (edited by J. Irvine) p. 138. Livingstone, Edinburgh.

Kordon, C., and Glowinski, J. (1972): Role of hypothalamic monoaminergic neurones in the gonadotrophin release-regulating mechanisms. *Neuropharmacology,* 11:153–162.

Kruse, H. (1974): Neurotrope Wirkungen Von TRH, Vortrag 15. Deutscher Pharmakologen-Kongress, Mainz, Germany.

Legros, J. J., Servais, J., and Franchimont, P. (1973): Influence of LRH on LH response in patients with psychogenic impotence. Presented at the 4th International Congress of Psychoneuroendocrinology, Berkeley.

Moss, R. L., and McCann, S. M. (1973): Induction of mating behavior in rats by luteinizing hormone-releasing factor. *Science,* 181:177–179.

Pfaff, D. W. (1973): Luteinizing hormone-releasing factor potentiates lordosis behavior in hypophysectomized ovariectomized female rats. *Science,* 182:1148–1149.

Plotnikoff, N. P., Prange, A. J., Breese, G. R., Anderson, M. S., and Wilson, I. C. (1974): The effects of thyrotropin-releasing hormone on DOPA response in normal, hypophysectomized, and thyroidectomized animals. In: *The Thyroid Axis, Drugs, and Behavior,* edited by A. J. Prange. Raven Press, New York.

Rubin, R. T., Kales, A., and Odell, W. (1973): Secretion of LH and FSH during sleep in man. In: *Hormones and Brain Function,* pp. 521–526. Budapest.

Veremeulen, A., (1973): Testosterone in plasma. A physiopathological study. In: *Verhandelingen van de Koninklijke Academie voor Genees-Kunde van Belgie.* Vol. 35, pp. 95–180.

Zitrin, A. (1974): Sexual function in hyperthyroidism. Presented to the 1st International Symposium on the pharmacology of sexual behavior, Cagliari.

Sexual Behavior: Pharmacology and Biochemistry, edited by M. Sandler and G. L.
Gessa. Raven Press, New York © 1975.

Neuroendocrine Regulation of Gonadotropin Secretion and Sexual Motivation After L-Tryptophan Administration in Man

Markku T. Hyyppä, Sirkka Falck, Helena Aukia, and Urpo K. Rinne

Department of Neurology, University of Turku, SF-20520 Turku 52, Finland

Many recent findings point to the importance of brain monoamines for copulatory behavior and sexual motivation in experimental animals. In 1964 Meyerson
proposed that increased serotoninergic tone has an antagonistic effect on copulatory behavior in female rats (Meyerson, 1964). This has been confirmed for both
female and male rats (Malmnäs and Meyerson, 1972; Malmnäs, 1973). More
recently, parachlorophenylalanine (PCPA), a drug that decreases brain serotonin
(5-HT) levels by inhibiting tryptophan hydroxylase enzyme activity, has been
shown to increase the sexual motivation of female rats (Meyerson, Eliasson,
Lindström, Michanek, and Söderlund, 1973). Earlier reports from different
laboratories have suggested that PCPA increases sexual performance particularly
in male mammals (Shillito, 1969; Tagliamonte, Tagliamonte, Gessa, and Brodie,
1969; Sheard, 1969; Ahlenius, Eriksson, Larsson, Modigh, and Sodersten, 1971).
It was also reported from our laboratory that PCPA when administered neonatally can permanently increase sexual activity of rats (Hyyppä, Lampinen, and
Lehtinen, 1972). Opposing opinions have also been presented; for example,
Whalen and Luttge (1970) have not agreed with the results drawn from experiments in animals, and in their critical review Zitrin and his co-workers have
emphasized the fact that no clear-cut evidence has ever been published demonstrating an increase of sexual interest in patients or normal volunteers treated
with PCPA (Zitrin et al., 1973). Although the role of PCPA in producing deviations of sexual behavior may be open to doubt, there exists a little more evidence
in favor of the "indoleamine hypothesis": indoleaminergic axon terminals can
be destroyed (for refs., see Baumgarten and Schlossberger, 1973) and serotonin
synthesis depleted selectively (Hyyppä, Cardinali, Baumgarten, and Wurtman,
1973) by 5,6-dihydroxytryptamine (5,6-DHT), and this drug also increases
copulatory activity of male rats concomitantly with a selective decrease of brain
serotonin (DaPrada, Carruba, O'Brien, Saner, and Pletscher, 1972).

Indoleaminergic mechanisms in neuroendocrine integration areas, i.e., in the
hypothalamus, pineal, and related limbic areas, regulate gonadotropin secretion
(for refs., see Kamberi, 1973). Most of the investigations in this field point to an
inhibitory role of 5-HT in luteinizing hormone (LH) secretion (O'Steen, 1965;
Kordon, Gogan, Hery, and Rotsztejn, 1971; Labhsetwar, 1971). Contrary results

have been obtained concerning the effect of 5-HT on follicle-stimulating hormone (FSH) levels (Brown, 1971; Kamberi, 1973). However, very little is known about brain 5-HT and gonadotropin secretion in man.

An investigator who wants to study the effects of increased or decreased indoleaminergic tone on human reproduction physiology faces certain restrictions: there are few ways to modify 5-HT metabolism *selectively* in brain indoleaminergic neurons. In the present study L-tryptophan (TP) loading has been regarded as the best method for the following reasons: (1) L-tryptophan is an essential amino acid; (2) it has very few pharmacologic side effects even in higher dosage, and it has been studied for some years in depressed patients (Murphy, Baker, Goodwin, Miller, Kotin, and Bunney, 1974); (3) it is taken up by indoleaminergic neurons, which metabolize it to 5-HT very rapidly (Aghajanian and Asher, 1971; Hyyppä et al., 1973); (4) it is more specific than the immediate precursor of serotonin, 5-hydroxytryptophan (5-HTP), because it is hydroxylated by a specific enzyme localized perhaps only in indoleaminergic nerve terminals (Kuhar, Roth, and Aghajanian, 1971); (5) the rate of synthesis of 5-HT in the brain is regulated principally by the availability of L-tryptophan (Wurtman and Fernström, 1972; Knott and Curzon, 1972; Tagliamonte, Biggio, Vargiu, and Gessa, 1973). Consequently, the present report studies the effects of an increased indoleaminergic tone produced by L-tryptophan treatment on neuroendocrine control of gonadotropin secretion as well as on sexual motivation.

MATERIAL AND METHODS

Patients

Ten male and nine female volunteers, aged 23 to 49 (mean 31.5 years) who suffered from multiple sclerosis (MS) were admitted to the hospital (Department of Neurology, Turku University Hospital) for at least 7 days. Within the first 2 days oral L-tryptophan treatment was started to study its effect on the course of the MS disease (Hyyppä et al., *unpublished observations*). After 30 days of treatment with L-tryptophan, the patients were examined again as outpatients. For the following 30 days, the tryptophan was replaced by placebo in capsules similar to L-tryptophan (Leiras, Finland). In the preliminary study, L-tryptophan was given to subjects three times daily in a dosage of 500 mg together with a decarboxylase inhibitor (50 mg; Ro 4–4602, Hoffmann-LaRoche, Switzerland). Subsequently patients were treated with a higher dose of L-tryptophan (2 g four times daily) without a decarboxylase inhibitor. Diagnoses were based on accepted international criteria, and all patients were informed according to the Helsinki Declaration, and did not know when placebo was administered instead of L-tryptophan. The patients were not permitted to take any other drug during the treatment period. All specimen sampling was made after a 10-hr fasting period, and all patients were examined and nursed routinely during their stay in hospital.

Laboratory Analyses

Immunoreactive levels of FSH and LH in plasma were assayed by a double antibody solid phase (DASP) radioimmunoassay (Den Hollander, Schuurs, and Van Hell, 1972), with some modifications of our own (to be published in detail subsequently). Purified gonadotropins, their antibodies, and reference standards (LER-907) were donated by the National Institute of Arthritis and Metabolic Diseases. Plasma was collected at 8:00 A.M. for 2 successive days, and radioimmunoassays were performed twice on each sample, with all samples always analyzed simultaneously. Results are expressed as mIU per ml, with 2 mIU of FSH and 6 mIU of LH equivalent to 100 ng of LER-907 in the immunoassay.

Tryptophan, 5-HIAA, and HVA were determined in the CSF of patients before and during L-tryptophan treatment. Before lumbar puncture, patients were confined to bed for the previous 3 hr. CSF sampling took place 10 hr after the last dose of L-tryptophan. L-Tryptophan was analyzed according to Denckla and Dewey (1967), 5-HIAA according to Ashcroft and Sharman (1962), and HVA according to Andén, Roos, and Werdinius (1963).

Sexual Motivation Tests

Sexual motivation was tested by our method (described in detail by Hyyppä, Falck, and Rinne, *this volume*) before and during L-tryptophan treatment, and also during the placebo period. In spite of the fact that most of the subjects were very anxious to participate in the sexual motivation study, only three men and four women were randomly chosen for this preliminary examination. Statistical analyses included paired and unpaired Student's t-tests.

RESULTS

Tryptophan concentrations in the CSF were 0.52 ± 0.02 $\mu g/ml$ (mean $\pm$ s.e.) before treatment. During treatment, a 44% increase occurred, to a level of 0.75 ± 0.08 $\mu g/ml$. The difference is highly significant ($p < 0.001$) (Table 1). When tryptophan was given together with decarboxylase inhibitor, no statistically significant differences were noted in 5-HIAA and HVA concentrations. However, 5-HIAA levels were markedly increased in certain patients 10 hr after L-tryptophan and Ro 4–4602 administration, with an average elevation of 69% ($p < 0.05$, paired Student's t-test). HVA remained unchanged (Table 1). In a group in which L-tryptophan was given alone in a dose four times higher (2,000 mg), a significant increase in 5-HIAA levels was apparent ($p < 0.001$, paired Student's t-test), but in this series, the subjects were more equally matched by symptoms of MS (Table 1).

Results for FSH plasma levels during L-tryptophan treatment are given separately for men and women in Table 2. It will be seen that FSH values for men

TABLE 1. *Effect of L-tryptophan on concentrations of tryptophan, 5-HIAA, and HVA in CSF of MS patients**

	L-Tryptophan (2 g)		
5-HIAA	+ 39	(4)	$p < 0.001$
	L-Tryptophan (0.5 g) + 50 mg of decarboxylase inhibitor		
Tryptophan	+ 44	(9)	$p < 0.001$
5-HIAA	+ 69	(9)	$p < 0.05$
HVA	± 0	(9)	n.s.

* CSF was collected 10 hr after L-tryptophan administration. Values are given as percentage changes from control levels. Number of patients is given in parentheses. Measurements of statistical significance were calculated according to the paired Student's *t*-test.

TABLE 2. *Effect of chronic tryptophan treatment on plasma gonadotropin levels (mIU/ml; mean ± s.e.)*

Plasma level/time		Men	Women
FSH	Before	10.4 ± 3.3 (10)	9.3 ± 3.6 (9)
	During	10.3 ± 2.5 (10)	12.9 ± 7.2 (9)
LH	Before	4.4 (10)	7.2 ± 6.4 (9)
	During	3.5 (10)*	5.5 ± 3.7 (9)

* According to paired Student's *t*-test the decrease approaches significance at $p < 0.05$ level ($t = 1.722$). L-Tryptophan + decarboxylase inhibitor were given 10 hr before collection of plasma samples which took place at 8:00 A.M.

TABLE 3. *Mean estimates of feelings among MS patients during the pornographic film at the first (I) (without tryptophan) and second (II) (with tryptophan) session*

Variables of sexual motivation	Group I	Group II
Pleasurable feelings	5.0	6.0
Unpleasurable feelings	3.0	3.8
Sexual excitement	4.1	5.1
Insulted	1.8	2.0
Shocked	2.1	2.5

are very constant with a narrow standard deviation whereas in women FSH levels vary with the menstrual cycle and the standard deviation is high. No observations on stage of cycle were made. (These values were within the normal range, according to the literature.) LH plasma levels, however, tended to be lower in male patients treated with L-tryptophan. Statistical significance was not reached, but the *t*-value according to the paired Student's *t*-test was very close to $p < 0.05$. In women, a high standard deviation was again found because of a high ovulatory peak observed in one of the subjects before treatment. Other fluctuations during the cycle are greater for LH than for FSH levels (see Austin and Short, 1972).

Table 3 shows some variables of sexual motivation after a pornographic film. No general change of the sexual parameters tested in the study was found in the overall patient group. Working capacity, measured in this group in addition, did not show alterations during the treatment with L-tryptophan.

DISCUSSION

The effect of L-tryptophan administration was biochemically controlled by measuring the concentrations of tryptophan, 5-HIAA, and HVA in the CSF of the patients. Tryptophan and 5-HIAA levels were markedly elevated 10 hr after the last dose of L-tryptophan, but HVA levels did not appear to vary significantly. Similar observations have been published by others (Eccleston, Ashcroft, and Crawford, 1970) concerning tryptophan and 5-HIAA changes, and although the tryptophan concentration rose more quickly, maximum levels were reached within a similar time in the study of van Praag, Fleutge, Korf, Dols, and Schut (1973). In our investigation, we did not use the probenecid technique as an index of brain amine turnover, because in rats (Tagliamonte, Tagliamonte, Perez-Cruet, and Stern, 1971) as well as more recently in humans, probenecid has been shown to increase plasma-free tryptophan levels (Lewander and Sjöström, 1973). This leads to an increased brain serotonin synthesis (Wurtman and Fernstrom, 1972; Hyyppä et al., 1973). In our opinion loading with L-tryptophan is a relatively physiologic way of accelerating brain serotonin synthesis without further pharmacologic manipulation. As a result of the increased availability of tryptophan, CNS serotonin turnover is accelerated (Wurtman and Fernstrom, 1972; Knott and Curzon, 1972; Hyyppä et al., 1973), a fact indicated by the elevated serotonin metabolite, 5-HIAA, in the CSF.

Only plasma LH levels, of the gonadotropins measured in this study, showed any notable change. As might have been expected from experimental studies, this change was toward lower levels. Among recent observations those of Kamberi and his co-workers (1973), of Kordon and his co-workers (1971), of Labhsetwar (1971), and of Brown (1971) support most favorably the suggestion that an increased brain serotoninergic tone is necessary to inhibit gonadotropin secretion in experimental animals. This seems to be the case even in humans. Our preliminary investigations, in which L-tryptophan was used as stimulator of indoleamines in the neuroendocrine control of pituitary hormones, have shown a *highly significant decrease* of plasma LH levels 1 hr after L-tryptophan loading (Hyyppä et al., unpublished results). In the present study, we have noted a response similar to the L-DOPA response, which is lacking some hours after treatment but present in the 2 hr following administration. L-Tryptophan, however, has a slight action on plasma LH levels even 10 hr after loading. Plasma FSH was unaffected, a finding which fits well with experimental observations. An increase of FSH has been found (Brown, 1971) but a decrease has also been reported (Kamberi, 1973). These variations in findings are due to different methods by which indoleamine tone in the CNS has been modified in a variety of experimental situations. Most of them can be criticized strongly because of the pharmacologic nature of most of the techniques employed.

Sexual motivation and working capacity did not alter significantly in our study. According to our hypothesis, L-tryptophan should cause a decrease of sexual motivation if it is possible to extrapolate from animal experiments. Although indoleaminergic tone was increased in patients treated with L-tryptophan, no changes in behavior were found. In this chapter we do not show the individual variations, which are interesting because of the different backgrounds of the subjects. L-Tryptophan has been used in depressed patients and many aspects of its effects have been discussed in the psychiatric literature (see Murphy et al., 1974). The immediate precursor of brain serotonin, 5-HTP, has also been given to chronic schizophrenic patients; it was assumed that psychologic changes found in this study stemmed directly or indirectly from increased brain serotonin (Wyatt, Vaughan, Galanter, Kaplan, and Green, 1972). To our knowledge, no sexual behavioral parameters have previously been published in patients treated with serotonin precursors.

Pharmacologic manipulations can perhaps accelerate brain indoleaminergic transmission but there exist serious doubts about their specificity. In addition, 5-HTP is also nonspecific because it is converted to serotonin within cells that normally do not contain serotonin (Moir and Eccleston, 1968), and this leads to changes in the metabolism of other amines. 5-HTP can stimulate the release of brain norepinephrine *in vitro* (Feers and Wirz-Justice, 1971) and *in vivo* (Okada, Saito, Fujieda, and Yamashita, 1972). Usually this possibility has not been checked in studies which have used psychopharmacologic drugs to accelerate brain serotonin turnover. Our study did not show changes in HVA concentration, which presumably excludes the possibility of dopamine metabolism being affected.

We generally presume that an increased indoleaminergic tone does not decrease sexual motivation in MS patients. No correlation analyses are included in the present study. These are, however, a necessary step in future work, because they might throw light on the general problem of parallel changes in sexual behavior and hormonal changes in the body. Whether brain indoleamine metabolism, gonadotropin secretion and sexual motivation can be correlated in humans awaits further information.

ACKNOWLEDGMENT

This work was supported by a grant (73-M30) from The Population Council to M.T.H.

REFERENCES

Aghajanian, G. K., and Asher, I. M. (1971): Histochemical fluorescence of raphe neurons: Selective enhancement by tryptophan. *Science,* 172:1159–1161.

Ahlenius, S., Eriksson, H., Larsson, K., Modigh, K., and Sodersten, P. (1971): Mating behavior in the male rat treated with *p*-chlorophenylalanine methyl ester alone and in combination with pargyline. *Psychopharmacologia,* 20:383–388.

Andén, N.-E., Roos, B.-E., and Werdinius, B. (1963): On the occurrence of homovanillic acid in brain and cerebrospinal fluid and its determination by a fluorometric method. *Life Sci.* (I), 7:448–458.

Ashcroft, G. W., and Sharman, D. F. (1962): Drug-induced changes in the concentration of 5-OR indolyl compounds in cerebrospinal fluid and caudate nucleus. *Br. J. Pharmacol.,* 19:153–160.

Austin, C. R., and Short, R. V. (1972): *Hormones in Mammals.* Cambridge Univ. Press, New York.

Baumgarten, H. G., and Schlossberger, H. G. (1973): Effects of 5,6-dihydroxytryptamine on brain monoamine neurons in the rat. In: *Serotonin and Behavior,* edited by J. Barchas and E. Usdin. Academic Press, New York.

Brown, P. S. (1971): Pituitary follicle-stimulating hormone in immature female rats treated with drugs that inhibit the synthesis or antagonise the actions of catecholamines and 5-hydroxytryptamine. *Neuroendocrinology,* 7:183–192.

DaPrada, M., Carruba, M., O'Brien, R. A., Saner, A., and Pletscher, A. (1972): The effect of 5,6-dihydroxytryptamine on sexual behaviour of male rats. *Eur. J. Pharmacol.,* 19:288–290.

Denckla, W. D., and Dewey, H. K. (1967): The determination of tryptophan in plasma, liver and urine. *J. Lab. Clin. Med.,* 69:160.

Eccleston, D., Ashcroft, G. W., and Crawford, T. B. B. (1970): Effect of tryptophan administration on 5-HIAA in cerebrospinal fluid in man. *J. Neurol. Neurosurg. Psychiatry,* 33:269–272.

Feers, H., and Wirz-Justice, A. (1971): The effect of 5-hydroxytryptophan on the efflux of noradrenaline from brain slices. *Experientia,* 27:880–881.

Den Hollander, F. C., Schuurs, A. H., and Van Hell, H. (1972): Radioimmunoassays for human gonadotrophins and insulin employing a "double-antibody solid-phase" technique. *J. Immunol. Meth.,* 1:247–262.

Hyyppä, M., Lampinen, P., and Lehtinen, P. (1972): Alteration in the sexual behaviour of male and female rats after neonatal administration of *p*-chlorophenylalanine. *Psychopharmacologia,* 25: 152–161.

Hyyppä, M., Cardinali, D. P., Baumgarten, H. G., and Wurtman, R. J. (1973): Rapid accumulation of H[3]-serotonin in brains of rats receiving intraperitoneal H[3]-tryptophan: effects of 5,6-dihydroxytryptamine or female sex hormones. *J. Neural Transm.,* 34:111–124.

Kamberi, I. A. (1973): The role of brain monoamines and pineal indoles in the secretion of gonadotrophins and gonadotrophin-releasing hormones. *Prog. Brain Res.,* 39:261–278.

Knott, P. J., and Curzon, G. (1972): Free tryptophan in plasma and brain tryptophan metabolism. *Nature,* 239:452–453.

Kordon, C., Gogan, F., Hery, M., and Rotsztejn, W. H. (1971): Interference of serotonin-containing neurons with pituitary gonadotrophins release-regulation. Hormones and antagonists. *Gynecol. Invest.,* 2:116–121.

Kuhar, M. J., Roth, R. H., and Aghajanian, G. K. (1971): Selective reduction of tryptophan hydroxylase activity in rat forebrain after midbrain raphe lesions. *Brain Res.,* 35:167–176.

Labhsetwar, A. P. (1971): Effects of serotonin on spontaneous ovulation: A theory for the dual hypothalamic control of ovulation. *Acta Endocrinol.,* 68:334–344.

Lewander, T., and Sjöström, R. (1973): Increase in the plasma concentration of free tryptophan caused by probenecid in humans. *Psychopharmacologia,* 33:81–86.

Malmnäs, C. O. (1973): Monoaminergic influence of testosterone-activated copulatory behavior in the castrated male rat. *Acta Physiol. Scand. [Suppl.],* 395.

Malmnäs, C. O., and Meyerson, B. J. (1972): Monoamines and copulatory activity in the castrated male rat. *Acta Pharmacol. Toxicol.,* 31, Suppl., 1–23.

Meyerson, B. (1964): Central nervous monoamines and hormone induced estrous behaviour in the spayed rat. *Acta Physiol. Scand. [Suppl.],* 241.

Meyerson, B. J., Eliasson, M., Lindström, L., Michanek, A., and Söderlund, A. (1973): Monoamines and female sexual behaviour. In: *Psychopharmacology, Sexual Disorders and Drug Abuse,* edited by T. A. Ban, J. R. Boissier, G. J. Gessa, H. Heimann, L. Hollister, H. E. Lehmann, I. Munkvad, H. Steinberg, F. Sulser, A. Sundswall, and O. Vinar. Czechoslovakia Medical Press, Prague, Czechoslovakia.

Moir, A. T. B., and Eccleston, D. (1968): The effects of precursor loading in the cerebral metabolism of 5-hydroxyindoles. *J. Neurochem.,* 15:1093–1108.

Murphy, D. L., Baker, M., Goodwin, F. K., Miller, H., Kotin, J., and Bunney, W. E., Jr. (1974): L-Tryptophan in affective disorders: Indoleamine changes and differential clinical effects. *Psychopharmacologia,* 34:11–20.

Okada, F., Saito, Y., Fujieda, T., and Yamashita, I. (1972): Monoamine changes in the brain of rats injected with L-5-hydroxytryptophan. *Nature,* 238:355–356.

O'Steen, W. K. (1965): Suppression of ovarian activity in immature rats by serotonin. *Endocrinology,* 77:937–939.

Van Praag, H. M., Flentge, F., Korf, J., Dols, L. C. W., and Schut, T. (1973): The influence of probenecid on the metabolism of serotonin, dopamine and their precursors in man. *Psychopharmacologia,* 33:141–151.

Sheard, M. (1969): The effect of *p*-chlorophenylalanine on behavior in rats: Relation to brain serotonin and 5-hydroxyindoleacetic acid. *Brain Res.,* 15:524–528.

Shillito, E. E. (1969): The effect of *p*-chlorophenylalanine on social interactions of male rats. *Br. J. Pharmacol.,* 36:193–194.

Tagliamonte, A., Tagliamonte, P., Gessa, G. L., and Brodie, B. B. (1969): Compulsive sexual activity induced by *p*-chlorophenylalanine in normal and pinealectomized male rats. *Science,* 166:1433–1435.

Tagliamonte, A., Biggio, G., Vargiu, L., and Gessa, G. L. (1973): Free tryptophan in serum controls brain tryptophan level and serotonin synthesis. *Life Sci. II,* 12:277–287.

Tagliamonte, A., Tagliamonte, P., Perez-Cruet, J., and Stern, S. (1971): Effect of psychotropic drugs on tryptophan concentration in the rat brain. *J. Pharmacol. Exp. Ther.,* 177:475–480.

Whalen, R. E., and Luttge, G. W. (1970): *p*-Chlorophenylalanine methyl ester: An aphrodisiac? *Science,* 169:1000–1001.

Wurtman, R. J., and Fernstrom, J. D. (1972): Tryptophan, L-tyrosine, and the control of brain monoamine biosynthesis. In: *Perspectives in Neuropharmacology,* edited by S. H. Snyder. Oxford Univ. Press, New York.

Wyatt, R. J., Vaughan, T., Galanter, M., Kaplan, J., and Green, R. (1972): Behavioral changes of chronic schizophrenic patients given L-5-hydroxytryptophan. *Science,* 177:1124–1126.

Zitrin, A., Dement, W. C., and Barchas, J. D. (1973): Brain serotonin and male sexual behavior. In: *Contemporary Sexual Behavior: Critical Issues in the 1970s,* edited by J. Zubin and J. Money. The Johns Hopkins Univ. Press, Baltimore, Maryland.

Sexual Behavior: Pharmacology and Biochemistry, edited by M. Sandler and G. L. Gessa. Raven Press, New York © 1975.

Is L-DOPA An Aphrodisiac in Patients with Parkinson's Disease?

Markku T. Hyyppä, Sirkka C. Falck, and Urpo K. Rinne

Department of Neurology, University of Turku, SF-20520 Turku 52, Finland

Undoubtedly the most effective treatment in Parkinson's disease is L-dihydroxyphenylalanine (L-DOPA). In combination with a so-called peripheral decarboxylase enzyme inhibitor, it has an even more beneficial effect on the disease than when it is used alone (Rinne, 1972). However, L-DOPA with or without decarboxylase inhibitor causes clinical side effects, depending on dosage, administration schedule, etc. Among those side effects first identified some years ago were that some patients felt sexual excitement and enhanced libidinal drive after 2 to 3 months of L-DOPA treatment (Hyyppä, Rinne, and Sonninen, 1970). These findings were confirmed by others in the same year (Calne and Sandler, 1970; Jenkins and Groh, 1970) and later (Benkert, Crombach, and Kockett, 1972; Sathananthan, Angrist, and Gerson, 1973). In order to explain the possible significance of L-DOPA treatment in the sexual excitement, a series of studies in rats was initiated. Sexual behavior and brain monoamine metabolism were determined during L-DOPA treatment, but in spite of expected variations in the contents of brain monoamines, changes in sexual behavior were not found, (Hyyppä, Lehtinen and Rinne, 1971; Hyyppä, Lehtinen, and Rinne, 1973). Reports from other laboratories have confirmed this observation (Malmnäs, 1973; Benkert, 1973). In addition a controversial report has been published by Da Prada, Carruba, Saner, O'Brien, and Pletscher (1973). Therefore, it is still not clear whether or not L-DOPA has any aphrodisiac effect in parkinsonian patients. In order to test this possibility, a group of parkinsonian patients was chosen to be clinically diagnosed according to general criteria. These patients were tested for their sexual motivation before, during, and after L-DOPA and decarboxylase inhibitor treatment.

MATERIAL AND METHODS

This study on 11 patients with diagnosed Parkinson's disease was carried out under double-blind conditions at the Department of Neurology of Turku University Hospital, Turku, Finland.

This research was designed so that the patients acted as their own controls (Liberman, Davis, Owens, and Moore, 1973). All attended out-patient's clinic and were admitted to hospital only for 3 days, at the beginning of the treatment period. The patients were tested (1) before the initiation of medication, (2) during medication 3 months after the initiation, and (3) 3 months after termination of medication. This design enabled comparisons to be made among and within the different experimental conditions.

Among the subjects, five received L-DOPA and decarboxylase inhibitor (Ro 8–0576 and Ro 8–0577) and six received L-DOPA alone from Hoffman-LaRoche, Switzerland). The patients were asked to stop any former anticholinergic medication 3 days before the initiation of L-DOPA treatment, and were thereafter not allowed to take other drugs for parkinsonism. L-DOPA treatment was started according to our routine schedule of increasing dosage until the beneficial level of treatment for parkinsonian symptoms is reached (Rinne, 1972).

The first session with the subject was initiated with an interview based on a standardized questionnaire that covered different background variables, sexual experiences, and habits. Sexual arousal was measured in terms of frequency of intercourse and orgasm (Whalen, 1966). After the interview, patients were given an attitude scale measuring their attitudes of guilt toward sex (Leiman and Epstein, 1961). They had to decide the degree of agreement with each of 12 statements. "Strongly approve" in a liberal direction was scored as one point, "approve" as two points, "partially approve" as three points, "undecided" as four points, "partially disapprove" as five points, "disapprove" as six points, and "strongly disapprove" as seven points. Minimal guilt-score was therefore 12 points and maximal score 84 points. The sexual stimulation consisted of the presentation of an erotic color film for 5 min. The film graphically displayed sexual intercourse between a male and a female. Naken genitals were seen also in close-up pictures. During intercourse, the female was in a position above the male. The film was lacking romantic components. Peripheral skin temperature was registered from the right index finger during the film, and measurements before and immediately after the film were compared (Adamson, Romano, Vurdick, Corman, and Chebib, 1971). After the film the patients were asked to report their pleasurable, unpleasurable and sexual feelings during the film along an 11-graded scale, from no feelings at all (one point) to extremely strong feelings (11 points). Furthermore, they were asked to report if they had felt shocked or insulted during the film and to mention any other feeling experienced during the film. Finally the patients were administered seven TAT pictures, 6GF, 9BM, 10, 12M, 12BG, 14, and 20; the responses were scored with regard to quantity of sexual responses and quality of the sexual content according to Clark (1952).

During the interview, patients were asked to estimate their working capacity along an 11-graded scale. The score of zero suggested that the patient considered himself no longer to have any capacity at all for his former job or occupation. The score 10 suggested that the patient considered himself to have a normal working capacity.

Spearman rank correlation coefficients were calculated between all these different variables separately for the three experimental conditions. In these calculations, three patients who refused to take part in the sexual stimulation test were excluded.

Differences between the conditions were assessed by Student's *t*-tests.

RESULTS

Background Variables

After the first session, 10 patients were excluded because they refused totally or partially to cooperate, and others were in such poor physical condition or so demented that testing was impossible. Among the 11 patients from whom complete data were obtained, there were three women, however, who did not take part in the sexual stimulation test. All four men and the remaining four women took part, that is, watched the erotic film.

Age

The average age of the patients was 59.9 years and ranged between 44 and 75 years. The women were on an average 65.6 years old; the average of the men was 53.7 years.

Education

All the male subjects had completed basic primary education. In addition to this, two of them had received vocational training. One man was a farmer and one an unskilled worker. Three men were pensioners, but the fourth was in full-time employment. The men had attended school for an average of 5.75 years and the women for 2.92 years. The low figures for the women were affected by the fact that the two oldest women had not attended school at all, except for an ambulatory school that had lasted for 6 weeks. Furthermore, two other women had received only 2 years of primary education. Three of the women had always been housewives, and among the four with paid jobs, three were pensioners and the fourth was pensioned during the time of treatment. The youngest and last pensioned woman had received a junior high school education and one year of vocational education.

Marriage

All men were married, and three of them considered their marriages to be quite or very happy. The one who was neither happy nor unhappy in his marriage had, 2 years after the death of his first wife, remarried "out of convenience," that is, because of consideration for his four small children. This couple had sexual problems, that is, they had a fear of sexual life because of the illness of the man.

Among the women the oldest (75 years) and the youngest (55 years) were unmarried. In her youth, the oldest woman was engaged for 8 years and gave birth to her only child during that time. Two of the women were widows. One of them had been a widow for 25 years, and the other for 11 years. One woman had been divorced for 11 years.

The men had on an average three children and the women 2.4 children. All men had children, one woman was childless, one had an adopted child, and one had given birth to seven children.

Sexual habits

At the time of the first individual session, when the patients were tested before the treatment, all of the men had a regular sexual life, with an average of one intercourse a week. Four women no longer had any sexual life, one woman (the youngest) lacked a partner temporarily, and only one had a regular sexual life with intercourse once a month. The subjects were also asked how often they wished to have intercourse or what frequency corresponded to their sexual needs. On the part of the men, the ideal frequency accorded with the actual frequency of intercourse. The woman who temporarily lacked a partner had need for intercourse twice a week, and the only woman with a regular sexual life desired two or three intercourses a month instead of her actual frequency. The four women without sexual lives had no sexual needs. These four women had also been dissatisfied with their sexual lives and two of them had never experienced orgasm. Only the youngest woman reached orgasm during almost every intercourse. Two women had reached orgasm approximately every second time, and two others very rarely.

The men had their first intercourse on an average at the age of 22.7 years. The earliest age was 20 and the latest 27 years. For the women the variation was somewhat broader. One woman had had her first experience with intercourse at the age of 17; the latest age was 30. On an average, the women were 21.8 years at the time of their first intercourse.

All patients were heterosexual.

Effects of Treatment

The second session, when the patients were administered the tests during the treatment, took place 3 months after the initiation of medication. Two men and three women had received L-DOPA and decarboxylase inhibitor, while others had received L-DOPA alone.

On this occasion, all men reported a general improvement of health. One male patient, treated with L-DOPA and decarboxylase inhibitor, found the medication most helpful, but could not report any sexual effects of the treatment. On the contrary, his frequency of intercourse had decreased from one intercourse a week to one intercourse a month. Only one man, treated with L-DOPA alone, reported increased libido, but showed no changes in the frequency of intercourse, nor in any other sexual respect. Three men had observed improved motor performance and one markedly decreased tremor. Two men had been in a better mood. One male, however, had felt very tired, was emotionally very labile, and burst easily into tears. TAT picture No. 10 provoked him to cry, reminding him of the close relationship between him and his mother. One man reported slight memory disturbances; another had had a headache in the mornings, perhaps related to the insomnia also reported by him. On the other hand one man had slept better than before.

Five women reported improvement in their health. Two had been treated with L-DOPA and decarboxylase inhibitor. In three postmenopausal women, vaginal bleedings occurred during the latter part of the treatment period. Only one of them had received L-DOPA with decarboxylase inhibitor. The average of the women who had vaginal bleeding was 63.3 years. Two women who did not have any vaginal bleeding were treated with L-DOPA and decarboxylase inhibitor. Apart from the general improvement in health shown by five female patients, three women showed improved motor performance, one slept better, one was in a better frame of mind, one was almost completely free from tremor, one felt more calm, one reported that her ability to concentrate was improved, and one reported an increased incentive for work. Among the negative effects, depression was seen in one female patient during the second session. One woman reported memory disturbances, one visual disturbances, one suffered from stiffness in the mornings, and two of the women could not report improvement in any respect.

Certain changes in the sexual habits of the women occurred during the treatment. One woman with vaginal bleeding who had been treated with L-DOPA and decarboxylase inhibitor had resumed her sexual life and had had intercourse once during the treatment period. Her ideal frequency of intercourse was, however, once a month. She was 58 years old, but her husband was 70 years old and suffered from congestive heart failure. The second woman with bleeding had had intercourse once a month, which corresponded to her ideal frequency and also to the frequency reported before medication. The third woman with vaginal bleeding was the one who reported increased incentive for work but she had no sexual needs at all. She had been without sexual life for 11 years. One woman (the youngest) treated with L-DOPA and decarboxylase inhibitor had reestablished her connections with her partner and had now had intercourse once a month. She had enjoyed sex more than usual and was the only woman who had experienced orgasm during the treatment period.

Aftertreatment

The third session, when the patients were tested 3 months after the end of medication, showed the following changes: one male patient treated with L-DOPA and decarboxylase inhibitor reported that his ideal frequency of intercourse was twice as high as the actual frequency. Earlier these frequencies had been in accordance with each other. Two other men showed a lowered ideal frequency of intercourse. The fourth male patient reported no sexual changes at all.

More sexual changes were observed among the women. The woman who had resumed her sexual life during the medication had no longer any desire or inclination to continue it, although she had had intercourse once during the 3 months after finishing medication. One woman, who had desired intercourse once a month both before and during treatment, now reported that she had no desire for sex at all.

Three patients reported continued improvement of health, whereas two patients were in a worse condition. The tremor of four patients had increased, and two felt depressed. In contrast, three patients were in a better mood, two of whom showed euphoric features. One reported a decreased interest in sex. Six patients showed various kinds of symptoms, impaired motor performance, dry mouth, insomnia, pressure in the chest, palpitations and anxiety, increased salivation, vertigo, and reduced memory. One of the male patients developed a psychosis that expressed itself in compulsive thoughts and in extremely aggressive and antisocial behavior.

Subjective Estimates of Working Capacity

The results from the subjective estimates of working capacity varied widely among the subjects. In the first session, almost all scale values were represented, from one to 10 points. The average estimate for working capacity was 5.45 ± 3.34.

In the second session, during treatment, the average working capacity was somewhat higher, 6.27 ± 2.41.

On the third occasion, after treatment, the average working capacity was 5.00 ± 2.33.

Student's t-tests between the various sessions showed no significant differences. A comparison between the two experimental groups did not show any significant differences.

Graphical representations of both individual estimates and average estimates of working capacity in the two experimental groups are seen in Fig. 1.

Attitudes Toward Sex

The results showed that the guilt scores before medication were on an average 37.81 with variation between 12 and 52 points. For the period during medication, the average guilt scores were 38.72 with a variation between 17 and 55 points. On the third occasion after the end of medication, the average was 44.3 points with a variation between 20 and 62 points. Only the difference between the first and third sessions was significant, but the difference between the second and the third session approached significance.

Graphic representations of individual ratings of attitudes toward sex, before, during, and after treatment can be seen in Fig. 2.

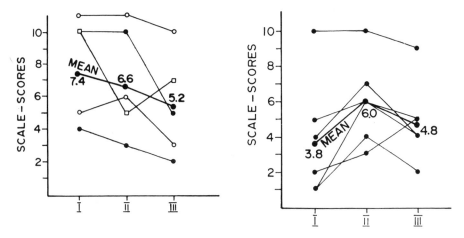

FIG. 1. *(Left)* Subjective estimates of working capacity in the L-DOPA + decarboxylase inhibitor groups. Individual estimates and average estimate of the group. *(Right)* Subjective estimates of working capacity in the L-DOPA group. Individual estimates and average estimate of the group.

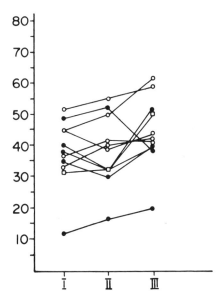

FIG. 2. Subjective ratings of guilty attitudes to sex, before (I), during (II), and after (III) treatment. Individual scores. Filled circles represent group treated with L-DOPA + decarboxylase inhibitor; open circles and squares represent group treated with L-DOPA alone.

Sexual Responses to TAT Pictures

The seven TAT pictures were exhibited after the presentation of the visual sexual stimulation. The subjects who refused to take part in the sexual stimulation test were given TAT, as well.

The mean number of sexual responses per subject was 3.1 in the the first session and 1.8 in the second and 2.1 in the third. No difference in the number of sexual responses between those who participated and those who did not participate in the sexual stimulation test could be observed. Neither were there any significant differences between the experimental groups nor between males and females.

Subjective Estimates of Emotions During the Film

Differences between the sessions were not significant, but there was a tendency for the unpleasurable feelings to increase from occasion to occasion, from 3.5 points to 4.5 points and finally to 5 points. The average estimates of the feelings experienced during the film are seen in Table 1.

TABLE 1. *Mean estimates of feelings during the film on the first (I), second (II), and third (III) showing*

Variables of sexual motivation	Group I	Group II	Group III
Pleasurable feelings	4.2	3.5	3.8
Unpleasurable feelings	3.5	4.5	5.0
Sexual excitement	3.1	3.8	3.7
Insulted	1.0	1.1	1.0
Shocked	1.7	1.1	1.6

It should be mentioned that one female patient was quite taken by the film and enjoyed it unrestrainedly every time she saw it. She had maximum estimates of pleasurable feelings on all three occasions, and her estimate of sexual excitement was 7 before treatment, 11 during treatment and 9 after treatment. She was the youngest female with the lowest guilt score, and had been treated with L-DOPA and decarboxylase inhibitor.

Spearman Rank Correlation Coefficients Between Variables

The highest correlation was found between pleasurable feelings and sexual excitement. This correlation was 0.74 before treatment, 0.74 during treatment and 0.95 after treatment. There was also very high correlations between education and age of the patients, between education and sexual excitement, and education and pleasurable feelings. Tables 2–4 show correlation coefficients between variables before, during, and after treatment.

METHODOLOGIC COMMENTS

The most complete theoretic integration of sexual behavior has been made by Beach (1956, 1965). Sexual drive or appetite has been seen as the result of

TABLE 2. *Spearman rank correlation coefficients showing the relationship between variables before medication*

	Parameters	1	2	3	4	5	6	7
	Education	0.41	−0.28	0.62	0.26	0.48	0.22	0.90
7	Age	0.41	−0.19	0.38	0.36	0.48	−0.13	
6	TAT responses	0.64	−0.60	0.39	0.10	0.00		
5	Guilt score	0.22	0.31	0.06	0.46			
4	Working capacity	0.24	0.32	−0.11				
3	Sexual excitement	0.74	−0.20					
2	Unpleasurable feelings	−0.41						

TABLE 3. *Spearman rank correlation coefficients showing the relationship between variables during medication*

	Parameters	1	2	3	4	5	6	7
	Education	0.65	−0.44	0.81	−0.02	0.49	0.27	0.90
7	Age	0.61	−0.73	0.52	0.06	0.65	0.10	
6	TAT responses	0.67	−0.41	0.67	0.43	0.43		
5	Guilt score	0.72	−0.76	0.32	0.23			
4	Working capacity	0.28	−0.05	0.00				
3	Sexual excitement	0.74	−0.07					
2	Unpleasurable feelings	−0.86						

TABLE 4. *Spearman rank correlation coefficients showing the relationship between variables after termination of medication*

	Parameters	1	2	3	4	5	6	7
	Education	0.80	−0.42	0.92	−0.02	0.49	0.51	0.90
7	Age	0.61	−0.60	0.74	0.41	0.77	0.28	
6	TAT responses	0.61	−0.56	0.54	0.73	0.55		
5	Guilt score	0.61	−0.55	0.48	0.54			
4	Working capacity	0.08	−0.16	0.33				
3	Sexual excitement	0.95	−0.66					
2	Unpleasurable feelings	−0.86						

adequate stimulation of a relaxed, normal animal. Beach emphasizes the role of symbolic stimuli which enable arousal to occur at the mere thought of sex. He presumes that outward stimuli are of far greater importance for sexual behavior than for any other primary drive.

The theory presented by Whalen (1966), who has collaborated with Beach, suggests that both human and animal sexual motivation is controlled by both biologic and experiential determinants. Sexual motivation is said to consist of two components, sexual arousal and sexual arousability. The sexual motivation of an individual might be presented by a specification of these two components. Sexual arousal is indicated by the degree of excitement and maximal arousal is characterized by the occurrence of orgasm. Sexual arousability is defined as the speed at which an individual reaches maximum arousal, and might be measured by behavioral or verbal report measures.

The distinction between sexual arousal and sexual arousability provides a practical starting point for at least the physiologic measurement of sexual motivation. A theory of sexual motivation based on several principles of general motivation has been developed by Hardy (1964). According to Hardy, the affective bases upon which sexual motivation is built or the circumstances which are adequate to strengthen or increase sexual "appetite" are (1) the pleasurable excitement of arousal and (2) the intense pleasure accompanying orgasm and the relaxation which follows. This "appetitional" theory correlates with the experiential determinants.

It can be said that modern theories of sexual motivation tend to emphasize hormonal determinants in sexual behavior of animals and experiential determinants of human sexual behavior. In his attempt to measure experimentally induced levels of sexual drive Epstein (1962) followed the same procedure as Clark (1952). Epstein found a significant direct relationship between sexual stimulation and sexual responses to TAT. There was, however, no significant relationship between drive and inhibition; nevertheless, there was a more direct relationship between stimulus and response under conditions of low rather than of high inhibition. These findings support the results of Mussen and Scodel (1955), but not the results of Clark (1952), who found an indirect relationship between drive and sexual responses to TAT. This discrepancy has been explained by Kinsey as being due to socioeconomic variables. Epstein's subjects, who came from lower socioeconomic backgrounds, were probably less inhibited than Clark's, who derived from the middle and upper middle classes.

It can generally be said that the relationship between drive and thematic sexual response is direct when inhibition is low and indirect when inhibition is high.

In their study of sex, Epstein and Smith (1957) noted a significant relationship between sexual response to TAT and frequency of orgasm. Furthermore, Leiman and Epstein (1961) found that when guilt was high, there was an indirect relationship between deprivation and sexual response, and when the guilt-score was low the relationship was direct. Leiman and Epstein (1961) also found evidence for the view that TAT pictures of relatively low sexual relevance best measured drive, whereas pictures of relatively high sexual relevance best measured guilt.

The findings in our study were in accordance with those of Leiman and Epstein concerning the relationship between deprivation and guilt. On the contrary, the pictures of high sexual relevance provoked significantly more sexual responses than did the pictures of low sexual relevance. Sexual responses on TAT correlated in a highly positive manner with pleasurable feelings and sexual excitement during the film.

The assumption that changes in peripheral skin temperature can be taken as evidence for sexual arousal is based on Masters' and Johnson's (1966) findings that vasodilatation is a sign of sexual arousal. Wenger, Averill, and Smith (1968) found a significant decrease of finger temperature in their study of responses to erotic literature. Adamson et al. (1971), however, found no support for the difference they had postulated between sexual and dystrophic arousal. The skin-temperature apparatus used in the present study was not sensitive enough to provide us with reliable data.

Generally, it can be said that visual sexual stimulation such as that provided by erotic films can induce sexual arousal (Kinsey, Pomeroy, Martin, and Geb-hardt, 1953; Masters and Johnson, 1966; Levi, 1969; Smidt, Sigusch, and Schäfer, 1973) in both male and female, but the fact remains that there is still no foolproof method of measuring sexual arousal (Money and Athanasiou, 1973).

The measurements in this study were mainly based on subjective estimates along graded scales, the assumption being that subjects do not remember their scores on a scale from occasion to occasion as easily as they can remember their answers to direct questions.

Hormonal effects on sexual arousal are still not wholly understood. Money (1961) has carried out extensive clinical studies on their role. His conclusion is that they do not seem to determine the direction of sexual preference but that they can have considerable consequences for the strength of sexual drive and arousability. Although it seems likely that the sex hormones are a relevant meas-ure of sexual arousal, there seem to be no direct observations available on their interrelationship.

DISCUSSION AND CONCLUSION

In spite of the behavioral changes observed during L-DOPA treatment which may well be related to sexual motivation, specific conclusions cannot yet be drawn about an aphrodisiac action of L-DOPA in parkinsonian patients, for several reasons. (1) The population investigated was very small and heterogeneous; (2) the data obtained seemed to be much influenced by background variables; and (3) the methods for measuring sexual arousal are still at an early stage of develop-ment and little is known about the effects of a variety of sexual stimuli on different individuals or groups of chronically ill people. A general conclusion which may be drawn, however, is that socioeconomic and psychologic factors determine sexual motivation in human beings so much that it is very difficult, even with a very potent neuropharmacologic drug such as L-DOPA, to influence the sexual motivation of humans.

Recent studies on L-DOPA show that it increases the level of arousal of patients suffering from Parkinson's disease (Horvach and Meares, 1974). L-DOPA treatment increases psychotic symptomatology, and one behavioral effect noted in nonschizophrenic patients is hypersexuality (Sathananthan et al., 1973). The drug may have some beneficial effect even on sexually impotent patients for an increase in libido was noted in two out of 10 subjects (Benkert et al., 1972), while temporarily increased libido was observed in about 20% of parkinsonian patients treated with L-DOPA for more than 1 month (Hyyppä et al., 1970).

Any changes in sexual behavior are generally seen at the beginning of the improvement stage of parkinsonian symptoms, and they later disappear in spite of the continued beneficial influence of L-DOPA on the central nervous system. An interesting observation is that reports of increased sexuality occur when symptoms of the disease can still be seen. Later, when parkinsonian symptoms have disappeared because of the L-DOPA treatment, patients no longer report increasing sexuality.

Estimates of working capacity point to a tendency toward improvement during treatment. This argues in favor of the transient beneficial action of L-DOPA on sexual motivation being related to the general improvement of treated patients.

The fact that the guilt scores increased step by step from the first to the third session perhaps points to the possible discrepancy between actual sexual performance and worsening of clinical symptoms after terminating L-DOPA treatment.

Finally, the fact that three women, among whom two were treated with L-DOPA alone, showed postmenopausal vaginal bleeding points to probable hormonal disturbances caused by L-DOPA. Whether these changes are of central origin needs to be elucidated by radioimmunologic determinations of plasma gonadotrophins and sex steroids after L-DOPA loading. Although chronic treatment with L-DOPA does not seem to cause visible alterations in blood levels of pituitary hormones (Lundberg, 1972), it is very likely that L-DOPA acts through neuroendocrine regulation mechanisms on the hypothalamohypophysial system even in chronically treated parkinsonian patients.

ACKNOWLEDGMENT

This study has been supported by a grant (73–M30) from The Population Council, New York, to M.T.H.

REFERENCES

Adamson, J. D., Romano, K. R., Vurdick, J. A., Corman, C. L., and Chebib, F. S. (1971): Physiological responses to sexual and unpleasant film stimuli. *J. Psychosom. Res.,* 16:153–162.

Beach, F. A. (1956): Characteristics of masculine sex drive. *Nebr. Sym. Mot.,* 4:1–32.

Beach, F. A. (1965): *Sex and Behavior.* Wiley, New York.

Benkert, O., Crombach, G., and Kockott, G. (1972): Effect of L-dopa on sexually impotent patients. *Psychopharmacologia,* 23:91–95.

Benkert, O. (1973): Pharmacological experiments to stimulate human sexual behavior. In: *Psycho-pharmacology Sexual Disorders and Drug Abuse*, edited by T. A. Ban, J. R. Boissier, G. J. Gessa, H. Heimann, L. Hollister, H. E. Lehmann, I. Munkvad, H. Steinberg, F. Sulser, A. Sulser, A. Sundswall, and O. Vinar. North-Holland Publ. Co., Copenhagen.

Calne, D. B., and Sandler, M. (1970): L-Dopa and Parkinsonism. *Nature*, 226:21–24.

Clark, R. A. (1952): The projective measurement of experimentally induced levels of sexual motivation. *J. Exp. Psychol.*, 44:391–399.

Da Prada, M., Carruba, M., Saner, A., O'Brien, R. A., and Pletscher, A. (1973): The action of L-dopa on sexual behavior of male rats. *Brain Res.*, 55:383–389.

Epstein, S. (1962): The measurement of drive and conflict in humans. In: *Nebraska Symposium on Motivation*, edited by M. R. Jones. University of Nebraska Press, Lincoln, Nebraska.

Epstein, S., and Smith, R. (1957): Thematic apperception, Rorschach content, and ratings of sexual attractiveness of women as measures of the sex drive. *J. Consult. Psychol.*, 21:473–478.

Hardy, K. R. (1964): An appetitional theory of sexual motivation. *Psychol. Rev.*, 71:1–18.

Horvath, T. B., and Meares, R. A. (1974): L-Dopa and arousal. *J. Neurol. Neurosurg. Psychiatry*, 37:416–421.

Hyyppä, M. T., Lehtinen, P., and Rinne, U. K. (1971): Effect of L-dopa on the hypothalamic, pineal and striatal monoamines and on the sexual behaviour of the rat. *Brain Res.*, 30:265–272.

Hyyppä, M. T., Lehtinen, P., and Rinne, U. K. (1973): L-Dopa: Its action on sexual behaviour and brain monoamines of the rat. In: *Hormones and Brain Function*, edited by K. Lissak. Plenum, New York.

Hyyppä, M., Rinne, U. K., and Sonninen, V. (1970): The activating effect of L-dopa treatment on sexual functions and its experimental background. *Acta Neurol. Scand. [Suppl.* 46], 43:223–224.

Jenkins, R. B., and Groh, R. H. (1970): Mental symptoms in parkinsonian patients treated with L-DOPA. *Lancet*, 2, 177–180.

Kinsey, A., Pomeroy, W., Martin, C., and Gebhardt, P. (1953): Sexual behavior in the human female. Saunders, Philadelphia, Pennsylvania.

Leiman, A. H., and Epstein, S. (1961): Thematic sexual responses as related to sexual drive and guilt. *J. Abnorm. Psychol.*, 63:169–175.

Levi, L. (1969): Sympatho-adrenomedullary activity, diuresis and emotional reactions during visual sexual stimulation in human females and males. *Psychosom. Med.*, 31:251.

Liberman, R., Davis, J., Owens, B., and Moore, J. (1973): Research design for analyzing drug-environment-behavior interactions. *J. Nerv. Ment. Dis.*, 156:432–439.

Lundberg, P. O. (1972): Blood levels of FSH, LH, TSH, and GH in parkinsonian patients before and during L-dopa treatment. *Acta Neurol. Scand.*, 48:427–432.

Malmnäs, C. O. (1973): Monoaminergic influence of testosterone-activated copulatory behavior in the castrated rat. *Acta Physiol., Scand.*, Suppl. 395.

Masters, W., and Johnson, V. (1966): Human sexual response. Little, Brown, Boston, Massachusetts.

Money, J. (1961): Sex hormones and other variables in human eroticism. In: *Sex and Internal Secretions*, edited by W. C. Young, Vol. VIII. Williams & Wilkins, Baltimore, Maryland.

Money, J., and Athanasiou, R. (1973): Pornography: Review and bibliographic annotations. *Am. J. Obstet. Gynecol.*, 115:130–146.

Mussen, D., and Scodel, A. (1955): The effects of sexual stimulation under varying conditions on TAT sexual responsiveness. *J. Consult. Psychol.*, 63:169–175.

Rinne, U. K. (1972): Recent advances in the treatment of Parkinsonism with drugs. *Acta Neurol. Scand.* 48 [Suppl. 51]:59–103.

Sathananthan, G., Angrist, B. M., and Gerson, S. (1973): Response threshold to L-dopa in psychiatric patients. *Biol. Psychiat.*, 7:139–146.

Schmidt, G., Sigusch, V., and Schäfer, S. (1973): Responses to reading erotic stories: Male–female differences. *Arch. Sex. Behav.*, 2:181–199.

Wenger, M. A., Averill, J. R., and Smith, D. D. B. (1968): Autonomic activity during sexual arousal. *Psychophysiology*, 4:468–478.

Whalen, R. E. (1966): Sexual motivation. *Psychol. Rev.*, 73:151–163.

Sexual Behavior: Pharmacology and Biochemistry, edited by M. Sandler and G. L.
Gessa. Raven Press, New York © 1975.

Prenatal and Pubertal Influence of Androgen on Behavior: Human Clinical Syndromes

John Money

Johns Hopkins University School of Medicine and Hospital, Baltimore, Maryland 21205

To the best of my knowledge, there are not yet any diagnosable human clinical syndromes in which discrepancies of sexual behavior can be systematically related to discrepancies of biogenic amine function, or vice versa. Nor are there syndromes of discrepant sexual behavior that can be related systematically to discrepancies of hormonal function, recent efforts to correlate homosexuality with steroid levels notwithstanding. In contrast, there are some syndromes of discrepant hormonal function that, because they bear either a positive or a negative relationship to sexual behavior, including reports of imagery, are instructive in showing the influence of hormones on sexual behavior. Except for hormonal changes induced for therapeutic reasons, naturally occurring endocrinologic syndromes provide the only ethical way of studying the hormone-behavior equation in human sexuality. The syndromes[1] I have selected for this brief chapter are the congenital adrenogenital syndrome of female hermaphroditism; virilism in the female with an adrenal tumor; spontaneous gynecomastia of adolescence in the male; precocious puberty in the male and female; and, in conclusion, a nonsyndrome, i.e., normal copulatory play of childhood. These syndromes serve to illustrate, as do others mentioned only in passing, four principles. The first is the principle of prenatal hormonal effects that predispose to sexually dimorphic behavior later in development. The second is the principle of postnatal social effects on gender dimorphic behavior and gender identity.[2] The third is the principle of pubertal hormone effects on the release threshold but not the imagistic stimulus of sexual behavior. The fourth is the principle of the rehearsal in prepubertal play of the sexually dimorphic behavior of postpuberty.

---

[1] For a more complete description of these syndromes, and for bibliographic details of original reports of behavioral findings see Money, J., and Ehrhardt, A. A. (1972): *Man and Woman, Boy and Girl: The Differentiation and Dimorphism of Gender Identity from Conception to Maturity.* Baltimore, Johns Hopkins Univ. Press.

[2] As used here, gender is a difficult word to translate into most European languages, especially in the term, gender identity. I originally borrowed the term gender from grammar so that the term, sex, could be reserved for behavior which engages the organs of the groin in some way or degree. Gender behavior is more generalized and refers to any behavior that is sexually dimorphic or sexually stereotyped as masculine or feminine. Verbal and gestural gender behavior constitute the raw data of the observing scientist. Gender identity is an inferential construct from these data. Like thinking, gender identity can be experienced directly as a raw datum only by the person reporting it.

ADRENOGENITAL SYNDROME OF FEMALE HERMAPHRODITISM

Etiologically, the relevant feature of the adrenogenital syndrome for present purposes is that a female with the genetic condition is born with masculinized external genitalia, as well as with ovaries and müllerian organs. In extreme cases there are a normal-appearing penis and empty scrotum. In less extreme cases, there is hypospadias of the clitorine penis. In both instances there are recorded instances of sex assignment as a boy, and others of assignment as a girl. Therefore, science has been provided with a series of matched pairs of individuals who are concordant for genetic sex, prenatal hormonal history, and morphology, but who are discordant for sex assignment, postnatal biography, and therapeutic history. In consequence, one has an opportunity to examine the prenatal hormonal, the postnatal social, and the pubertal hormonal principles of the differentiation of gender dimorphic behavior and gender identity as male or female.

For mnemonic purposes, I have dubbed the prenatal hormonal principle in the adrenogenital syndrome the Adam principle. For example, if an adrenogenital genetic female hermaphrodite is prenatally androgenized so as to have a large phallus at birth, and is assigned as a male, and is then given concordant masculine hormonal therapy plus whatever surgical correction is required, then gender dimorphic behavior and identity differentiate as masculine. Except for sterility, the boy grows up to be a man, indistinguishable from other men in appearance, demeanor, imagery, attitude, and sexuality. His masculine behavioral dimorphism and identity are able to survive despite the possible insult, as a result of incongruous endocrine mismanagement at the age of puberty, of growing breasts and menstruating through the penis. In that circumstance, the primary concern of one such boy was to have his body masculinized. He abhorred the idea of changing to live as a girl.

In the corresponding case of an adrenogenital genetic female hermaphrodite—the other member of a matched pair—who is diagnostically recognized at birth and assigned as a girl, and then is surgically and hormonally treated concordantly, gender dimorphic behavior and identity differentiate as feminine, but with the "hue" of tomboyism. The characteristics of behavior that constitute tomboyism are listed in Table 1. Tomboyism is not stigmatizing, but is a legitimate variant of the cultural stereotype of femininity in today's world. Tomboyish behavior and interests are seen in adrenogenital girls whose abnormally high adrenal androgen level is correctly regulated from birth onward by means of cortisone therapy. It is also found in older patients who grew up in the precortisone era. Such women are particularly instructive for science insofar as the majority have demonstrated a feminine behavioral dimorphism and identity differentiated concordantly with their sex of rearing, in defiance of their extremely masculinized physique. A small minority have reported a lesbian preference in erotic activity, and still others have reported bisexual dreaming. Requests for sex reassignment have been exceptionally rare. They were made by individuals for whom both genital appearance and rearing were sexually ambiguous. In one

TABLE 1. *History, incidence, or frequency of activities and preferences related to tomboyism in 15 teenaged girls with the early-treated adrenogenital syndrome*

Outdoor vigor	♠
Athletic abilities	♠
Body contact sports	♠
Kinesis	♠
Known as tomboy	♠
Doll play	♢
Boys' toys	♠
Unisex clothes	♠
Nondomestic career	♠

♠ = Trait found in ≥ 80% of the girls.

matched pair the requested reassignment was made from male-to-female-to-male in one case, and from male-to-female in the other. The genetic, gonadal, and hormonal sex, the same in each case, did not automatically program the developmental course of gender dimorphic behavior and identity toward the request for reassignment.

Pairs of adrenogenital hermaphrodites, matched for concordance of prenatal history and discordance of postnatal history have their counterpart in matched pairs of male hermaphrodites—also in matched pairs of genetic males with a micropenis, and, in one case, even in a matched pair of identical genetic male twins of whom one suffered ablatio penis in a circumcision accident—one assigned and reared as a boy, the other as a girl. All such matched pairs exemplify the two principles of gender dimorphic behavioral and identity differentiation. First is the Adam principle (as opposed to its counterpart, the Adam-insufficiency principle) of a prenatal androgenic factor predisposing to tomboyism or "boyism." Second is the principle of postnatal programming of behavioral dimorphism in a manner analogous to the postnatal programming of native language. Postnatal programming determines whether prenatal programming will become incorporated into a masculine or feminine final program of behavioral and identity dimorphism; it does not autonomously preordain masculinity or femininity.

SYNDROMES OF INCONGRUOUS PUBERTY

As indicated in the foregoing section, among hermaphrodites, there are some cases in which the physique of puberty develops contrary to the sex assignment and the juvenile differentiation of gender dimorphism of behavior and identity. The evidence of these cases can be augmented with evidence from nonhermaphroditic cases of incongruous puberty, as exemplified by gross gynecomastia in genitally normal males, and by virilizing hirsutism in genitally normal females, such as may result from a virilizing tumor.

The sum total of evidence from such cases can be supplemented further with evidence from syndromes of pubertal failure and precocity. The principle that then emerges may be called the threshold principle: the hormones of puberty lower the threshold and facilitate the expression of erotic interest, imagery, and behavior, but they do not program the content of that erotic interest, imagery, or behavior.

Clinical evidence points to the conclusion that androgen in human beings is a libido hormone for each sex. Estrogen and progestin both act as androgen-depleting hormones in human males. Their erotic or libidinal roles in human females still remain to be elucidated—they could conceivably exert a more powerful influence indirectly by way of pheromone release, for example, than directly by way of libido.

SYNDROMES OF SEXUAL PRECOCITY

Regardless of etiology, sexual precocity has as its final common pathway the release of pubertal hormones and the premature onset of somatic puberty. In consequence, there is a disparity between physique age and chronologic age, with social age precisely parallel to neither. Erotic age, as manifested in erotic behavior and imagery, parallels social age rather than either chronologic age or hormonal and physique age. In other words, precocious hormonal puberty does not itself directly program the content of erotic imagery and behavior. It changes the threshold for the release of erotic imagery and behavior, the content of which is then socially programmed on the biographic basis of social age and experience.

JUVENILE EROTIC REHEARSAL

For all the importance of their threshold effect, the hormones of puberty are not imperative for sexual behavior. For those whose research preoccupation is the pharmacology of sexual behavior, it is wise always to keep in mind the fact of prepubertal sexual rehearsal play, which stands as much in need of scientific explanation as does postpubertal, adult sexual behavior. Juvenile sexual play rehearsal is particularly prominent in infant primates. In man it requires ethnographic studies of societies lacking a sexual taboo to reveal the extent of juvenile sexual rehearsal play in our own species—including copulatory rehearsal play during the misnamed latency period. Closer to home, I have in my possession a series of color transparencies taken from the window of a high-rise apartment building in a metropolitan neighborhood. In a children's swimming pool area below, a half-grown girl acts as matchmaker to a boy and girl of around seven years of age. The pair undress, and on a park bench engage in a very authentic demonstration of copulation.

Where today is the scientist who would dare challenge our society's sexual taboo in order to study the sexuality of children at play?

ACKNOWLEDGMENTS

This work was supported by USPHS Grant No. HD00325 and by funds from the Grant Foundation, New York.

Sexual Behavior: Pharmacology and Biochemistry, edited by M. Sandler and G. L.
Gessa. Raven Press, New York © 1975.

Aphrodisiac Effect of Testosterone in Parachlorophenylalanine-Treated Sexually Deficient Men

Federigo Sicuteri, Enrico Del Bene, and Bruno Anselmi

Department of Clinical Pharmacology, Headache Center, University of Florence, Florence, Italy

Migraine and related headaches have been termed essential or idiopathic from the lack of a convincing explanation of the pain mechanism involved. Our group at first suggested the implication of 5-hydroxytryptamine (5-HT) in the pathogenesis of migraine, and consequently introduced the antiserotonin drugs in the therapy of this disease (Sicuteri, 1959). Recently the serotonin theory of migraine has become better "focused"; the peripheral (vascular and/or biochemical) origin of the pain has been denied and the possibility of a central mechanism involving 5-HT brain modulation and inhibition of central sensitive input has been proposed (Sicuteri, Anselmi, and Del Bianco, 1973; Sicuteri, Anselmi, Del Bene, and Galli, 1974). The 5-HT theory of essential headache is supported by animal investigations which demonstrate that a deficiency of brain 5-HT induces hyperalgesia, which can be corrected by 5-hydroxytryptophan (Harvey and Lints, 1965; Tenen, 1967). Modifying monoamine turnover in the brainstem of migraine sufferers, apart from provoking pain, may provide an explanation for nonpainful phenomena of the migraine attack, such as nausea, vomiting, mood instability, shivering, fever, and disturbances of sleep and water balance. Sex is also involved: stage of menstrual cycle and pregnancy influence the course of a headache. Sexual activity may be depressed or abolished in about one-half of serious migraine headache cases. In headache an instability of brain 5-HT turnover has been suggested; migraine sufferers appear to be more vulnerable than normal subjects to 5-HT depleting drugs such as reserpine and parachlorophenylalanine (PCPA) (Sicuteri et al., 1973). During clinical trials with PCPA, a well-known inhibitor of 5-HT synthesis, sexual excitation was sporadically reported by migraine sufferers; their response appeared to be different from that of normal subjects and of intestinal carcinoid patients (Engelman, Lovenberg, and Sjoerdsma, 1967).

With the aim of improving the sexual deficiency of headache sufferers, we are investigating the possibility of potentiating the mild sexual excitatory effects of PCPA with other drugs. In this chapter, investigations on the aphrodisiac effects of testosterone during PCPA treatment are reported, as an extension of some preliminary observations (Sicuteri, 1974).

METHODS

Patients

In- or outpatients of the Headache Center of the Department of Clinical Pharmacology of the University of Florence complaining of a strongly reduced or abolished libido volunteered to take part in this investigation. They were informed about the object and risks of the treatment, were assured of strict surveillance, and were cautioned against the possible side effects of PCPA. Sixteen male patients, aged from 40 to 65 years, took part.

Drugs

PCPA was administered orally in capsules of 0.2 g, to a total of 15 mg/kg daily; testosterone propionate (TST) was injected intramuscularly, a total dose of about 350 μg/kg being given daily. Oral placebo-stimulating PCPA and intramuscular placebo-stimulating TST were administered.

Treatment

Each patient received medication for 30 days; this period was divided into three subperiods (decades) of 10 days: in the first, only placebo, oral or muscular or both, was administered; in the second, oral PCPA and muscular placebo; in the third, oral PCPA and muscular TST. The number of daily erections was taken as an index of drug effectiveness.

Side Effects

A number of tests were performed on each patient: platelet and white count, including eosinophils, red cell sedimentation rate, enzyme measurements indicative of possible liver damage, and other routine blood examinations. Sleep and body temperature were observed and the onset of paresthesia or pains in the trunk or limbs particularly taken note of.

RESULTS

As shown in Fig. 1, TST plus PCPA treatment (third decade) provoked a highly significant increase in number of erections, compared with second decade (PCPA and placebo) and first decade (placebo only). The erections were almost exclusively nocturnal, with a lively accompaniment of sexual fantasy. The stages of intercourse in these patients, usually shortened or precipitate, tended to return to normal. An improvement of mood and consequently of behavior and of facial

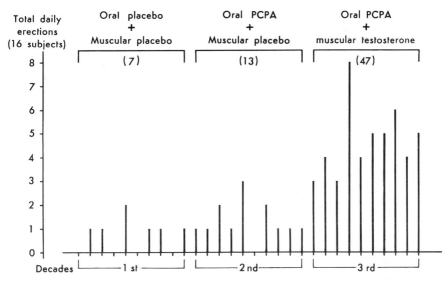

FIG. 1. Aphrodisiac effect of treatment with placebo, parachlorophenylalanine, and parachloro-phenylalanine plus testosterone (PCPA) each for 10-day periods (decades) in sexually deficient men. In brackets are the total number of erections for each decade. Only in the third decade is the number of erections greater than that of the other two decades; the difference is highly significant ($p > 0.001$).

expression, sometimes dramatic, was noted after the PCPA–TST combination had started to take effect.

During PCPA treatment, with or without TST, four patients complained of pain in the legs and trunk; in three, an increase of blood eosinophils was noted—small increases of red cell sedimentation rate and body temperature were observed in two patients. In no case were PCPA side effects severe enough to compel interruption of treatment.

COMMENT

As previously reported, the pharmacologic combination of PCPA and TST appears to be effective in correcting sexual deficiency in man (Sicuteri, 1974). Unfortunately, the side effects of PCPA, which are frequent, discourage the use of this drug in the current therapy of reduced libido and sexual decline in mature or aging men. On the credit side, however, is the duration of the aphrodisiac effect of the combined treatment. In 11 patients, it has been continued for about 1 month. Benefit was maintained, and when treatment was interrupted in six patients, there was no falling off of effect for several months.

One of the most surprising effects was a striking improvement in psychologic condition: the subjects appeared more lively, sociable, and younger. Such an antidepressant action of PCPA–TST treatment stems from the sexual improvement; it was only observed when the treatment successfully countered reduction in libido. It merits attention because it may be more striking than might have been expected from the power of suggestion alone.

In a previous report in which sexual activity after TST, PCPA, and PCPA–TST treatment were compared (Sicuteri, 1974), TST alone was unable to correct the sexual deficiency as dramatically as PCPA–TST. The results of the present investigation confirm this finding and are in agreement with experimental studies which indicate unequivocally that PCPA–TST treatment increases sexual activity in normal and castrated animals (Tagliamonte, Tagliamonte, Gessa, and Brodie, 1969; Gessa, Tagliamonte, Tagliamonte and Brodie, 1970).

The mild PCPA aphrodisiac effect, which has been observed in migraine sufferers but not in normal subjects or carcinoid patients, might provide further support for the hypothesis of an instability of brain 5-HT turnover in these patients.

Even though the frequency of PCPA side effects discourages its use in the treatment of deficient libido, the availability of new and less toxic 5-HT synthesis inhibitors in the future might provide real progress in the treatment of sexual deficiency. The present study suggests that 5-HT may play an inhibitory role at brain level in the production of sexual deficit: the lowering of 5-HT brain concentration seems to sensitize central structures involved in the sexual stimulation, thereby facilitating a trigger action of TST.

SUMMARY

A decline or disappearance of libido and sexual activity is frequently observed in sufferers from severe migraine for which the mechanism of production of 5-HT has been implicated. An open controlled study in 16 men, suffering from this illness and complaining of sexual deficiency has been carried out with placebo, PCPA, and TST. Whereas PCPA and TST, given separately, result in mild sexual stimulation, the conjoint treatment of PCPA + TST exhibits a clear aphrodisiac effect. Although such treatment must be discouraged because of PCPA side effects, there is promise for the future when new and less toxic 5-HT synthesis inhibitors become available.

ACKNOWLEDGMENTS

This work was supported by a grant from the National Research Council, Rome. Thanks are due to the Marxer Company (Ivrea, Italy) for having placed at our disposal sufficient quantities of parachlorophenylalanine, placebo, and testosterone for this investigation.

REFERENCES

Engelman, K., Lovenberg, W., and Sjoerdsma, A. (1967): Inhibition of serotonin synthesis by para-chlorophenylalanine in patients with the carcinoid syndrome. *New Engl. J. Med.,* 277:1103.

Gessa, G. L., Tagliamonte, A., Tagliamonte, P., and Brodie, B. B. (1970): Essential role of testosterone in the sexual stimulation induced by *p*-chlorophenylalanine in male animals. *Nature,* 227: 616–617.

Harvey, J. A., and Lints, C. E. (1965): Lesions in the medial forebrain bundle: Delayed effects on the sensitivity to electric shock. *Science,* 148:250–252.

Sicuteri, F. (1959): Prophylactic and therapeutic properties of 1-methyl-lysergic acid butanolamide in migraine. *Int. Arch. Allergy Appl. Immunol.,* 15:300–307.

Sicuteri, F. (1974): The influence of tryptophan and parachlorophenylalanine on the sexual activity in man. *1st. Int. Mg. Tryptophan Metabolism: Biochemistry, Pathology and Regulation, Padova,* Absts. p. 31, May 1974 *(in press).*

Sicuteri, F. (1974): Serotonin and sex in man. *Pharmacol. Res. Commun.,* 4:403–411.

Sicuteri, F., Anselmi, B., and Del Bianco, P. L. (1973): 5-Hydroxytryptamine supersensitivity as a new theory of headache and central pain: A clinical pharmacological approach with *p*-chlorophenylalanine. *Psychopharmacologia,* 29:347–356.

Sicuteri, F., Anselmi, B., Del Bene, E., and Galli, P. (1974): 5-Hydroxytryptamine and pain modulation in man: A clinical pharmacological approach with tryptophan and parachlorophenylalanine. *1st. Int. Mg. Tryptophan Metabolism: Biochemistry, Pathology and Regulation, Padova,* Absts. p. 21, May 1974 *(in press).*

Tagliamonte, A., Tagliamonte, P., Gessa, G. L., and Brodie, B. B. (1969): Compulsive sexual activity induced by *p*-chlorophenylalanine in normal and pinealectomized male rats. *Science,* 166:1433–1435.

Tenen, S. S. (1967): The effects of *p*-chlorophenylalanine, a serotonin depletor, on avoidance acquisition, pain sensitivity and related behaviour in the rat. *Psychopharmacologia,* 10:204–219.

SUBJECT INDEX

A

Acetylcholine, 99
  effect on male sexual behavior,
    111
Adequacy, sexual
  analysis of, 94
Adrenalectomy
  effect on female sexual recep-
    tivity, 182
Adrenergic mediation
  cholinergic mediation and
    effect on male sexual behavior,
      99-100
Adrenergic substance(s)
  action blocking in male sexual
    behavior, 102, 103, 104
  exogenous
    action of in male sexual
      behavior, 102, 103
Adrenocorticotropic hormone
  (ACTH)
  effect of
    on adaptive responses, 269
    on behavior, 269
    EEG changes from, 248
    induction of stretching-yawn-
      ing syndrome, 247-248
    on lordosis, 39
    on sexual stimulation, 247
  injection of
    intracerebral or intrathecal
      sexual stimulation by,
        248-249
  intraventricular
    effects of, 260
      copulatory behavior, 269
    on LH levels, 260, 264, 265,
      266

  on LRH release, 261-263,
    264, 265
  on sexual behavior, 260
  like peptides
    behavioral receptors for localiza-
      tion of, 254-255
  effect of
    on adaptive responses, 269
    on copulatory behavior, 274
    induction of sexual excite-
      ment, 264
    induction of stretching-yawn-
      syndrome, 259, 266
    on sexual behavior, physio-
      logic significance of,
        255-256
    on sexual response, 249, 250-
      252
    in hypothalamus, induction of
      stretching-yawning syndrome
      and sexual stimulation,
        253-254
  secretion of
    inhibition of, 143
    modulation of, 144
    stimulation of, induction of
      lordosis behavior, 142-143
  sexual response to
    permissive role of testosterone
      in, 252-253
Adrenocorticotropic hormone[1-24],
  259-266
Adrenocorticotropic hormone[4-10],
  260-274
β-Adrenocorticotropic hormone
  effect of
    on copulatory pattern, 294